PowerPoint® Advanced
Presentation Techniques

PowerPoint® Advanced Presentation Techniques

Faithe Wempen

WILEY

Wiley Publishing, Inc.

PowerPoint® Advanced Presentation Techniques

Published by
Wiley Publishing, Inc.
10475 Crosspoint Boulevard
Indianapolis, IN 46256
www.wiley.com

ISBN: 0-7645-6881-7

Manufactured in the United States of America

10 9 8 7 6 5 4

For general information on our other products and services or to obtain technical support, please contact our Customer Care Department within the U.S. at (800) 762-2974, outside the U.S. at (317) 572-3993 or fax (317) 572-4002.

Wiley also publishes its books in a variety of electronic formats. Some content that appears in print may not be available in electronic books.

Library of Congress Cataloging-in-Publication Data

ISBN: 0-764-56881-7

Wiley Publishing, Inc. is a trademark of Wiley Publishing, Inc.

Credits

To Margaret, for the usual reasons.

Acknowledgments

Thanks to the wonderful editorial team at Wiley for another job well done, including the always cheerful and well-organized Katie Mohr, my acquisitions editor.

One of the fun things about the computer book publishing industry is that you tend to run into the same people repeatedly in different capacities. This book was a great example of that, as I was reunited with former co-worker Mark Enochs, a talented editor from "the old days" a decade or so ago, when I was an in-house editorial manager for another publisher. Other familiar names on this book's credits page include Mary Beth Wakefield, who knows more about book production than *anybody*, and Richard Swadley and Joe Wikert, who were already veteran managers in the industry when I was brand-new to it, back in the early 1990s. It's a pleasure to work with such an experienced, professional staff who knows how to make the editorial and production process run smoothly.

When I was asked to write this book, my first request was to get Echo Swinford, a Microsoft PowerPoint MVP, lined up to be my technical editor. She did an outstanding job once again on this book, as she did on my previous book, *The PowerPoint 2003 Bible*.

I'd also like to thank the entire Microsoft PowerPoint MVP community for the wonderful work they do in helping the PowerPoint user community, especially Shyam Pillai, Geetesh Bajaj, and Sonia Coleman. This book is peppered with references to add-ins and articles that they have made available on the Web. Several of the MVPs have also graciously consented to let me use some of their templates and add-ins on the CD that accompanies this book. You guys rock.

Contents at a Glance

Contents

Introduction

PowerPoint is pretty easy to learn if all you want to do is toss up a few bulleted lists. Anyone who has had some basic word-processing training can do that.

The difficulty comes when you want to start doing things that aren't quite so ho-hum—when you really want to motivate and excite an audience with your presentation materials. PowerPoint certainly has enough powerful features to help you with that, but most people aren't familiar enough with the deeper levels of the program to access those features easily—and by "easily," I mean without wasting an entire workday fiddling with it!

That's where this book comes in.

Who This Book Is for

First of all, who this book is *not* for: it's not for someone who is new to computers and needs to be told how to double-click a mouse or open a menu. There are a lot of books on the market today for those types of users, and I won't try to write another one of those here.

This book is something you may not have seen before—a no-nonsense, no-jargon guide for the intermediate to advanced user. It won't insult your intelligence, but it also won't go way over your head or assume that you are a programmer. It simply describes and illustrates the most useful advanced features of PowerPoint and provides tips for implementing them in your own work.

How This Book Is Organized

This book is organized into parts, which are groups of chapters that deal with a common general theme. In each part I've attempted to avoid the obvious and focus only on the cool features that will help you become more effective and efficient as a professional PowerPoint user.

Here's what you'll find:

◆ *Part I: The Big-Picture Design.* This part starts out with an extremely compressed introduction to PowerPoint for those who may need a review (Chapter 1). Then it moves right into creating your own templates and color schemes and managing slide masters and layouts.

◆ *Part II: Conveying the Message.* The chapters in this part provide guidance for importing and exporting text, using automatic versus manual text boxes, and arranging text in tabular or worksheet form including importing and linking with Excel.

◆ *Part III: Still Images.* This part covers still graphics of all kinds. It explains the drawing tools in PowerPoint including the special fill effects available, covers strategies for effective use of bitmap images without unduly increasing file size, and explains how to use the Clip Organizer to create large catalogs of artwork. Advanced strategies for formatting charts and modifying diagrams are also covered.

◆ *Part IV: Motion Images and Effects.* This part tackles the extremely powerful and complex topic of slide animation, including transitions, preset animations, and custom animation techniques. It also includes help for working with sound effects, soundtracks, and narration, and working with full-motion video clips.

◆ *Part V: Preparing and Presenting a Show.* Presenting a show is much more than just clicking the mouse to advance to the next slide! Learn about custom shows, automatic timing rehearsal, presenting using a multi-monitor configuration, and packaging presentations on CD. This part also covers advanced formatting techniques for handouts including exporting them to Word, and techniques for preparing a presentation for publication on the Web including creating clickable hyperlink buttons.

◆ *Part VI: Extending PowerPoint.* This part explains how to make PowerPoint your own by customizing menus and toolbars and writing macros. It also gives you a peek at the world of add-ins.

In addition, check out these appendices:

◆ *Appendix A* explains what's new in PowerPoint 2003 and how changing between versions can affect your existing presentations.

◆ *Appendix B* points you to some helpful Internet resources, which are also available on the companion Web site for this book.

◆ *Appendix C* tells you about the goodies on the CD that accompanies this book.

Special Features

Every chapter in this book opens with a quick look at what's in the chapter and closes with a summary. Along the way, you'll also find icons to draw your attention to specific items. Here's what the icons mean:

Notes provide extra information about a topic, perhaps some technical tidbit or background explanation.

Tips offer ideas for getting the most out of a feature.

 Warnings point out how to avoid pitfalls.

 Xrefs point you to other parts of the book for more detail on a particular topic.

Good luck with PowerPoint 2003! I hope you have as much fun reading this book as I had writing it. If you would like to let me know what you thought of the book, good or bad, you can e-mail me at faithe@wempen.com. I'd like to hear from you!

PowerPoint® Advanced Presentation Techniques

Part I

The Big Picture Design

Chapter 1

PowerPoint in a Nutshell

IN THIS CHAPTER

- ◆ Why use PowerPoint?
- ◆ The PowerPoint interface
- ◆ Working with views
- ◆ Controlling the display
- ◆ Using content placeholders
- ◆ Selecting and manipulating slides
- ◆ Managing presentation files

NEW TO POWERPOINT? Start here. Before diving head-first into some of the more advanced topics in the rest of the book, let's spend a few pages reviewing some of the basic "must-knows" about the application.

Why Use PowerPoint?

I was talking to a new acquaintance recently at a party who had just discovered PowerPoint. As a graphic artist back in the 1980s for one of the "big three" TV networks, she had spent many years creating presentation graphics and overlays for commercials and TV shows. She was so excited about PowerPoint's capabilities! "With PowerPoint, I can do in 2 minutes by myself what it would take a staff of 20 people a whole week to do," she told me.

That's PowerPoint's appeal, in a nutshell. It does all these amazing graphical things that make presentation graphics really shine, and it does them so easily and quickly that it puts the power of creation in almost anyone's hands.

PowerPoint is a very popular tool among people who give presentations as part of their jobs, as well as for their support staff. With PowerPoint, you can create visual aids that will help get the message across to an audience, whatever that message may be and whatever format it may be presented in. The following are just a few of the types of presentations you can have:

- ◆ *Speaker-led*: The most traditional kind of presentation is a live speech presented at a podium. For live presentations, you can use PowerPoint to create overhead transparencies, 35 mm slides, or computer-based shows that can help the lecturer emphasize key points.

- ◆ *Self-running*: Over the last several years, advances in technology have made it possible to give several other kinds of presentations, and PowerPoint has kept pace nicely. You can use PowerPoint to create kiosk shows, for example, which are self-running presentations that provide information in an unattended location. You have probably seen such presentations listing meeting times and rooms in hotel lobbies and giving sales presentations at trade show booths.

- ◆ *Internet*: The Internet has also made several other presentation formats possible. You can use PowerPoint to create a show that you can store on a Web or intranet server so that people can watch it at their own leisure from anywhere in the world.

Can you create presentation support materials without PowerPoint? Certainly. You could make a Word document where each page was a "slide," or you could create a Web-based presentation with Web page creation software like Microsoft FrontPage or Macromedia Dreamweaver, for example. But it wouldn't be nearly as easy as it is with PowerPoint, and the results would probably not be as professional. PowerPoint is somewhat of a one-trick pony in the business software arena. It does one thing really well: *make presentation materials.*

 PowerPoint 2003 is a member of the Microsoft Office 2003 suite of programs. A *suite* is a group of programs designed by a single manufacturer to work well together. Like its siblings Word (the word processor), Excel (the spreadsheet), Outlook (the personal organizer and e-mail manager), and Access (the database), PowerPoint has a well-defined role in the family. Because PowerPoint is so tightly integrated with the other Microsoft Office 2003 components, you can easily share information among them. For example, if you have created a graph in Excel, you can use that graph on a PowerPoint slide. It goes the other way too. You can, for example, take the handouts from your PowerPoint presentation and export them to Word, where you can dress them up with Word's powerful document formatting commands. Virtually any piece of data in any Office program can be linked to any other Office program, so you never have to worry about your data being in the wrong format.

The PowerPoint Interface

PowerPoint is a fairly typical Windows-based program in many ways. It contains the same basic elements that you expect to see: title bar, menu bar, window controls, and so on. And like all Office 2003 applications, it has a task pane that provides shortcuts for common activities. Here's a quick rundown of some basic elements, which are shown in Figure 1-1.

◆ *Toolbars*: The Standard and Formatting toolbars appear at the top, and the Drawing toolbar at the bottom, by default. Other toolbars come and go automatically as needed, and they can also be displayed or hidden by right-clicking any visible toolbar and choosing from the menu that appears.

◆ *Task pane*: This pane pops up on its own for certain activities as well as when PowerPoint starts. You can also display or hide it manually from the View menu.

◆ *Slide pane*: This is where the PowerPoint slide(s) that you are working on appear.

◆ *View buttons*: Near the bottom left corner of the screen are some tiny icons for switching back and forth between the various views. (More on views shortly.)

◆ *Tabs*: In Normal view (which is shown in Figure 1-1), the left-hand pane has two tabs: Outline and Slides. (In this book I refer to that pane as the Outline/Slides pane.) Each shows a different view of the list of slides in the presentation.

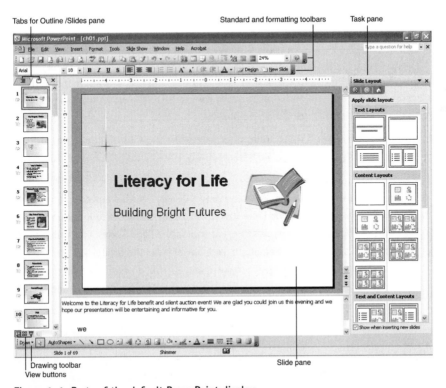

Figure 1-1: Parts of the default PowerPoint display.

If you have only a single row of toolbar buttons at the top of your screen, the Standard and Formatting toolbars are probably all bunched up on a single row together. That's the default for PowerPoint (unfortunately, in my opinion). To place them on two separate rows, choose Tools ⇨ Customize, and on the Options tab, mark the Show Standard and Formatting toolbars on two rows checkbox. Another default setting you will probably want to change before going much further is to turn off the Personalized Menus feature. It's the one that hides some of the menu commands when you first open menus. To turn that off, choose Tools ⇨ Customize again, and on the Options tab, mark the Always show full menus checkbox.

Working with Views

A *view* is a way of displaying your presentation on-screen. PowerPoint comes with several views because at different times during the creation process, it is helpful to look at the presentation in different ways. For example, when you are adding a graphic to a slide, you will want to be able to work closely with that individual slide, but when you need to rearrange the slide order, you will want to see the entire presentation as a whole.

PowerPoint offers the following views:

◆ *Normal*: This is a combination of several resizable panes, so you can see the presentation in multiple ways at once. Normal is the default view and was shown in Figure 1-1. Each of the panes in Normal view has its own scroll bar, so you can move around in the outline, the slide, and the Notes panes independently of the other panes.

◆ *Slide Sorter*: This is a light-table type overhead view of all the slides in your presentation, laid out in rows, suitable for big-picture rearranging (see Figure 1-2).

Here's a funny little quirk. Even if you choose to show the Standard and Formatting toolbars on two rows, the two toolbars in Slide Sorter view will still appear on a single row by default. In Slide Sorter view, the toolbars at the top are Standard and Slide Sorter. To make them appear on two rows as shown in Figure 1-2, drag the Slide Sorter toolbar down below the Standard toolbar by dragging its "handle"—that is, the vertical row of dots at its left end.

◆ *Notes Page*: This is a view with the slide at the top of the page and a text box below it for typed notes to yourself. (You can print these notes pages to use during your speech.) See Figure 1-3.

Standard toolbar

Slide Sorter toolbar

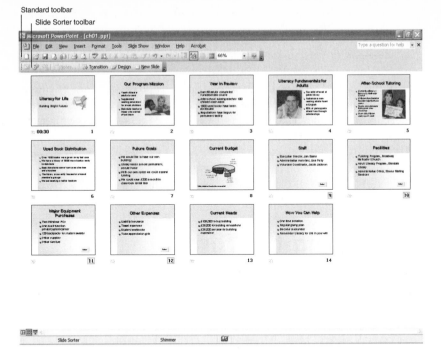

Figure 1-2: The Slide Sorter view.

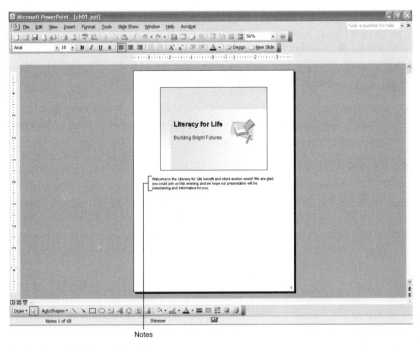

Notes

Figure 1-3: The Notes Page view.

◆ *Slide Show*: This is the view you use to show the presentation to an audience on a computer screen. Each slide fills the entire screen in its turn.

In some earlier versions of PowerPoint there were also Outline and Slide views, but these have been combined into Normal view. The tabs in the Outline/Slides pane in the Normal view switch back and forth between viewing the presentation's text outline and viewing thumbnail images of the slides, and these serve the same purpose as those older views did. You can resize the space allocation among the panes by dragging the borders between them.

There are two ways to change the view: open the View menu and select a view, or click one of the View buttons in the bottom left corner of the screen, as pointed out in Figure 1-1. All of the views are available in both places except Notes Page; it can be accessed only from the View menu.

Controlling the Display

As with anything, it's easier to work with PowerPoint when you can clearly see what you're doing. Here are some tips for making the display show the elements you want to see.

Customizing the Normal View Panes

In Normal view, you can adjust the sizes of the panes relative to one another by dragging the borders between them. To get rid of one of the panes entirely, drag the border between it and the adjacent pane so that it is as small as possible. For example, in Figure 1-4 I've dragged the bar between the Slide pane and the Notes pane down all the way to the bottom, so the Notes pane is completely hidden, and I've increased the width of the Outline tab's section. The Outline/Slides pane also has an X in its top-right corner that you can click to close it.

To restore any panes you've hidden, reselect Normal view from the View menu. This does not restore the sizes of any panes you resized, nor does it reopen the task pane. (Choose View⇨Task Pane to do that.)

Setting the Zoom

If you need a closer look at your presentation, you can zoom the view in or out to accommodate almost any situation. For example, if you have trouble placing a graphic exactly at the same vertical level as some text in a box adjacent to it, you might zoom in for more precision. You can view your work at various magnifications on-screen without changing the size of the surrounding tools or the size of the print on the printout.

In a single-pane view like Notes Page or Slide Sorter, a single zoom setting affects the entire work area. In Normal view, each of the panes has its own individual zoom. To set the zoom for the Outline/Slides pane only, for example, select that pane first by clicking inside it, and then choose a zoom level. Or to zoom only in the slide pane, click it first.

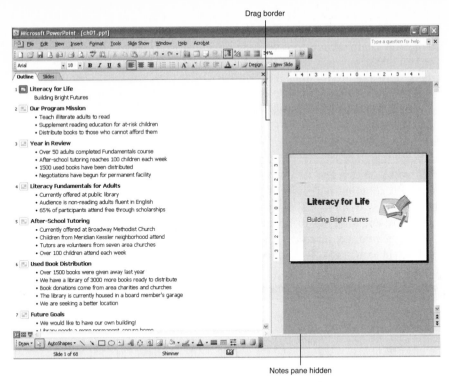

Figure 1-4: You can customize Normal view by dragging the dividers between panes.

 Instead of clicking a pane in the Normal view to switch to it, you can press F6 to move clockwise among the panes or Shift+F6 to move counterclockwise. You can also use Ctrl+Shift+Tab to switch between the Slides and Outline tabs of the Outline/Slides pane.

The easiest way to set the zoom level is to open the Zoom drop-down list on the Standard toolbar and choose a new level, as shown in Figure 1-5. You can also type

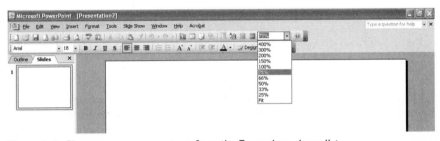

Figure 1-5: Choose a zoom percentage from the Zoom drop-down list.

a specific zoom percentage into that box; you aren't limited to the choices on the list. (However, some panes do limit you to 100% as the highest zoom level.)

The default zoom setting for the Slide pane (Normal view) is Fit, which means the zoom dynamically adjusts so that the entire slide fits in the Slide pane and is as large as possible. If you drag the dividers between the panes to redistribute the screen space, the size of the slide in the Slide pane adjusts too, so that you continue to see the whole slide. You can change the zoom to whatever you like and then return to the default by choosing Fit as the zoom amount.

The larger the zoom number, the larger things appear on-screen. A zoom of 10% would make the slide so tiny you couldn't read it. A zoom of 400% would make the slide so big that a few letters on a slide would fill the entire pane. The main advantage to zooming out is to fit more on the screen at once. For example, if you're working with a lot of slides in Slide Sorter view and normally can see three slides per row, zooming out to 33% might let you see eight or more slides on each row. The disadvantage, of course, is that if the slides get too small, as shown in Figure 1-6, you can't read the text or tell the slides apart from each other.

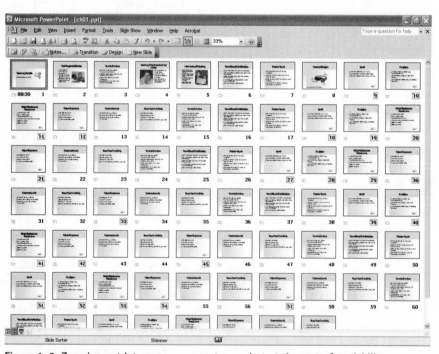

Figure 1-6: Zooming out lets you see more at once, but at the cost of readability.

Another way to control the zoom is with the Zoom dialog box. Select View➪Zoom to open it. Make your selection, as shown in Figure 1-7, by clicking the appropriate button, and then click OK. Notice that you can type a precise zoom percentage in the Percent text box. This is the same as typing a percentage directly into the Zoom text box on the Standard toolbar.

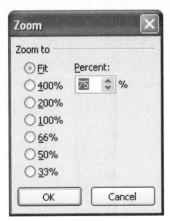

Figure 1-7: You can control the zoom with this Zoom
dialog box rather than the list on the toolbar, if you prefer.

Displaying and Hiding Screen Elements

PowerPoint has a lot of optional screen elements that you may (or may not) find
useful, depending on what you're up to at the moment. In the following sections I'll
show you the most common ones and explain how to toggle them on and off.

RULERS

Vertical and horizontal rules around the Slide pane can help you place objects more
precisely. The rulers aren't displayed by default, however; you have to turn them
on. To do so, select View⇨Ruler. Do the same thing again to turn them off. Rulers
are available only in Normal and Notes Page views.

Rulers help with positioning no matter what content type you are working with,
but when you're editing text in a text frame, they have an additional purpose as
well. The horizontal ruler shows the frame's paragraph indents, and you can drag
the indent markers on the ruler just like in Word (see Figure 1-8). Control those
indents more precisely by holding the *Ctrl* key while dragging them.

Notice in Figure 1-8 that the rulers start with 0 as the spot in the top-left corner of
the selected frame, and they run down to the right from there. When an object other
than a text frame is selected, or when no object is selected at all, the ruler's numbering changes. It starts with 0 at the center of the slide vertically and horizontally
and runs out in both directions from those midpoints.

GRID AND GUIDES

Guides are on-screen dotted lines that can help you line up objects on a slide. For
example, if you want to center some text exactly in the middle of the slide, you can
place the object exactly at the intersection of the guide lines. With the ruler alone
you would have to eyeball it, but with the guides you can be very precise. Guides
are available in the same views as rulers: Normal and Notes Pages. Figure 1-9 shows
one vertical and one horizontal guide line.

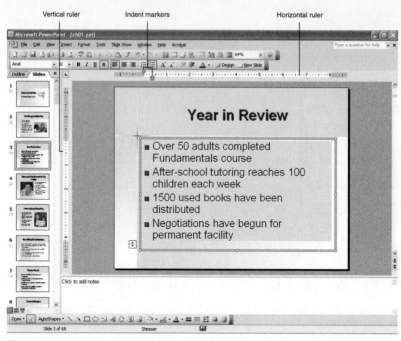

Figure 1-8: Rulers can help you place objects precisely and can also help set and change paragraph indents in a text frame.

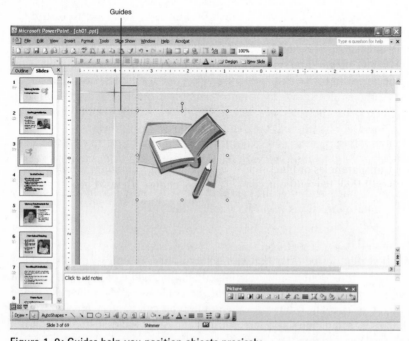

Figure 1-9: Guides help you position objects precisely.

The *grid* is a group of evenly spaced lines like those on a piece of graph paper. When you drag objects around on a slide, they snap to this grid automatically, to help you get things aligned with one another. The Snap feature is on by default, although, by default, the grid's lines are invisible.

The settings for both guides and the grid are controlled from the Grid and Guides dialog box. Choose View ⇨ Grid and Guide (or press Ctrl+G) and then use the settings there to turn the features on/off and change their settings (see Figure 1-10).

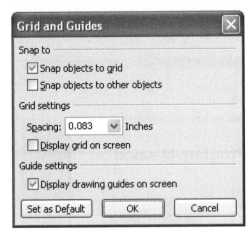

Figure 1-10: Adjust grid and guide settings in this dialog box.

 A shortcut for displaying or hiding guides is to press Alt+F9. To use more guides than just the default two, hold down Ctrl as you drag one of the guide lines; a duplicate will be created of it, up to eight in total in either direction.

DISPLAYING OR HIDING COLORS

Most of the time you will work with your presentation in color, but if you are eventually going to present the presentation in black and white or grayscale (for example, on overhead transparencies or black-and-white handouts), you might want to check to see what it will look like without color. To do so, choose View ⇨ Color/Grayscale and then choose Color, Grayscale, or Pure Black and White.

 This Pure Black and White option is especially useful when you are preparing slides that will eventually be faxed, because most fax machines fax only in pure black and white. Something that looks great on a color screen could look like a shapeless blob on a black-and-white fax.

When you choose Grayscale or Pure Black and White, a Grayscale View toolbar appears. From it you can open a drop-down list of various types of grayscale and black-and-white settings. Select an object, and then choose the setting that shows the selected object to best advantage; PowerPoint will remember that setting when printing or outputting the presentation to a grayscale or black-and-white source (see Figure 1-11). When you are finished, click the Close Grayscale View button on the Grayscale View toolbar, or choose View⇨Color/Grayscale⇨Color. Changing the Black and White or Grayscale settings doesn't affect the colors on the slides; it only affects how the slides will look and print in black and white or grayscale.

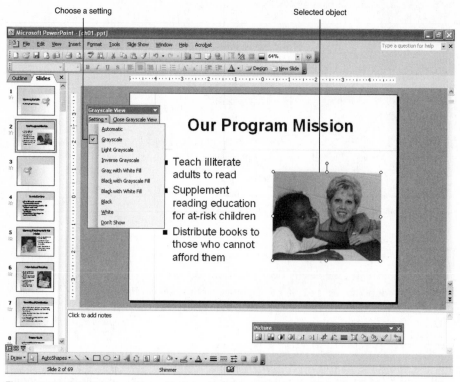

Figure 1-11: Select a grayscale or black-and-white option for individual objects.

DISPLAYING OR HIDING THE TASK PANE

The task pane is a separate pane that sometimes appears to the right of the other PowerPoint panes. Its content depends on the activity you are performing. Many activities that used to be contained in dialog boxes in earlier versions of PowerPoint are now accessed from the task pane instead, such as changing the design template and the slide layout.

To display the task pane, choose View⇨Task Pane or choose a command that requires it to be open (such as Format⇨Slide Layout). To hide the task pane, click the Close (X) button in its upper-right corner.

Once the task pane is open, you can switch among all the available task pane pages by opening its menu. As you can see in Figure 1-12, there are many task pane pages, and just like with any other panes in PowerPoint, you can resize the task pane to take up more or less space on-screen; just drag its border.

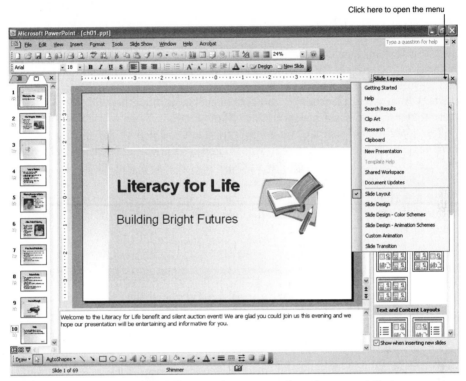

Figure 1-12: Switch among the different task pane pages from the menu at the top.

TIP The Getting Started task pane opens automatically each time you start Power-Point. If you want to suppress that, choose Tools ⇨ Options and on the View tab, deselect the Startup Task Pane checkbox. While you're there, check out some of the other viewing options you can control there, such as whether or not to show the status bar and vertical ruler.

Using Content Placeholders

Slides are based on *layouts*. The default layout for the first slide in the presentation is Title; the default layout for all subsequent slides is Title and Text.

You'll learn more about layouts in Chapter 3; I'm bringing them up now only because the layout controls the type and positioning of the *content placeholders* on the slides. Whenever you see a dotted-line box with something in it like "Click to add..." something, that's a text placeholder. There are other kinds of content placeholders too, such as placeholders for graphics, charts, tables, and so on.

Text Placeholders

To use a text placeholder, just click in it and type the text. Anything you type in them will appear on the Outline tab, and vice versa. (That is, anything you type on the Outline tab will show up on a slide in a text placeholder.) When you delete all the text from a text placeholder, the default message "Click here..." returns. (The placeholder text does not appear in Slide Show view.)

Text placeholders have an AutoFit feature that's enabled by default. If you type more text in a placeholder box than will fit, PowerPoint will automatically decrease the size of the text and change the line spacing so that it will all fit. If you then delete some of the text later, it will reenlarge the text.

For a text placeholder that has been AutoFitted, an AutoFit icon appears in the bottom left corner. You can click that icon to change the AutoFit behavior (see Figure 1-13).

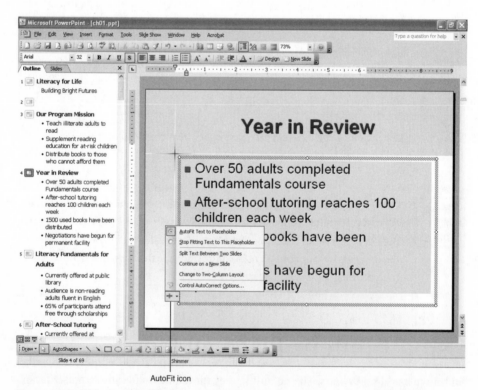

Figure 1-13: Click the AutoFit icon to control the AutoFit setting of a text placeholder.

A text placeholder box is not the only kind of text box you can have on a slide. You can also manually add a text box using the Text Box tool on the Drawing toolbar. The text in such a text box does *not* appear on the outline.

Chapter 5 discusses the pros and cons of using text placeholders versus manual text boxes.

Graphic Object Placeholders

Some slide layouts have placeholders for graphic objects. Of these, some have a placeholder for one specific type of graphic, such as clip art, while others have a grid of six icons and enable you to insert any of the six different object types. Figure 1-14 shows one of these multi-purpose placeholders.

To use the graphic placeholder shown in Figure 1-14, you would click one of the six icons. From there, a task pane or a dialog box appears asking for the specifications or settings for that object. Just follow the prompts.

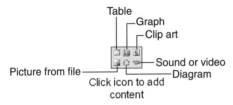

Figure 1-14: Some layouts have a multi-purpose graphic object placeholder like this one.

You can also place graphics of all kinds on a slide manually, independent of any placeholder. You'll learn those techniques in Part III of the book. When you do manually insert a graphic on a slide, PowerPoint's AutoLayout feature tries to be helpful by changing the slide's layout to one that includes a placeholder for that type of graphic, and placing the manually inserted graphic into that placeholder. If that's what you want, great. If not, you can reverse the action by clicking the AutoLayout icon (which shows up automatically in the bottom-right corner of the inserted object) and choosing Undo Automatic Layout, as shown in Figure 1-15.

Adding and Deleting Slides

You can type slide text in the Outline pane to add new slides to the presentation. To promote a line of text to be its own slide, press Shift+Tab; to indent text to be subordinate to the text above it, press Tab. All new slides added using this method have the default Title and Text layout.

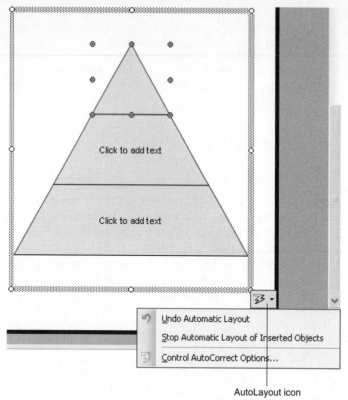

Click to add text

Click to add text

Undo Automatic Layout

Stop Automatic Layout of Inserted Objects

Control AutoCorrect Options...

AutoLayout icon

Figure 1-15: You can undo an AutoLayout, if desired.

Chapter 4 discusses text manipulation in the Outline pane in more detail.

You can also add new slides with the New Slide button on the Formatting toolbar. Clicking this button opens the Slide Layout task pane, from which you can select any layout desired (see Figure 1-16).

To delete a slide, display or select the slide and then choose Edit⇨Delete Slide. (There are other methods too; you can select it in the Slides pane or in Slide Sorter view, and press the Delete key on the keyboard, for example. You can also right-click it and choose Delete Slide.)

Selecting Slides

PowerPoint has three broad types of commands: those that operate on a single slide, those that operate on a selected group of slides, and those that operate on the entire

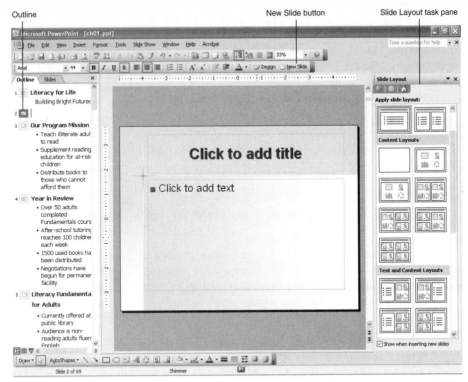

Figure 1-16: Add a new slide either by typing in the Outline pane or by clicking the New Slide button.

presentation file. Most of the single-slide commands, such as a command that inserts an object on a slide, are executed from Normal view. In Normal view you see only a single slide at a time, so selecting the slide is not an issue. The selected slide is simply the one that is displayed.

Most of the "group of slides" commands, such as deleting, moving, and applying a transition effect, are best performed in Slide Sorter view. Because you see multiple slides at a time in that view, you must select the slides you want to affect. (You can do this from the Slides pane in Normal view too, but it's a little more awkward.)

Here are the options for selecting slides in Slide Sorter view (or the Slides pane in Normal view):

◆ To select a single slide, click it.

◆ To select multiple slides, hold down the Ctrl key as you click each one. A selected slide will show a shaded border around it.

◆ To select a contiguous group of slides, click the first one and then hold down the *Shift* key as you click the last one. All the slides in between will be selected as well.

◆ To cancel the selection of multiple slides, click anywhere away from the selected slides.

Saving Presentation Files

In PowerPoint, the standard operations, such as saving work, are just like in any other Office application. To save, click the Save button on the Standard toolbar or choose File⇨Save. To save the presentation under a different name or location, or as a different type, use File⇨Save As. No surprises there.

In most cases you'll want to save PowerPoint presentation files in the default format: Presentation (*.ppt). There are lots of alternatives available, though, and Table 1-1 summarizes them. If you decide you want to save in PowerPoint format, you have three choices:

◆ Presentation (PowerPoint 2003) format is very versatile. It is compatible with all PowerPoint versions 97 and above (97, 2000, 2002, and 2003), and it preserves all features.

◆ PowerPoint 97–2003 and 95 format adds compatibility for PowerPoint 95 to the mix, but it also greatly increases the file size. That's because in 97 and higher, graphics are compressed, but in 95 they are not. Therefore, the presentations saved in this format must support both. All features are preserved, although many of them will not be visible in the earlier PowerPoint versions.

◆ Presentation for Review format is not an option when you first save the file, but if you use Save As to save it again, you will have access to it. It's almost exactly the same as Presentation format, but it keeps track of changes made to e-mailed copies so you can merge the changes later. Don't use this unless you need to, because the file size grows until you merge the changes each time someone else's revisions are added.

Although all of these formats retain all features of PowerPoint 2003, other people using earlier versions of PowerPoint to view them might not see things exactly the same as they were created. See Appendix A for a complete analysis of what doesn't work in which earlier version.

TABLE 1-1 FORMATS IN WHICH YOU CAN SAVE POWERPOINT SLIDES

Format	Extension	Notes
Presentations		
Presentation	PPT	The default. Use in most cases. Can be opened in PowerPoint 97 and higher.
PowerPoint 97-2003 & 95	PPT	For use in a variety of earlier versions of PowerPoint, including PowerPoint 95. Results in a large file because it contains the uncompressed images needed to support PowerPoint 95. Retains all PowerPoint 2003 features.

Format	Extension	Notes
Single File Web Page	MHT, MHTML	Web-based, but all elements in a single file. Suitable for use as an e-mail attachment. May lose some animation effects.
Web Page	HTM, HTML	Creates a plain-text HTM file and pulls out each graphic element in a separate file. Suitable for posting on a Web site. May lose some animation effects.
Presentation for Review	PPT	Creates a normal PowerPoint file but sets it up to track revisions from multiple revisers. Not an option when saving initially.
Design Template	POT	Creates a template that can be used for formatting future PowerPoint presentations you create.
PowerPoint Show	PPS	Just like a normal presentation file except it has a different extension and opens by default in Slide Show view instead of Normal view.
Graphics/Others		
PowerPoint Add-In	PPA	Stores any Visual Basic for Applications (VBA) code associated with the presentation as an add-in.
GIF Graphics Interchange Format	GIF	Static graphic. GIFs are limited to 256 colors.
PNG Portable Network Graphics Format	PNG	Static graphic. Similar to GIF except without the color depth limitation.
JPEG File Interchange Format	JPG, JPEG	Static graphic. JPEG files can be very small, making them good for Web use.
Tagged Image File Format	TIF, TIFF	Static graphic. A high-quality file format suitable for slides with high-resolution photos.
Device Independent Bitmap	BMP	Static graphic. BMP is the native format for Windows graphics, including Windows background wallpaper.

Continued

TABLE 1-1 FORMATS IN WHICH YOU CAN SAVE POWERPOINT SLIDES *(Continued)*

Format	Extension	Notes
Windows Metafile	WMF	Static graphic. A vector-based format, so it can later be resized without distortion. Not Mac-compatible.
Enhanced Windows Metafile	EMF	Enhanced version of WMF, not compatible with 16-bit applications. Also vector-based and non-Mac-compatible.
Outline/RTF	RTF	Text and text formatting only; excludes all non-text elements. Only text in slide placeholders will be converted to the outline. Text in the Notes area and in manually placed text boxes is not included.

The MultiSave add-in by Shyam Pillai allows you to save a PowerPoint presentation in many formats simultaneously; this can be useful if you need to make copies in different formats and keep all the copies synchronized. Download it from http://officeone.mvps.org/multisave/multisave.html.

At that same Web site is a Sequential Save add-in that creates a backup of the last saved version of a presentation before overwrites it with changes. See www.mvps.org/skp/seqsave.htm.

Presentation Basics: Some Tips

Before you start diving into the multimedia presentation building in the rest of the book, you'll need some basic presentation-building skills. I'm assuming that many of you already came to this book with those, and I hope that this chapter has helped the rest of you come up to speed.

Following is some related info I haven't touched on here that might be useful to a beginner:

- ◆ You're not completely alone in this presentation-building thing. PowerPoint comes with lots of templates that give you a jumpstart on a presentation; see Chapter 2 to learn more about them.

- ◆ For almost every type of content, you have a choice of using a layout with a placeholder or inserting the object manually. It's usually best to use the placeholder. See Chapter 3 for more information about layouts.

◆ If you find yourself making the same changes to every slide in the presentation, save yourself some time—use the Slide Master. Anything you do to the Slide Master automatically trickles down to every slide in the presentation. Chapter 3 explains the Slide Master.

◆ PowerPoint may not be your favorite program for text editing, and it need not be. You can create the presentation text in some other program, like Word, and then import it into a presentation. See Chapter 4 to learn how to do that.

◆ Slide content exists in frames that float over the top of the slide. There are text frames, graphics frames, and so on. Every framed object can be moved (drag it by its middle, or by its border but not on a selection handle), resized (drag it by a selection handle), or deleted (select the frame and press Delete). Chapter 7 explains manipulating graphics, and the information there applies to most other types of objects as well.

Chapter 2

Working with Templates and Color Schemes

THE TEMPLATE CONTROLS the overall look and feel of a presentation—background, colors, fonts, object placement, and so on. PowerPoint comes with a lot of templates to choose from, and you can also get them from other sources (like the CD with this book!) or create your own. Or do without one altogether, if that suits your purposes.

In this chapter, you'll learn what a template consists of, and how to apply one to a presentation. Each template has at least one color scheme, so next we'll look at how color schemes simplify the process of selecting colors for a presentation, and you'll learn how to apply, modify, and create color schemes. The chapter winds up by looking at ways to create your own templates.

What a Template Provides

A *template* is like a set of clothes in which you dress your presentation's content. Different templates can give very different overall impressions about the content, just like different outfits can make a person look different.

All templates provide formatting to the presentation, such as background, fonts, and color schemes. In addition, some templates also provide sample content on which to base a new presentation. Both kinds are stored in the same template format—with a POT extension. Let's take a look at these two ways of using templates individually.

Design Templates

A basic template is also known as a *design template*. Design templates do not provide sample content to the presentation—only formatting. A design template typically provides the following:

◆ Background graphics, usually consistent for all slides

◆ A font scheme consisting of one or more typefaces and sizes assigned to the various outline levels

◆ Artwork for graphical bullet characters (in some templates)

◆ Several color schemes—sets of colors chosen to work well together—from which to choose

◆ Preset placements for text placeholder boxes that allow the text to interact gracefully with any background images or designs

Figure 2-1 shows a typical slide in a presentation created with a design template.

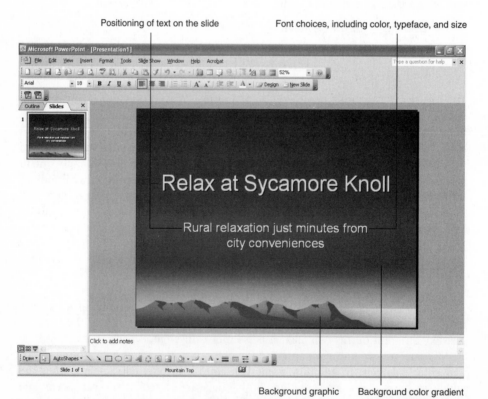

Figure 2-1: Many of the formatting choices on this slide were made by the design template.

You can choose a design template when creating a new presentation, or you can apply a design template to a presentation later at any time. Changing the design template does not alter the content on the slides (but it may make the content move around a bit, depending on the design template's positioning of text placeholders).

Presentation Templates

There's also another kind of template, known as a *presentation template.* It not only contains all the formatting elements of a design template, but it also contains pre-made slides with sample content. Figure 2-2 shows a new presentation that has been created using a presentation template.

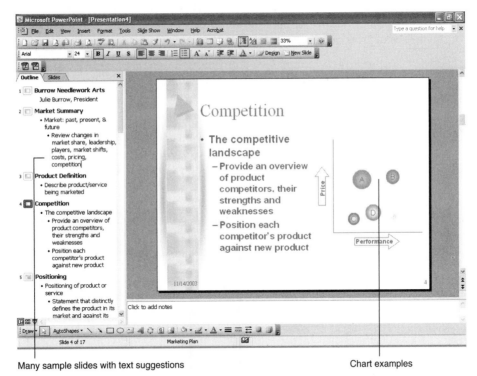

Many sample slides with text suggestions   Chart examples

Figure 2-2: A presentation based on a presentation template contains many sample slides.

The AutoContent Wizard in PowerPoint employs presentation templates to help you build a new presentation with sample content. Let's call these "content templates" (because that's what Microsoft calls them). You can also apply a content template to an existing presentation—essentially treating it as if it were a design template—but you get only the formatting and design features, not the sample slides.

Creating a New Presentation Based on a Template

If you're starting a new presentation, you have the following choices:

◆ **Use the AutoContent Wizard.** *Pros:* Sample content based on a topic you select helps you to avoid mental blocks and gets you off to the right start. *Cons:* A design template comes with the sample content, but you don't get to preview it before making your selection. Therefore, you will probably end up changing the design template after the initial creation.

◆ **Base it on an existing presentation or template file.** *Pros:* Same benefit of sample content as with AutoContent Wizard, but faster. *Cons:* Unlike AutoContent Wizard, no opportunity to select slide dimensions or input title text. (You can do these things later though.)

◆ **Create a new presentation based on a design template.** *Pros:* It's easy to pick a template visually, so you don't have to fumble around trying lots of different ones. *Cons:* There's no sample content, so you must create all the slides except the first one on your own. (It starts you off with a title slide.)

◆ **Create a plain blank presentation.** *Pros:* Since there's no design to get in your way, you can focus on pure content. You can worry about the design later. *Cons:* The results are not very attractive. You will probably want to apply a design template later.

The following sections detail each of these options.

Starting a New Presentation with the AutoContent Wizard

Use the AutoContent Wizard whenever you need some help with the content of the presentation. The makers of PowerPoint recognize that not everyone is a whiz at business protocol, and lots of times people are thrown into the awkward position of having to make a presentation that they don't know how to make. For example, suppose your boss tells you to prepare a presentation that will explain your company's products and services to potential clients. *Where do you start? What slides should you include? How long should it be?* Using the AutoContent Wizard creates a sample that you can use as a starting point.

To use the AutoContent Wizard, perform the following steps:

1. Choose File➪New. The New Presentation task pane appears.

2. Click From AutoContent Wizard. The AutoContent Wizard runs. Click Next to begin it.

3. Choose a presentation topic. There are categories to choose from, or you can choose the All category to see the entire list at once, as shown in Figure 2-3. Make your selection and click Next.

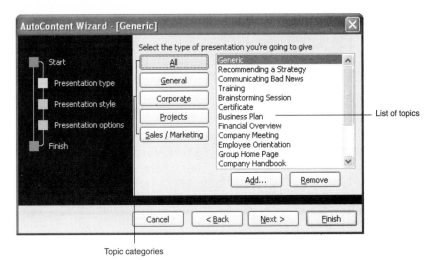

Figure 2–3: Select a presentation template by topic—not by design—through the AutoContent Wizard.

4. Choose the type of output you will use (for example, on-screen presentation or 35 mm slides). Then click Next.

5. Type a title for the presentation in the Presentation Title box.

6. If you want a repeated footer on every slide, type it in the Footer box.

7. By default, the date and slide number will appear at the bottom of every slide; clear the checkboxes for those features if you don't want that. Then, click Next.

8. Click Finish. The presentation opens, including sample content, as shown in Figure 2-4. You're ready to start editing the text to customize it for your own needs. You probably already know enough about text editing to get started with that; see Chapter 4 for more tips for working with text.

 Notice in Figure 2-4 that there's a placeholder on the first slide that says "Your Logo Here." Not all presentation templates have that placeholder. (In fact, this one I happened to choose for Figure 2-4 is one of the few that does.) This is a text box, but you can replace it with a graphic, if desired. See Chapters 7 through 9 for information about graphics.

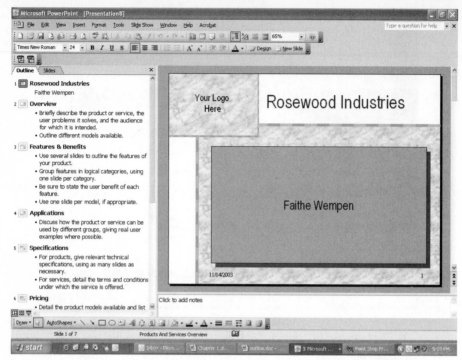

Figure 2-4: A products and services presentation created with the AutoContent Wizard.

Notice also that the wizard puts your name in the subtitle box on the title slide (the first slide). It pulls your name from its information about the registered user of this copy of PowerPoint. If you want some other name to appear from now on in new presentations you create using the wizard, choose Tools➪Options and enter a different name on the General tab.

You might have noticed in Figure 2-3 that there's an Add button below the list of templates. This enables you to create your own presentation templates with sample content and add them to the AutoContent Wizard. I'll explain the process toward the end of this chapter, when I'm talking about creating your own templates.

Adding a Template to the AutoContent Wizard

The AutoContent Wizard will work with any template, not just the elite set that it comes with. To add a template to the AutoContent Wizard, follow these steps:

1. Start the AutoContent Wizard as usual.

2. On the screen where you select the desired template, make sure the category is displayed in which you want to place the template, and then click Add (see Figure 2-5).

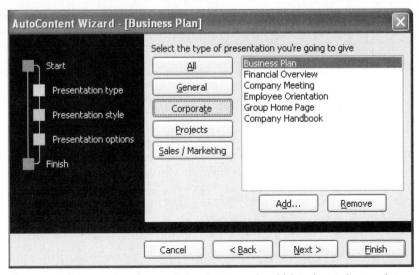

Figure 2-5: Select an AutoContent Wizard category in which to insert the template.

3. The Select Presentation Template dialog box appears, with the default location of your user templates displayed. Select the desired template and click OK. The template is added to the chosen category in the AutoContent Wizard, and is available from that point forward for use there.

TIP You might notice that all the other template names in the AutoContent Wizard are nicely capitalized with spaces. That's because their file names are actually written that way. (Check it out for yourself; look in the 1033 folder.) You can rename your own templates using that same convention to make them blend better with the others.

Basing a New Presentation on a Content Template

If you want to start a new presentation based on a content template's sample content but you find the AutoContent Wizard too time-consuming, consider this method instead.

You can base a new presentation on any existing presentation or template. This basically does the same thing as the AutoContent Wizard except it doesn't ask for the title and it doesn't prompt you for the slide size. To do this, follow these steps:

1. Choose File⇨New to display the New Presentation task pane.

2. Click From Existing Presentation.

3. Change the location to the folder containing the template on which you want to base the new one. The ones that the AutoContent Wizard uses, for example, are stored in `C:\Program Files\Microsoft Office\Templates\1033`.

4. Select the desired template and click Create New. A new presentation opens with the same sample content as in that template.

This procedure works equally well for basing a new presentation on a template or on another presentation. Some people avoid using template (POT) files altogether and simply maintain a generic presentation with boilerplate text and base each new presentation upon it.

Starting a New Presentation from a Design Template

Don't need any help deciding what to say? Then starting with a design template is a good choice, as follows:

1. Choose File➪New. The New Presentation task pane appears.

2. Click From Design Template. A new blank presentation appears, and the Slide Design task pane opens.

3. Click the desired design from the task pane, as shown in Figure 2-6; then close the task pane if desired to give yourself more room or leave it open if you want to experiment with some others. (You can always click the Design button on the Formatting toolbar to redisplay the task pane later.)

TIP If you almost always start a new presentation with a certain template, select it on the template list, open its menu (click the down arrow next to it or right-click it) and choose Use for All Presentations. This moves it up near the top of the list of templates and sets new presentations to be based upon it. To go back to how things were before, select the blank template (Default Design) and choose Use for All Presentations.

When you start with a design template, you get a single slide that uses the Title layout. Your name is not filled in automatically anywhere; you must manually click in the placeholder boxes and type the text you want.

New Slide You'll need to add some more slides, of course. To do so, you can click the New Slide button on the Formatting toolbar (or press Ctrl+M), or you can display the Outline pane and type text in the outline.

Only one slide

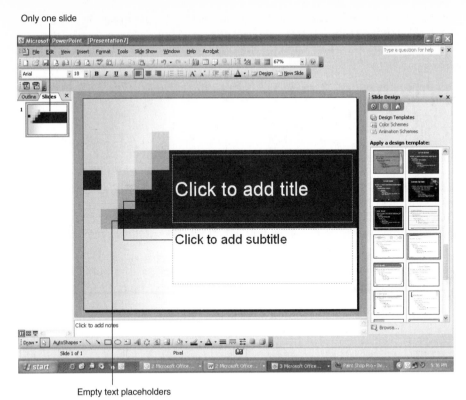

Empty text placeholders

Figure 2-6: A template applied to a new blank presentation.

For a detailed discussion of the outlining tools, turn to Chapter 4.

XREF

Starting a Blank Presentation

A blank presentation is just like one that uses a design template except that the template it happens to employ is a totally plain one with no background or text colors (just black and white), no background, and a very plain font (Arial).

There are several ways to create a new blank presentation. One is to use the steps in the preceding section to start one based on a design template, and then pick Default Design as the template of choice.

Another method is to click the New button on the Standard toolbar. (This is the easier way, obviously.) When you do it this way, the Slide Layout task pane appears instead of the Slide Design task pane, so you can insert more slides and choose their layouts.

Yet another method is to open the New Presentation task pane (choose File⇨New) and select Blank Presentation from the task pane.

Applying a Template to an Existing Presentation

 Design There's no commitment when selecting a design template in PowerPoint, because you can change to a different one any time. To do so, click the Design button on the Formatting toolbar; the Slide Design task pane reopens, and you can pick a different one.

You can apply different templates to different slides in the same presentation, if you like. To apply a design template only to certain slides, follow these steps:

1. Click the Design button to display the Slide Design task pane if it is not already displayed.

2. Select the slides that should have the different design template applied.

 To select more than one slide, click the slides you want in the Slides pane (while holding down the Ctrl key), or select their text in the Outline pane, or switch to Slide Sorter and select them from there.

3. Point to the desired template in the task pane; a down arrow appears to its right, as shown in Figure 2-7.

4. Click the down arrow to open a menu, and click Apply to Selected Slides.

When you switch to a different template after starting a presentation from a presentation template (with sample content), some of the graphics provided by the original template may remain, even though they aren't appropriate for the new design. If that happens, simply select them, and then delete them by pressing the Delete key.

Using a content template as a design template

The content templates have their own unique designs, and some of them are pretty interesting. Even if you aren't interested in the sample content, you might want to use some of their designs in your own presentations.

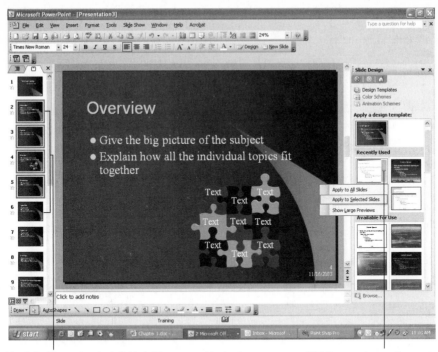

Use Ctrl+click to select the individual slides you want to change.   Click the arrow to open the menu.

Figure 2-7: Apply a different template to selected slides, if desired.

There's one minor glitch with that idea, however: by default, the presentation templates do not show up in the list of designs in the Slide Design pane. Therefore, you'll need to do the following:

1. Click the Browse hyperlink at the bottom of the Slide Design task pane. The Apply Design Template dialog box opens.

2. Navigate to this path (assuming C: is the hard disk where Office is installed):

   ```
   C:\Program Files\Microsoft Office\Templates\1033
   ```

3. Click one of the presentation designs. A preview of it appears to the right of the list, as shown in Figure 2-8. If it doesn't, click the View button (to the immediate left of Tools) and choose Preview.

4. Click Apply to apply the presentation template as if it were a design template. You won't get any sample slides—just design attributes.

 Why is the folder called 1033? It has to do with international support within Office applications. Items that are country-specific go in folders for that country, and 1033 is the numeric code for United States of America.

Switch to the 1033 folder.

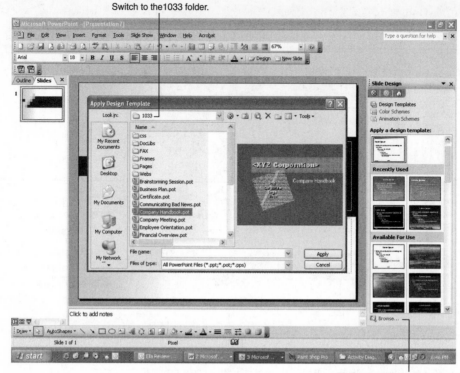

Click here to open dialog box.

Figure 2-8: Select a presentation template for use as a design template.

Applying User Templates and Third-Party Templates

Applying templates from other sources is just like applying a content template (see Figure 2-8); the only difference is the location of the file. Just follow the steps in the preceding section and navigate to wherever you have stored it. If you're applying a template you created yourself, it's probably in `C:\Documents and Settings\Your Name\Application Data\Microsoft\Templates`, which is the default location for user-created templates. (I'll tell you more about creating your own templates later in this chapter.)

Many third-party templates that you can buy will have a Setup utility that installs them in the same folder as PowerPoint's regular design templates (`C:\Program Files\Microsoft Office\Templates\Presentation Designs`) so that they show up automatically in the Slide Design task pane. You can manually move or copy them there if you like; see the next section to learn more about file locations and what templates to store in what places.

Microsoft is one obvious source of additional templates. At the bottom of the list of templates in the Slide Design task pane is a "Design Templates on Microsoft

Office Online" box. Click it to open a Web browser and connect to Microsoft's Office Online Web site, where you can find more templates for free download. There are many third-party sources of templates as well. This book's CD includes several dozen, and you can download many more at both free and pay sites all over the Web.

Understanding and Changing Template File Locations

Here's something curious (and handy). When you open the Apply Design Template dialog box, it points to the default location for user templates—that is, the templates you create yourself. There are shortcuts there to the Presentation Designs and the 1033 folders, however, so you can get to those folders easily from there. To test this for yourself, try this:

1. Click Browse in the Slide Design task pane to open the Apply Design Template dialog box.

2. From the Apply Design Template dialog box, open the Look in list. Notice it's pointing to your own user template folder. (Mine is `C:\Documents and Settings\Faithe Wempen\Application Data\Microsoft\Templates`). Notice that there are at least two folders there: 1033 and Presentation Designs.

3. Now double-click the 1033 folder and then reopen the Look in list. Notice that the path has completely changed.

Here are the template location rules, in a nutshell:

◆ When you create and save your own templates (which you'll learn to do later in this chapter), they're saved by default in `C:\Documents and Settings\Your Name\Application Data\Microsoft\Templates` where Your Name is the user name with which you are logged onto Windows. This folder also holds shortcuts to the two other template folders described next.

◆ When PowerPoint is deciding which templates to display in the Slide Design task pane, it looks in this folder: `C:\Program Files\Microsoft Office\Templates\Presentation Designs`.

◆ When PowerPoint is deciding which templates to display in the AutoContent Wizard, it looks in this folder: `C:\Program Files\ Microsoft Office\Templates\1033`. However, just placing a template file in that location is not enough to make the AutoContent Wizard see it; you must add it to the AutoContent Wizard, as described later in this chapter.

If you want different templates to appear in different places, it's simply a matter of moving or copying them into one of the three folders on the list in the preceding section.

For example, to narrow down the templates that appear in the Slide Design task pane so you don't have to wade through so many, move some of Power-Point's default templates out of `C:\Program Files\Microsoft Office\Templates \Presentation Designs`. You can create a Backup folder within it, for example, and then move the unwanted templates into there. You can also delete unwanted templates entirely, but what if you someday want them again? You would have to reinstall PowerPoint (or manually extract them from the Setup CD) to get them back. Therefore, it's better to just move them out of the way.

Another example—if you want the presentation templates (that is, the ones with sample content) to also be available for use as design templates, copy them from `C:\ Program Files\Microsoft Office\Templates\1033` to `C:\Program Files\ Microsoft Office\Templates\Presentation Designs`. Don't move them, because then the AutoContent Wizard would not have them to work with.

By default, the templates you create yourself may not appear in the Slide Design task pane. To make them appear there, move or copy them into `C:\ Program Files\Microsoft Office\Templates\Presentation Designs` from wherever you saved them (probably `C:\Documents and Settings\Your Name\ Application Data\Microsoft\Templates`).

 If you put your templates in folders in the `Program Files\Microsoft Office\Templates\Presentation Designs` folder, each folder will appear as a tab in the New Presentation dialog box. (To open the New Presentation dialog box, click Templates on My Computer in the New Presentation task pane.) Actually, you don't even have to store the templates in that location; you can just put shortcuts to the real locations there. Here's a great article that explains it in more detail: `www.soniacoleman.com/Tutorials/ PowerPoint/powerpoint_2003_templates.htm`.

Working with Color Schemes

To achieve the perfect look for your presentation, you will probably want to experiment with color choices. You can probably see the trouble coming a mile away, though—if you change one color, some other color probably won't look good next to it, and then you'll end up changing *that* color, and so on, until you've wasted several hours making corrections manually on every single slide.

To avoid that kind of hassle, PowerPoint employs *color schemes*. A color scheme is a set of eight colors that are carefully chosen to look good with one another and to offer appropriate levels of contrast—so your text won't be a similar color to the background on which it's placed, for example. Each of the eight colors is assigned a named position:

- *Color 1: Background.* This color appears as the background on the slides.

- *Color 2: Text and lines.* All text on the slide except the slide title will appear in this color. Also, if you draw any AutoShapes, their outside borders will be this color.

- *Color 3: Shadows.* If any elements are shadowed with the Shadow feature (Drawing toolbar, see Chapter 7), the shadow's default color is Color 3.

- *Color 4: Title text.* This is the color for text that appears in title placeholders.

- *Color 5: Fills.* When you draw any AutoShapes (see Chapter 7), their fill will be this color.

- *Color 6: Accent.* For templates that use accent colors, this will be one of the colors used.

- *Color 7: Accent and Hyperlink.* A secondary accent color, plus the color for hyperlinks that have not been followed.

- *Color 8: Accent and Followed Hyperlink.* Another secondary accent color, plus the color for hyperlinks that have been followed.

Figure 2-9 shows a slide with the color numbers pointed out, so you can see how PowerPoint uses these color placeholders. Different templates may use them differently in minor ways.

 Some of the colors in Figure 2-9 are not at full strength—they are set to have 50% transparency. The Transparency setting for an object determines how much of whatever is underneath an object should show through. You'll learn all about it in Chapter 7, when we dig into graphics in detail.

One of the most common uses for color schemes is to prepare "light" and "dark" versions of the same presentation. Sometimes a presenter does not know the conditions in the presentation room in advance—will a light background or a dark one be more appropriate? By testing the presentation with multiple color schemes in advance, you can know which schemes will work well with it and be ready to switch to an alternate scheme quickly when conditions dictate.

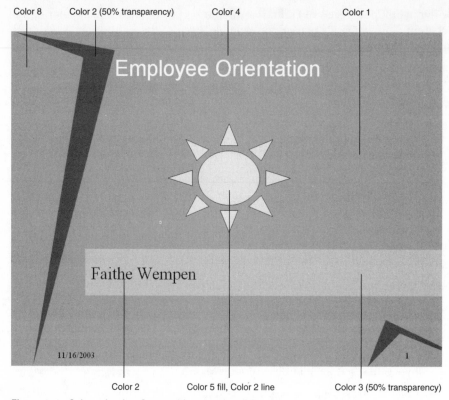

Figure 2-9: Color selection for an object on the slide.

Selecting a Color Scheme

Each template comes with a default color scheme, and in most cases several alternative color schemes too. That means that if a certain template is perfect except for the colors, you can simply switch to a different color scheme—without giving up any of the other design elements of that template.

The color schemes available depend on the template. Some templates have lots of color schemes; others have only a few.

Before selecting a color scheme, you should be happy with your choice of templates. If you switch to a different template later, your color scheme choice will be wiped out, so make sure the template is correct first. Then, do the following to see what color scheme choices that template offers:

1. Click the Design button to open the Slide Design task pane if it is not already displayed.

2. Click the Color Schemes hyperlink near the top of the task pane. Thumbnail images of various color schemes appear, as shown in Figure 2-10.

3. Click the color scheme to apply; it is immediately applied. Try several, if needed, to find the one that looks best. Then, close the task pane.

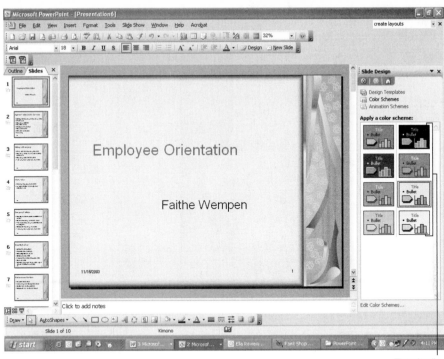

Thumbnails

Figure 2-10: Select from among the alternative color schemes that the template provides.

Applying a Color Scheme to Individual Slides

As with slide designs, you can also apply a color scheme to only the selected slides, if you prefer. Point to the color scheme, so that an arrow appears to its right, and then click that arrow to open a menu. Then choose Apply to Selected Slides, as shown in Figure 2-11.

Color scheme can be copied from one slide to another via Format Painter. In Normal view, make sure that the left-hand pane shows the slide thumbnails, as shown in Figure 2-11. Then click one of the slides that has the desired color scheme, click the Format Painter button, and then click the slide that needs its color scheme changed.

To switch all slides back to a common color scheme, simply reapply the color scheme by clicking on it in the task pane.

Customizing a Color Scheme

As I said before, some templates are much more generous in the number of color schemes they provide than others. If none of the color schemes suits you, customize one.

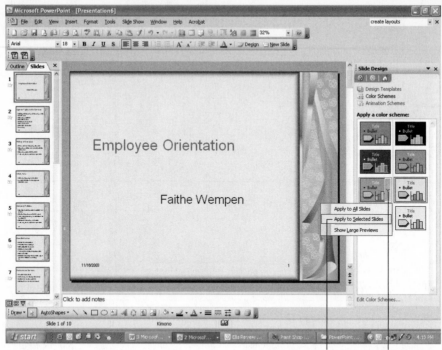

Apply to Selected Slides Click the arrow
to open the menu.

Figure 2-11: Select a different color scheme for some or all slides.

When you customize a color scheme, you redefine one or more of the color numbers as a different choice. For example, you could redefine Color 1's definition in order to change the color of the background plus any other images that are formatted using Color 1. (See *Using Scheme Colors for Individual Object Formatting* later in this chapter for details about how that might occur.)

It's best to start with the color scheme that is closest to what you want, because then you'll have fewer changes to make. To customize a color scheme, follow these steps:

1. In the Slide Design task pane, make sure Color Schemes is selected and the available schemes appear.

2. (Optional) To apply the scheme to certain slides only, select them.

3. Click the color scheme that is closest to what you want. It is applied to all slides.

4. Click the Edit Color Schemes hyperlink at the bottom of the task pane. The Edit Color Scheme dialog box opens, as shown in Figure 2-12.

5. Click a colored square representing a color you want to change, and click the Change Color button. The Color dialog box appears. Its exact name depends on the colored square you chose. For example, it's Background Color in Figure 2-13.

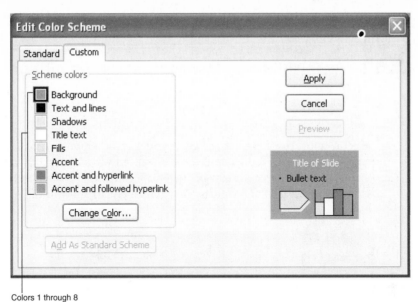

Colors 1 through 8

Figure 2-12: Edit the color scheme by redefining one or more of the color placeholders.

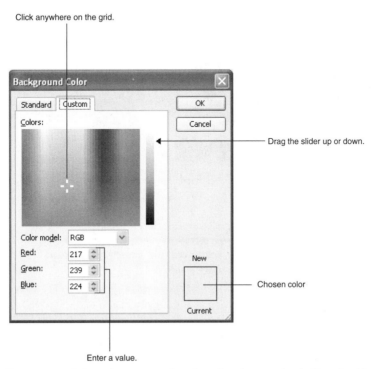

Figure 2-13: Select the exact color that the chosen placeholder should display for all objects formatted with it.

There are two tabs in the Color dialog box. If the current selection is a custom color, the Custom tab will appear at first, as shown in Figure 2-13. If the current color is a standard color, the Standard tab will appear first. You can select from either.

6. Select a color. You can click the color you want or enter an exact value by number. I'll explain more about these advanced ways of picking a color in Chapter 7; for now you might be better off going to the Standard tab and selecting one of the solid colored hexagons there, as shown in Figure 2-14.

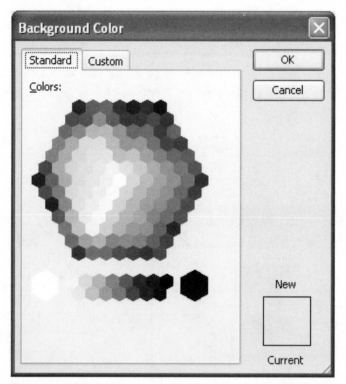

Figure 2-14: Select the exact color that the chosen placeholder should display for all objects formatted with it.

7. Click OK.

8. Repeat steps 4-7 for each color to change. Click Preview if you desire to see the color choices previewed on the slide behind the dialog box.

9. When you're finished, click Apply. (Or, click Cancel to reject all the changes you've made.)

Saving a Custom Color Scheme

Saving the color scheme is easy. After making your changes to the color scheme, but before clicking Apply (step 9 in the preceding steps), click the Add as Standard Scheme button. It's added to the color scheme thumbnails in the Slide Design pane. There's no need to name it.

Actually, the color scheme gets saved in the current presentation even if you don't click Add as Standard Scheme. This is a quirk (a.k.a. "feature") in PowerPoint 2003.

Using Scheme Colors for Individual Object Formatting

Whenever there is an opportunity to select a color for an object in PowerPoint, the drop-down list shows the scheme's colors on its first row. Below that are menu items for opening dialog boxes (which I'll get into a bit later). Figure 2-15 shows a typical list.

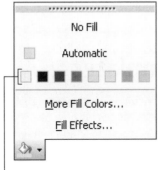

Scheme colors

Figure 2-15: Color selection for an object on the slide.

If you have chosen any non-scheme colors for any objects in the presentation (which I'll get into in Chapter 7), they will appear on menus in a row immediately below the scheme colors. In Figure 2-16, for example, there is one non-scheme color that has been used. Use non-scheme colors sparingly, as they don't automatically change when you apply a different color scheme.

Here are a couple of inexpensive add-ins that deal with color schemes.

The Palette Toolbar add-inthat gives you more control over color scheme management and lets you create color schemes of up to 96 colors each. You can read about it and download a demo at www.rdpslides.com/pptools/FAQ00015.htm.

If you need to copy color schemes between presentations, try the Color Scheme Manager add-in at www.mvps.org/skp/csm.htm. It lets you create a master-database of color schemes and assign names to them.

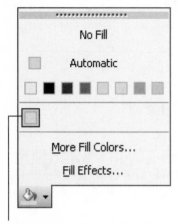

No Fill

Automatic

More Fill Colors...

Fill Effects...

Another color used in the presentation

Figure 2-16: Non-scheme colors appear on a separate row.

Creating Your Own Templates

Creating your own templates can be as easy or as difficult as you make it. The actual saving of the file as a template is very simple; the variable part is how much design work you want to put into the template. Do you just want to modify an existing template slightly and save it under a new name? Or, are you thinking of building your own masterpiece including custom graphics and sample content? There's a big difference. Since this is only Chapter 2, let's think "small" for the moment, and as you read more of this book and learn how to do more things, you can expand your custom template's feature set.

When saving a template, PowerPoint makes no distinction between templates with or without sample content. If there are slides in the template, PowerPoint will use them if starting a new presentation based on it (through AutoContent Wizard, for example) but will ignore them if changing the design of an existing presentation. The distinction is all in where you store the templates and how you employ them.

Creating a Design Template

A design template should not include any sample content. If you base a new presentation on a design template that does have sample content, PowerPoint will include it, so don't include any "junk" slides in your template. Work only with the Slide Master when making changes to the file that you will save as a template.

 You'll learn about the Slide Master in Chapter 3.

Suppose you want to base a new design template on an existing one. There are two ways to go about it. You can either open the original template (POT) file, or start a new presentation based on it. Either way, you then make your changes to the master slides and save the file as a new template (POT).

Where to save it? That depends on how you want to use it. The default location is `C:\Documents and Settings\Your Name\Application Data\ Microsoft\ Templates`. See *Applying User Templates and Third-Party Templates* earlier in the chapter.

If you want it to appear in the Slide Design task pane, however, you should save it in `C:\Program Files\Microsoft Office\Templates\Presentation Designs` instead.

Here's a play-by-play of the process:

1. Open an existing template file, or start a new presentation based on the desired template.

2. Switch to Slide Master view (see Chapter 3) and make any design changes to the template as desired.

3. (Optional) Display the Slide Design task pane and edit the color schemes for the template as desired.

4. Choose File⇨Save As. Change the Save As type to Design Template (*.pot) and save the template in the appropriate location. Figure 2-17 shows the file being saved to the default location for user templates. Then close the file.

Creating a Presentation (Content) Template

Making a content template is similar to making a design template except that instead of just editing the Slide Master (again, see Chapter 3), you also create some sample slides. I won't get into the process of creating slides here, as it's addressed in Part II of the book. Here's what to do:

1. Follow steps 1–3 in the steps in the preceding section.

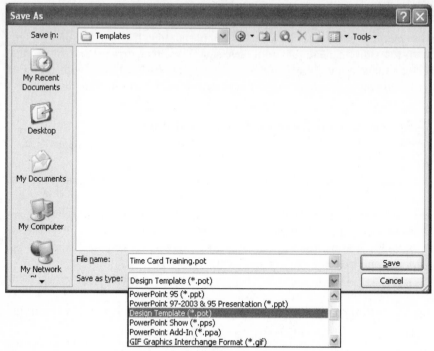

Figure 2-17: Save a file as a Design Template to reuse it repeatedly later.

2. Close Slide Master view if it is still open, and add the desired slides to the presentation.

3. Choose File➪Save As. Change the Save As type to Design Template (*.pot) and save the template in the default location for user templates (C:\ Documents and Settings\Your Name\Application Data\ Microsoft\ Templates).

If you plan to save the template in a location other than the default for user templates, change the Save As type setting to Design Template (*.pot) before you change the save location. When you select Design Template, the file location automatically changes back to the default save location, even if you've already manually selected a different one.

Tips for Effective Templates

Now that you know how templates are created and maintained, try these ideas in your work:

◆ The default storage location for user templates is specific to you as a Windows user. If someone else logs into the same PC using a different name, they won't be able to access your templates. Therefore, if you want to share your templates with other users of the local PC, store them in a folder that everyone can access. Then, create a shortcut to that folder in the default Templates folder so you can access it quickly.

◆ The above idea also goes for sharing your templates on a network. You can place them on a centrally accessible network drive, and then create a shortcut to that network location in the default Templates folder for easy access to it.

◆ If your company requires that certain elements always exist on every presentation, such as the company's name or logo, add it to the Microsoft-supplied templates. Open each one's template file (POT), edit the Slide Master to include the required text or graphic, and then save it back to its original location.

◆ Clean up the AutoContent Wizard by removing any templates from it that you never use. This does not delete the templates from the hard disk—it only removes them from the wizard. To do so, click the template and click Remove in the Wizard (on the screen shown in Figure 2-5). You can always add them back in later if you decide you want them there.

◆ Take advantage of the multiple masters feature in PowerPoint 2003 to create different masters that use different color schemes. Chapter 3 covers masters in great detail.

Additional Template Sources

There are plenty of interesting templates on the CD that accompanies this book, and many more are available online. Here are some sources to get you started:

◆ PowerPoint Backgrounds: www.powerpointbackgrounds.com/index.htm

◆ Sonia Colema: www.soniacoleman.com

◆ PowerPointed.com: www.powerpointed.com/001100/back/

◆ PowerFinish: www.powerfinish.com/index.html

You can always search regular search engines online for "PowerPoint templates" or "PowerPoint backgrounds."

Summary

In this chapter you learned how to apply templates and color schemes to make your presentations more professional-looking and easier to create. Even though the topic was probably not new to you, I hope you picked up a tip or two! The next chapter continues along these same lines by looking at masters and layouts, two other powerful ways of shaping a presentation's look-and-feel.

Chapter 3

Working with Masters and Layouts

IN THIS CHAPTER

- ◆ Working with slide layouts
- ◆ Understanding masters
- ◆ Editing the Slide Master layout
- ◆ Manually editing master elements
- ◆ Managing multiple masters

IN CHAPTER 2 YOU LEARNED about design templates that make broad, sweeping changes to the formatting of a presentation in a few simple clicks. When you apply a different design template to a presentation, what you're really doing is changing the formatting of that presentation's *masters*. Masters are sets of rules that PowerPoint refers to when formatting and displaying the text from the outline. In this chapter you'll learn how slides derive their layouts and other formatting and find out how to customize the masters in your templates.

Working with Slide Layouts

In Chapter 1 I introduced the concept of slide layouts very briefly. A *slide layout* is an arrangement of text and/or graphic placeholders. The layout you choose tells PowerPoint where on the slide your text should appear.

The Default Layouts

The default layout for the first slide in the presentation is Title Slide. This layout has two placeholders: one for the title of the presentation and one for the subtitle (see Figure 3-1).

The default layout for all other slides in the presentation is Title and Text. This layout also has two placeholders: a title across the top (for the individual slide's title, not the overall presentation title) and a large text box in the center where the text is automatically formatted in bulleted paragraphs (see Figure 3-2). Whenever you insert a new slide (by using the New Slide button on the toolbar or typing in

Title Slide layout

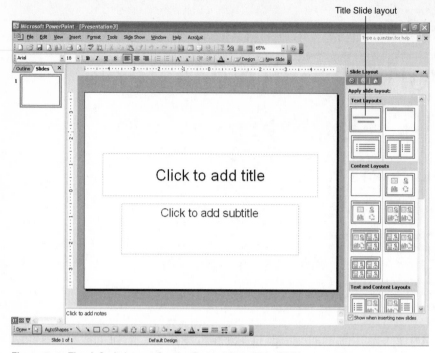

Figure 3-1: The default layout for the first slide is Title Slide.

Title and Text layout

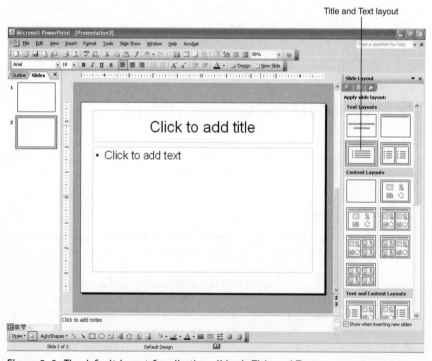

Figure 3-2: The default layout for all other slides is Title and Text.

the Outline pane—both of which are covered in Chapter 4), the resulting slide starts out in this Title and Text layout. If you want a different layout, it's up to you to select something else.

 TIP An add-in is available that enables you to change the default layout for the first slide in new presentations to something other than Title Slide. Download the add-in from http://officeone.mvps.org/sdsl/sdsl.html. Once it's installed, use Tools ➪ Set Default Slide Layout.

 NOTE The exact positioning of the placeholder text boxes on these two layouts (Title Slide and Title and Text) comes directly from the Title Master and Slide Master, respectively. That's why applying a different design template to a presentation sometimes shifts the text around on certain slides.

Choosing a Different Slide Layout

Most of the other slide layouts available in PowerPoint include more than just text. You would select a different layout whenever you wanted non-text content to supplement your words, such as clip art, video clips, or diagrams.

There is also a slide layout with a table placeholder. Even though you and I would consider a table to be "text," PowerPoint considers it to be a type of graphic object that serves as a text container.

To select a different layout for an existing slide:

1. Select the slide.

2. Choose Format ➪ Slide Layout. The Slide Layout task pane appears (see Figure 3-3).

3. Click the desired layout.

4. Close the task pane (or leave it open, your choice).

There are two kinds of placeholders on slide layouts (besides text): single-type and multi-type. The single-type ones insert one kind of object, such as a table or graph. The multi-type placeholders have six little icons and can be used for any of those six types of content.

 XREF I explained the content placeholders in Chapter 1, so turn back there if you need some more information.

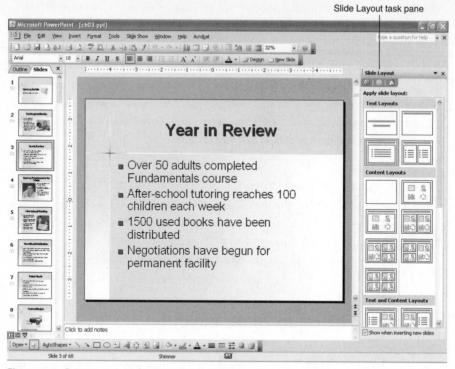

Figure 3-3: Select a layout from the Slide Layout task pane.

When you insert a new slide with the New Slide button on the toolbar, the Slide Layout task pane opens automatically. It does not do so when you create a new slide via the Outline pane, however. To choose a different layout after typing text in the Outline pane, you must choose Format⇨Slide Layout to open the Slide Layout task pane manually.

TIP One of the most annoying things about changing the slide layout for me is that there's no toolbar button. You have to go through the menu system for it. You can fix this, however, by adding a button to the toolbar yourself. See Chapter 18 to learn how.

AutoLayout and Text/Graphics Interaction

Throughout much of the second and third parts of this book, you'll learn various ways of inserting various types of content on a slide. You can use one of these placeholder layouts if you want, but it's not required; you can also manually insert items on any type of slide layout. For example, you could start with a plain Title and Text layout and then manually place a piece of clip art on top of it.

So why use a placeholder layout for non-text elements, if it's not required? One reason is that using the placeholders makes it easier to change to a different slide layout later without having to manually reposition anything. For example, suppose you start out with a Title, Text and Clip Art layout, as shown on the left side of Figure 3-4, and then you change it to a Title, Clip Art, and Text layout, as shown on the right side of Figure 3-4. Since you used the layout originally to position the clip art, the clip art moves gracefully to the other side when you apply the new layout. If the clip art had been manually placed on the slide and then the new layout applied, you might have had to manually move the clip.

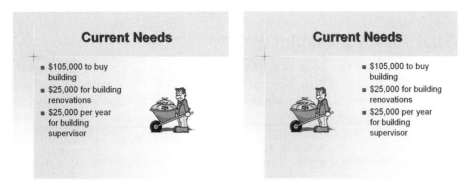

Figure 3-4: The same content using two different slide layouts.

So why did I say "might" in that last sentence? Because PowerPoint tries its best to save you from yourself. It has an *AutoLayout* feature that attempts to plug your existing content into the appropriate layout, whenever possible. It works with some object types (but not all).

To check it out, try the following experiment:

1. Create a new presentation, and insert a new slide in it that uses the Title and Text layout (the default bulleted list one from Figure 3-2). Type a bit of text in each of the placeholder boxes, just so you'll have something there.

2. Manually insert a piece of clip art (Insert➪Picture➪Clip Art). Any one will do. Notice that PowerPoint plops it down in the center of the slide, on top of the text box.

3. Delete the clip art (press Delete). We've learned from this experiment that PowerPoint does not do the AutoLayout thing for clip art.

4. Click the Insert Diagram or Organization Chart button in the Drawing toolbar. Click any of the diagram types and click OK. This time, PowerPoint switches to a different slide layout automatically and places the diagram to the right of the text box.

5. Notice the AutoLayout icon in the bottom right corner of the diagram. Click it to open a menu, and from there choose Undo Automatic Layout. The

diagram moves to the center of the slide, and the layout switches back to the default Title and Text layout.

If you don't like AutoLayout, you can turn it off completely in either of the two following ways:

◆ Click the AutoLayout icon after an AutoLayout operation has taken place and choose Stop Automatic Layout of Inserted Objects.

◆ Choose Tools➪AutoCorrect Options, and on the AutoFormat As You Type tab, clear the Automatic layout for inserted objects checkbox.

What About a Blank Layout?

Sometimes it can make sense to start with a Blank layout or a Title Only layout and then add the objects to the slide manually. The Blank layout gives you a totally empty canvas on which you can use the drawing tools, insert a collage of pictures, place manual text boxes, or insert any other combination of content. The Title Only layout does the same thing except it retains a placeholder for a title at the top consistent with the other slides in the presentation.

When you switch to a Blank or Title Only layout after having inserted content in placeholders in some other layout, that content remains but is converted to manual objects. (This is not just with those two types of layout—it happens any time you switch to a layout that does not include a placeholder for some content that you already have in place.) For example, try this experiment:

1. Create a new slide with Title, Text, and Clip Art. Type some text in both of the text placeholder boxes, and insert a piece of clip art in the art placeholder.

2. Switch to the Title Only layout. The text box and clip art remain, but their positions change, indicating they are no longer being constrained by placeholders.

3. View the Outline pane. Notice that the text appears there, even though it is not officially in a placeholder.

4. Switch to Title and Text layout. Notice that the text comes back into the text placeholder, and the clip art also remains but not in a placeholder.

5. Delete the bulleted text. Notice that the text placeholder appears to take its place.

6. Delete the clip art. No clip-art placeholder appears to take its place because the current slide layout has none for clip art.

One thing you might not have expected in the preceding steps is that in step 3, the text appears in the outline even though it's not part of a placeholder. Remember, earlier I told you that only placeholder text shows up in the outline, not text from manual text boxes? Well, that's still true. In step 3, the text is in a special class of text box. It's not really manual, because we didn't create it ourselves, but it's not really a placeholder box either. Let's call it an orphaned text box. It retains its ties to the outline because it could spring back into full placeholder-type membership at any moment should you choose to apply a layout that contained a text placeholder.

Understanding Masters

A *master* is a formatting and layout template—a set of specifications—that apply to all the slides in the presentation of a certain type. You've heard the word "template" before in Chapter 2, but there it related to a file with a POT extension. Here we're using the word template in a different sense. However, the two meanings are related.

When you apply a different design template to the presentation (that is, apply a different design through the Slide Design task pane), the new formatting settings apply to all the slides in the presentation by default. However, PowerPoint does not select each individual slide and apply that design to it; instead PowerPoint applies the settings to the Slide Master and Title Master, and then the settings apply automatically to each of the individual slides.

There are actually four different masters in PowerPoint:

◆ *Slide*: This master controls slides using all layouts except Title Slide.

◆ *Title*: This master controls slides using the Title Slide layout.

◆ *Notes*: This master controls the layout of Notes Page view and printouts of notes pages.

◆ *Handouts*: This master controls the layout of handouts printed through PowerPoint. There are separate layouts for each style of handouts (one, two, three, four, six, and nine slides, plus outline).

The Slide and Title Masters are edited within a single view called Slide Master, but the Notes Master and Handouts Master each have their own separate views. Chapter 17 explores the Notes Master and Handouts Master in detail, so in this chapter we'll stick with the Slide Master view as our focus.

 For some design templates, there may be a separate Title Master command on the View ➪ Master menu that jumps you into Slide Master view with the Title Master selected.

Exploring Slide Master View

The best way to understand masters is to take a look at them. Choose View ➪ Master ➪ Slide Master to enter Slide Master view, as shown in Figure 3-5.

Notice in Figure 3-5 that there are two thumbnail slides at the left. The top one is for the Slide Master, which is what you're seeing in Figure 3-5. Click the one immediately beneath it; that's the Title Master, as shown in Figure 3-6.

Slide Master

Figure 3-5: Viewing the Slide Master.

Connecting line between Slide and Title Masters

Title Master   Slide Master View toolbar

Figure 3-6: Viewing the Title Master.

Slide Master view has a floating Slide Master View toolbar, which you can see in Figures 3-5 and 3-6. To leave Slide Master view, click the Close Master View button on that toolbar. I'll explain the other buttons on this toolbar later in the chapter.

Slide Master view also shows placeholder boxes for each of the layout elements that carries over to each slide. Some of these are common to both the Slide Master and the Title Master. For example, when comparing Figures 3-5 and 3-6, you'll notice that both have a "Click to edit Master title style" placeholder, as well as Date Area, Footer Area, and Number Area placeholders. The main difference between the two is that the Slide Master has a "Click to edit master text styles" area where you set up the formatting for slide text, whereas the Title Master has a "Click to edit Master subtitle style" area, where you set up the formatting for the title slide's subtitle.

 As with other views, the divider between the thumbnails pane and the main editing pane is resizable; drag it left or right to change the proportions as desired.

Slide and Title Master Interaction

Notice the gray line that ties the Slide Master and Title Master together. It indicates that these two are related. This becomes important when you start working with multiple sets of masters in a single presentation (which is covered later in the chapter).

Most types of changes you make to the Slide Master, such as color and font choices, will trickle down to the Title Master. (Other changes, such as placeholder repositioning, do not.) This enables you to make changes at the master level only once, rather than having to duplicate your changes for both the Slide and Title Masters.

There are some exceptions—not all kinds of formatting transfer automatically between the Slide Master and the Title Master. Table 3-1 lists some effects and whether or not they transfer automatically.

Note that it does *not* work the same going the other direction—that is, from Title Master to Slide Master. Changes you make to the Title Master do not apply automatically to the Slide Master. This is by design; it allows you to have different formatting for your title slides than for your other slides. Therefore, if you want to make changes that apply to both, you can make them to the Slide Master to save time.

Master Settings versus Individual Slide Settings

Any formatting you do to an individual slide overrides the formatting on the Slide Master or Title Master. For example, suppose you set the background color on the Slide Master to green, and then on an individual slide you set the background color to blue. That particular slide will have a blue background, but any slides for which

TABLE 3-1 AUTOMATIC FORMATTING TRANSFER BETWEEN SLIDE MASTER AND
TITLE MASTER

Feature	Copies from Slide Master to Title Master?
Color scheme	Yes
Slide design	Yes
Font, Size, Attributes, Color of Title placeholder	Yes
Font, Size, Attributes, Color of Text placeholder	Yes, modifies the subtitle
Slide background color	Yes
Slide background graphic	Yes
Background in text placeholder box	No
Positioning of text placeholders	No
Deletion of text placeholders	No
Addition of clip art or other objects	No
Vertical or horizontal alignment of slide title placeholder	No

you have not explicitly chosen a background color will still be green. The same goes for fonts, positioning, and all other formatting attributes.

Other Ways to Modify the Slide/Title Masters

The most straightforward and obvious way to modify a master is to do it from Slide Master View, as shown in Figure 3-6. That's the method we'll use in most of this chapter.

However, certain other commands in PowerPoint also can make changes to the Slide Master, without opening its view. Some features have an Apply to All Slides option that makes the change on the Slide Master and Title Master. You saw this in Chapter 2 with the slide designs and color schemes, for example. Table 3-2 lists some of the features that you can apply to the Slide Master and Title Master without opening up the Master view.

Editing the Slide Master Layout

Now that you are familiar with the concepts of the Slide and Title Masters, let's start looking at some of the ways you can edit them. We'll start with something obvious: positioning of objects.

TABLE 3-2 SLIDE AND TITLE MASTER CHANGES YOU CAN MAKE WITHOUT USING MASTER VIEW

Feature	How to apply
Color Scheme	Choose from Color Schemes in the Slide Design task pane; your choice automatically applies to Slide and Title Masters.
Slide Design	Choose from the Slide Design task pane; your choice automatically applies to Slide and Title Masters.
Slide Transition	Choose from the Slide Transition task pane, and then click Apply to All.
Animation Scheme	Choose from Animation Schemes in the Slide Design task pane, and then click Apply to All.
Background	Choose Format⇨Background, select a background, and click Apply to All.

Modifying Text Placeholder Positions

The text placeholder positioning determines where the text will appear on each slide. The Title placeholder is usually at the top of each slide, and the Text placeholder is usually below it. However, each design template has its own ideas about exactly where the text placeholders should be positioned. To see this for yourself, display the Slide Design task pane and switch rapidly between several different slide designs. You can see the text placeholders jump around to different spots.

The Text placeholder usually takes up nearly the entire slide, but if you need to make room for a graphic or other repeated element on each slide, you may want to change its size and/or position. For example, in Figure 3-7 I've made the Text placeholder narrower so that I can place a graphic to its right.

To modify a text placeholder, resize it on the Slide Master or Title Master as you would any text box. Click the outside of its frame to select it; selection handles appear around the outside. Then, to resize the text placeholder, drag one of its selection handles. Or, to move the text placeholder, position the mouse pointer over the border—but *not* on a selection handle—and drag.

Deleting and Restoring Placeholders on Masters

To delete a placeholder from a master, click its border and then press Delete. If there are any slides in the presentation that rely on the deleted placeholder to hold some of their existing content, that content will remain but will be converted to an "orphaned" object. The orphaned object will retain the same text, but its formatting will probably change.

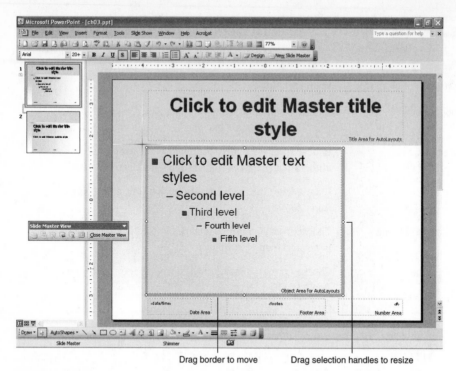

Figure 3-7: Drag the text placeholder boxes on a Slide or Title Master to move or resize them the same way as you would any object on any slide.

If you customize a master by deleting one or more of the placeholders on it, you can get those placeholders back at any time. To do so, click the Master Layout button on the Slide Master View toolbar, or choose Format⇨Master Layout. This opens a dialog box containing check boxes for all the placeholders. Any that have been deleted have open check boxes; mark those check boxes to replace those deleted items (see Figure 3-8).

Figure 3-8: Restoring deleted items from the Slide Master.

TIP It is not necessary to delete the Date Area, Footer Area, or Number Area place-holders from the Slide Master layout if you don't want to use them; you can leave the placeholders intact but turn off their display in the Header and Footer dialog box. See *Changing Header and Footer Elements* later in this chapter to learn how.

Here's an experiment that will show you the effect of deleting and restoring a text placeholder:

1. Start a new presentation using the AutoContent Wizard for a Training presentation.

2. Display Slide Master view, and delete the main text placeholder in the center.

3. Close Slide Master view and page through the slides. Notice that each text box now has a white background and appears to be totally blank with some yellow bullet circles. That's because the text is set to appear white.

4. Select one of the orphaned text boxes on one of the slides and apply a black background fill to it. The text on the slide comes into view.

5. Switch back to the Slide Master view.

6. Choose Format⇨Master Layout. Mark the Text checkbox and click OK. Then close Slide Master view.

7. Switch to Slide Sorter view and examine the slides. All the slides have changed back to the default formatting for their text except the one you manually modified in step 4; it retains its black background.

8. Close the presentation without saving your changes.

Changing Header and Footer Elements

The Date Area, Footer Area, and Number Area on the Slide and Title Masters enable you to control where those elements will appear on each slide. For example, you could move any of those elements to the top of the slide, swap their places, or make any other positioning changes.

You can also format those placeholder boxes to change the fonts used for each of those elements. The settings governing each of those three placeholders varies depending on the design template in use. See *Changing Text Formatting* later in this chapter for information on specifying a font for a placeholder box.

All three areas are controlled from the Header and Footer dialog box. Choose View⇨Header and Footer (either in Slide Master view or outside of it; it doesn't matter). Then on the Slide tab, change the settings of each of the three placeholder types (see Figure 3-9).

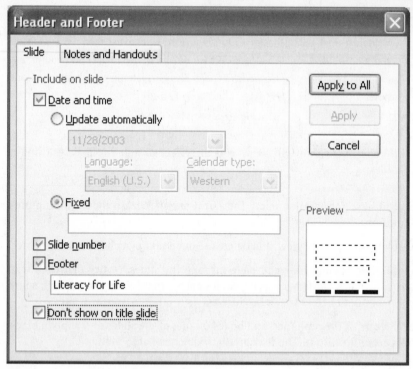

Figure 3-9: Choose the placeholders to display.

Here are the specifics on each of the three elements.

DATE AND TIME

Date and Time is enabled by default. Depending on the design template, it may be set either to Update Automatically or Fixed:

◆ Update Automatically pulls the current date from the computer's clock and formats it in whatever format you choose from the drop-down list. You can also select a Language and a Calendar Type setting (although unless you are presenting in some other country than the one for which your version of PowerPoint was written, this is probably not an issue).

◆ Fixed prints whatever you enter in the Fixed text box in the Date area. By default, the Fixed text box is empty, so it appears as if the Date and Time feature had been turned off. It's actually on, but blank.

TIP In addition to (or instead of) placing the date on each slide, you might want to insert the current date or time on one individual slide—perhaps as part of a sentence in a text box, for example. To do so, display that individual slide, position the insertion point where you want it, and choose Insert ➪ Date and Time. Then select the format you want and click OK.

When you put an automatically updated date/time code on the slide master, it updates at the beginning of the presentation but does not keep updating in real time throughout the slide show. If you want a real-time clock that shows the current time on each slide during the show, try the Auto-DateTime add-in,found at `http://officeone.mvps.org/autodatetime/autodatetime.html`.

SLIDE NUMBER

This option shows the slide number on each slide, wherever the Number Area box is positioned.

By default, slide numbering starts with 1. You can start with some other number if you like; choose File ➪ Page Setup and change the value in the Number Slides From box.

You can format the font size and other attributes used for the number by formatting the placeholder in the Number Area box, but you cannot change to a different style of numbering (such as Roman or letters). The automatic slide numbers are strictly Arabic-style in PowerPoint.

The slide number can be inserted on an individual slide, either instead of or in addition to the numbering on the Slide Master. To do so, display that slide, position the insertion point, and then choose Insert ➪ Slide Number. This places a code for the slide number, so that if the slide's number changes, the reference will change too.

Check out `www.rdpslides.com/pptfaq/FAQ00548.htm` for a handy add-in that enables you to number slides, including the total number of slides—for example, in a 10-slide presentation, page 2 would be numbered "2 of 10."

FOOTER

The footer is enabled by default in most design templates, but is blank. Enter the desired text in the Footer box in the Header and Footer dialog box. The Footer checkbox is handy because it enables you to suppress the footer (by clearing the checkbox) without deleting the text in the Footer text box, so you can retain your footer text for later use.

DON'T SHOW ON TITLE SLIDE

This checkbox suppresses the date/time, page number, and footer on the title slide. Many people like to hide those elements on the title slide for a cleaner look and to avoid repeated information (for example, if the current date appears in the subtitle box on the title slide).

Manually Editing Master Elements

Besides dragging placeholder boxes around, what can you do to the Slide and Title Masters? Plenty. Just about anything you can do to an individual slide, you can do to the masters. Here are just a few examples.

Changing Text Formatting

To change the text formatting used in the presentation's text placeholders, change them for the placeholder text on the Slide Master. The changes you make to the Slide Master will automatically apply to the associated Title Master too. You can change the font (typeface), size, color, and other attributes like bold, italic, shadow, and so on.

You probably already know how to make font changes, but just in case you need one or two refreshers, Table 3-3 summarizes the procedures for various types of text formatting. Also see the section *Formatting Text* in Chapter 5 for more formatting procedures.

TABLE 3-3 TEXT FORMATTING REVIEW

To accomplish this:	Do this:
Change the font	Format⇨Font or Font drop-down list on toolbar
Change the font size	Format⇨Font or Font Size drop-down list on toolbar
Apply/remove Bold, Italic, Underline, or Shadow	Format⇨Font or buttons on Formatting toolbar
Apply/remove Emboss, Superscript, or Subscript	Format⇨Font
Change the font color	Format⇨Font or Text Color drop-down list on toolbar
Change text alignment within the placeholder box	Format⇨Alignment or alignment buttons on toolbar

Changing the Background

Most of the design templates that come with PowerPoint include some sort of background graphic decoration. You can stick with the background provided, modify it, create your own, or go backgroundless.

There are several ways you can go when it comes to slide backgrounds as follows:

◆ You can choose a design template that comes with a background you like, and then customize it as needed.

◆ You can start with a background provided by a design template and then dissect and modify it.

◆ You can delete any background graphic provided and use a solid color background.

◆ You can delete any background graphic provided and use a fill effect such as gradient, pattern, picture, or texture as the background.

◆ You can create your own background by combining lines and shapes with PowerPoint's drawing tools.

 Most of the background graphics are either transparent or use one of the scheme colors as their fill (see Chapter 2 for information about scheme colors). Therefore, changing the color scheme also changes the color of the background graphic. Keep that in mind if you are creating your own backgrounds; it's better to use scheme colors or transparency than to choose fixed colors that might clash with a color scheme you apply later.

ANATOMY OF A BACKGROUND

Before you start getting into the complexities of background modification and creation, it might help to break down one of PowerPoint's provided backgrounds and see how the good folks at Microsoft constructed it. This experiment might be a springboard for your own ideas and/or might help you figure out how to customize the background to meet your needs.

Try the following as an experiment:

1. Start a new, blank presentation and apply the Radial.pot design template to it.

2. Open Slide Master view and select the background graphic behind the title area on the Slide Master—not the Title Master (see Figure 3-10).

3. On the Drawing toolbar, choose Draw ⇨ Ungroup. Now each of the shapes and lines that comprise the background graphic have their own individual

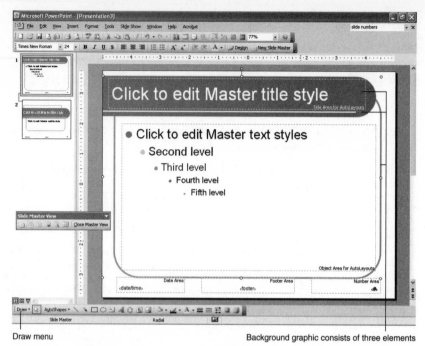

Draw menu

Background graphic consists of three elements

Figure 3-10: Apply Radial.pot to a blank presentation and then select the background graphic on the Slide Master.

frames. This particular background graphic consists of three separate elements: the purple shape behind the title, the white underline beneath the title, and the green oval line that runs around the outside.

TIP Actually, you can select an object within a group without having to ungroup it, but only certain formatting commands work on it when it's selected that way. Click one to select the group, then click again on the individual object inside the group. It appears with gray selection handles, indicating that that object is selected. You can't resize it, but you can change its border and fill. Chapter 7 covers border and fill formatting.

4. Click in the blank white area to deselect everything. Then click once on the purple shape behind the title.

5. Choose Draw⇨Change AutoShape⇨Basic Shapes, and then click the octagon (second shape in second row). The purple shape changes to an elongated octagon (see Figure 3-11).

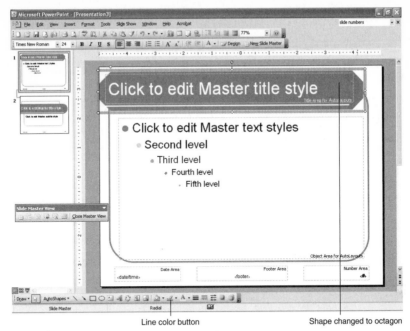

Figure 3-11: Background graphics constructed of AutoShapes can be edited freely using PowerPoint's own drawing tools.

6. Click the green border to select it. Then open the Line Color menu from the Drawing toolbar and select the second-from-the-right color in the color scheme (brown). The line changes to brown.

7. Regroup the objects (choose Draw⇨Regroup). You do not have to select all the objects; PowerPoint remembers what all was in the group.

8. Close Slide Master View.

9. Close the presentation without saving your changes to it.

As you learned from the preceding steps, backgrounds provided in PowerPoint are in many cases just simple AutoShapes grouped together. You can change them at will by ungrouping and modifying them. See Chapter 7 for more help with the drawing tools.

Some of the backgrounds are more than just AutoShapes, however. For example, the background in the slide shown in Figure 3-12 includes a graphic of several clocks. There is also a frame with a gradient shadow along its right edge.

This background can also be dissected by using the Draw⇨Ungroup command on it. In Figure 3-13, I've broken apart the two elements—a graphic and a transparent rectangle with a partial gradient fill—so you can see them separately; take a look at Figure 3-13 and then look back at Figure 3-12 to see how they work together to give the illusion that there is a shadow behind the graphic.

This entire panel is a single graphic image.   The shadow is a separate graphic.

Figure 3-12: Some backgrounds include external graphic images, not just AutoShapes.

There is one final type of background provided in some of PowerPoint's templates, and that's a full-slide image. For example, many of the backgrounds that look like water or clouds are actually single large images. These can't be selected or ungrouped in the Slide Master; they must be edited through the Background dialog box (Format⇨Background). You'll see one of these later in the chapter in the section *Selecting a Picture Background*.

DELETING A BACKGROUND GRAPHIC
First things first—to delete a background graphic, do either of the following:

◆ Display the Slide Master, select the background, and press Delete.

◆ While *not* in Slide Master View, choose Format⇨Background, mark the Omit background graphics from Master checkbox (see Figure 3-14), and click OK.

SELECTING A SOLID COLOR BACKGROUND
You can't delete the color from the background, but you can change it to a different color (like white, for example). To do that, choose Format⇨Background and select the desired color or effect. Remember, though, that changing to a fixed color means that color will stick even if you switch to a different color scheme. Therefore, it's usually better to allow the color scheme to select the background color, or at least

Figure 3-13: The background from Figure 3-12, dissected
into its two parts.

Figure 3-14: You can remove background graphics from
the Background dialog box

to use one of the scheme's other colors for it. You can also modify the background color in the current color scheme, as you learned in Chapter 2. That would make the color change in the current presentation and would allow it to change if you changed the color scheme later.

SELECTING A FILL EFFECT AS A BACKGROUND

I'm saving the main discussion of fill effects for Chapter 7, so jump ahead there if you're eager to play with gradients, textures, or patterns as backgrounds. Suffice now to say that these are really cool effects and that you will need to master them before you can consider yourself really proficient at background creation.

SELECTING A PICTURE BACKGROUND

A picture background fills the entire "behind" of each slide with a single graphic image. As I mentioned earlier, PowerPoint uses this technique for some of the design template backgrounds.

To see how one works, do this experiment:

1. Start a new, blank presentation and apply the Ocean.pot template.

2. Choose Format⇨Background.

3. Open the drop-down list in the Background dialog box and choose Fill Effects.

4. Click the Picture tab. Notice that the current background appears as a picture here (see Figure 3-15).

5. Click Select Picture. The Select Picture dialog box opens. The default location shown is the My Pictures folder.

6. Navigate to the folder containing the picture you want to use. For this experiment, open the Sample Pictures folder (within My Pictures) and choose Sunset. Then click Insert.

7. Click OK in the Fill Effects dialog box to use the chosen picture.

8. In the Background dialog box, click Apply to All. Notice that the picture is all-blue, whereas the original was a vibrant red.

9. Choose Color Schemes from the Slide Design task pane to open the Color Schemes in the task pane, and select the yellow-background scheme. The picture changes to all-yellow.

10. Close the presentation file without saving your changes.

 Notice what happened in step 8. When you use Apply to All, the image appears as a background "wash," as you saw. If you had used Apply instead of Apply to All, the picture would have stayed with its original colors. So if you want the original colors, you have to insert the picture for each slide individually.

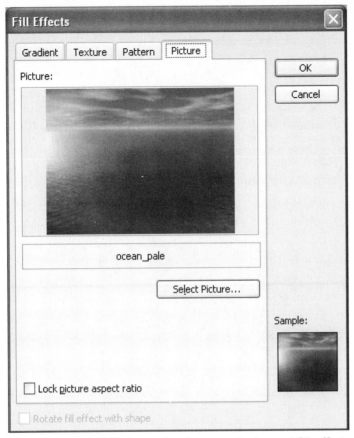

Figure 3-15: PowerPoint has used a picture as a background fill effect in the current design template.

CREATING YOUR OWN BACKGROUND

Now that you have seen how backgrounds work, you're probably itching to create your own. If you come up with some good ones, you might even be able to sell them to other PowerPoint users!

Check out some of the backgrounds on the CD that comes with this book; they were created by expert users who are in that very business.

The specifics of background-creation will depend on your vision of the finished product, of course, but here are some general steps:

1. Set the background color to either a solid color or a gradient or pattern. Use scheme colors whenever possible.

    or

Choose a background texture or picture. Picture backgrounds were covered in the preceding section.

For details on textures, gradients, and patterns, see Chapter 7.

2. In Slide Master View, create background graphics using PowerPoint's drawing tools, layering and formatting objects as needed to create the desired images.

Using the drawing tools is a huge and important topic, because you can use drawn lines and shapes to accent and enhance almost any presentation design.

3. Add any graphics from files that you need to supplement the graphics drawn with the drawing tools.

4. When you're finished, select and group all the graphics into a single object (with Draw⇨Group). This isn't necessary, strictly speaking, but it does make them easier to work with.

5. Exit from Slide Master View and save the file as a template (see Chapter 2).

Changing Bullet Characters

You can use anything from a simple round dot to a full-fledged graphic from any source. Each slide can have its own different bullet characters, but it's better in most cases to stick with a consistent bullet character across all slides. And whenever you want something applied to all slides, where do you apply it? That's right, to the Slide Master.

Decide upon your slide design template first, before changing the bullet characters. Most design templates apply their own bullet styles.

On the Slide Master, you'll notice several levels of bulleted lists. By formatting the placeholders there with the desired bullet character, you automatically assign them to all text placeholder boxes on all slides where bullets are employed.

The choice of first-level bullet character is especially important since it's the one that your audience will see most often. However, the other bullet levels are important too because they must be complementary to the top-level bullet character in style.

APPLYING A BASIC BULLET CHARACTER

To change the bullet character for an outline level (just the basic bullet, nothing fancy), do the following:

1. From the Slide Master, click in the line representing the outline level for which you want to change the bullet character.

2. Choose Format➪Bullets and Numbering. The Bullets and Numbering dialog box opens.

3. Make sure the Bulleted tab is displayed. If it isn't, click it.

4. Click one of the other bullet styles shown (see Figure 3-16).

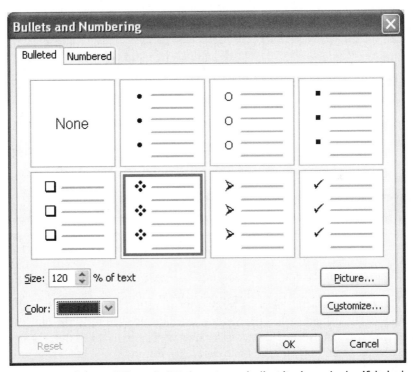

Figure 3-16: Select a different bullet character, and adjust its size and color, if desired.

5. (Optional) To change the size of the bullet in relation to the text, change the value in the Size box.

6. (Optional) To change the color of the bullet, change the color in the Color box.

7. Click OK.

CHOOSING AN ALTERNATIVE BULLET CHARACTER

The seven bullet character choices that appear in the Bullets and Numbering dialog box are just the tip of the iceberg. You can choose any character from any font on your system as the bullet, including any of the special fonts like Wingdings.

To select a different character, from the Bullets and Numbering dialog box, click the Customize button. The Symbol dialog box opens (see Figure 3-17). Choose a font from the Font list, click the desired bullet character, and click OK.

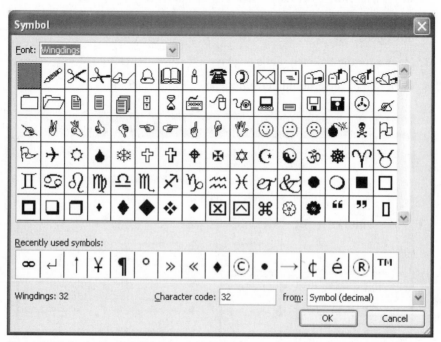

Figure 3-17: In the Symbol dialog box, choose any character from any font as the bullet character.

The bullet character takes its formatting from the line of text that it supports. For example, if the text has the Shadow attribute applied to it, the bullet character will too. You can't format the bullet character differently from the text in terms of shadowing or bolding, but you can make it a different size and color through the Bullets and Numbering dialog box as you saw in Figure 3-16.

Try these fonts as bullet character sets: Symbol, Wingdings (1-3), Webdings, Bookshelf Symbol, Zapf Dingbats (if available), MS Outlook, MS Reference Specialty, Marlett, and MT Extra.

If you use an unusual font for the bullet character, embed TrueType fonts when saving (see Chapter 2). You will need to test the embedding before distributing the presentation widely, however. If possible, test it by opening it on a PC that does not have that font. Reason: PowerPoint 2003 has a nasty quirk introduced by Microsoft's legal department that prevents you from editing a presentation with embedded fonts that have some certain types of restrictions on them. You can't even use Format ➪ Replace Fonts to remove the offending font—the presentation becomes totally uneditable on that PC.

CHOOSING A PICTURE BULLET

Picture bullets give great flexibility to PowerPoint's bulleted list feature! You can use any picture as your bullet character, in any size.

PowerPoint's Clip Organizer comes with hundreds of small graphics suitable for use as bullets, so you may not need to look any further than that. To select a bullet character from the Clip Organizer, click the Picture button in the Bullets and Numbering dialog box. This opens the Picture Bullet dialog box shown in Figure 3-18. From here just click the graphic you want and click OK.

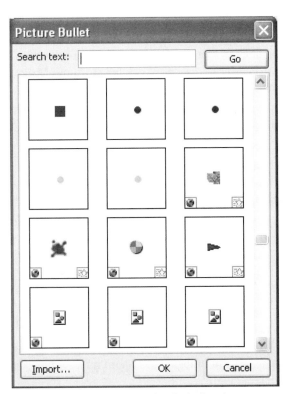

Figure 3-18: Select a picture for the bullet character.

Chapter 9 will tell you all about the Clip Organizer, but for now here's what you need to know:

◆ The clips with a little globe in the bottom left corner are located on the Internet (at Microsoft's Web site). When you choose one of these, it will subsequently be downloaded to your hard disk for use. Download time is minimal since the graphics are so tiny. These do not appear in the Picture Bullet dialog box if you are not connected to the Internet.

◆ The clips with a little star in the bottom right corner have some sort of animation effect associated with them, such that when they're used in a presentation, they do something other than just sit there. (The exact effect varies, so you have to try each one out to see what it does.)

◆ The clips with neither a globe nor a star are plain, static bullet characters that are already located on your hard disk and ready for use.

If none of the bullet characters suit you, you can import your own. To do so, from the Picture Bullet dialog box shown in Figure 3-18, click Import. Then select the file containing the graphic you want to use and click Add. The clip is then inserted into the Picture Bullet dialog box, and you can select it from there as you would any of Microsoft's own bullet graphics.

 If you use a very large graphic file as a bullet character, you'll increase the overall size of your PowerPoint file dramatically. Resize and resave any graphics files in a third-party graphics editing application so that they are approximately the size you plan on using in the presentation (somewhere around 30 pixels high would be ample for a bullet character).

Managing Multiple Masters

You can have more than one set of Slide Masters and Title Masters in Power-Point 2003, which gives you more flexibility in creating long or complex presentations. You might want to have two Title Master layouts, for example—one for the very first slide in the show and one for the title slides that indicate sections within the show. Or, you might want to have two Slide Master layouts, one for slides with lots of text and one for slides with only a few words of text. It's all up to you.

In this part of the chapter you'll be working extensively with the Slide Master View toolbar. Review the button names shown in Figure 3-19, and refer to it as you read the following sections.

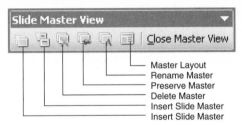

Figure 3-19: Slide Master View toolbar.

Creating Additional Slide and Title Masters

 To create an additional Slide Maser, click the Insert New Slide Master button on the Slide Master View toolbar. The new master appears in the left pane, below the original slide and title masters. By default it is totally blank, but you can apply one of the other design templates to it.

You can also create a new slide master by displaying the Slide Design task pane and clicking a design there (while still in Slide Master View).

Notice that by default, the new Slide Master does not have an associated Title Master. You can create one for it by selecting it and then clicking the Insert New Title Master button. This button is available only when a Slide Master is selected that does not already have an associated Title Master.

Slide Masters and Title Masters always have a one-to-one relationship, so if you want an additional Title Master, you must first create an additional Slide Master. (You can format it exactly the same as the other Slide Masters, however, if that is helpful.) Figure 3-20 shows an additional Slide Master and Title Master.

> **TIP** One easy way to create a new set of masters is to select existing ones and copy them (Ctrl+C) then paste them (Ctrl+V).

If you know that you want to apply a certain design template to the alternative Slide Master, and you know that you will also want an alternative Title Master, here's a shortcut: from Slide Master view, open the Slide Design task pane and open the menu for the desired design (use its arrow button or right-click it). On its menu, choose Add Design (see Figure 3-21). This creates a new Slide Master/Title Master pair with that design.

Copying a Master

When you create new masters as described previously, they are completely blank and plain. Perhaps you would rather start with a copy of the existing master and modify it. To copy a master, select it and choose Edit⇨Copy and then Edit⇨Paste.

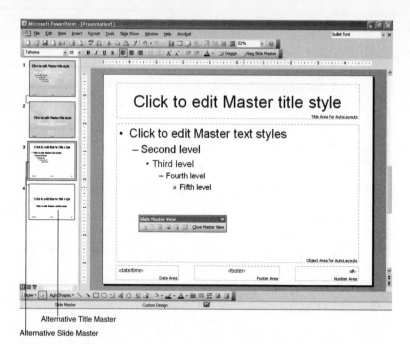

Alternative Title Master

Alternative Slide Master

Figure 3-20: Another set of masters has been added; they are blank by default with plain Arial font.

Click the arrow to open a design template's menu.

Figure 3-21: To create a new pair of masters based on a certain design, choose Add Design from that design's menu in the Slide Design pane.

Renaming a Master

The default name for a new master is "Custom Design," but you will probably want to give yours a more descriptive name. For example, you might call your alternative Slide Master something like Master for Backup Slides. To rename a master, select it, click the Rename Master button on the Slide Master View toolbar, and then type the new name.

Deleting a Master

To delete a master, select it, and press Delete or click the Delete Master button on the Slide Master View toolbar. If you delete a Title Master, its associated Slide Master remains. However, if you delete the Slide Master, the Title Master is deleted too.

When you delete a master, any slides that used it change over to the first remaining master. If you deleted an alternative, the affected slides change to the main master set. If you delete the main master set, the slides change to the first alternative master set in the Slides pane in Slide Master view.

Preserving Alternative Masters

If a master does not have any slides associated with it, PowerPoint will delete it. Suppose, for example, that you created an alternative master and then applied it to several slides, but then you deleted those slides. The alternative master will go away unless you elect to preserve it.

When a master is preserved, a pushpin symbol appears next to it in the Slides pane at the left. To toggle a master's preservation status, select it and click the Preserve Master button on the Slide Master View toolbar.

Using an Alternative Master for New Slides

After you have created the alternative masters you want, and saved them by closing Slide Master View and returning to the presentation, you will probably want to apply the alternative master(s) to some slides.

By default, all slides use the primary set of masters (Slide and Title). To switch to an alternative set for a slide, do the following:

1. Open the Slide Design task pane. In the Used in This Presentation section at the top, there should be two designs: your original and your alternative.

2. To apply the alternative to certain slides, select those slides in the Slides pane on the left. Then click the down arrow next to the alternative design and choose Apply to Selected Slides (see Figure 3-22).

The alternative Slide Master will be applied if the slides use any layout except Title Slide; any title slides will receive the alternative Title Master.

Figure 3–22: Apply an alternative master to selected slides.

Summary

In this chapter you learned all about using slide layouts and masters to simplify layout and formatting across a multi-slide presentation. The larger and more complex your presentations, the more useful these features become. This ends Part I of the book; in the next part we'll be looking at some ways to simplify text entry and formatting.

Part II

Conveying the Message

Chapter 4

Importing and Organizing Text

IN THIS CHAPTER

◆ Importing text from Word

◆ Importing text from other presentations

◆ Importing text from other sources

◆ Working with the Outlining tools

TYPING A FEW LINES OF TEXT on a PowerPoint slide is easy, right? Just click and type. The tricky stuff comes in when you have a great deal of text to manage, especially if you've already typed it in some other application or presentation and don't want to waste your time retyping it. In this chapter you'll learn some shortcuts for importing text from various sources and organizing it in the Outline pane in PowerPoint.

Importing Text from Word

Many people find Word a better tool for typing text than PowerPoint, because Word is designed specifically for text whereas PowerPoint is more multi-purpose.

It's fairly easy to import text from a Word document into PowerPoint, but unless you format it correctly in Word beforehand, there will be lots of cleanup work to do after the import. The following sections explain how to prepare the text in Word, how to import it into PowerPoint, and how to check for and fix any problems afterward.

Preparing a Word Document to Be Imported into PowerPoint

Technically, PowerPoint will take any text from any Word document, but it won't be pretty. Suppose, for example, you have a Word document consisting of a series of paragraphs. When you import it into PowerPoint, it might look something like Figure 4-1.

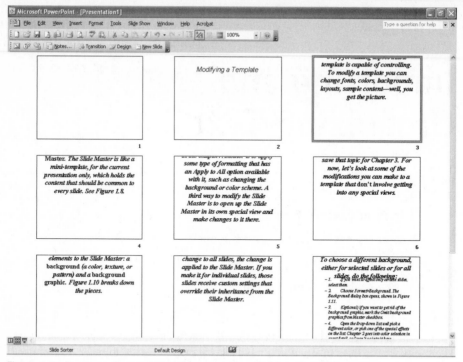

Figure 4-1: A paragraph-style Word document imported into PowerPoint as is.

Figure 4-1 is a prime example of what happens if you *don't* prepare a document in Word before you import it into PowerPoint. PowerPoint makes each heading a slide title, but the document shown in Figure 4-1 had only one heading. It then puts each paragraph on its own slide, but it doesn't fit them into the text placeholders. It tries to fit the numbered list on a single slide, but there isn't room. Pretty much a train wreck, isn't it? Figure 4-1 also illustrates an important point to remember: *regular paragraph-style text does not work very well in PowerPoint.* PowerPoint is all about short, snappy bulleted lists and headings.

A good Word document for PowerPoint importing uses heading styles consistently, with the top-level heading style (Heading 1) used for each line that should become a slide title and lower level heading styles (Heading 2, Heading 3, and so on) for each of the bullet points within each slide. There should not be any paragraph text (that is, text that does not have a Heading style). Figure 4-2 shows a document in Word that would import nicely into PowerPoint.

The best way to generate a Word document comprised exclusively of headings is to work in Outline view (choose View⇨Outline). In Outline view, each heading level has a different amount of indent so you can clearly see the relationships among the headings. Figure 4-3 shows the document from Figure 4-2 in Outline view in Word. In fact, when PowerPoint imports from Word, it considers it a "Word Outline," indicating that it is interested primarily in the heading-based outline organization of the document.

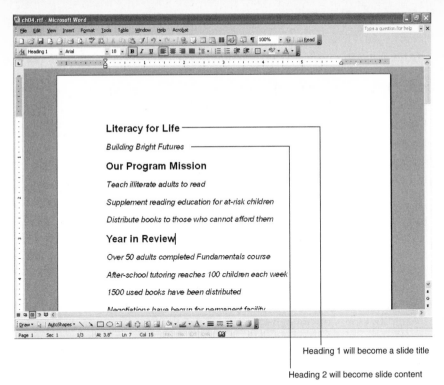

Heading 1 will become a slide title

Heading 2 will become slide content

Figure 4-2: This Word document would import well into PowerPoint because of its consistent use of heading styles for the text.

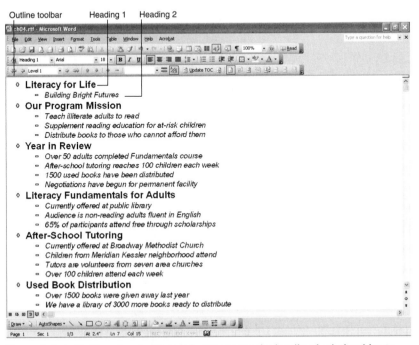

Figure 4-3: In Outline view in Word it is easy to see the headings' relationships to one another.

To change a paragraph of text between outline levels in Outline view in Word, press Tab (to demote) or Shift+Tab (to promote) while the insertion point is anywhere within that paragraph. This also changes the style applied to that paragraph to the corresponding heading style.

Following are some other tips for preparing a Word document for PowerPoint import:

◆ Stick with the basic styles only—just Heading 1, Heading 2, and so on.

◆ Delete all blank lines above the first heading; if you don't, you will have blank slides at the beginning of your presentation.

◆ Strip off as much manual formatting as possible from the text in Word, so that PowerPoint's design templates will be free to format the text consistently. To strip off formatting in Word, select the text and press Ctrl+spacebar.

◆ Do not leave blank lines between paragraphs. These will translate into blank slides or blank bulleted items in PowerPoint.

◆ Delete any graphic elements, such as clip art, pictures, charts, and so on. These will not transfer over to PowerPoint anyway and may confuse PowerPoint's Import utility.

The Word document can be saved in Word's native format or in Rich Text Format (*.rtf). Either works fine for importing text into PowerPoint. RTF is a very portable format, so it would be useful if you planned on importing this text not only into PowerPoint but also into some non-Microsoft and/or non-Windows applications.

 TIP You don' t really need Word to create an outline for import into PowerPoint. A plain-text editor will work just fine, like Notepad, or any other word-processing program. Each line that should be a title slide should start at the left margin; first-level bullet paragraphs should be preceded by a single tab; second-level bullets should be preceded by two tabs; and so on.

Bringing Text from a Word Outline into PowerPoint

Now that your outline is prepared in Word, it's a snap to import it into PowerPoint. There are two ways to do it. You can use the Slides from Outline command to import the text into an existing presentation file, or you can open a Word or RTF document as a new presentation.

IMPORTING WORD TEXT INTO AN EXISTING PRESENTATION
Use this method if you already have started the presentation and have some text or formatting settings you want to keep.

To import a Word outline, follow these steps:

1. Open the presentation into which you want to import.

2. Display the Outline pane (at the left) and click where you want the new slides to be imported.

3. Choose Insert ⇨ Slides from Outline. The Insert Outline dialog box appears (see Figure 4-4).

4. Select the document from which you want to import and click Import. The outline of the Word document is inserted into the outline of the presentation, with all Heading 1-styled paragraphs becoming slide titles.

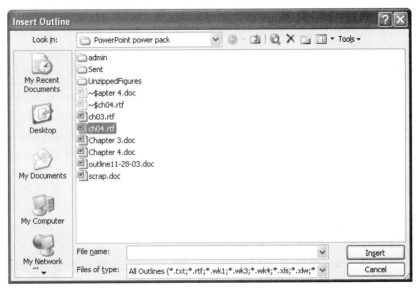

Figure 4-4: Select the Word document (or other outline file format) and click Insert.

 You can also import tables from Word, and they become PowerPoint tables. However, they don't get imported when using the Slides from Outline command described here. See Chapter 6 for details about working with tables.

OPENING A WORD DOCUMENT AS A NEW PRESENTATION
Use this method if you want to start a new presentation based on a Word outline—that is, if you do not already have a presentation started.

To create a new presentation from a Word document, follow these steps:

1. Choose File ⇨ Open. The Open dialog box appears.

2. Change the Files of type drop-down list's setting to All Outlines.

3. Select the document and click Open. The outline becomes a PowerPoint presentation, with all Heading 1—styled paragraphs becoming slide titles.

 PowerPoint can't open or insert your outline in PowerPoint if it is currently open in Word. This limitation is an issue only for Word files, not plain text or RTF format.

Post-Import Cleanup

After importing text from an outline, there will probably be a few minor corrections you need to make. Run through this checklist:

◆ The first slide in the presentation may be a blank one. If it is, delete it.

◆ The first slide in the presentation might not have the Title Slide layout applied to it; apply that layout, if needed (see Chapter 3).

◆ There might not be a design template applied; choose one, if needed (see Chapter 2).

◆ Some of the text might contain manual formatting that interferes with the formatting of the design template and makes for inconsistency. Remove any manual formatting that you notice. (One way to do this is to select all the text in the Outline pane by pressing Ctrl+A and then Ctrl+spacebar.)

◆ If some of the text is too long to fit comfortably on the slide, change to a different slide layout, such as the two-column bulleted list, if needed. You might also split the content into two or more slides.

◆ There might be some blank bullet points on some slides (if you missed deleting all the extra paragraph breaks in Word before the import). Delete them.

Importing Text from Other Presentations

If the desired text is already in some other PowerPoint presentation, you can import slides from that presentation into your existing one. You can import any number of slides at once, from one to an entire presentation; however, if you want the entire presentation, it would be easier to simply open the presentation file in PowerPoint and then save it with a new name.

To copy slides from an existing presentation into the current one, follow these steps:

1. Choose Insert ⇨ Slides from Files. The Slide Finder window opens.

2. Click the Browse button and locate the presentation file you want to copy from; then click OK. The slides in the selected presentation appear in the Slide Finder window, as shown in Figure 4-5.

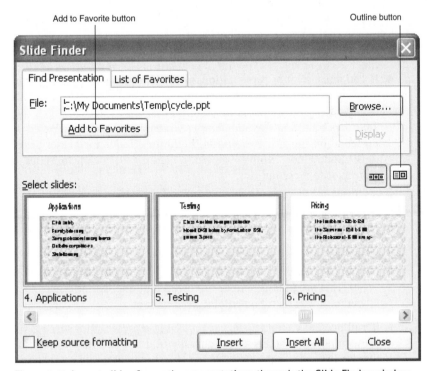

Figure 4-5: Import slides from other presentations through the Slide Finder window.

3. (Optional) If you want the copied slides to retain their formatting rather than conforming to the design template specified in the current presentation, mark the Keep Source Formatting checkbox.

4. Select the slide(s) you want. To select more than one slide, hold down Ctrl as you click on each slide. By default, you see the slides in thumbnail view in the Slide Finder window, but you can switch to an Outline view that shows the slide titles by clicking the Outline button (indicated in Figure 4-5).

Clicking away from the slides does not deselect them as it would in other views; you have to actually toggle a slide selection off by clicking it again. You also can't use Shift to select a range of contiguous slides as you would in other views; only Ctrl works.

5. After selecting the desired slides, click Insert. The slides are inserted into the presentation.

You need not import the slides exactly into the positions you want them; you can move them around after the import. The easiest method is to switch to Slide Sorter view and drag-and-drop them where you want them. Another way is to move the text using the Outline pane, explained later in this chapter.

Here are a few additional tips for importing content from other presentation:

◆ If you make a lot of presentations with some slides in common, consider creating a presentation file or group of files that will serve as a "library" from which you can copy the boilerplate slides as needed. Click the Add to Favorites button in the Slide Finder window to make the selected presentation file easier to find in the future. Notice the List of Favorites tab in the Slide Finder window shown in Figure 4-5; click it for quick access to any favorite presentations.

◆ Sometimes when you have a corrupt PowerPoint file, you can retrieve the slides from it by importing the slides into a new, blank presentation using Insert⇨Slides⇨From File.

◆ Another way to retrieve slides from a corrupt PowerPoint file is to open it in a program called Impress in the OpenOffice suite (www.openoffice .org). This program is similar to PowerPoint and can often open PowerPoint files that PowerPoint itself cannot.

◆ If you need to combine slides from multiple presentations into a single presentation file, here's a shortcut way of doing it. From Windows, choose Start⇨Run, and in the Open dialog box, type **powerpnt –i** followed by the names of the presentation files in quotation marks (full paths), separated by spaces. So, for example, to open File1.ppt, File2.ppt, and File3.ppt, all of which are stored in a folder called C:\Files, you would type **powerpnt –i** "C:\Files\File1.ppt" "C:\Files\File2.ppt" "C:\Files\File3.ppt".

Importing Text from Other Sources

PowerPoint accepts text from a variety of sources, including some that you might not expect. It deals with that text in different ways, depending on its origin. For example, it handles an Excel worksheet differently than it would handle a plain-text file or a Word table. The following sections look at some of the more popular data sources.

Importing from Other Word Processing Applications

In addition to Word, PowerPoint also imports from plain-text files, WordPerfect (various versions), Microsoft Works, and Rich Text Format (RTF). The procedure is the same as described earlier in the chapter under "Importing Text from Word" except you change the Files of type setting in the Insert Outline dialog box to match the type of file you are importing from (or choose All Outlines as the file type to see all file formats that can contain outlines). As with the Word import, the better you prepare the file before importing it, the less cleanup there will be to do afterward. You can also open text files from a variety of word-processing applications as new PowerPoint presentations, as described in "Opening a Word Document as a New Presentation" earlier in the chapter.

Some formats import better than others. For example, plain text will not import with any sense of where the breaks between slides should be since there are no heading styles to rely on; you will need to promote certain lines to slide titles in the Outline pane in PowerPoint after the import. However, as I mentioned earlier, you can simulate outline levels in a plain-text file with tab stops, and the tab stops do make the outline levels import correctly from plain text or any other type of file.

Importing from Web Pages

PowerPoint accepts imported text from several Web page formats, including HTML (*.html and *.htm) and MHTML (*.mht). It helps if the data is in an orderly outline format, or, if it was originally created from a PowerPoint file, in that there will be less cleanup needed.

There are several ways to import from a Web page:

◆ Open a Web page file as a presentation (File ⇨ Open).

◆ Insert the text from the Web page as an outline (Insert ⇨ Slides from Outline).

◆ Insert slides from the Web page (Insert ⇨ Slides from File), which works best if the Web page is set up as a presentation (for example, if it was originally a PowerPoint presentation but was saved as a Web page at some point).

 See Chapter 17 for more information about working with Web pages in Power-Point (including saving as a Web page and playing PowerPoint presentations on the Web).

Here are a few additional tips for importing content from Web pages:

◆ When importing from a Web page, don't expect the content to show up formatted the same way it was on the Web. We're talking strictly about text here. If you want an exact duplicate of the Web page's look, take a "picture" of the page with Shift+PrintScreen and then paste it into PowerPoint (Ctrl+V) as a graphic.

◆ Don't paste HTML text directly into PowerPoint with copy-and-paste, or you may get additional HTML tags you don't want, including tabs that might cause your presentation to try to log onto the Web every time you open it.

◆ If you are importing an outline from an MHT-format Web page that contains pictures, the pictures will be imported into PowerPoint too. If you don't want them, delete them.

◆ If you need to show a live Web page from within PowerPoint, try Shyam Pillai's free Lie Web add-in, at www.mvps.org/skp/liveweb.htm.

Importing from Excel and Other Spreadsheets

In Chapter 6 you will learn how to include spreadsheet data on a PowerPoint slide. That's *not* what we're talking about here. Rather, here we're talking about a spreadsheet program being used to construct a text-only outline, much like an outline in Word or any other word-processing application. Granted, it's not an ideal tool, but some people do use it for outline building.

An outline in Excel might look something like Figure 4-6. You can import it as an outline with the same Insert⇨Slides from Outline command as for Word. The default file type of All Outlines should catch Excel files as well as Word; if All Outlines is not the current setting, you can either select it or select Microsoft Excel Worksheet.

When you open an Excel workbook as a new presentation file, you get a dialog box like the one in Figure 4-7 asking whether you want to use the entire workbook or only certain sheets or certain ranges.

One drawback of importing from a spreadsheet is that there is no way in most spreadsheet programs of distinguishing between outline levels. In Figure 4-6, I had designated the slide titles by making the text bold, but when PowerPoint imports the text, it ignores such indicators. Therefore, each spreadsheet row becomes its own slide, and you must go through the outline in PowerPoint and demote any lines that should be subordinate to the one(s) above.

Another drawback—PowerPoint doesn't recognize named ranges as valid import units. So, for example, if you want to import only the text in a certain named range, there's no good way. You must import either the whole sheet or the whole workbook.

Working with the Outlining Tools

The Outline pane is a great place to edit text, especially when you want to peruse the text from multiple slides at once and move text around. You might want to make the Outline pane larger in Normal view by dragging the line between the panes, so you have more space for the outline.

You may also wish to set the Zoom higher for the Outline pane, so that the text appears larger on-screen for easier viewing. The default is 33%, but 50% might be better, especially if you have a small monitor or are running Windows at a high display resolution.

One final thing: you will probably want to turn on the Outlining toolbar, which contains buttons for manipulating the outline more easily. To do so, choose View⇨Toolbars⇨Outlining.

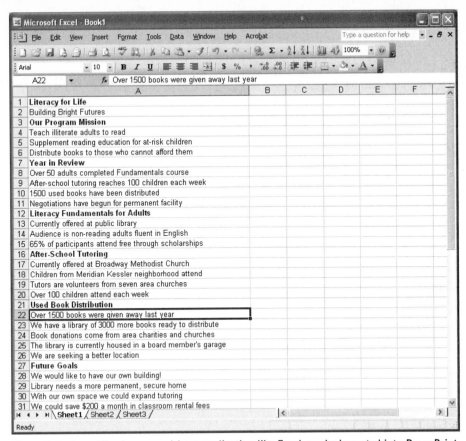

Figure 4-6: An outline in a spreadsheet application like Excel can be imported into PowerPoint too.

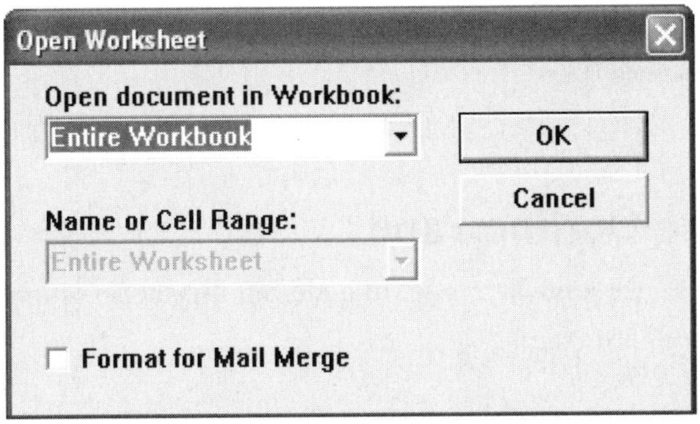

Figure 4-7: Specify which sheet(s) should be imported from a multi-sheet workbook file.

Figure 4-8 shows Normal view adjusted for optimal outline viewing with the Outline pane's zoom set to 50% and the Outlining toolbar displayed.

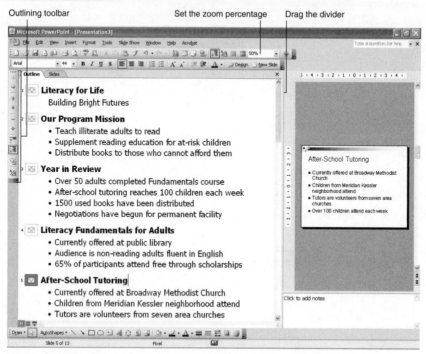

Figure 4-8: Before working with the outline, you might want to adjust the display settings as shown here.

Drag the Outlining toolbar by its handle (the dots at the top) into the center of the screen to make it a floating toolbar, which may perhaps be more handy depending on your work style.

Selecting Text in the Outline Pane

Drag across text to select it, just like anywhere else. In addition, use the selection shortcuts in Table 4-1.

By default when you drag across a few characters of a word, the entire word becomes selected. To change this behavior, choose Tools ⇨ Options, and on the Edit tab, deselect the When selecting, automatically select entire word checkbox.

TABLE 4-1 SELECTING TEXT IN THE OUTLINE PANE

To select this:	Do this:
Word	Double-click
A paragraph and any subordinate text	Triple-click
Entire slide and all its text	Click the slide icon to the left of the text
All text on all slides	Press Ctrl+A
From insertion point to end of line	Shift+End
From insertion point to beginning of line	Shift+Home
From insertion point to end of presentation	Ctrl+Shift+End
From insertion point to beginning of presentation	Ctrl+Shift+Home
Slide's icon (to the left of its text) but not the text itself	Shift+Page Down or Shift+Page Up, or double-click the slide icon
From insertion point to beginning of slide	Ctrl+Shift+up arrow. Repeat the up arrow to select entire additional slides above
From insertion point to end of slide	Ctrl+Shift+down arrow. Repeat the up arrow to select entire additional slides below

 TIP To move the insertion point to the beginning or end of the outline without selecting anything, try these shortcuts: Ctrl+Home to beginning, Ctrl+End to the end.

Expanding and Collapsing the Outline

By default the entire outline is expanded, so all text is visible. Collapsing the outline can help you see the big picture better, especially in a long presentation with many slides. When you collapse the outline, only the top-level headings show; the others are hidden. You can specify exactly which levels should be expanded and which should be collapsed.

There are two ways to collapse and expand outlines: one item at a time or everything at once. For example, you can collapse all the bullet points beneath a certain slide title, or you can collapse all bullet points beneath all slide titles.

To collapse all levels on the current slide, click the Collapse button on the Outlining toolbar, press Alt+Shift+minus sign, or double-click the slide's icon.

To collapse the entire outline except level 1 (the slide titles), click the Collapse All button or press Alt+Shift+1.

To expand everything on the current slide, click the Expand button or press Alt+Shift+plus sign or double-click its icon. (Double-clicking the icon toggles between collapsed and expanded views.)

To expand the entire outline, click the Expand All button or press Alt+Shift+9.

Promoting and Demoting Outline Text

Promoting and demoting on a PowerPoint outline is the same as in Word: press Tab to demote (or Alt+Shift+right arrow) and Shift+Tab (or Alt+Shift+left arrow) to promote.

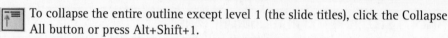 You can also use the buttons on the Outlining toolbar to promote and demote. The Demote button is the right-pointing arrow; the Promote button is the left-pointing arrow.

Rearranging Outline Text

Each icon to the left of a slide in the Outline pane represents the slide itself and everything on it. One way to rearrange slides is to drag a slide's icon up or down. As you drag, a horizontal line appears showing where it is going, as shown in Figure 4-9.

You can also drag individual paragraphs up or down within a slide, or from one slide to another. Simply select the paragraph and then position the mouse pointer over it so the pointer becomes an arrow with a small box and drag up or down.

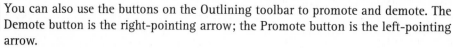 The Move Up and Move Down buttons on the Outlining toolbar can also be used. First, select the text to be moved and then click one of those buttons.

One last method: the keyboard. Press Alt+Shift+up arrow to move the selection up, or Alt+Shift+down arrow to move it down.

Other Outlining Options

The Outlining toolbar has two other buttons we haven't looked at yet: Summary Slide and Show Formatting. Neither is an integral part of outlining in PowerPoint, but some may find them useful.

The Summary Slide button creates a summary slide that contains the titles of the slides that follow it, or if you select a group of contiguous slides, it creates a summary slide with their titles on it. This is useful for creating transition slides in a long or complex show. Selected slides must use a layout containing a title placeholder in order for the Summary Slide feature to be available.

Show Formatting toggles between showing and hiding text formatting in the Outline pane. It is off by default. For presentations that use plain Arial font anyway, there won't be much difference. Turning on the display of formatting may be helpful in proofreading for inconsistent formatting, especially in a presentation where the content has been assembled from multiple sources.

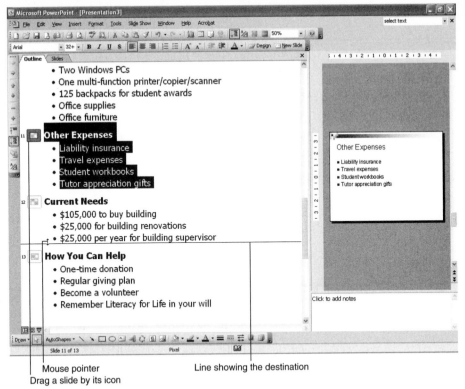

Mouse pointer
Drag a slide by its icon

Line showing the destination

Figure 4-9: Drag-and-drop slides by dragging the icon to the left of their title text.

Summary

In this chapter you learned about importing and managing text in PowerPoint, including working with the Outlining toolbar tools. The next chapter continues our look at text by exploring some of the layout and formatting features you can apply to your text.

Chapter 5

Attractive Text Placement

IN THIS CHAPTER

- ◆ Text box types
- ◆ Creating a manual text box
- ◆ Selecting a text box
- ◆ Sizing and positioning a text box
- ◆ Text box border and fill
- ◆ Formatting text
- ◆ Positioning text
- ◆ Deleting and restoring text boxes
- ◆ Applying an AutoShape to a text box

YOU'VE PROBABLY SEEN some tedious PowerPoint presentations before, right? You know—the kind where every slide uses the same old Title and Text layout, and each slide has the same boring three-to-five bullet points. This chapter presents some ideas and alternatives that can help you avoid Boring Presentation Syndrome, even without graphics.

Text Box Types

A text box is just a frame that holds text, right? But there are actually two distinct types of text boxes—text placeholder boxes and manual text boxes—and each has its own little quirks. So, before we get into any formatting specifics, let's review them.

Text Placeholder Box

This is the type of text box that appears on a slide layout with some instructions in it like "Click to add text." Its size and positioning is determined by the Slide Master and by the slide layout you have chosen for the slide.

Here are some of the qualities that differentiate a text placeholder from a manual text box:

◆ You cannot create new text placeholder boxes on your own; they come only from applying slide layouts (Format⇨Slide Layout; see Chapter 3).

◆ If you delete all the text from this type of text box, the placeholder instructions return (in Normal view, but not in Slide Show view).

◆ This type of text box begins as a fixed size on the slide (as determined by the placeholder on the Slide Master), regardless of the amount of text in it. You can resize it freely.

◆ AutoFit is turned on by default, so that if you type more text than will fit, or resize it so that the existing text will no longer fit, the text will shrink in size so it continues to fit.

◆ The text you type in a text placeholder box appears in the Outline pane.

◆ A rotation handle does *not* appear at the top of the text placeholder box when selected. (However, you can still rotate it, by using the Draw⇨Rotate or Flip⇨Free Rotate commands.)

As mentioned in Chapter 3, when you switch to a different layout that does not contain an equivalent text placeholder, this type of text box goes away if it was empty. If it contained text, it stays on the slide as an orphaned text box (similar to a manual text box described next, except that it appears in the outline). If you then apply another layout that does contain an equivalent text placeholder, it reattaches itself to the placeholder.

Manual Text Box

A manual text box is one that you create yourself using the Text Box tool on the Drawing toolbar. You can place a text box anywhere using this tool—in any location on any slide—regardless of the layout chosen. This type of text box ignores the slide's layout completely and just "does its own thing." Figure 5-1 shows a placeholder text box and a manual text box so you can see the difference.

Here are the unique qualities of a manual text box:

◆ You can create one anywhere and as many as you like, regardless of the layout chosen.

◆ If you delete all the text from a manual text box, the text box remains empty or disappears completely. There are no placeholder instructions.

◆ A manual text box starts out small (vertically) and expands as you type more text in it.

◆ Text does not AutoFit; the text box simply gets longer and longer to make room for more text.

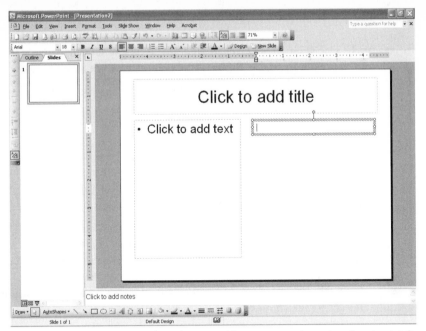

Figure 5-1: A placeholder text box (on the left) and a manual text box (on the right).

◆ A manual text box cannot be resized such that the text in it no longer fits; PowerPoint will refuse to make it shorter vertically until you delete some text from it.

◆ A rotation handle appears at the top, for easy rotation.

◆ The text you type in a manual text box does *not* appear in the Outline pane.

 You can also create an AutoShape, as described in Chapter 7, and then add text to it. This has the same end result as creating a manual text box and then applying an AutoShape to it, a procedure I'll explain later in this chapter.

Creating a Manual Text Box

Remember, manual text box content doesn't show up in the Outline pane, so you probably won't want to use manual text boxes as the main staple of your presentation's diet. You will more likely use manual text boxes sparingly, to add little comments or embellishments.

To create a manual text box, do the following:

1. Make sure there is sufficient blank space on the current slide for the text box you want to create. Resize other elements as needed.

2. Click the Text Box button on the Drawing toolbar. The mouse pointer changes to a crosshair.

3. Do one of the following:

   ■ Click where you want the top-left corner of the text box to begin. A text box will be created that is exactly one character in height and width, and it will expand as you type. Text wrap will be turned off, so you must press Enter to start a new line (or turn text wrap on).

   ■ Drag a rectangle where you want the text box to be. PowerPoint will create a new text box of the width you specify, starting with its top-left corner where you initially clicked. It will ignore the height you specified when dragging, and the box will begin with one line of height only. Text wrap will be turned on, so as you type more text, the box's bottom border will move down.

4. Type in the text box. If you do not type in the text box before you click away from it, and if it has no border or fill applied, it disappears.

Once a manual text box has been created, you can resize it, reposition it, delete it, flip it, add a border and/or fill to it, align it with other objects on the slide, apply an AutoShape to it, format its text, and so on. Lots of possibilities! I'll cover many of these options in the remainder of this chapter.

Selecting a Text Box

This topic might seem like a no-brainer on the surface. Just click it, right? Well, almost. There are two "selected" states that a text box can be in. One is that the box itself is selected, and the other is that the insertion point is within the box. There is a subtle difference, but it's evident when issuing certain commands. For example, if the insertion point is in the text box and you press Delete, PowerPoint deletes the single character to the right of the insertion point, but if the entire text box is selected and you press Delete, it deletes the entire text box.

To select the entire text box, click its border. You can tell it's selected because the border will consist of dots, as shown in Figure 5-2.

To move the insertion point within the text box, click inside the text box. You can tell the insertion point is there because you'll see it flashing inside (obviously!) but also because the box's border will consist of diagonal lines, as shown in Figure 5-3.

In the rest of the chapter, when I say "Select the text box," I mean the first way, so that the box itself is selected, the border is dotted, and the insertion point is *not*

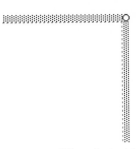

Figure 5-2: When the text box itself is selected, the border consists of dots.

Figure 5-3: When the insertion point is in the text box, the border consists of diagonal lines.

flashing within it. For most of these activities coming up, it does not make any difference, but in a few cases it does.

TIP Having trouble selecting a text box's border? Click inside it and then press Esc.

Sizing and Positioning a Text Box

You're probably already familiar with the drag-and-drop methods of sizing and positioning objects in PowerPoint, and they work just fine for text boxes. However, there are a few quirks, and some alternative methods involving dialog boxes and precise settings, so check out the following sections if you're interested in the finer points.

Sizing

All text boxes can be resized; just drag their selection handles (the white circles around the border). However, the type of text box and the amount of content it contains make a difference in these ways:

◆ By default, a text placeholder box will AutoFit the text if you make the box smaller, such that the text no longer will fit. If you turn AutoFit off for it (see the following note), the text will run out the bottom of the box. AutoFit is not available in manual text boxes.

◆ By default, a manual text box has the Resize AutoShape to Fit Text option turned on, which causes the following behaviors:

■ You cannot decrease its height if it would mean that the text would no longer fit.

■ You cannot expand its height beyond what is necessary to hold the current text within it.

To turn those behaviors off, double-click the text box's border and deselect the Resize AutoShape to Fit Text checkbox on the Text Box tab. You can then resize the text box vertically as desired. That feature is turned off by default for text placeholder boxes, but you can turn it on for them in the same way.

 To turn AutoFit off for a placeholder box, click its AutoFit icon (in its bottom left corner when it is selected) and choose Stop Fitting Text to This Placeholder. The AutoFit icon remains. To turn AutoFit back on, click the AutoFit icon again and choose AutoFit Text to Placeholder. See the *AutoFit* section later in this chapter for more information.

For more precise resizing, you might want to use the Format dialog box. (Its exact name varies depending on the type of text box.) To do this, follow these steps:

1. Double-click the text box's border. Its Format dialog box appears (Format Placeholder for a placeholder box or Format Text Box for a text box).

2. Click the Size tab (see Figure 5-4).

3. Enter a precise Height and Width in the boxes provided. Measurements are in inches.

4. Click OK.

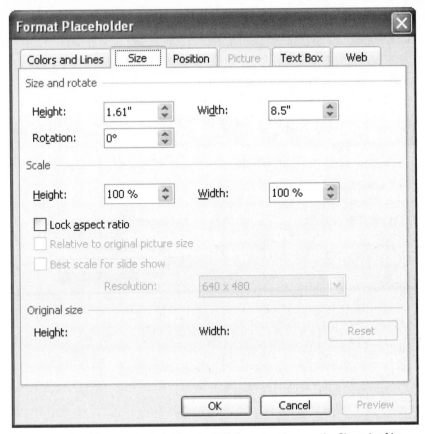

Figure 5-4: Specify a precise height and width for a text box on the Size tab of its Format dialog box.

TIP Here are two alternative methods of opening the Format dialog box for a manual text box: (1) right-click its border and choose Format Text Box; and (2) select it and then choose Format ⇨ Text Box. For a text placeholder box, do the same in each alternative except substitute Placeholder for Text Box.

Moving

To move a text box, select it and then drag the border with the mouse. Don't drag on a selection handle (white circle), but anywhere else on the border is fair game.

There is also a dialog box method for moving, useful when precise positioning is important (for example, to position the same item on multiple slides in exactly the same spot on each).

For the dialog box method, follow these steps:

1. Double-click the text box's border. Its Format dialog box appears (Format Placeholder for a placeholder box or Format Text Box for a text box).

2. Click the Position tab (see Figure 5-5).

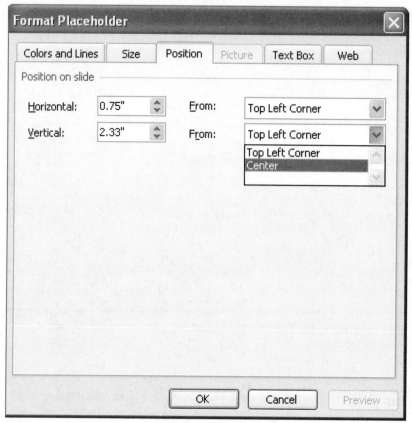

Figure 5-5: Specify a precise position for the text box, either in relation to its top-left corner or in relation to its center.

3. Enter a precise position measurement for vertical and horizontal positioning. Use the associated drop-down list for each to specify where the measurement begins: Top-Left Corner or Center.

4. Click OK.

Rotating

Text boxes can be rotated to create tilted text. The text inside rotates as the box itself rotates. (There are other ways of tilting text, such as creating WordArt, but let's assume for the moment that you want a real rotated text box.) This can be useful for whimsical or artsy special effects, but I wouldn't recommend it for the bulk of your presentation—unless you want the audience to be watching you with their heads cocked to the side, that is!

Dragging a rotation handle is useful when you want to rotate by "eyeballing it." To rotate a manual text box, drag its rotation handle. That's the green circle at its top when it is selected (see Figure 5-6).

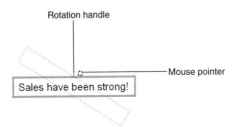

Figure 5-6: Rotate a manual text box by dragging its rotation handle.

A text placeholder box does not have a rotation handle, but you can still rotate it with drag-and-drop. Do the following:

1. Select the text placeholder box.

2. On the Drawing toolbar, choose Draw⇨Rotate or Flip⇨Free Rotate. Green circles replace the white circles in the corners of the text box.

3. Position the mouse pointer over any of the green circles and drag to rotate the box (see Figure 5-7).

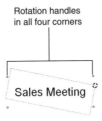

Figure 5-7: Rotate a text placeholder box by entering Free Rotate mode and then dragging a corner.

4. Press Esc or click elsewhere on the slide to cancel the rotation mode when finished.

You might have noticed on the Draw menu in step 2 that there are other rotation commands: Rotate Left and Rotate Right. These rotate by 90 degrees in the specified direction, and are useful if you want the object to be exactly perpendicular to its current position, or exactly upside down (in which case, you would rotate it twice in the same direction).

You can also rotate a precise amount via a dialog box method. This is useful when creating a graphic that must be rotated exactly the same as another graphic, for example. Here are the steps for the dialog box method:

1. Double-click the text box's border. Its Format dialog box appears (Format Placeholder for a placeholder box or Format Text Box for a text box).

2. Click the Size tab (which you saw back in Figure 5-4).

3. Enter a number in the Rotation text box (or use the up/down increment buttons to change the value).

4. Click OK.

Rotational position as specified in step 3 is in relation to the original; it is not incremental. So, for example, if you rotate it 45 degrees and close the dialog box, then reenter the dialog box and enter 90 for the rotation, the total rotation will be 90 degrees from the original, not 135 degrees.

Flipping

Flipping an object creates a mirror image of it. You can flip either vertically or horizontally. However, flipping a text box does not exactly create a mirror image of it, in that the text does not appear backwards the way it would if you held it up to real mirror. The text continues to appear in normal left-to-right orientation, and all the letters appear normally.

So what does flipping do, then?

For a text box in its default rotation setting (that is, the text is straight across), horizontal flipping does nothing. If you think about it, it makes sense. The mirror image from side-to-side of a text box would be an identical text box except the text would be backwards, but since PowerPoint doesn't allow the text to be backward, so there's no change.

If you need a mirrored text box that includes mirrored (backward) text, copy it and then use Paste Special to paste it. In the Paste Special dialog box, choose one of the image formats. Then, flip the image.

Vertical flipping turns the box upside down, so that the letters are upside down, as shown in Figure 5-8. Notice that the text still runs normally, but you have to stand on your head to read it. (In this example, I've made a copy and flipped the copy so you can see the original at the same time.)

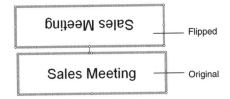

Figure 5-8: The result of flipping a text box vertically.

To flip a text box, follow these steps:

1. Select the text box.

2. On the Drawing toolbar, choose Draw⇨Rotate or Flip⇨Flip Vertical or Flip Horizontal.

If you have rotated the text box, the result of flipping horizontally changes a bit. Again, if you think about it, it makes sense; a text box that angles 45 degrees to the left, when flipped, should angle 45 degrees to the right... right? Figure 5-9 shows the result of flipping such a text box horizontally.

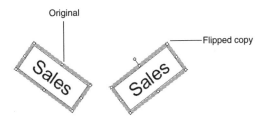

Figure 5-9: The result of flipping a rotated text box horizontally.

Notice in Figure 5-9 that the copy has a rotation handle and the original does not. The original was a text placeholder box, but when I copied it, the copy was a manual text box. Remember, you cannot create text placeholder boxes; they come only from slide layouts. A copy of a placeholder is "created," so it is a manual text box by definition.

 Flipping also makes a difference if you have applied an AutoShape to the text box, because the AutoShape flips too. See *Applying an AutoShape to a Text Box* near the end of this chapter.

Text Box Border and Fill

By default, a text box has no border and no fill. "No border" means that there is no line around the outside of the text box. "No fill" means that its background is transparent, so whatever is behind it shows through.

These defaults work well most of the time, because on a typical slide you want the text to appear to be floating over the background, without any obvious division between it and the rest of the slide. However, in the process of creating your own special effects and designs, you might decide that a border and/or fill is a good idea.

When using a border or fill, the size of the text box becomes more of an issue because the audience can clearly see where the text box's boundaries are. (When it's transparent and borderless, they can't tell, so it doesn't matter.) Therefore, you might want to change the size and/or positioning of the text box after applying a border or fill to it.

If you want the border or fill to appear on every slide in the presentation, make the changes described in the following sections to the Slide Master (see Chapter 3). If you want them on only an individual slide, work with the text boxes on just that slide.

 TIP If you want a border and/or fill to apply to multiple—but not all—text boxes on multiple slides, use Format Painter to copy the formatting from one box to another.

Setting a Text Box Border

A text box's border can have these attributes:

- ◆ *Line color*: Choose one of the scheme colors (recommended) or a specific color or pattern. Your audience won't be able to notice a pattern unless the line is really thick, though; the line will simply look broken or dotted.

- ◆ *Line style*: If chosen from the Line Style button on the Drawing toolbar, this includes both the type of line (single, double, and so on) and its weight (thickness). If chosen from the Format dialog box, style and weight are separately configurable settings.

- ◆ *Dash style*: The default is a solid line, but you can choose a dashed or dotted line instead.

You can set a text box's border either using the buttons on the Drawing toolbar or using the Format dialog box for the text box.

TOOLBAR METHOD

If you use the toolbar, you must make three separate choices for the border. Select the text box and then do the following:

1. 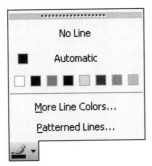 Open the Line Color button's menu and choose a color, as shown in Figure 5-10. Scheme colors (top row of colored squares) are best, if possible, because they change automatically when you change to a different color scheme. For more information about line formatting, see Chapter 7.

Figure 5-10: Choose a color for the border.

2. Open the Line Style button's menu and choose a line style, as shown in Figure 5-11. Notice that line weights and line styles are all mixed

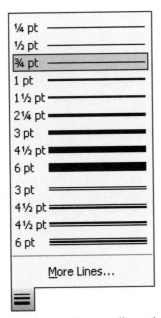

Figure 5-11: Choose a line style for the border.

together on this menu. If the combination you want doesn't appear, choose More Lines to open the Format dialog box (see the next section, *Dialog Box Method*).

3.   Open the Dash Style button's menu and choose a dash style—or, skip this to stick with the solid line.

DIALOG BOX METHOD

The dialog box method's main advantage is that the line style and line weight are separate so you have more combinations to choose from. A default weight was assigned when you made your selection from the Style list, but you can change it.

To set the text box border via dialog box, follow these steps:

1. Double-click the text box's border. Its Format dialog box appears (Format Placeholder for a placeholder box or Format Text Box for a text box).

2. Click the Colors and Lines tab.

3. In the Line area, use the Color, Style, and Dash drop-down lists to make your selections for the border.

4. Increment the Weight setting up or down as needed to adjust the line weight.

5. Click OK.

 TIP To make your chosen border style the default, mark the Default for new objects checkbox. (This is also the case for the text box fill you choose, described in the following section.)

Setting a Text Box Fill

The fill is the background color, pattern, or image for the text box. Each text box could have a different fill—in theory. However, that would be pretty ugly! For best results, stick with the same fill for the text boxes on every slide unless there is a compelling reason to make a change for an individual slide.

The same fill effects are available for text boxes as for backgrounds (discussed in Chapter 3, and again for objects in Chapter 7). These include solid color, gradient, pattern, texture, and picture. The "No Fill" setting, which is the default, is for the box to be transparent. (See Figure 5-12.)

TOOLBAR METHOD

To fill a text box via toolbar, select the text box and then open the Fill Color button's menu (from the Drawing toolbar) and choose a color or effect. Same deal as with the line—scheme colors are best, if possible. Fill Effects opens the Fill Effects dialog box, where you can choose from among the special effects. I'll cover these effects more thoroughly in Chapter 7.

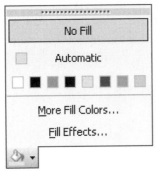

Figure 5-12: Choose a fill color for the text box.

DIALOG BOX METHOD

The dialog box method of filling a text box has one advantage: it allows you to set a transparency amount for the fill. A partially transparent fill allowsthe background to show through to some extent. A completely transparent fill is equivalent to having no fill at all. A completely opaque (non-transparent) fill is a complete fill with no background peeking through. Figure 5-13 shows the difference between a 0% fill, 50% fill, and 100% fill when placed on a picture background. At higher transparencies than 0%, the color appears as a semi-transparent "wash" over the background.

Text box fill: bright blue with 0% transparency

Text box fill: bright blue with 75% transparency

Text box fill: bright blue with 100% transparency

Figure 5-13: Examples of various fill transparency settings.

Here are the steps for the dialog box method:

1. Double-click the text box's border. Its Format dialog box appears (Format Placeholder for a placeholder box or Format Text Box for a text box).

2. Click the Colors and Lines tab.

3. In the Fill section, open the Color drop-down list and choose the desired fill color or effect.

4. Drag the Transparency slider or enter a transparency percentage in its text box (see Figure 5-14).

5. Click OK. If you don't like the results, do it over again. (You can also click Preview instead of OK to apply the change without closing the dialog box, as a bit of a timesaver if you're not sure what results you will get with a particular setting.)

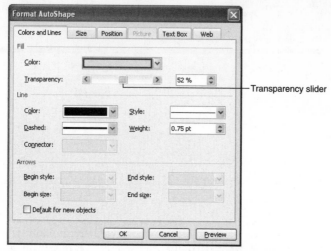

Transparency slider

Figure 5-14: Applying a fill color from the Format dialog box
enables you to set a transparency amount as well as a fill.

Applying a Shadow or 3-D Effect to a Text Box

Shadows and 3-D effects are mutually exclusive; you can choose one or the other
but not both.

 Both of these features make the text box look as if it were set apart from the slide
background, and remember, earlier I said that it's actually relatively uncommon
to want that; most of the time your text boxes will blend seamlessly into the slide
background. So use these effects strategically and sparingly on text boxes.

The Shadow button on the Drawing toolbar opens a menu; pick the direction
that the shadow should extend from the object and select the length of the
shadow. One of the little quirks (or, as Microsoft calls them, "features") of a shadow
is that if you apply it to a text box with no fill, the text within the text box receives
the shadow. If the text box has a fill applied, however, the shadow applies to the
outside of the text box. Figure 5-15 shows some examples, as well as the Shadow
button's menu. For more options, choose Shadow Settings from the menu to display
the Shadow Settings toolbar.

 The Shadow Settings toolbar is discussed in more detail in Chapter 7.

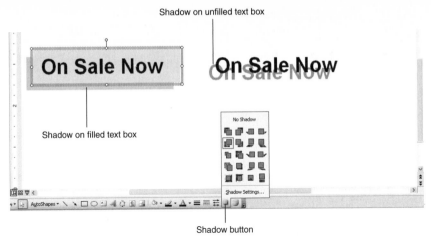

Figure 5-15: Shadows apply to the text in an unfilled text box or to the outside border in a filled text box.

 3-D effects can be applied only to text boxes that have either a line or a fill (or both); when you select an unfilled, unbordered text box, the 3-D effects will not be available. Click the 3-D button on the Drawing toolbar and choose the angle and depth you want. (Or, choose 3-D Settings to display the 3-D Settings toolbar with more options, covered in Chapter 7.) See Figure 5-16.

> **TIP** There is a way around that "filled/bordered only" rule. Choose a fill color for the text box, but then set its Transparency setting to 100%. (See the preceding section, *Setting a Text Box Fill.*) This makes the background of the 3-D object transparent, so it's almost like there's no fill. However, the sides of the 3-D effect are still solid and appear in the color that you chose for the fill (see Figure 5-17).

Formatting Text

I'm assuming you already know the basics of text formatting in PowerPoint, but here's the briefest of reviews.

As with nearly everything else, there's the toolbar method and the dialog box method. Figure 5-18 points out the buttons involved in the toolbar method, including font, font size, attributes (such as bold), color, and so on. All are found on the Formatting toolbar.

For the dialog box method, choose Format➪Font. In the Font dialog box, shown in Figure 5-19, you have all the same text formatting options as with the toolbar method plus the following extras:

Figure 5-16: A 3-D effect applied to a filled text box.

Figure 5-17: A 3-D effect applied to a filled text box that has 100% transparency.

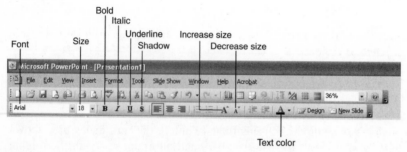

Figure 5-18: Toolbar buttons and lists for text formatting.

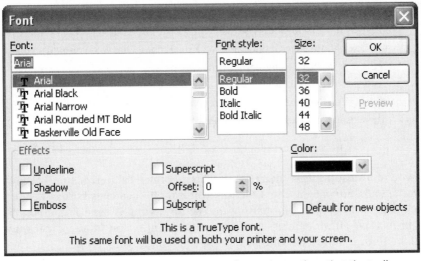

Figure 5-19: The Font dialog box has extra text formatting options that the toolbar does not provide.

◆ Emboss

◆ Superscript (and user-definable amount of offset)

◆ Subscript

◆ Ability to set the current settings as the default for new objects

If you use emboss, superscript, or subscript frequently, consider adding buttons for them to the toolbar as explained in Chapter 18.

The Small Caps font attribute is not available in PowerPoint. (You may be familiar with it from Word.) However, an add-in is available that simulates the Small Caps attribute. It is the RnR Starter Kit add-in set on the CD that accompanies this book. That add-in set gives you an Edit toolbar, and one of the buttons on that toolbar is Small Caps.

One thing you *don't* get with the dialog box method is the preview of the fonts. On the Font drop-down list on the Formatting toolbar, notice that the fonts (well, most of them) appear on the list in their own style of lettering. You don't get that with the Font dialog box's list of them.

TIP If you need to include a certain unusual font in the presentation that not everyone may have, embed it. (When saving, click the Tools button in the Save As dialog box, choose Save Options, and mark the Embed TrueType Fonts checkbox.) If the font cannot be embedded, but it's imperative that you use it, use a thirdparty vector graphic program such as Adobe Illustrator to create a graphic text object that uses that font, and then save it as an EMF or WMF format graphic. Then insert that graphic into PowerPoint.

As you're formatting text, don't forget about Format Painter! It's one of my favorite tools. Format some text the way you want it, then click Format Painter, and click the text to copy the formatting to. The formatting is copied, and Format Painter turns itself off. Or, double-click the Format Painter icon to turn the feature on until you turn it off (by clicking the button again or pressing Esc).

Positioning Text

Besides changing how the text looks (for example, formatting it), you can also change where it sits. There are lots of text-positioning settings in PowerPoint—some of them familiar, others perhaps not. The following sections describe them.

AutoFit Text

AutoFit Text shrinks the font size of the text, if needed, so that it continues to fit in the box. It kicks in whenever you type more text in the box than will fit at the default size.

One important thing to remember about AutoFit Text is that the font size has not really been changed for the text in a strict sense. The text box's content is all uniformly shrunk down to fit, and incidentally that has involved reducing the text size. If you delete some of the text in the text box, the text will enlarge itself to fill the newly available space, up to its original size. (It won't enlarge higher than its original size with AutoFit.)

To explore AutoFit, do the following:

1. Start a new Title and Text slide, and type eight bulleted paragraphs in it. (Each can have a single word in it; no need to get fancy.) Notice the font size reported on the Formatting toolbar.

2. Type two more bulleted paragraphs in the text box. Notice that AutoFit kicks in and makes all the text smaller. Notice also that an AutoFit icon appears in the bottom left corner of the text box.

3. Click the AutoFit icon to open its menu, as shown in Figure 5-20.

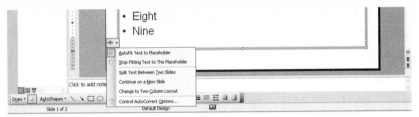

Figure 5-20: AutoFit settings for a text placeholder box.

4. Click Stop Fitting Text to This Placeholder. The text returns to its default size and overflows the text box.

5. Click the AutoFit icon again and choose Change to Two-Column Layout. The change occurs.

6. Press Ctrl+Z to undo that last action, click the text box to select it again, and then click the AutoFit icon again and choose AutoFit Text to Placeholder. AutoFit turns back on again for that text box.

7. Click the AutoFit icon again and choose Control AutoCorrect Options. The AutoCorrect dialog box opens.

8. In the Apply as you Type section, notice the two AutoFit options for title and text placeholders (see Figure 5-21). If you don't like AutoFit and want to turn it off, clear these checkboxes; otherwise leave them marked.

9. Click OK.

You can also access the AutoCorrect dialog box with the Tools ⇨ AutoCorrect Options menu command.

Text Alignment

Each paragraph has its own horizontal alignment setting, such as Left, Right, Center, or Justify. You can choose these with the Alignment buttons on the Formatting toolbar (see Figure 5-22).

Justify is an alignment in which the text aligns both with the right and left margins of the text box, and space is added between words and letters to make that happen. Many newspapers use this alignment. It works best for long lines of text where there is a lot of text in which to spread out the extra spacing. Most people don't use it in presentations because it makes the text a bit harder to read.

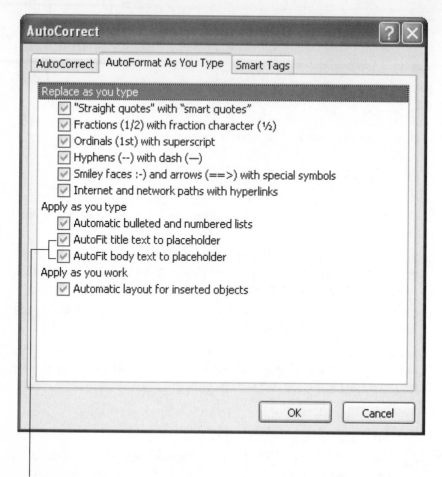

AutoFit options

Figure 5-21: Turn AutoFit on/off in the AutoCorrect dialog box.

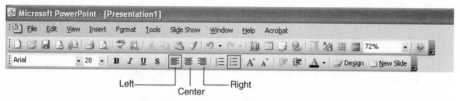

Left — Center — Right

Figure 5-22: Buttons for horizontal text alignment on the Formatting toolbar.

You can also change the alignment from the Format menu by choosing Format➪Alignment and then choosing an alignment from the submenu. The Justify alignment is not available by default from the Formatting toolbar, so you must use the menu method for it (or add it to the toolbar yourself, as explained in Chapter 18).

Internal Margins

A slide does not have any particular margins; content appears on the slide wherever you put it. However, each text box has its own internal margins—in other words, the amount of space between the edge of the text box and where the text starts.

To set the internal margins for a text box, follow these steps:

1. Double-click the border of the text box to open its Format dialog box.

2. Click the Text Box tab.

3. Enter margin settings in the Internal margin section (see Figure 5-23).

4. Click OK.

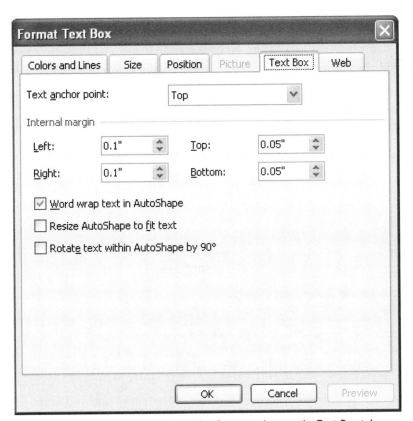

Figure 5-23: Change the internal margins for a text box on the Text Box tab.

Notice the three checkboxes at the bottom of the Text Box tab, shown in Figure 5-23. Why would they say "AutoShape?" It's because PowerPoint considers text boxes to be AutoShapes, much like the drawn shapes from the Drawing toolbar.

Here's what each of these checkboxes does:

◆ *Word wrap text in AutoShape*: This setting is responsible for the text wrapping to the next line when it hits the right margin of the text box. If you turn it off, the text will extend past the right margin.

◆ *Resize AutoShape to fit text*: This feature makes the text box exactly as tall as it needs to be for the text it contains. It's turned on by default for manual text boxes, and off by default for text placeholder boxes. When it is on, you will be unable to vertically resize the text box manually.

◆ *Rotate text within AutoShape by 90°*: This setting makes the text appear turned on its side, running from bottom to top.

Vertical Alignment

You might have noticed in the preceding section that I skipped over one of the settings: Text Anchor Point. This is the vertical alignment setting for the text box. (Well, sort of.)

The text anchor point is the point where the text begins. The default is Top. Figure 5-24 shows some of the other possible settings.

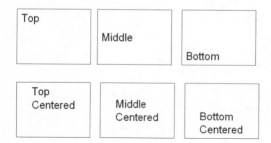

Figure 5-24: Text anchor point settings.

Notice in Figure 5-24 the difference between Top and Top Centered (and each of the other pairs). Top Centered is *not* the same as a top vertical alignment and a centered horizontal alignment. If the text were centered horizontally, then each individual line would be centered. With the Top Centered setting, the longest line of text is centered within the text box, but all the other lines left-align with it (or conform to whatever the horizontal alignment setting is for that paragraph).

 Text anchor point is an important setting if the text box is larger than it needs to be to accommodate the text, but not so important if the text box is sized such that the text exactly fits. The text boxes in Figure 5-24 are all larger than they need to be, so the extra space in the text box is positioned differently according to the text anchor point setting. But remember that in most manual text boxes, by default the Resize AutoShape to Fit Text setting is enabled (Text Box tab of Format Text Box dialog box), so that the vertical size of the text box is always adjusted for an exact fit. Therefore, in a box like that you will see no difference between, for example, Top and Bottom anchor points.

About that default I mentioned in the previous note . . . it's actually a bit more complicated. If you click and drag when you create a manual text box, Resize AutoShape to Fit Text is indeed enabled, but if you click to create a default-sized text box when creating a manual one, it's not enabled by default.

Line Spacing

There are three line spacing settings:

◆ *Paragraph*: spacing between lines in a paragraph

◆ *Before*: spacing before the first line of a paragraph

◆ *After*: spacing after the last line of a paragraph

All of these are set from the Line Spacing dialog box (choose Format⇨Line Spacing), shown in Figure 5-25. You can set them in either lines or points. If you use the Lines unit of measurement, the actual amount of spacing is based on the font used in the paragraph. If you use the Points unit of measurement, it's a fixed amount regardless of the size of the text.

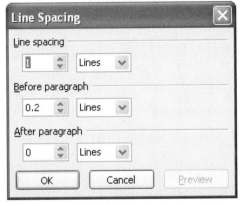

Figure 5-25: Adjust line spacing before, within, and after a paragraph.

Bullets and Numbering

 To remove the bullet entirely from a paragraph, select the paragraph and click the Bullets button on the Formatting toolbar. This toggles the default bullet on/off.

To choose a different bullet character, choose Format⇨Bullets and Numbering and make your selection on the Bullets tab.

Chapter 3 explained the process of selecting an alternate bullet character in detail, in the section *Changing Bullet Characters.*

To type sub-bullets beneath a bulleted paragraph, press Enter to start a new paragraph and then press Tab; PowerPoint changes the bullet character and indents to the next level. See the next section for more information about indentation.

The same process applies for numbered lists. You can convert a bulleted or unbulleted paragraph to a numbered one by clicking the Numbering button on the Formatting toolbar. Or, choose Format⇨Bullets and Numbering and set up any advanced options on the Numbered tab (see Figure 5-26).

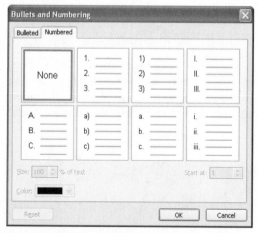

Figure 5-26: Use the Bullets and Numbering dialog box to set up custom bullet characters or different numbering styles.

Tabs and Indents

Tab stops and indents are very different in PowerPoint than in other applications you might have worked with before, like Word.

One big difference is that indent markers apply to the entire text box in PowerPoint, not to individual paragraphs. Another is that the text box can have multiple levels of indent markers—one set for each level of bulleted or numbered lists in that text box.

INDENT MARKERS

To understand how indent markers work, take a peek at the indent markers and tab stops in Slide Master view, as shown in Figure 5-27. In Slide Master view, we see all the indent markers at once.

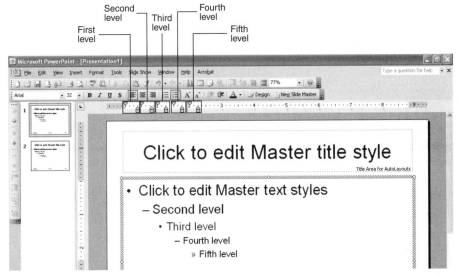

Figure 5-27: Indent markers on the horizontal ruler in Slide Master view—one set for each bulleted list level.

Notice that for each bulleted list level, there are separate indent markers:

▽ *First line indent.* This down-pointing triangle represents the positioning of the first line. If it's a bulleted paragraph, it represents the positioning of the bullet character. Drag it to the left or right to adjust it.

△ *Hanging indent.* This up-pointing triangle represents the positioning of the second and *subsequent* lines in a multi-line paragraph. There is sometimes a left-aligned tab stop at this same position as well, indicating where the first line's *text* will begin if a bullet character is placed at the first line indent location (see the preceding example). If it is a single-line paragraph and not bulleted (or numbered), this indent is ignored. Drag it to the left or right to adjust it.

TIP For more precise control while dragging indent markers, hold down the Ctrl key as you drag.

☐ *Left indent.* This rectangle controls both of the triangles as a single unit. If you want to move both triangles and maintain the spacing between them, you would drag this rectangle to the left or right.

When you press *Tab* at the beginning of a paragraph, PowerPoint changes the paragraph's status to the next-lesser outline level. For example, if it was a first-level bullet, it changes it to a second-level one.

TAB STOPS

Notice that there are faint gray lines every 1/2 inch under the ruler. These are the default tab stops. They are evenly spaced tab stops that are in effect for any paragraphs for which you do not set custom tab stops. You can drag one of those little gray lines to the left or right to change their interval.

 The default tab stops in PowerPoint are left-aligned stops; you don't have a choice of alignments for them. If you need more complex alignment options, place a custom tab stop.

To set a custom tab stop, click the ruler. By default, the tab stop is a left-aligned one, but you can click the tab indicator at the far left end of the ruler (looks like an L when it's set for the default of Left) to toggle through the available types and then click the ruler when it displays the type you want.

EXPERIMENTING WITH INDENTS AND TAB STOPS

From Slide Master view, try this experiment to familiarize yourself with tabs and indents. (It's a rather long experiment, but valuable, I promise.)

1. Click in the main text box (where the bullets are.) The indent markers appear on the ruler.

2. Position the mouse pointer over the third Left Indent marker (rectangle) on the ruler, and drag it two inches to the right. Notice that all the indent markers to its right move with it.

3. Now drag the same Left Indent marker back 1 inch to the left. Notice that the indent markers to its right do *not* move this time. This tells us that those indent markers that moved in step 1 were not tied to this set specifically; they just moved because they had to get out of the way.

4. Still working with the third (middle) set of indent markers, drag the First line indent marker (top triangle) to the right so that it lines up with the Hanging indent marker (bottom triangle).

5. Drag the Hanging indent marker (top triangle) 1/2 inch to the right, so that the First-line indent is once again offset from it.

6. Close Slide Master view, and display a blank slide that has the Title and Text layout. (Insert one, if needed.) Notice that you see only the first set of indent markers on the ruler when you click in the Text Placeholder.

7. Type a few words, and then press the Tab key. Notice below the ruler, to the right of the last indent marker, there are evenly spaced faint gray marks. Those are the tab default stops, and the insertion point has moved to the first available one after your typed text.

8. Point to the tab stop marker that the insertion point is aligned with, and drag it slightly to the left or right. The insertion point moves too.

9. Type a few more words. Then press Enter. PowerPoint begins a new bulleted paragraph.

10. Press the Tab key. The paragraph changes to a second-level bulleted item, and now there are two sets of indent markers on the ruler.

11. Press the Tab key again. The paragraph changes to a third-level bulleted item, and now there are three sets of indent markers. The text will be near the middle of the slide because of the indents.

12. Press Shift+Tab. The paragraph changes back to a second-level bulleted item, and the third set of indent markers on the ruler disappears, leaving only two.

Discard the presentation file when you're done with the experiment; there's no need to save it.

Deleting and Restoring Text Boxes

To delete a text box, select it and press Delete. But remember how at the beginning of this chapter I differentiated between a text box itself being selected and the insertion point being in the box? Here's one of those cases where it matters. Make sure that the text box itself is selected (it should have a dotted border) before pressing Delete.

Pressing Delete with the insertion point inside just deletes whatever character is to the left of the insertion point.

There's a difference between deleting a manual text box and a text placeholder box, as follows:

◆ When you select a text placeholder box that contains text and press Delete, the box will be replaced by a default-formatted empty placeholder text box.

◆ When you select a text placeholder that is empty and press Delete, the placeholder box is deleted.

◆ When you select any manual text box (containing text or not) and press Delete, the text box is immediately deleted.

To get a placeholder text box back that you've deleted, reapply the slide layout (or apply a different slide layout that contains the type of text box you want).

Applying an AutoShape to a Text Box

Normally, we think of AutoShapes as the drawn lines and shapes created with the Drawing toolbar's tools, but PowerPoint also considers text boxes to be AutoShapes too. As a consequence of that assumption, almost anything that you can do to an AutoShape, you can do to a text box. You've seen that throughout this chapter; a lot of what we've done here, we'll do again in Chapter 7 when working with drawn shapes.

PowerPoint sees a text box as an AutoShape without the "shape"—that is, a frame around a shape that doesn't have any line or fill. You can apply an AutoShape to any text box (actually PowerPoint calls it "changing" the shape) to use an AutoShape as a frame around the text.

In Chapter 7 you'll learn how you can add text to an AutoShape; this is the flip side of that. Actually, the results you get are the same either way; you can start with the text box or with the AutoShape. The advantage of starting with the text box is that you can apply an AutoShape to either a text placeholder or a manual text box. The AutoShape-first method always produces a manual text box.

To apply an AutoShape to a text box, follow these steps:

1. Select the text box.

2. On the Drawing toolbar, choose Draw⇨Change AutoShape and then select a category of shape and a specific shape. The shape is applied to the text box, but you won't be able to see it yet.

3. Use the Line Color button on the Drawing toolbar to select a line color for the AutoShape. And/or, use the Fill Color button on the Drawing toolbar to select a fill color for it. Figure 5-28 shows an example of both a line and fill color assigned to a subtitle placeholder on a title slide that has an AutoShape arrow applied to it.

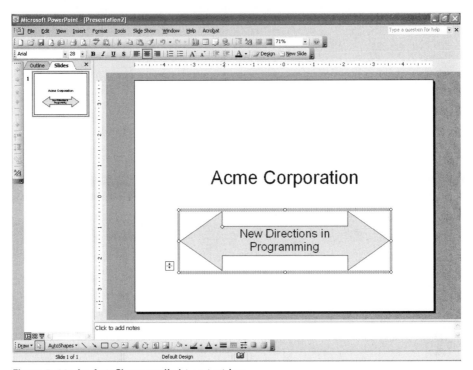

Figure 5-28: An AutoShape applied to a text box.

To remove the AutoShape, simply set its border and shading to No Line and No Fill, respectively.

Summary

In this chapter you learned many techniques for formatting and positioning place-holder and manual text boxes on slides. Now you can tackle any type of text box! But we're not quite through with text yet; in Chapter 6 we'll look at text in tabular form—PowerPoint tables, Word tables, Excel worksheets, and more.

Chapter 6

Tables and Worksheet Grids

IN THIS CHAPTER

◆ Creating a new table

◆ Selecting rows, columns, and cells

◆ Editing a table's structure

◆ Formatting table cells

◆ Copying tables from Word

◆ Copying worksheet cells from Excel

◆ Linking and embedding Excel data

TABULAR DATA—in other words, data in a grid of rows and columns—can be typed directly into a table or imported from other applications. Much of the formatting you learned about in Chapter 5 also applies, but there are also some special considerations for tabular data as well. In this chapter you'll learn how to create and manage PowerPoint tables and how to insert tabular data from other sources.

Creating a New Table

A table is a great way to organize little bits of data into a meaningful picture. For example, you might use a table to show sales results for several salespeople or to contain a multi-column list of team member names.

There are four ways to create a new table in PowerPoint as follows:

◆ Use a layout placeholder.

◆ Use the Insert menu.

◆ Use the Table button on the Standard toolbar.

◆ Use the Tables and Borders toolbar to draw a table.

Each method has its fans, so I'll explain all of them and you can take your pick. 133

Tables are like manual text boxes in PowerPoint, in that they hold text but the text does not appear in the Outline pane. Therefore, you would not want to put data in a table that was essential to the outline if you were planning on printing and using the outline separately from the slide show itself.

Using a Slide Layout Placeholder

Table is one of the six types of content available from the multi-type placeholder on a slide layout. One way to insert a table, then, is to change to a layout containing that placeholder and then click the Table icon, as shown in Figure 6-1.

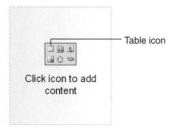

Table icon

Click icon to add
content

Figure 6-1: Click the Table icon in a slide layout.

There is also a separate Title and Table slide layout, near the bottom of the list of layouts in the task pane. It provides a slide title and one big table that fills the rest of the slide. Select that layout for a slide and then double-click the table placeholder, as shown in Figure 6-2. (Notice that it's a double click here, whereas with the multi-type placeholder you use a single click to activate.)

Either way, when you activate the placeholder, the Insert Table dialog box appears (see Figure 6-3). You enter the number of rows and columns you want and click OK.

Because you started with a placeholder, the resulting table will be fit into that placeholder area. The rows and columns will be squashed as needed to make that happen.

Inserting a Table with the Insert Menu

The Insert menu method (Insert⇨Table) opens the same Insert Table dialog box as does the placeholder method described in the preceding section.

If AutoLayout is enabled (and it is by default), the slide's layout will change to one that includes a placeholder for a table, and the table will be placed in it. Table 6-1 details the AutoLayout modifications that occur when you add a table to an empty slide that uses various layouts.

 If PowerPoint changes to a different layout, the AutoLayout icon appears next to the inserted table. Click the icon to open its menu and then choose Undo

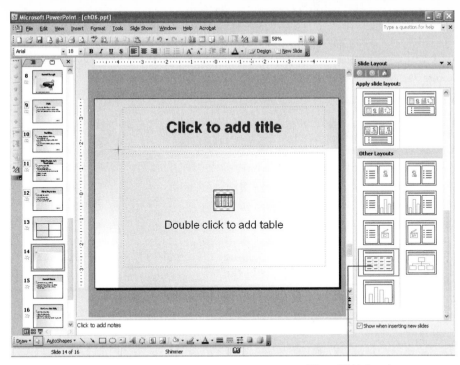

Title and Table layout

Figure 6-2: The Title and Table placeholder is suitable for a large table.

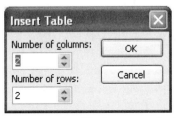

Figure 6-3: Specify the rows and columns desired for the
table to be inserted.

AutoLayout, if desired. You can also undo the AutoLayout by issuing the Undo command immediately after the insertion (Edit⇨Undo, Undo button on toolbar, or Ctrl+Z).

If AutoLayout did not change the layout, or if you undid it, the inserted table appears centered on the slide vertically and horizontally, ignoring all existing content on the slide, as in Figure 6-4 where it has been inserted on a blank slide. You will probably want to move and resize the table to place it exactly where you want it.

TABLE 6-1 LAYOUT CHANGES MADE BY AUTOLAYOUT WHEN INSERTING A TABLE

Original layout	Changes to:
Title Only	Title and Table
Title and Text	Title and Table
Title and Two-Column Text	Title, Text, and Content, and the table appears in the Content placeholder
Title, Text, and Content	No change, but the table appears in the Content placeholder
Title, Content, and Text	Same as above
Title, Text, and ___	Table takes the place of the non-text placeholder, whatever it might be
Title, ___, and Text	Same as above
Title Slide	No change; table appears on top of existing placeholders
Blank slide	No change; table appears centered on slide

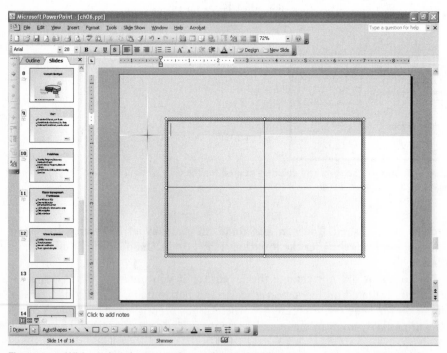

Figure 6-4: Without AutoLayout active, an inserted table appears centered on the slide.

Inserting a Table with the Table Button

Here's an alternative to the menu method. The Insert Table button on the Standard toolbar opens a drop-down grid when you click it. You then drag your mouse across the grid to specify the number of rows and columns you want, as shown in Figure 6-5, and PowerPoint inserts a table based on that specification. Other than the method of specifying rows and columns, this method is identical to the Insert menu method. The same issues apply regarding placeholders versus free-floating tables, as described in the preceding sections.

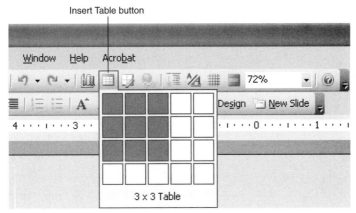

Figure 6-5: Another way to insert a table is to drag across the desired number of rows and columns from the Table button.

Drawing a Table

I've saved the most fun method for last. Drawing a table enables you to use your mouse pointer like a pencil to create every row and column in the table in exactly the positions you want. You can even create unequal numbers of rows and columns. This method is a good one whenever you want a table that is non-standard in some way—different row heights, column widths, different numbers of columns in some rows than others, and so on.

First, you'll need to display the Tables and Borders toolbar, as shown in Figure 6-6. To do so, click the Tables and Borders button on the Standard toolbar or choose View ➪ Toolbars ➪ Tables and Borders. Table 6-2 describes the buttons on that toolbar; you'll learn more about many of them in the remainder of this chapter.

Figure 6-6: The Tables and Borders toolbar.

TABLE 6-2 TABLES AND BORDERS TOOLBAR BUTTONS

Button	Name	Description
	Draw Table	Turns the mouse pointer into a pencil for drawing table lines
	Eraser	Turns the mouse pointer into an eraser for removing table lines
	Border Style	Opens a list of line styles for table borders
1 pt	Border Width	Opens a list of line widths for table borders
	Border Color	Opens a list of colors for table borders
	Borders	Opens a list of border sides, so you can place or remove the border from one or more sides of the table or individual cells
	Fill Color	Opens a list of colors for filling the insides of the cells
Table	Table	Opens a menu of commands for selecting, inserting, and deleting rows
	Merge Cells	Combines two or more cells into a single cell
	Split Cell	Splits the current cell into two cells
	Align Top	Sets the vertical alignment for the selected cells to Top
	Center Vertically	Sets the vertical alignment for the selected cells to Center
	Align Bottom	Sets the vertical alignment for the selected cells to Bottom
	Distribute Rows Evenly	Resizes rows so that they are all the same
	Distribute Columns Evenly	Resizes columns so that they are all the same

TIP The Tables and Borders toolbar is a floating toolbar by default but can be dragged to dock at the top, bottom, left, or right, as can any other toolbar.

After displaying the Tables and Borders toolbar, you'll notice that the mouse pointer is a pencil and the Draw Table button is selected on the toolbar. PowerPoint is ready for you to draw the table. If for some reason the mouse pointer does not appear as a pencil, click the Draw Table button to enable it.

Use your mouse "pencil" to drag a rectangle delineating the outside border of the table. You can draw it anywhere on the slide. The result will be a single-cell table, as shown in Figure 6-7.

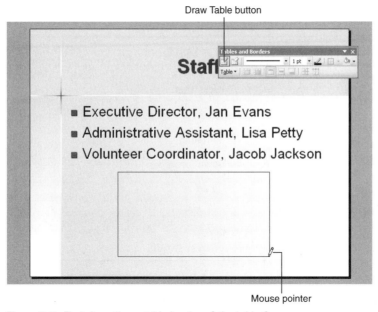

Figure 6-7: First draw the outside border of the table frame.

Now draw the row and column borders, still using the mouse as a pencil. When you begin to drag vertically or horizontally, PowerPoint will lock into that and keep the line exactly vertical or horizontal and straight. You can create entire rows and columns or partial ones. When you are done, press Esc to turn the mouse pointer back to a normal arrow again.

Figure 6-8 shows an example of a table created by drawing. If you need to make some changes to your drawing (for example, erase or move some lines), see *Editing a Table's Structure* later in this chapter.

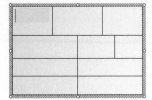

Figure 6-8: This table, created with the Draw Table feature, is free from normal conventions regarding row and column numbers and sizes.

Moving Around in a Table

Each cell is like a little text box. To type in a cell, click in it and type. Pretty simple! You can also move between cells with the keyboard; Table 6-3 lists the keyboard shortcuts for moving the insertion point around in a table.

TABLE 6-3 MOVING THE INSERTION POINT IN A TABLE

To move to:	Press this:
Next cell	Tab
Previous cell	Shift+Tab
Next row	Down arrow
Previous row	Up arrow
Tab stop within cell	Ctrl+Tab
New paragraph within same cell	Enter

Selecting Rows, Columns, and Cells

If you want to apply formatting to one or more cells, or issue a command that acts upon them such as Copy or Delete, you must first select the cells to be affected.

To select a single cell, move the insertion point into it by clicking inside the cell. Any commands you issue at that point will act on that individual cell and its contents, not on the whole table, row, or column. Drag across multiple cells to select them.

To select an entire row or column, click any cell in a current row or column, and then choose Table ⇨ Select Row or Table ⇨ Select Column. The Table menu is accessed from the Tables and Borders toolbar, not the normal menu bar. You can also select an entire row or column by dragging across it. Figure 6-9 shows a selected column.

There are two ways to select the entire table—or rather, two senses in which the entire table can be said to be "selected:"

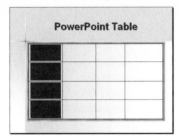

Figure 6-9: A table with a column selected.

◆ When all cells in the table are selected, they all appear with black backgrounds as shown in Figure 6-9, and any text formatting commands you apply at that point will affect all text in the table. To do this kind of selection, press Ctrl+A.

◆ When the table itself is selected, its frame is selected, but the cursor is not anywhere within the table and no cells appear selected. To do this kind of selection, right-click the table and choose Select Table or click the outer border of the table. You would do this kind of selection before moving or resizing the table, for example.

If this sounds familiar, it should—it's the same as the two kinds of "selected" involved with a text box from Chapter 4.

Editing a Table's Structure

Now let's look at some ways of modifying the table after creating it.

Resizing the Overall Table

Dragging the selection handles on a table's outer frame resizes it, as with any other framed object in PowerPoint. All the rows and columns maintain their spacing proportional to one another as you resize.

Inserting or Deleting Rows and Columns

Here's an easy way of creating a new row at the bottom of the table: position the insertion point in the bottom right cell and press Tab.

Need something more complicated than that? The Table menu (on the Tables and Borders toolbar) contains the following commands that help you insert and remove rows and columns, as shown in Figure 6-10:

◆ *Insert Columns to the Left*: Adds a new column to the left of the column containing the insertion point.

◆ *Insert Columns to the Right*: Same as previous command, except it inserts to the right of the insertion point.

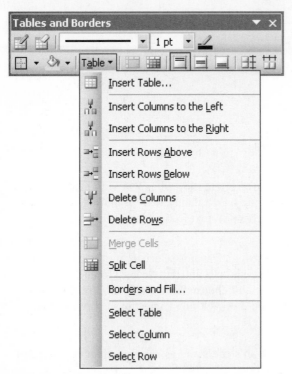

Figure 6-10: The Table menu provides commands that insert and delete rows and columns in the table.

◆ *Insert Rows Above*: Adds a new row above the one containing the insertion point.

◆ *Insert Rows Below*: Same as previous command, except it inserts the row below the current row.

◆ *Delete Columns*: Deletes the column containing the insertion point.

◆ *Delete Rows*: Deletes the row containing the insertion point.

If you prefer buttons to menus, you might want to edit the Tables and Borders toolbar to add buttons for inserting and deleting rows and columns. See Chapter 19 for details.

You can use any of the Insert or Delete commands from the Table menu on multiple rows or columns at a time. Simply select more than one before issuing the command. When you have more than one row or column selected and you insert, PowerPoint inserts the same number of items that were selected. For example, if you select two columns and then choose Insert Columns to the Right, it inserts two columns to the right of the selected ones.

Adding and removing rows and columns changes the overall size of the table, as can resizing rows and columns (covered in *Formatting Table Cells* later in the chapter). After adding rows or columns or increasing the size of a row or column, your table could start running off the slide. PowerPoint does not warn you when your table exceeds the slide's area; you have to watch for that yourself. You can resize the table by dragging its outer border's selection handles.

Merging and Splitting Cells

If you need more rows or columns in some spots than others, try the Merge Cells and Split Cell commands.

Here are some ways to merge cells:

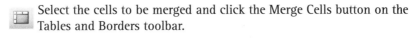 Click the Eraser button on the Tables and Borders toolbar, and then click the line you want to erase. The cells on either side of the deleted line will be merged.

Select the cells to be merged and click the Merge Cells button on the Tables and Borders toolbar.

◆ Select the cells to be merged and choose Table⇨Merge Cells.

◆ Select the cells to be merged, and then right-click any of them and choose Merge Cells.

Here are some ways to split cells:

Click the Draw Table button on the Tables and Borders toolbar, and draw a line in the cell you want to split. Press Esc to turn the drawing feature off again when finished.

Select the cell to be split and click the Split Cell button on the Tables and Borders toolbar.

◆ Select the cell to be split and choose Table⇨Split Cell.

Formatting Table Cells

Now that you have the correct quantity of cells in the table, and in the correct arrangement, let's take a look at the ways you can format them.

Changing Row Height and Column Width

You might want a row to be a different height or a column a different width than the others in the table. To resize a row or column, follow these steps:

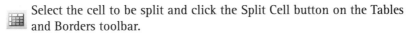

1. Position the mouse pointer on the border below the row or to the right of the column that you want to resize. The mouse pointer turns into a line with arrows on each side of it.

2. Holding down the mouse button, drag the row or column to a new height or width. A dotted line appears, as shown in Figure 6-11, showing where it will go.

3. Release the mouse button.

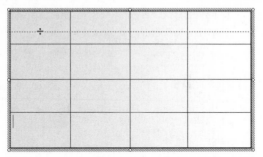

Figure 6-11: Resize the rows or columns of your table as needed to eliminate wasted space or to make room for longer text strings.

 The Distribute Rows Evenly and Distribute Columns Evenly buttons on the Tables and Borders toolbar adjust each row or column in the selected range so that the available space is occupied evenly among them. This is handy especiallyif you have drawn the table yourself rather than allowed PowerPoint to create it initially. (If PowerPoint creates the table, the rows and columns are already of equal height and width by default.)

Table Margins and Alignment

Remember, PowerPoint does not have any margins per se on a slide; everything is in a frame. An individual frame does have internal margins, however.

You can specify the internal margins for cells from the Format Table dialog box as follows:

1. Select the cells to which the setting should apply. To apply to the entire table, select the entire table.

2. Choose Format⇨Table. The Format Table dialog box opens, as shown in Figure 6-12.

3. Click the Text Box tab.

4. Enter Left, Right, Top, and Bottom margins.

5. From the Text Alignment box, choose a default alignment for the cells of the table (Top, Middle, Bottom, Top Centered, Middle Centered, or Bottom Centered). You can override this setting for individual cells as needed, as you would any text box (see Chapter 5).

6. Click OK.

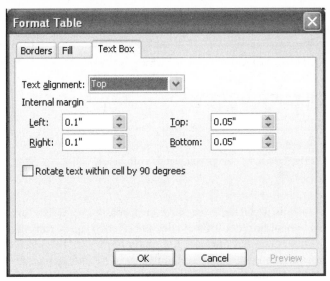

Figure 6-12: Use the Format Table dialog box to set table margins and default alignment.

Even though the Format Table dialog box appears to refer to the entire table, not individual cells, the alignment and margin settings you make on the Text Box tab will apply only to the cells that you selected prior to opening the dialog box, not to the entire table. If you want to affect the entire table, select it first.

Applying Borders

The border lines around each cell are very important because they separate the data in each cell. By default, there's a 1-point (that's 1/72 of an inch) border around each side of each cell, but you can make some or all borders fatter, a different line style (dashed, for example), a different color, or remove them altogether to create your own effects. Here are some examples:

◆ To make a list of names appear to be floating in multiple columns on the slide (that is, to make it look as if they are not really in a table at all but just lined up extremely well), remove all table borders. In Figure 6-13, for example, the borders on the top row (Q1, Q2, Q3) have been removed, and the column headings appear to be floating above the grid.

◆ To create a header row at the top, make the border beneath the first row of cells darker or thicker than the others. In Figure 6-13, the line between the column headings and the first row of months has been assigned a 6-point line.

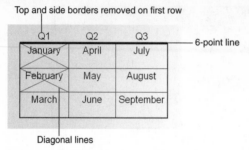

Top and side borders removed on first row

6-point line

Diagonal lines

Figure 6-13: Here are some things you can do with border formatting.

◆ To make it look as if certain items have been crossed off a list, format those cells with diagonal borders. This creates the effect of an X running through each cell. (These diagonal lines are not really borders in the sense that they don't go around the edge of the cell, but they're treated as borders in PowerPoint.) In Figure 6-13, January and February both have diagonal borders applied.

When you apply a top, bottom, left, or right border, those positions refer to the entire selected block of cells if you have more than one cell selected. For example, suppose you select two adjacent cells in a row and apply a left border. The border applies only to the leftmost of the two cells. If you want the same border applied to the line between the cells too, you must apply an Inside Vertical border.

TOOLBAR METHOD

The Tables and Borders toolbar has several buttons for applying table borders, as you saw in Table 6-2. Follow these steps:

1. Select the cell(s) that you want to format.

2. Select a border style from the Border Style button's list. The default is solid, but you can choose a variety of dotted or dashed lines.

3. Select a border thickness from the Border Width drop-down list. The default is 1 point.

4. Click the Border Color button and choose a different color for the border, if desired. The colors that appear on the palette are the colors from the current color scheme in the presentation. You can also choose More Border Colors.

5. Click the down arrow next to the Border Sides button to open its drop-down list of borders (see Figure 6-14). Then, click the button for the border positioning you want to apply. For example, to place the border on all sides of all selected cells, click the All Borders button, which is the one that looks like a window pane.

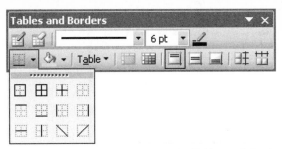

Figure 6-14: Use the controls on the Tables and Borders toolbar to format the border of each cell in the table.

TIP Any time you see a menu with dots at the top of it, like the Border Sides menu in Figure 6-14, you can drag it off to the side to make it into a floating toolbar.

6. If you need to apply the border to any other sides, repeat step 5. If you need to turn the border off for any side that currently has a border, click the button for that side to toggle it off.

DIALOG BOX METHOD

For more control over the borders, use the Format Table dialog box as follows:

1. Select the cell(s) to affect.

2. Choose Format⇨Table. The Format Table dialog box opens.

3. Click the Borders tab.

4. Choose a border style, color, and width.

5. Click the buttons surrounding the sample to turn the border for each side on or off individually. The sample shows the effect (see Figure 6-15).

6. If you want differently styled borders on some sides, repeat steps 3 through 5.

7. Click OK to finish.

Applying Fills

By default, table cells have a transparent background so that the color of the slide beneath shows through. Most of the time, this looks very nice, and you should not need to change it. Sometimes, however, you might want a different color background for some or all of the cells in the table.

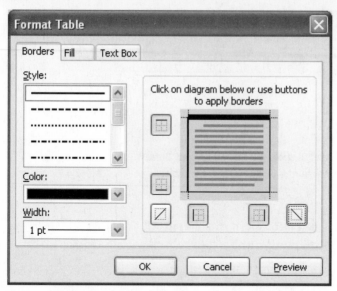

Figure 6-15: The Format Table dialog box lets you specify formatting for the border on each side of each cell.

To change the color of the cells, follow these steps:

1. Select the cell(s) to affect, or to apply the same color to all the cells, select the table's outer border.

2. Click the down arrow next to the Fill Color button on the Tables and Borders toolbar. A palette of colors opens.

3. Select the color you want. Or to remove the background fill, choose No Fill instead of a color. This is the same color palette as in earlier chapters when you were selecting a fill for text boxes and backgrounds.

You can also use a dialog box method. Choose Format⇨Table, and use the Fill tab of the Format Table dialog box to select a color. The benefit of doing this is that a Semi-transparent checkbox is available there, so you can have a semi-transparent fill (see Figure 6-16).

 The Color drop-down list on the Fill tab of the Format Table dialog box lacks a No Fill command. Instead, there is a Fill Color checkbox there; deselecting that checkbox is the same as choosing No Fill.

As with text boxes and background, you can also choose More Fill Colors to choose a different color, or choose Fill Effects to choose gradients, patterns, or other special effects, just like with text boxes and backgrounds.

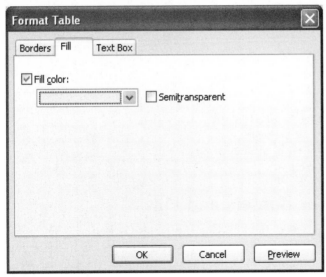

Figure 6-16: Mark the Semitransparent checkbox, if desired, on the Fill tab of the Format Table dialog box.

When you fill a table with a color, picture, texture, or pattern, each cell gets its own individual fill. That means that, for example, if you fill with a picture of a dog, and the table has nine cells, you'll see nine dogs (see Figure 6-17).

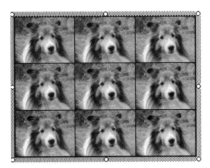

Figure 6-17: When you apply a picture fill to a table in general, each cell gets its own copy of the picture.

If you want a single copy of the picture to fill the entire area behind the table, make the table background transparent (by deselecting the Fill Color checkbox on the Format Table dialog box's Fill tab), and then place the picture as a separate object on the slide, behind the table. Then, use the Draw ⇨ Order ⇨ Send to Back command from the Drawing toolbar to move the picture's position in the stack to the back (see Figure 6-18).

Figure 6-18: When you make the table background transparent and then place the picture behind it as a separate object, a single copy of the picture can serve as the background for the entire table.

Special Effects for Borders and Fills

One extra option that appears on the Fill menu for tables (as well as many other objects) is Background. Setting the fill color to Background makes it match the background color or fill for the slide. Isn't this the same thing as transparent? Well, sort of, but not exactly. If you are stacking items in layers on the slides, and the table's background is transparent, it will show whatever is behind it, whether that's the background or some intervening object(s). If you set the fill to Background, the table's background will always match the slide's background, and any intervening objects in the stack will be masked. Figures 6-19 and 6-20 show the difference.

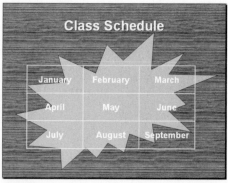

Figure 6-19: When the table's fill is transparent, any objects between the table and the background show through.

Many times I have wished for the ability to apply a 3-D or shadow effect to a table, but PowerPoint does not allow it. One way I have at least partially gotten around this has been to apply a different thickness of border to two sides of a table's outer frame, giving the illusion of a shadow (if you don't look too closely). For example, in Figure 6-21, the right and bottom border is 6-point gray while the rest of the borders are $1/2$-point black. Change the border thickness for each individual cell to simulate a shadow effect for each one. Another method is to apply a fill and then place a shaded AutoShape underneath in the stack.

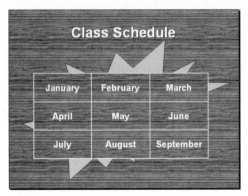

Figure 6-20: When the table's fill is set to Background, the table's fill shows exactly what the slide background shows, and any intervening items are masked.

January	February	March
April	May	June
July	August	September

Figure 6-21: Using a different thickness of border for two sides can simulate a shadow effect.

Here's a sneaky way around the "no shadow" limitation for tables in PowerPoint. PowerPoint does allow you to apply shadows to pictures, right? And also to imported objects from other programs, such as Excel. So here's what you can do:

1. Type your table in Excel.

2. Apply the borders around the desired cells in Excel.

3. Copy the desired range in Excel to the Clipboard.

4. Start a new Title Only or Title and Text slide in PowerPoint.

5. Paste the copied Excel cells onto the new slide. Warning: it won't look very pretty at this point.

6. Click the Paste Options icon near the bottom right corner of the pasted cells, to open its menu, and choose Picture of Table (see Figure 6-22). Now you have a picture of the table.

7. Drag the selection handles of the pasted table picture to enlarge it as needed. The text will enlarge along with the table itself. (Since it is a graphic, can't control its font directly. If you want to change the font or formatting, go back to Excel, make the changes there, and then recopy the table.)

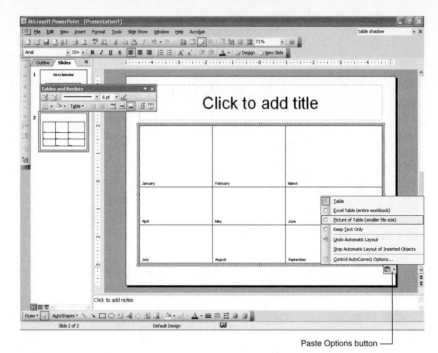

Paste Options button

Figure 6-22: Change the paste option for the pasted Excel cells to Picture of Table, so PowerPoint will treat the pasted object as a graphic.

8. Click the Shadow button on the Drawing toolbar and apply a shadow. Since the object is transparent, each character of text will appear individually shadowed.

9. Apply a fill to the object (white, for example). The shadow will move to the outer border of the object. Voila, you've just created a table with a shadow!

If you want a 3-D table, as shown in Figure 6-23, you'll have to fudge that as well. This time we'll use AutoShapes. You might need to complete Chapter 7 first,

Figure 6-23: Group 3-D rectangles together and add text to each of them to create the illusion of a 3-D table.

to learn how to do some of these steps:

1. Create a rectangle with the drawing tools (see Chapter 7) and apply a 3-D effect to it. Right-click it, choose Add Text, and type some text in it.

2. Copy it as many times as needed until you have enough copies for every cell in your table.

3. Arrange the rectangles in a table-like grid. Use the Align and Distribute commands as needed on the Drawing toolbar's Draw menu.

4. Arrange the stacking order of the rectangles (using the Draw⇨Order menu command) as needed.

5. Type different text in each rectangle.

6. Select them all, and group them (using the Draw⇨Group menu command) into a single object.

 For more on how to use PowerPoint's drawing tools, turn to Chapter 7.

Copying Tables from Word

If a table already exists in Word, you can copy it into PowerPoint. PowerPoint will convert the Word table to a PowerPoint table by default, but you can override that behavior, if desired. (To keep it as a Word table, use Edit⇨Paste Special and then paste it as a Microsoft Word Document Object.)

Assuming you don't mind that it's converted to a PowerPoint table upon import, simply select the table in Word, copy it to the Clipboard (Ctrl+C), and then paste it onto a slide in PowerPoint (Ctrl+V). Then one of the following occurs:

◆ If there is a suitable placeholder on the slide already (that is, any of the multi-type content placeholders, or a table placeholder), and it doesn't have any data in it yet, the Word table will go into it. The table will be sized to fit that placeholder's area. If you don't want the table to go into the placeholder, use the AutoLayout button's menu to undo it, or just press Ctrl+Z to undo the change.

◆ If there is not a suitable placeholder, but there is room on the slide for one (like on a Title Only layout, for example), PowerPoint will switch to a layout that has a table placeholder and will put the Word table into the placeholder as a PowerPoint table. Again, you can undo that with Ctrl+Z.

◆ If you insert the table on a completely blank slide, the table appears in the center of the slide, with no AutoLayout options.

♦ If there is no placeholder and no room for one because of existing content, PowerPoint will place the table on top of everything else as a new PowerPoint table, and it'll be up to you to move things around and resize them to make it fit.

If the Word table becomes part of a layout placeholder, it conforms to the size of that placeholder (but the text stays the same size). If the Word table becomes a free-floating object unattached to any placeholder, it becomes a PowerPoint table formatted with the original size and shape of the Word table.

Copying Worksheet Cells from Excel

Copying cells from an Excel worksheet is similar to copying a Word table into PowerPoint. PowerPoint converts the pasted cells into a PowerPoint table, and either places it in a placeholder or as a free-floating object depending on the existing slide content and layout. However, there are some important differences.

The most noticeable difference is the button that appears next to the pasted data after the paste. Rather than an AutoLayout icon, it's a Paste Options button, and it has a different menu with different commands, as shown in Figure 6-24.

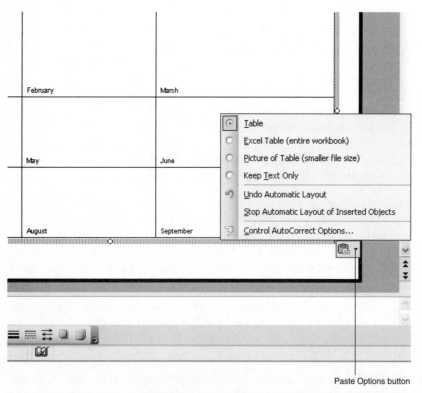

Paste Options button

Figure 6-24: Paste options after pasting worksheet data from Excel into PowerPoint.

Your paste option choices are the following:

◆ *Table*: This option converts the Excel data into a PowerPoint table.

◆ *Excel Table (entire workbook)*: This option embeds the entire Excel workbook into the PowerPoint presentation file, which makes the file much larger, but it does retain Excel functionality and access to other cells in the workbook that were not originally selected for the paste.

◆ *Picture of Table (smaller file size)*: This option embeds only the copied Excel cells, and it embeds them in a graphic format that does not allow further editing of the text.

◆ *Keep Text Only*: This option strips off all the row and column dividers and places all the text into a single text box.

Except for the Excel Table option, none of the preceding options do any linking or embedding. What's that, and why is it significant? Read the next section.

Linking and Embedding Excel Data

There are several ways of bringing foreign objects such as Excel data into your presentation. The method you choose depends on how you want the object to behave once it arrives. You can make the inserted content into a full citizen of the presentation in a PowerPoint table—that is, with no ties of any kind to its source—or, you can help it retain a connection to either the original data file or to the original application in which it was created.

Both of those latter options have a price, however, in terms of larger file size (in the case of embedding) and dependence on the availability of another file for updating (in the case of linking). Therefore, you should use linking and embedding strategically for specific purposes, and not as a general rule.

Embedding maintains the relationship between that data and its native application. In the case of Excel data, it would "remember" that it came from Excel, and you could double-click it within PowerPoint to edit it within Excel.

Linking maintains the relationship between that data and the original data file from which it was copied. When changes are made in the original, they are reflected in the copy in PowerPoint.

You can link or embed entire files or just snippets of files. There are separate procedures for each, which I'll outline in the following sections.

The information in these sections will serve you well when working with other types of content too, not just Excel, although I'll be focusing on Excel here.

Embedding Selected Cells from an Excel Worksheet

Technically, there is no such thing as embedding "selected cells" from a worksheet into PowerPoint. If you embed an existing file, you get the entire file—which impacts the size of the PowerPoint file, of course. However, you can *appear* to embed only selected cells, in that only selected cells will show up on your PowerPoint slide, and that's what you were really wanting after all, wasn't it?

You've already seen one way do to this. Do a simple copy-and-paste from Excel, and then click the Paste Options icon on the pasted cells in PowerPoint and choose Excel Table (entire workbook) from the menu (shown in Figure 6-24).

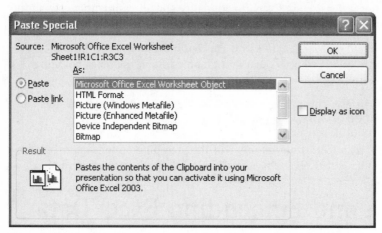

Figure 6-25: Use Paste Special to specify how the pasted item should appear, and then select Excel Object as the type.

Another way is with the Paste Special command, as follows:

◆ Copy normally in Excel.

◆ In PowerPoint, choose Edit⇨Paste Special.

◆ In the Paste Special dialog box, choose Paste.

◆ Select Microsoft Office Excel Worksheet Object as the type (see Figure 6-25).

◆ Click OK.

You will then be able to double-click the pasted object in PowerPoint to make Excel's menus and toolbars appear to help with its editing.

Embedding an Entire Excel Workbook

Again, technically all Excel embedding embeds an entire workbook, but in this case we are talking about *showing* the entire contents in PowerPoint. For example, if your Excel workbook file consists of a single worksheet with a single tabular range of cells, you might want to show it all.

To embed the entire contents of a saved workbook, do the following:

1. In PowerPoint, display the slide on which you want to place the embedded object.

2. Choose Insert⇨Object.

3. Click the Create from File button. The controls change to those shown in Figure 6-26.

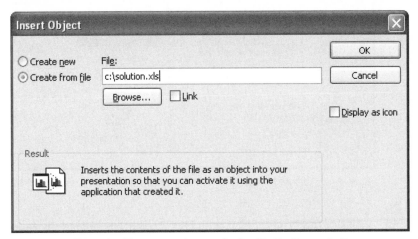

Figure 6-26: Enter the file name or browse for it with the Browse button.

4. Click Browse and use the Browse dialog box to locate the file you want; then click OK to accept the file name.

5. Click OK. The file is inserted on the slide.

You can tell that it is embedded, rather than simply copied, because when you double-click it, it opens in Excel. In contrast, when you double-click some Excel data that has been copied into PowerPoint as a PowerPoint table, the Format Table dialog box opens.

Embedding a New Excel Workbook

If you haven't already created the tabular data in Excel, you have your choice: you can use a PowerPoint table, or you can embed a new Excel object. I don't use embedded Excel worksheets for ordinary tables because of the increased file size, but I do use them whenever I need to perform calculations within a table because of Excel's extensive collection of functions.

To embed a new Excel worksheet, do the following:

1. Display the slide on which you want to put it.

2. Choose Insert⇨Object.

3. Click Create New. A list of available object types appears. This list comes from the installed applications on your system, so yours will be different than the ones shown in Figure 6-27.

4. Click Microsoft Excel Worksheet and click OK.

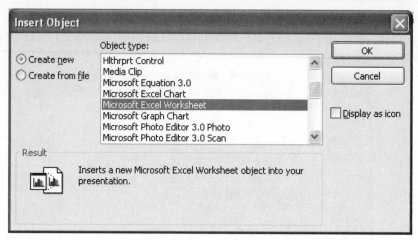

Figure 6-27: Choose Microsoft Excel Worksheet as the type of new object to embed.

5. A frame appears on the slide with Excel cells inside it. Type the data into the cells. Resize it as needed to show more or fewer cells. Notice that the menus and toolbars are Excel's, not PowerPoint's, while the object is active.

6. Click away from the object to return control to PowerPoint.

7. Move and resize the object on the slide as necessary.

Linking Selected Cells from an Excel Worksheet

Linking maintains a relationship to the original data file, so you would do this only if you thought that the Excel copy was going to change and you wanted those changes to be reflected in PowerPoint.

To link selected cells from an existing worksheet, follow the steps under *Embedding Selected Cells from an Excel Worksheet* except in step 3, click Paste Link instead of Paste. Everything else is the same.

Use linking only when its unique functionality is required. Linking is not a good general-purpose practice because the link relies on both files remaining in the same location (or, at least in relation to one another). For example, if you link to an Excel file called Solution.xls that's in the same folder as your PowerPoint file, and then you move Solution.xls somewhere else, PowerPoint won't be able to find it, and an error will appear when you open the PowerPoint file. (You can redirect the link, which I'll explain later in the chapter, but it's still a pain.) Linking also makes the process of opening and closing the PowerPoint file take longer because the links have to be updated.

Linking an Entire Workbook

To link the entire workbook, follow the steps under *Embedding an Entire Excel Workbook* earlier in the chapter, but mark the Link checkbox before clicking OK in the last step.

Editing an Embedded Excel Workbook

When an embedded worksheet is selected, you can choose Edit⇨Worksheet Object or right-click and choose Worksheet Object to see a menu of things you can do to it as follows:

◆ *Edit*: This option activates the object with Excel's menus and toolbars within PowerPoint. You can also do the same thing by double-clicking the object on the slide.

◆ *Open*: This option opens the object in the full-blown Excel window, outside of PowerPoint.

◆ *Convert*: This option allows you to convert the object to some other format. For an Excel worksheet, the only option is Excel Chart. Do this if you want to show the data graphically rather than as a table.

The above also work with linked workbook data except the command on the Edit menu is Linked Worksheet Object.

Managing Workbook Links

Working with linked data from Excel? Here are some things you can do to it.

UPDATING LINKS

Links are automatically updated each time you open your PowerPoint file. However, updating these links slows down the file opening considerably, so if you have to open and close the file frequently, you might want to set the link updating to Manual. That way the links are updated only when you issue a command to update them.

To set a link to update manually, follow these steps:

1. Choose Edit⇨Links. The Links dialog box appears (see Figure 6-28). If the Links command does not appear on the Edit menu, there are no links.

2. Click the link you want to change, and click the Manual button.

3. If you want to manually update a link now, select it and click the Update Now button.

4. Click OK to close the dialog box.

5. Save the presentation to save the changes to the link settings.

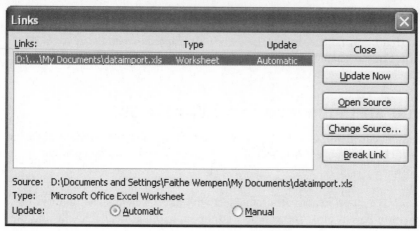

Figure 6-28: You can change the update setting for a link here.

When you set a link to manual, you have to open the Links dialog box and click Update Now each time you want to update it, or right-click the object and choose Update Link for its shortcut menu.

BREAKING A LINK

When you break a link, the object remains in the presentation, but it becomes a picture. So, for example, if you break the link for an Excel worksheet object, it becomes a picture of a worksheet object. You can't edit it in Excel anymore; when you double-click it, a Format Picture dialog box appears. The embedding information disappears too.

To break a link, reopen the Links dialog box (refer to Figure 6-28), click the link to break, and then click Break Link. If a warning appears, click OK.

CHANGING THE REFERENCED LOCATION OF A LINK

If you move files around on your hard disk or move them to other disks, you might need to change the link location reference. For example, perhaps you are moving the presentation file to a ZIP disk, and you want to place the linked workbook file in a separate folder on the ZIP disk.

To change a link reference, do the following:

1. Copy or move the files where you want them. For example, if you are going to be transferring the presentation and linked files to a floppy, do that first.

2. In the copy location, open the PowerPoint presentation. You'll see an error about the linked files missing; ignore it.

3. Choose Edit➪Links. The Links dialog box appears.

4. Click the link you want to change and click Change Source. A Change Source dialog box opens.

5. Select the file to be linked from its new location and click Open. The link is updated.

6. In the Links dialog box, click Close.

7. Save your work.

If you change the location of the link to a different file (for example, a different workbook), the link will refer to the entire file, as if you had inserted it with Insert ⇨ Object. If you used Edit ⇨ Paste Special, Paste Link to insert only a part of the original file, that aspect might be lost and the entire file might appear as the object in the presentation. In such a situation it is better to delete the object and recreate the link from scratch.

Summary

In this chapter you learned how to create tables in PowerPoint and how to bring tabular data in from Excel and Word. We also looked at OLE and how to use it to create dynamic links to Excel data. The next lesson starts a whole new topic in the book—Graphics—by introducing you to graphic effects involving the drawing tools. Even if you have used the drawing tools before, you will likely pick up some tips and tricks here.

Part III

Still Images

Chapter 7

Drawing Tools and Graphic Effects

IN THIS CHAPTER

◆ The basics of vector graphics

◆ Drawing lines and shapes

◆ Creating WordArt

◆ Sizing and positioning objects

◆ Applying fill, shadow, and 3-D effects

◆ Modifying an AutoShape

◆ Rotating, flipping, layering, and grouping objects

POWERPOINT COMES WITH A SET of drawing tools that create simple lines and shapes on slides. It refers to these drawn lines and shapes as *AutoShapes,* and provides a whole host of formatting commands and options for them. They're so much fun to create and format with that you may wish you didn't have to bother with text!

PowerPoint is wonderfully consistent in the way it handles object formatting. The bulk of what you've learned in the earlier chapters about borders, fills, and positioning will serve you well here too. In this chapter I'll review that information—in case you're not reading the book from cover to cover—and I'll also bring up some additional formatting features that are handy when working with AutoShapes.

About Vector Graphics

The drawing tools create simple line-based vector graphics that are each a separate object on the slide. For example, if you make a drawing consisting of four rectangles, an oval, and several lines, each of those is separately movable or resizable. You can stack them to create a more complex drawing, format each one individually, and/or group them (by choosing Draw ⇨ Group) to create a single object that can be formatted, moved, and resized as a single unit.

A *vector graphic* is one that is based on a mathematical formula, like in geometry class. For example, if you draw a vector graphic line, the application stores the line start point, line end point, and line properties (width, color, and so on) as numeric values. When you move or resize the line, those numbers are updated. Clip art is also

165

a vector graphic type. In contrast, a scanned image or a photo is a bitmap graphic, in which each individual colored dot is represented by a separate numeric value.

 For more on clip art, turn to Chapter 9, and for more on scanned images photos, turn to Chapter 8.

The most important advantages of using vector graphics are the following:

◆ *Size.* Vector graphics don't take up much disk space to store because not every pixel of the image needs to be represented numerically.

◆ *Scalability.* When you resize a vector graphic, the math is recalculated and the shape is redrawn. That means the picture is never distorted and its lines never get jagged the way bitmap graphics do.

The main drawback to vector graphics is lack of realism No matter how good an artist you are, a vector graphic will always have a flat, cartoon quality to it.

3-D graphics programs such as AutoCAD are based on vector graphics too. They start out with a wireframe image of a 3-D object (such as a cube), combine it with other wireframe images to make an object, and then use a rendering tool to cover the wireframe with a color, pattern, or texture that makes it look like a real object. Many popular video games also use vector graphics, like *The Sims*, for example.

Drawing Lines and Shapes

The Drawing tools in PowerPoint are the same as in other Office applications. Word and Excel both have identical tool sets, for example.

The Drawing tools provide for five basic things you can draw. By combining these elements you can make a surprising variety of drawings:

Line

Arrow (that is, a line with an arrowhead on one or both ends)

Rectangle (hold down Ctrl for a perfect square)

Oval (hold down Ctrl for a perfect circle)

 AutoShapes (click to open a menu of shapes)

There are dozens of these pre-created shapes on the AutoShapes menu, including all kinds of block arrows, sunbursts, brackets, and flow-charting symbols. Table 7-1 shows each of the submenus and what's on them.

TABLE 7-1 MICROSOFT OFFICE AUTOSHAPES

Menu	Name	Description
	Lines	Freeform shapes or lines, or straight lines, with or without arrows, used to draw freehand or to call attention to certain objects.
	Connectors	Flow charting connectors that help create relationship lines between other objects.
	Basic Shapes	A variety of geometric shapes and simple symbols.
	Block Arrows	Arrows that are thicker than just lines, useful for flow charting or to call attention to another object. These arrows use both fill and border colors, unlike arrows created from lines.
	Flowchart	Standard flowchart symbols.
	Stars and Banners	Lively starbursts and swoops for calling attention to an object or text. Place text inside these shapes for extra impact.
	Callouts	Thought and speech bubbles for cartoons and explanatory boxes.
	Action Buttons	Buttons useful for moving from slide to slide in a user-interactive presentation.

To draw with one of the drawing tools, click it and then drag on the slide. If you need to draw more than one of a certain item, double-click its button rather than clicking it, and it will stay "on" until you turn it off (by clicking the button again or pressing Esc).

 Microsoft Office programs are inconsistent in the use of the term *AutoShape*, but don't let it confuse you. In some dialog boxes and in the Help system, *all* drawn objects, including manual text boxes, are generically referred to as AutoShapes, but there is also a special class of pre-drawn shapes called AutoShapes that are accessible from the AutoShapes button on the Drawing toolbar. In this chapter I use the term AutoShape generically to refer to any drawn shape, not just the ones that happen to be on the AutoShapes menu.

There are all kinds of uses for drawn lines and shapes. For example, you might draw a line with an arrow to point to an important part of a chart. The rectangles and ovals can be used to draw boxes or frames around important slide points or objects. Figure 7-1 shows a chart with an oval and a line enhancing its main point.

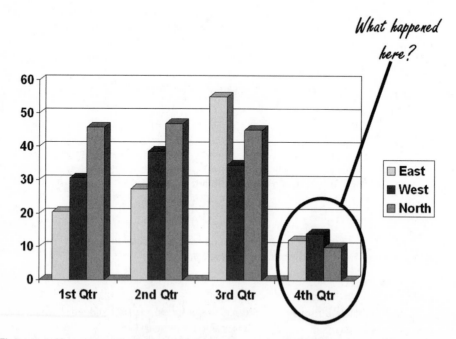

Figure 7-1: You can use simple lines and shapes to accentuate the content on a slide.

An arrow is the same as a line except there's an arrowhead on one or both ends. You can use the Arrow button to draw the line, or you can convert a regular line to an arrow by changing its properties in the Format AutoShape dialog box.

If you are artistically inclined, you can even attempt to create complete drawings with the drawing tools. Want some examples? Try the following experiment:

1. Insert a piece of clip art from the Clip Organizer (see Chapter 9, if needed).

2. Select the clip art and then choose Draw⇨Ungroup. A message appears asking if you want to convert it to a Microsoft Drawing object.

3. Click Yes, and then choose Draw⇨Ungroup again. The art will be broken down into its individual lines and shapes, as shown in Figure 7-2. Each individual line and shape has its own selection handles; that's why there are all those tiny white circles. (That's a lot of individual drawn objects.)

Figure 7-2: To see an example of what you can do with the drawing tools, deconstruct a piece of clip art.

4. Drag the individual lines and shapes away from the drawing one by one to deconstruct it.

 Interested in advanced experimentation with drawing Bezier curves via the drawing tools in PowerPoint? See this excellent online tutorial: www .echosvoice.com/beziercurves.htm.

Adding Text to an AutoShape

One of my favorite ways to use AutoShapes is to hold text. I mentioned this in Chapter 5, but here it is again. Any AutoShape can be used to hold text. Figure 7-3 shows an example of some starburst AutoShapes being used for text. To make an AutoShape text-capable, right-click it and choose Add Text. An insertion point appears in its center; type the text there.

Figure 7-3: You can use AutoShapes as text boxes.

Duplicating AutoShapes

Many times you might need multiple copies of the same AutoShape. Rather than trying to redraw exact copies, just duplicate the original one.

Here's a really cool feature that not many people know about: PowerPoint automatically equalizes the spacing between multiple pasted copies of a drawn shape if you use Edit➪Duplicate (Ctrl+D) instead of a regular copy-and-paste. To try this out, do the following:

1. Create an AutoShape. For this experiment try something odd-shaped like an arrow or chevron.

2. Choose Edit➪Duplicate or press Ctrl+D.

3. Move the copy so that it is positioned in relation to the original in the way that you want all copies to be spaced.

4. Duplicate again. The new copy appears with the same spacing.

5. Duplicate again several times. The new copies all get the same spacing. Pretty handy!

Creating WordArt

All of the Office 2003 applications have access to a program called WordArt that helps you create stylized, interesting-looking text. The text can be shaped, slanted, twisted, and all manner of other manipulations, so that it ends up looking more like a graphic than like text. Figure 7-4 shows some examples of WordArt.

Figure 7-4: Here are some examples of what you can do with WordArt.

Formatting-wise, most of what you can do to an AutoShape can also be done to WordArt, so most of the remainder of this chapter will apply to both. In addition, I'll include an extra section at the end of this chapter covering some of the advanced manipulations that are specific to WordArt.

You can create a piece of WordArt easily using some standard settings and then refine it to be exactly what you want using the various formatting techniques in the remainder of this chapter. Follow these steps to create some WordArt:

1. Display the slide you want to place the WordArt on.

2. Click the WordArt button on the Drawing toolbar. The WordArt Gallery dialog box appears (see Figure 7-5).

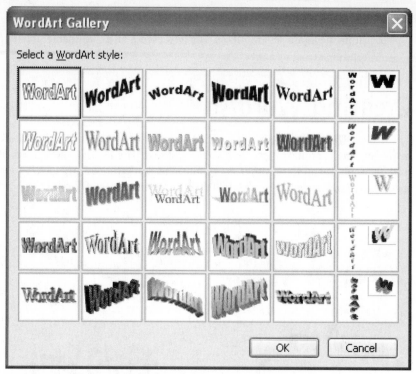

Figure 7-5: Choose an initial design from the WordArt Gallery.

3. Click one of the gallery designs. If there isn't one that matches exactly what you want, pick something similar; you can modify it later.

4. Click OK. The Edit WordArt Text dialog box appears.

5. Type the text you want. Choose a different font and size if desired, and/or click the Bold or Italic buttons.

6. Click OK. The finished WordArt appears on the slide. From here you can modify it as you would an AutoShape; the rest of the chapter explains how.

There are some minor differences in formatting WordArt and AutoShapes, and I'll point those out as we go along.

Changing WordArt Shape

The biggest thing that distinguishes WordArt from regular text is the ability to apply different shapes to it. To choose a different shape, click the WordArt Shape button on the WordArt toolbar, and select a shape from the menu that appears (see Figure 7-6).

Figure 7-6: Choose a different shape, if desired.

Editing WordArt Text

To change the WordArt text, double-click the WordArt object. The Edit WordArt Text dialog box appears. You can also click the Edit Text button on the WordArt toolbar instead, if desired (see Figure 7-6).

Advanced WordArt Formatting Techniques

In addition to the "biggies" of shape and text wording, there are many other options for manipulating WordArt. For example, you can toggle between having all the letters be the same height or not, toggle between making the letters run vertically or horizontally, and change the amount of white space between the letters. Table 7-2 describes the full set of buttons available on the WordArt toolbar.

TABLE 7-2 WORDART TOOLBAR BUTTONS

Button	Name	Description
	Insert WordArt	Opens the WordArt Gallery dialog box so you can create an additional WordArt object. Has no effect on the existing WordArt.
Edit Text...	WordArt Edit Text	Reopens the Edit WordArt Text dialog box for the current WordArt object. Can also be activated by double-clicking the WordArt object.
	WordArt Gallery	Reopens the WordArt Gallery dialog box for the current WordArt object. Useful for choosing a different style.

Continued

TABLE 7-2 WORDART TOOLBAR BUTTONS *(Continued)*

Button	Name	Description
	Format WordArt	Opens the Format WordArt dialog box, from which you can access a full range of options including sizing, position, colors, and so on. Many of the controls here are discussed later in this chapter for AutoShapes and work the same way.
	WordArt Shape	Opens a pop-up array of shapes you can choose for your WordArt, as shown in Figure 7-6.
	WordArt Same Letter Heights	Makes all the letters the same height. An interesting effect, but it may make the text difficult to read.
	WordArt Vertical Text	Toggles between vertical and horizontal text orientation.
	WordArt Alignment	Opens a shortcut menu of alignments (centered, right-aligned, and so on). Refers to the WordArt's position within its own frame, not in relation to the slide. Therefore, it is not that useful unless the WordArt does not completely fill its frame.
	WordArt Character Spacing	Changes the spacing between letters (normal, loose, tight, and so on).

In addition to using the buttons on the WordArt toolbar, you can also manipulate WordArt by doing the following:

◆ Drag a side selection handle on the WordArt to change its height/width proportions.

◆ Drag a yellow diamond to fine-tune the shape of the WordArt, such as adjusting the tilt of the letters.

◆ Apply shadows and 3-D effects to the WordArt, as described later in this chapter (*Adding Shadow Effects* and *Adding 3-D Effects*).

Sizing and Positioning Objects

By now, moving and sizing objects is old hat for you, right? Drag by a selection handle to resize, or by the border to move. It's the same as with text boxes (see Chapter 5). Here are some tips:

◆ *Proportional resizing*: Drag a corner selection handle rather than a side one.

◆ *Moving or resizing several objects at once*: Hold down Shift and click each one until all are selected; then move or resize as a group. You can also drag a "box" around a group of objects with the mouse pointer to select them all.

◆ *Specific positioning*: Right-click the object, choose Format AutoShape, and then on the Position tab, enter an exact position for it.

◆ *Specific sizing*: Right-click the object, choose Format AutoShape, and then on the Size tab, enter an exact size in inches or a percentage of the current size. You can choose to lock the aspect ratio (that is, the proportion of height to width), if desired (see Figure 7-7).

◆ *Cropping*: If you want to crop the object rather than resize it, use the Crop tool on the Picture toolbar.

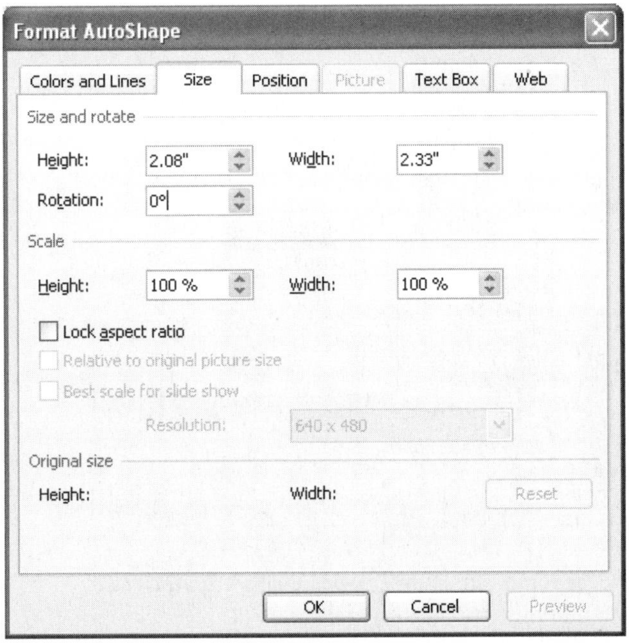

Figure 7-7: AutoShapes and WordArt can be sized precisely just like text boxes.

The Picture toolbar's Crop tool is covered in Chapter 8 in detail.

In addition to these basic sizing and positioning settings, PowerPoint also offers the following options for fine-tuning.

Nudging

To nudge something is just what it sounds like: to move it over slightly. The Nudge commands are located on the Drawing menu (on the Drawing toolbar). Select the object and apply the command (Up, Down, Left, or Right).

To convert the menu into a floating toolbar, drag it off onto the work area by the dots at the top (see Figure 7-8). This works for all the submenus off the Drawing menu (including Align or Distribute, covered in the following two sections).

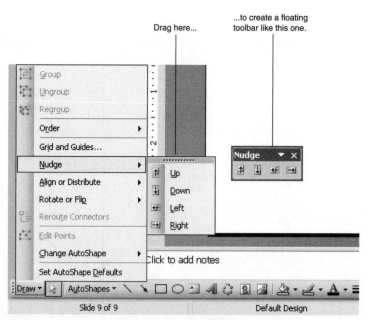

Figure 7-8: Use the Nudge controls from the Drawing toolbar's Draw menu or drag the controls off into their own floating toolbar.

You can also use the keyboard to nudge objects. Select an object and then use the arrow keys to move it.

The amount that each nudge moves depends on these factors:

◆ If Snap to Grid is turned on, each nudge moves the object by one place in the grid spacing. By default, the grid interval is .083 inches. To toggle Snap to Grid on/off or to change the grid spacing, choose Draw ⇨ Grid and Guides to display the Grid Settings dialog box.

◆ If Snap to Grid is turned off, each nudge moves in .01-inch increments.

Alignment and Distribution

You can align or distribute objects either in relation to the slide itself or in relation to other objects. Here are some examples:

◆ You can align an object to the top, bottom, left, right, or center of a slide. I have found the Center option to be especially handy in making an object appear in the exact center both vertically and horizontally.

◆ You can align two objects in relation to one another so they are at the same vertical or horizontal position. For example, you could align two pictures so that their tops form a straight line across the slide.

◆ You can distribute three or more objects so that the spacing between them is even. For example, if you have four objects in a horizontal row, Distribute would reallocate the space between them so there is the same amount of blank space between each.

 The commands on the Align or Distribute menu are not always available. You must have two or more objects selected for aligning, or you must make sure that the Relative to Slide command has a checkmark next to it. You must have three or more objects selected for distributing.

ALIGNING AN OBJECT IN RELATION TO THE SLIDE

To align a single object in relation to the slide, select the object and then choose Draw ⇨ Align or Distribute and then the desired Align command (see Figure 7-9).

The Relative to Slide command must have a checkmark next to it in order to align a single object. (Otherwise there is nothing for it to align with!) To check this, choose Draw ⇨ Align or Distribute. Choose Relative to Slide from the menu to toggle its checkbox on/off.

ALIGNING TWO OR MORE OBJECTS WITH ONE ANOTHER

You can also align two objects in relation to one another. This works by assigning the same setting to both objects. For example, in Figure 7-10, the objects are in their starting positions. Figure 7-11 shows what happened when I used the Draw ⇨ Align

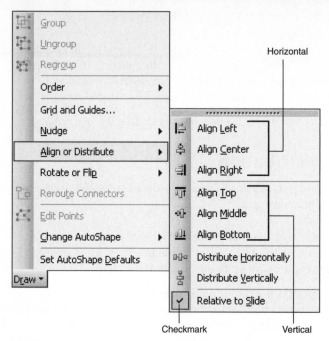

Figure 7-9: The Align or Distribute submenu offers a variety of options for making objects align in relation to one another.

Figure 7-10: The original positioning.

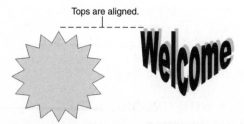

Figure 7-11: The positioning after applying the Align Top command.

or Distribute ⇨ Align Top command. The lower object moved up to the same vertical position as the higher one. If I had used Align Bottom, the higher objects would have been moved so that its bottom matched the lower one. If I had used Align Center, both objects would have moved to split the difference between the positions of their centers.

To align two or more objects with one another, you'll first need to turn off the Relative to Slide option if it's on. (It's on in Figure 7-9, for example.) Then, select all the objects, choose Draw ⇨ Align or Distribute, and then choose the desired alignment command.

If you use Align Top and the objects move to the very top of the slide, you have probably left the Relative to Slide option turned on. Undo (Ctrl+Z) and then select Draw ⇨ Align or Distribute ⇨ Relative to Slide to turn it off.

DISTRIBUTING OBJECTS

Distribution works only in relation to the slide or with three or more objects selected. When you distribute objects, you spread them evenly over a given space. For example, suppose you have just aligned three text boxes vertically, as shown in Figure 7-12, and now you want to even out the space between each box. You can apply the Distribute Horizontally command to create the uniform spacing shown in Figure 7-13.

Figure 7-12: The original positioning.

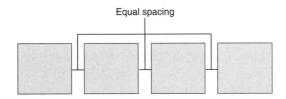

Figure 7-13: The positioning after applying the Distribute Horizontally command.

To distribute objects, select them (hold down Shift as you click each one), then choose Draw ⇨ Align or Distribute, and then either Distribute Vertically or Distribute Horizontally.

Formatting Lines and Borders

With an AutoShape (except for a line) or a piece of WordArt, there are three distinct areas: inside, outside, and the border between the two. You format the border with the Line tools, and you format the inside with the Fill tools. (The area outside the shape is defined by the slide background setting.)

A line, on the other hand, has only two areas: the line and the background on which it sits. To format a line, you work only with the Line tools in PowerPoint. The Fill tools are unavailable when a line is selected.

Since all drawn objects and WordArt use the Line settings, let's look at those first.

TIP Many people make the mistake of placing a transparent rectangle around an object when they want a border around it. This works, but it is inefficient. Because the rectangle and the object it frames are two separate objects, they move separately, so when you resize or move the object, the rectangle has to be moved and resized separately. You could group the objects, but that would be another step. A much simpler way to put a frame around an object is to simply select that object and apply a Line Color to it.

The fast and easy way to apply line formatting is with the Drawing toolbar buttons:

Line Color: The outside border around a shape, or the line itself for a line. Click the button face to apply the currently chosen color or click the down arrow to the right of the button to open a menu.

Line Style: The number and type of smaller lines that comprise the line. It might be a single line, or two or three thin rows running parallel to one another. Clicking the button opens a menu.

Dash Style: The spacing and shape of the dashes in its line (or its quality of being solid, without dashes of any kind). Clicking the button opens a menu.

Arrow Style: The presence or absence of an arrow at one or both ends of the line, and the arrow's size and shape. Clicking the button opens a menu.

There are a couple of minor drawbacks to using the toolbar method. One is that the Line Style list contains a combination of line styles and thicknesses. If the line style you want appears there in the wrong thickness, too bad. The other is that you can't apply a different arrowhead style to each end of a line; you get either the same style at both ends or a single-end arrow.

For the dialog box method, select the drawn object, and choose Format⇨Auto-Shape. Then click the Colors and Lines tab, and make your selections in the Line area (see Figure 7-14).

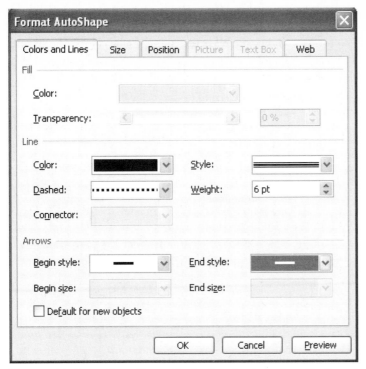

Figure 7-14: Formatting a line, or the border of a shape, from the Format AutoShape dialog box.

If you are formatting a line (not a shape), the Arrow area will also be available. The options here include both a style and a size for the beginning and the end of the line. So, for example, you can select an arrowhead style and then choose how large that arrowhead will be as two separate issues.

 TIP Which is the beginning of the line, and which is the end? When you initially draw that line, wherever you started is the beginning. If you don't remember, use trial-and-error; you have a 50% chance of being right.

Applying Solid or Semi-Transparent Fills

The default fill for a drawn shape is the fifth color in the active color scheme, but you can change it to any other color in the scheme, any specific solid color, or any of a variety of fill effects.

Let's look first at the solid color options. The easiest method is to select the shape and then open the menu for the Fill Color button on the Drawing toolbar, as shown in Figure 7-15. The top row of colored squares is the color scheme colors. The second row (if present) shows squares for any other colors you have already used in this presentation. No Fill makes it transparent, while Automatic resets the fill to the default (the fifth color in the active color scheme).

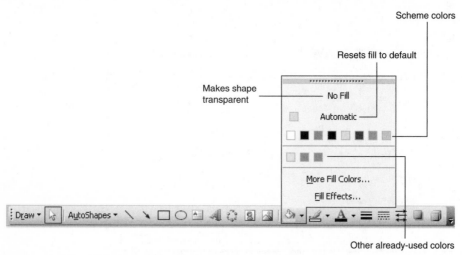

Figure 7-15: The Fill Color button offers a variety of colors on its menu.

A fill applied from the Fill Color button is completely non-transparent; it has 0% transparency set. That means that the shape completely obscures whatever is behind it. As I mentioned in Chapter 5, you can apply transparency to an object (you did it for a text box in Chapter 5) so that whatever is behind it shows through. Transparency is a slider that goes from 0% to 100%.

To set transparency, use the dialog box method. Select the object, choose Format⇨AutoShape, and then use the Transparency slider on the Colors and Lines tab (see Figure 7-16). Figure 7-17 shows the same shape with varying degrees of transparency applied. (Compare to Figure 5-14; it's the same thing as with text box transparency.) You can also access transparency settings by choosing More Fill Colors from the Fill button's drop-down list; the dialog box that appears has a Transparency slider in it.

Applying Fill Effects

The Fill Effects command on the Fill Color menu opens a Fill Effects dialog box with four tabs: Gradient, Texture, Pattern, and Picture. Each of these is a type of fill that you can use as an alternative to a solid color in an AutoShape or a piece of WordArt.

Format AutoShape   [X]

| Colors and Lines | Size | Position | Picture | Text Box | Web |

Fill

   Color: [_____] [v]

   Transparency: [<] [____▦____] [>] [54 %] [⬍]

Line

   Color: [████████] [v]   Style: [————————] [v]

   Dashed: [————————] [v]   Weight: [0.75 pt] [⬍]

   Connector: [_____] [v]

Arrows

   Begin style: [_____] [v]   End style: [_____] [v]

   Begin size: [_____] [v]   End size: [_____] [v]

   [ ] Default for new objects

[OK]   [Cancel]   [Preview]

Figure 7-16: Control the transparency of the fill from the Colors and Lines tab.

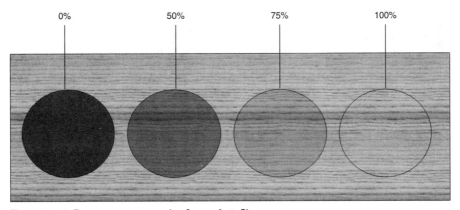

Figure 7-17: Transparency examples for an AutoShape.

Gradients

If you've ever watched a sunset (and who hasn't?), you know how the red of the sun slowly fades into the blue/black of the evening sky. You may not have thought of it quite this way before, but that's a gradient. Whenever one color turns gradually into another one, it's a gradient. Gradients are often used on large shapes on logos and on backgrounds. Figure 7-18 shows some WordArt with a gradient fill.

Figure 7-18: This gradient fades from black at the top to white at the bottom.

On the Gradient tab in the Fill Effects dialog box, you can choose three kinds of gradients:

◆ *One color*: This gradient uses one color plus either black or white or a shade of gray.

◆ *Two color*: This gradient uses two colors that you choose.

◆ *Preset*: This gradient option lets you select one of the preset color combinations that come with PowerPoint.

One thing that all three gradient types have in common is that you can choose whether the gradient should rotate when you rotate the AutoShape. For example, suppose you have an up-pointing block arrow that you have drawn with the Auto Shape tool. You then rotate it to be a left-pointing arrow. Should the gradient rotate too or stay fixed? Figure 7-19 shows the difference. Mark or clear the Rotate Fill Effect with Shape checkbox at the bottom of the dialog box to indicate your preference in this matter.

To set a one-color gradient, click the One Color option button and then select the color from the Color 1 drop-down list. Then drag the Dark/Light slider to adjust the gradient. If the slider is in the center, there will be no gradient. Drag it to Dark to make the chosen color a gradient with black, or drag it to Light to make the chosen color a gradient with white.

After selecting the color, adjust the Transparency sliders, if desired. Transparency can also be a gradient effect, making the transparency of an object gradually fade from one amount of transparency to another. The From slider specifies the beginning transparency and the To slider is for the ending transparency.

Finally, choose a shading style. Choose a category of style from the option buttons, and then click on the desired variant (see Figure 7-20).

When you select the Two Colors gradient option, the Light/Dark slider goes away and is replaced by a Color 2 drop-down list, as shown in Figure 7-21. Choose the second color you want from that list. Then, select the desired shading style.

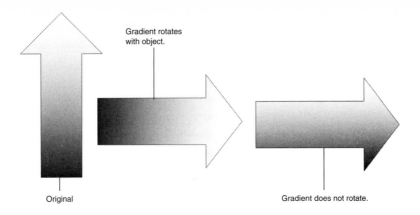

Figure 7-19: When a shape is rotated, the gradient will rotate too, or not, depending on your setting in the Fill Effects dialog box.

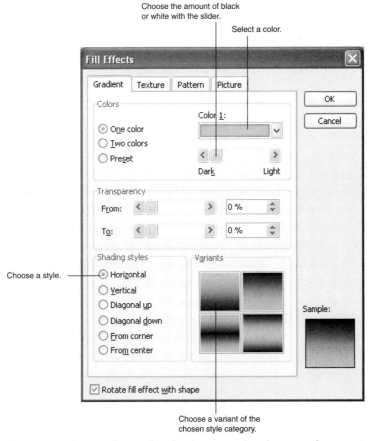

Figure 7-20: A one-color gradient involves one color plus a certain amount of either black or white.

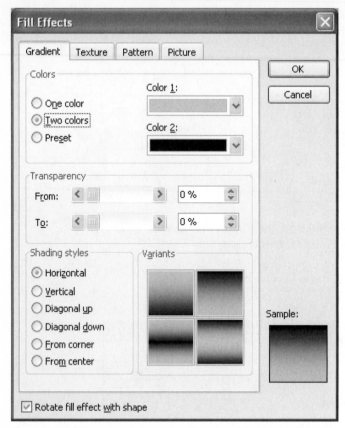

Figure 7-21: With the Two Colors gradient you select two different colors instead of one color plus black or white.

Preset gradients are nice timesavers. When you click the Preset option button, a Preset Colors drop-down list appears. You can select from a variety of preset multi-color gradients with picturesque names like Daybreak and Horizon.

Preset gradients are good for more than just convenience; some of these presets have several colors in them and can create effects that you cannot duplicate with the One-color or Two-colors options, such as the Rainbow I and Rainbow II presets.

Textures

On the Texture tab of the Fill Effects dialog box, you can choose from a variety of simulations of textured surfaces, such as marble, straw, sandpaper, and so on. Scroll through the list to find the one you want, select it, and click OK (see Figure 7-22).

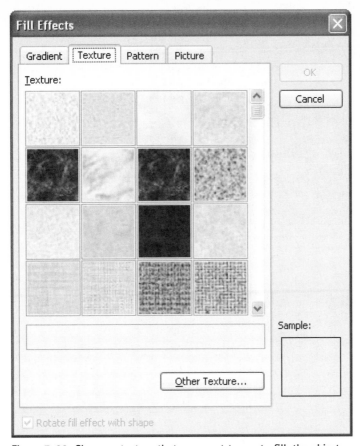

Figure 7-22: Choose a texture that you want to use to fill the object.

You can also specify any image that you want to use as a texture. The image will be tiled (repeated) as needed to fill the object. To do so, click Other Texture, select the image file, and click OK. For example, you could use any of the background bitmap images that come with Windows. You'll find them in the Windows folder on your hard disk. Figure 7-23 shows one of the background images from Windows XP used as a texture.

Patterns

Patterns are not as flashy as gradients or textures, but they have their uses. A pattern, simply stated, is an arrangement of lines or shapes of one color over a background of another color. For example, a pinstripe suit has a pattern of gray or white lines over a black, blue, or gray background. You get the idea.

To apply a pattern, click the Pattern tab in the Fill Effects dialog box and then click a pattern that you want to use (see Figure 7-24). You can choose the foreground and background colors from the drop-down lists at the bottom of the dialog box. If

Figure 7-23: A background texture from Windows has been imported here.

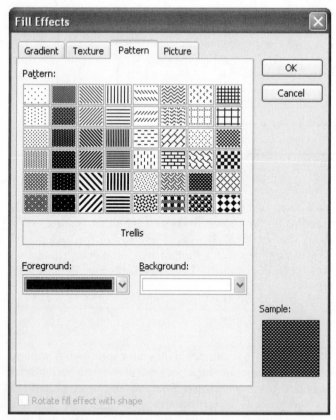

Figure 7-24: Choose the pattern you want, and select a foreground and background color.

you want the pattern colors to change when the color scheme changes, use scheme colors as your choices.

 Patterns make any text difficult to read. Don't apply a pattern to an AutoShape that is functioning as a text box unless you have a very compelling reason to do so. And if you do, make sure the pattern uses subtly contrasting colors and that the text is large, bold, and of a strongly contrasting color.

Pictures

You probably have at least one friend or acquaintance who is into scrapbooks, right? That person will probably tell you that pictures are much more interesting when they have unusual shapes.

You can use any AutoShape as a picture frame by applying a Picture fill to it. The AutoShape becomes a sort of matte for the picture, giving it some style. Figure 7-25 shows some examples.

To use a picture as a fill, click the Picture tab in the Fill Effects dialog box. There won't be any pictures there initially; don't worry. Click the Picture button, select the picture, and double-click it. Then, click OK to place the picture in the object.

Background Fill

This one is not a true "fill effect" in the sense that it is accessible only from the Format AutoShape menu (not from the Fill Effects dialog box like other fills), but it is an interesting and unusual effect to apply.

As I mentioned in Chapter 5 for text boxes, the "Background" fill choice on the Fill Color menu is somewhat like making the AutoShape completely transparent, since it makes the slide background show through. However, the Background setting obscures any objects that are between it and the background. Figure 7-26 shows an example. In this figure, the star has Background as its fill, and it is sitting on top of a text box containing the text. This is better than filling the star with the same pattern, gradient, or texture as the background because no matter where you move it on the slide, its background will continue to "match" with the slide's background.

Adding Shadow Effects

In Chapter 5 you learned about applying the Shadow effect to a text box, but you can also apply a shadow to any object, including any AutoShape. Further, the shadows you apply to these objects are much more versatile than the shadows that you apply to text. There are lots of special effect options. You can control the positioning of the shadow, control how far it appears to be away from the text, change the shadow color, and more.

Figure 7-25: Pictures placed in AutoShapes take on the AutoShape as a frame.

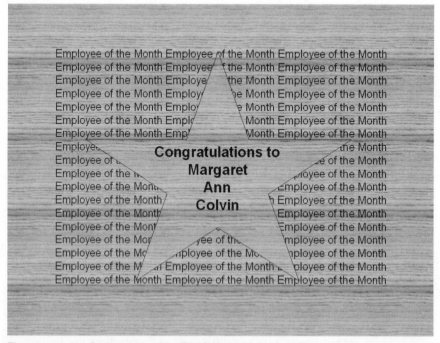

Figure 7-26: Use Background as the fill if you want the AutoShape to pick up the slide background but ignore any intervening objects.

On some object types, when you apply a shadow it clings to the object itself. For others the shadow clicks to the rectangular outer frame around the object. For some object types it depends on the transparency setting for the object background too. Here are some general rules:

◆ *AutoShapes and WordArt*: The shadow always clings to the shape, not its frame. If the shape is transparent, the shadow will change so that it's a shadow of the border around the outside, rather than of a solid shape (see Figure 7-27).

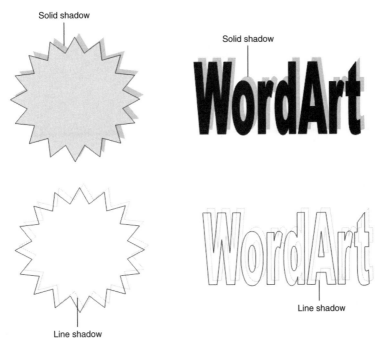

Figure 7–27: Results of applying a shadow to transparent and non–transparent AutoShapes and WordArt.

◆ *Bitmap images*: Photographs and other imported bitmap pictures always apply the shadow to the frame around the picture.

◆ *Clip art, text boxes, and charts*: If any of these have transparent background (no fill), the shadow applies directly to the object, but if there is a background, the shadow is then applied to the outer frame instead.

Clip art is covered in Chapter 9, and charts are covered in Chapter 11.

To apply a shadow to an object, click the object and then click the Shadow button on the Drawing toolbar. A pop-up menu appears, as shown in Figure 7-28. Click the button for the type of shadow you want, or to turn off a shadow, choose No Shadow.

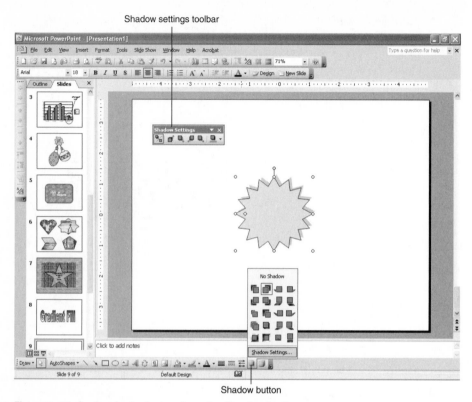

Figure 7-28: Apply a basic shadow from the Drawing toolbar.

Besides the simple buttons on the Shadow shortcut menu shown in Figure 7-28, there are several more sophisticated shadow controls. To see them, choose Shadow Settings from the pop-up menu. A Shadow Settings toolbar appears, containing controls that help you fine-tune the shadow. See Table 7-3 for an explanation of these controls.

Once you apply a basic shadow to an object, the Nudge buttons can help you increase or decrease the height and width of the shadow. For example, you might want to make a shadow more prominent, to make it more obvious that the shadow exists. The larger the shadow, the greater the effect of the object floating on the slide.

If you change the shadow color, make sure you stick with a color that is darker than the object. Lighter-colored shadows do not look realistic. (The exception is that for black text, you should use a gray shadow.)

TABLE 7-3 SHADOW SETTINGS TOOLBAR BUTTONS

Button	Name	Purpose
	Shadow On/Off	Toggles the shadow on/off
	Nudge Shadow Up	Moves the shadow up slightly
	Nudge Shadow Down	Moves the shadow down slightly
	Nudge Shadow Left	Moves the shadow to the left slightly
	Nudge Shadow Right	Moves the shadow to the right slightly
	Shadow Color	Opens a drop-down list of colors for the shadow

The Shadow Color button opens a drop-down list of colors in the scheme, as well as the More Shadow Colors option. It also contains a Semitransparent Shadow command (an on/off toggle which is On by default), so you can make the shadow more or less opaque.

If you want to experiment with the shadow feature, try the following experiment:

1. Create an AutoShape or some WordArt, and select it.

2. Click the Shadow button and then pick the first shadow on the first row.

3. Click the Shadow button again and click Shadow Settings.

4. On the Shadow Settings toolbar, click the Nudge Shadow Up button twice and then the Nudge Shadow Left button twice.

5. On the Shadow Settings toolbar, click the Shadow Color button and select a different color for the shadow.

6. Delete the object when you are finished experimenting.

Adding 3-D Effects

Although similar to shadows, 3-D effects can make an object look like it has sides, like it's ready to jump off the slide. You can use 3-D effects, for example, to make a circle look like a pillar or a rectangle look like a box. You can also create some interesting effects with WordArt by applying 3-D. Some of the WordArt Gallery samples already have 3-D applied to them, in fact. Figure 7-29 shows some examples of objects that have been enhanced with 3-D effects.

You can use either a shadow or a 3-D effect on an object, but not both. When you apply one, it cancels the other.

To apply a basic 3-D effect, select the object and click the 3-D button on the Drawing toolbar. A pop-up menu of effects appears. Click the button for the type of effect you want, or to turn the 3-D effect off, choose No 3-D (see Figure 7-30).

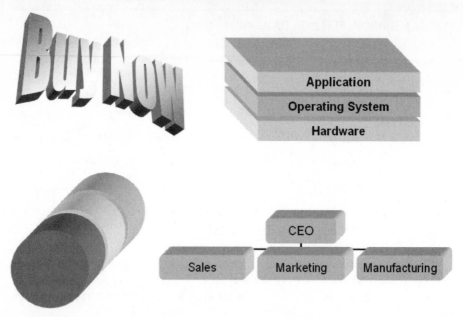

Figure 7-29: Some 3-D effects applied to various types of objects.

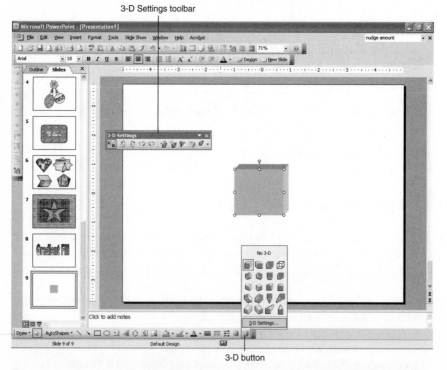

Figure 7-30: Choose a 3-D effect from the menu to apply to your object, or choose 3-D Settings to display the toolbar.

There is also a special toolbar for 3-D effects, which you can display by choosing 3-D Settings from the menu shown in Figure 7-30. Table 7-4 lists and describes its buttons.

TABLE 7-4 3-D SETTINGS TOOLBAR BUTTONS

Button	Name	Purpose
	3-D On/Off	Toggles the 3-D effect on/off
	Tilt Down	Rotates the shape down slightly
	Tilt Up	Rotates the shape up slightly
	Tilt Left	Rotates the shape left slightly
	Tilt Right	Rotates the shape right slightly
	Depth	Opens a list on which you can select the depth of the 3-D effect
	Direction	Opens a list on which you can select the direction of the 3-D effect
	Lighting	Opens a list on which you can select where the "light" is coming from for the object shading
	Surface	Opens a list of surface types for the object
	3-D Color	Opens a list of colors for the 3-D sides of the object

If you want to experiment with the 3-D settings, try the following:

1. Create an AutoShape or some WordArt, and select it.

2. Click the Shadow button and then pick the first shadow on the first row.

3. Click the 3-D button and pick the first 3-D setting on the first row. Notice that the shadow goes away.

4. Click the 3-D button and click 3-D Settings. The 3-D toolbar opens.

5. Click the Tilt Down button twice and the Tilt Left button twice.

6. Click the Depth button, and then click 72 pt.

7. Click the Direction button, and click the bottom right icon to switch the direction.

8. Click the Lighting button, and click the top left lighting option.

9. Click the Surface button, and then click Wireframe. Repeat to choose each of the other available options on the Surface button's menu, to see what they look like.

10. Open the 3-D Color button's list and choose a different color for the 3-D effect. Make it a dramatically different color, so you can see the effect more easily.

11. Delete the object when you are done experimenting with it.

Modifying an AutoShape

There are many ways to modify the shape of an AutoShape or WordArt object. The easiest is to simply drag a side selection handle to change its perspective.

In addition, most AutoShapes and WordArt can be twisted, stretched, and otherwise manipulated by dragging the yellow diamond on the shape. Figure 7-31 shows some examples of what you can do to a curved arrow, for instance. The original AutoShape is the one in the top left corner.

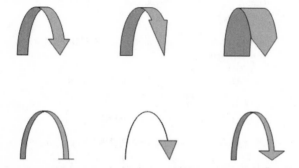

Figure 7-31: Some examples of how stretching an AutoShape can alter its appearance.

The key is in the adjustment handles on the object. Most AutoShapes have at least one yellow diamond on them. You can drag the yellow diamond to modify the shape. When you drag the diamond, you modify the thickness and size of the shape. For example, on a parallelogram you can change the amount of tilt, or on a block arrow you can change the thickness of the arrow shaft and the height of the arrowhead. Some shapes have only one adjustment handle; others have two or three. It depends on the type of shape and in what ways it can be modified. In Figure 7-32, the shape shown has two diamonds, and one of them is being dragged.

Rotating and Flipping

To rotate a shape 90° to the left or right, choose Draw ⇨ Rotate or Flip and then Rotate Left 90° or Rotate Right 90° (see Figure 7-33). You can apply these modifications serially, so, for example, you could rotate a shape 180° (90 plus 90) and then flip it.

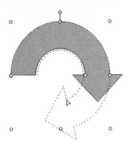

Figure 7-32: To stretch an AutoShape, drag a yellow diamond.

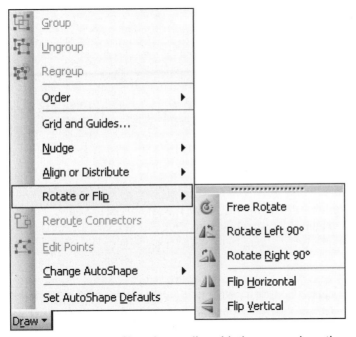

Figure 7-33: Rotate or flip a shape or line with the commands on the Draw menu.

You can also free-rotate a shape if you need a rotation other than 90° or a multiple of 90°. It works just like with text boxes (see Chapter 5). Simply select it and then drag its green rotation handle to rotate it. The mouse pointer becomes a set of circular arrows, as shown in Figure 7.34. Holding the Shift key while rotating will constrain the rotation to 15° increments.

Flipping an object changes it to a mirror image of itself, either vertically or horizontally. This can be useful if you need to use the same object twice or more on the same slide at different orientations. You might make several copies of an AutoShape

Rotation handle

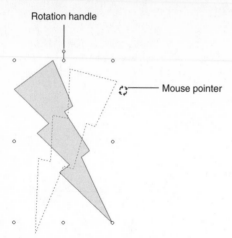

Mouse pointer

Figure 7-34: Drag the green circle—the rotation handle—to rotate an AutoShape.

and then flip some of them so that each points toward the center of the slide, for example.

To flip a shape vertically or horizontally, choose Draw⇨Rotate or Flip and then Flip Horizontal or Flip Vertical.

Working with Layers

You can stack objects on top of each other to create special effects, as you've already seen in this book. For example, you might create a logo by stacking a text box on top of an oval or rectangle.

TIP Remember, you can type text directly into an AutoShape; you don't have to place a text box on top of it necessarily. Right-click it, choose Add Text, and then type the text.

By default, objects stack in the order that you create them. For example, in Figure 7-35, the lightning bolt appears over the starburst because the starburst was created first. You can move the shapes around, but whenever they overlap they will continue to be stacked in the order shown.

If you need to reorder the objects in a stack, follow these steps:

1. Click an object. You can work with any object in the stack, although it may be difficult to select an object that is buried under another object.

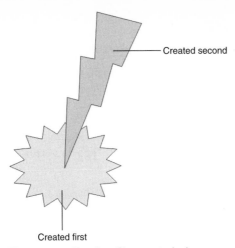

Created second

Created first

Figure 7-35: Two AutoShapes stacked.

2. Choose Draw⇨Order and then choose the command that reflects what you want to do with that object:

- Send to Back sends that object to the very back of the pile.

- Send Backward sends that object back one position in the pile (assuming there are more than two objects).

- Bring Forward brings that object forward one position.

- Bring to Front sends that object to the very front of the pile.

3. Repeat steps 1 and 2 for each object until all objects are in the order you want them.

Grouping Graphic Objects

You probably already know how to select multiple objects and work with them as a single unit, right? Just click each one while holding down Shift, or drag a box around them with your mouse.

If multiple objects are always going to be considered a single unit for formatting purposes, you can save yourself some time by grouping them. When you group two or more objects, those objects become a single object for the purposes of moving and resizing. You can always ungroup them later if you need to work with the objects separately. At the beginning of this chapter I showed you how to ungroup a piece of clip art, for example.

To group two or more objects, select them and then choose Draw⇨Group. To ungroup, select the object and choose Draw⇨Ungroup. If you later need to regroup the same items again, select any one of them and use Draw⇨Regroup.

Add-Ins for Working with Graphic Objects

Here are a few interesting add-ins available online that can enhance your capabilities for working with drawn objects. Some are free; some are not.

- ◆ *Shape Styles*. This add-in lets you create styles that apply formatting to drawn objects. The free version lets you save three styles; the pay version has no limit. www.rdpslides.com/pptools/FAQ00037.htm

- ◆ *Smooth Shadows*. Ever wanted to create a smooth gradient shadow behind a gradient-filled object? This add-in helps you with that. http:// officeone.mvps.org/smooth_shadows/smooth_shadows.html

- ◆ *Find and Replace Colors*. If you apply manual colors and fills to objects, and then want to search for and replace all instances of such formatting, use this add-in. www.mvps.org/skp/pptxp006.htm

- ◆ *Shape Console*. This add-in provides a floating window that shows the current selected shape(s). This is handy when you are trying to select one shape in a layered stack and you aren't sure when you've got it successfully. www.mvps.org/skp/sconsole.htm

Summary

In this chapter you learned how to format and manipulate AutoShapes and Word Art, two types of vector graphics that PowerPoint helps you create. But what about graphics that you acquire on your own, such as from a scanner or digital camera? In Chapter 8 we'll look at some techniques for integrating that type of art into a presentation.

Chapter 8

Working with Photographic Images

THERE ARE THREE BASIC CATEGORIES of still graphics you can work with in Power-Point. In Chapter 7 you learned about the first of these: drawn AutoShapes. The second is photographic images, covered in this chapter, and the third is clip art, covered in Chapter 9.

In this chapter you'll learn the ins and outs of using photographs in a PowerPoint presentation, including tips and tricks for preparing them beforehand, compressing them so they take up less disk space, and exporting pictures out of PowerPoint so that they can be saved separately.

Understanding Raster Graphics

There are two kinds of graphics in the computer world: *vector* and *raster.* As you learned in Chapter 7, vector graphics (AutoShapes, for example) are created with mathematical formulas. Some of the advantages of vector graphics are their small file size and the fact that they can be resized without losing any quality. The main disadvantage to a vector graphic is that it doesn't look "real." Even when an expert artist draws a vector graphic, you can still tell that it's a drawing, not a photograph. For example, perhaps you've seen the game *The Sims*? Those characters and objects are 3-D vector graphics. They look pretty good, but there's no way you would mistake them for real people and objects.

In this chapter, we'll be working with raster graphics. A raster graphic is made up of a very fine grid of individual colored *pixels* (dots). The grid is sometimes called a *bitmap*. Each pixel has a unique numeric value representing its color. Figure 8-1 shows a close-up of a raster image. You can create raster graphics from scratch with a "paint" program on a computer, but a more common way to acquire a raster graphic is by using a scanner or digital camera as an input device.

Each colored square is a pixel with a numeric value for its color.

Figure 8-1: A raster graphic, normal size (right) and zoomed in to show individual pixels (left).

 The term *bitmap* is sometimes used to refer generically to any raster graphic, but it is also a specific file format for raster graphics, with a BMP extension. This is the default file format for the Paint program that comes with Windows and for Windows desktop wallpaper.

Because there are so many individual pixels and each one must be represented numerically, raster graphics are much larger than vector graphics. They take longer to load into the PC's memory, take up more space when stored as separate files on disk, and make your PowerPoint presentation file much larger. A raster graphic can be compressed so that it takes up less space on disk, but the quality may suffer. Therefore, it's best to use vector graphics when you want simple lines, shapes, or cartoons and reserve raster graphics for situations where you need photographic quality.

The following sections explain some of the technical specifications behind raster graphics; you'll need this information to make the right decisions about the way you capture the images with your scanner or digital camera and the way you use them in PowerPoint.

Resolution

The term *resolution* has two subtly different meanings. One is the size of an image, expressed in the number of pixels of width and height, such as 800 × 600. The other meaning is the number of pixels per inch when the image is printed, such as 100 dots per inch (dpi). The former meaning is used mostly when referring to images of a fixed physical size, such as the display resolution of a monitor. In this book I'll mostly be referring to the latter meaning.

If you know the resolution of the picture (that is, the number of pixels in it), and the resolution of the printer on which it is to be printed (for example, 300 dpi), you can figure out how large the picture will be in inches when you print it. Suppose you have a picture that is 900 pixels square, and you print it on a 300 dpi printer. It will be three inches square on the printout.

RESOLUTION ON PREEXISTING GRAPHICS FILES

When you acquire an image file from an outside source, such as downloading it from a Web site or getting it from a CD of artwork, its resolution has already been determined. Whoever created the file originally made that decision. For example, if the image was originally scanned on a scanner, whoever scanned it chose the scan resolution—that is, the dpi setting. That determined how many individual pixels each inch of the original picture would be carved up into. At a 100 dpi scan, each inch of the picture is represented by 100 pixels vertically and horizontally. At 300 dpi, each inch of the picture is broken down into three times that many.

You can modify the picture in an image-editing program to change the number of dots per inch by resizing the image (see *Compressing Images* later in this chapter), and/or you can crop off one or more sides of the image.

 If you crop or decrease the size of an image in an image-editing program, save the changes under a different file name. Maintain the original in case you ever need it for some other purpose. Decreasing the image resolution decreases its dpi setting, which decreases its quality. You might not notice any quality degradation on-screen, but you will probably notice when printing it at a large size. That's because the average monitor displays only 96 dpi, but the average printer prints at 600 dpi or higher.

PowerPoint slides do not usually need to be printed at a professional-quality resolution, so image quality on a PowerPoint printout is not usually an issue. However, if you use the picture for something else later, such as printing it as a full-page color image on photo paper, a high dpi file can make a difference.

RESOLUTION ON GRAPHICS YOU SCAN YOURSELF

When you create an image file yourself by using a scanner, *you* choose the resolution, expressed in dots per inch (dpi), through the scanner software. For example, suppose you are scanning a 4-inch by 6-inch photo. If you scan it at 100 dpi, the scanner will break down each 1-inch section of the photo (horizontally and vertically) into 100 separate pieces and decide on a numeric value that best represents the color of each piece. The result will be a total number of pixels of $4 \times 100 \times 6 \times 100$, or 240,000 pixels. Assuming that each pixel requires 3 bytes of storage, the file will be approximately 720K in size. (The actual size will vary slightly depending on the file format.)

Now, suppose you scan the same photo at 200 dpi. The scanner will break down each 1-inch section of the photo into 200 pieces, so that the result will be $4 \times 200 \times 6 \times 200$ or 960,000 pixels. Assuming again that one pixel requires 3 bytes for storage, the file will be approximately 2.9MB in size. A big difference!

The higher the resolution in which you scan, the larger the file will be, but also the finer the detail of the scan. However, unless you are zooming in on the photo, you will not be able to tell a difference between 100 dpi and a higher resolution. That's because most computer monitors display at 96 dpi, so any resolution higher than that will not improve the output.

Let's look at an example. In Figure 8-2, you can see two copies of an image open in a graphics program. The same photo was scanned at 75 dots per inch (left) and 150 dots per inch (right). However, the difference between them is not significant when the two images are placed on a PowerPoint slide, as shown in Figure 8-3. The lower resolution image is at the top left, but there is no observable difference at the size at which they are being used.

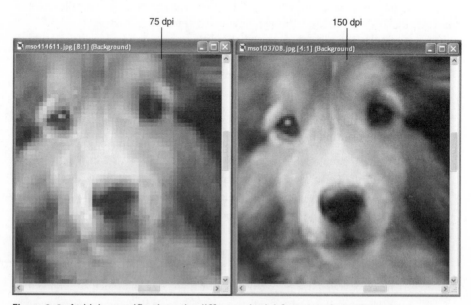

Figure 8-2: At high magnification, the difference in dpi for a scan is apparent.

75 dpi

150 dpi

Figure 8-3: When the image is used at normal size, there is virtually no difference between a high-dpi and a low-dpi scan.

RESOLUTION ON DIGITAL CAMERA PHOTOS

Top-quality digital cameras today take very high-resolution pictures, much higher than you will need for an on-screen PowerPoint presentation. At normal size and magnification, a high-resolution graphic file is overkill; it wastes disk space need-lessly. Therefore, you may want to adjust the camera's image size so that it takes lower-resolution pictures for your PowerPoint show.

If you think you might want to use those same pictures for some other purpose in the future, such as printing in a magazine or newsletter, then go ahead and take them with the camera's highest setting, but you should compress them in PowerPoint or resize them in a third-party image-editing program. See *Compressing Images* later in this chapter to learn how.

Color Depth

Color depth is the number of bits required to describe the color of a single pixel in the image. For example, in 1-bit color, a single binary digit represents each pixel. Each pixel is either black (1) or white (0). In 4-bit color, there are 16 possible colors because there are 16 possible combinations of 1s and 0s in a four-digit binary number. In 8-bit color there are 256 combinations.

For most file formats, the highest number of colors you can have in an image is 16.7 million colors, which is 24-bit color (also called "true color"). It uses 8 bits each for Red, Green, and Blue.

There is also 32-bit color, which has the same number of colors as 24-bit but adds 8 more bits for an Alpha Channel. The Alpha Channel is used to describe the amount of transparency for each pixel. This is not so much an issue for a single-layer graphic, but in a multi-layer graphic, such as you can create in high-end graphics programs like Photoshop, the extent to which a lower layer shows through an upper one is important.

 Here's a great article on alpha channel usage in PowerPoint by Geetesh Bajaj: www.indezine.com/products/powerpoint/ppalpha.html.

Scanners and Color Depth

If you are shopping for a scanner you will probably notice that they're advertised with higher numbers of bits than the graphics formats will support. This is for error correction. If there are extra bits, it can throw out the bad bits to account for "noise" and still end up with a full set of good bits. (Error correction in a scan is a rather complicated process, but fortunately your scanner driver software takes care of it for you.)

48-bit color is fairly new, and it's just like 24-bit color except it uses 16 rather than 8 bits to define each of the three channels: Red, Green, and Blue. It does not have an Alpha Channel bit. 48-bit color depth is not really necessary, as the human eye cannot detect the small differences it introduces. Of the graphics formats that PowerPoint supports, only PNG supports 48-bit color depth.

The higher the color depth, the larger the file size of the image. Photos look best when they are used at a color depth of 16-bit or higher; an 8-bit photo is noticeably less realistic. Most scanners and digital cameras produce images automatically at their maximum color depth.

I normally would not decrease the color depth of a photo to less than 24-bit unless there was an issue with lack of disk space that could not be solved any other way. To decrease the color depth you would need to open the graphic file in a third-party image-editing program, and use the command in that program for decreasing the number of colors. Before going through that, try compressing the images in the presentation (see *Compressing Images* later in the chapter) to see if that doesn't solve the problem.

File Format

Many scanners scan in JPEG format by default, but most will also support TIF format too, and some support other formats as well. Images you acquire from a digital camera will almost always be JPEG. Images from other sources may be any of dozens of graphic formats, including PCX, BMP, GIF, or PNG.

Different graphic formats can vary tremendously in the size and quality of the image they produce. The main differentiators between formats are the color depth they support and the type of compression they use (which determines the file size).

Remember, earlier how I explained that each pixel in a 24-bit color image requires 3 bytes? (That's derived by dividing 24 by 8 because there are 8 bits in a byte.) Then you multiply that by the height, and then by the width, to determine the image size? Well, that formula was not quite accurate because it does not take compression into account. *Compression* is an algorithm (basically a math formula) that decreases the amount of space that the file takes up on the disk by storing the data about the pixels more compactly. A file format will have one of these three states in regard to compression:

◆ *No compression*: The image is not compressed.

◆ *Lossless compression*: The image is compressed, but the algorithm for doing so does not throw out any pixels so there is no loss of image quality when the image is resized.

◆ *Lossy compression*: The image is compressed by recording less data about the pixels, such that when the image is resized there may be a loss of image quality.

Table 8-1 provides a brief guide to some of the most common graphics formats. Generally speaking, for most on-screen presentations JPEG should be your preferred choice for graphics because it is compact and Web-accessible (although PNG is also a good choice and uses lossless compression).

TABLE 8-1 POPULAR GRAPHICS FORMATS

Extension	Pronunciation	Compression	Notes
JPG or JPEG	"Jay-peg"	Yes	Stands for Joint Photographic Experts Group. Very small image size. Uses lossy compression. Common on the Web. Up to 24-bit.
GIF	"gif" or "jif"	Yes	Stands for Graphic Interchange Format. Limited to 8-bit (256 color).

Continued

TABLE 8-1 POPULAR GRAPHICS FORMATS *(Continued)*

Extension	Pronunciation	Compression	Notes
			Uses proprietary compression algorithm. Allows animated graphics, which are useful on the Web. Color depth limitation makes this format unsuitable for photos.
PNG	"ping"	Yes	Stands for Portable Network Graphic. An improvement on GIF. Up to 48-bit color depth. Lossless compression, but smaller file sizes than TIF. Public domain format.
BMP	"B-M-P" or "bump"	No	Default image type for Windows. Up to 24-bit. Used for Windows wallpaper and other Windows graphics.
PCX	"P-C-X"	Yes	There are different versions: 0, 2, and 5. Use version 5 for 24-bit support. Originally introduced by a company called ZSoft; sometimes called ZSoft Paintbrush format.
TIF or TIFF	"tiff"	Optional	Stands for Tagged Image Format. Supported by most scanners and digital cameras. Up to 48-bit. Uses lossless compression. Large file size but high quality.

TIP If you are not sure what format you will eventually use for an image, scan it in TIF format and keep the TIF copy on your hard disk. You can always save a copy in JPEG or other formats when you need them for specific projects. TIF format's compression is lossless, so it results in a high-quality image.

Importing Image Files into PowerPoint

Most of the choices you make regarding a raster image's resolution, color depth, and file type are done outside of PowerPoint, with your scanner or digital camera or with an image-editing program. Consequently, by the time you're ready to plop it into PowerPoint, the hard part is over.

Assuming you have already acquired the image (scanner, camera, or some other method), use the following steps to insert it in PowerPoint. If you have not yet acquired it, see the next section instead.

1. Display the slide on which you want to place the image.

2. Choose Insert⇨Picture⇨From File. The Insert Picture dialog box appears (see Figure 8-4).

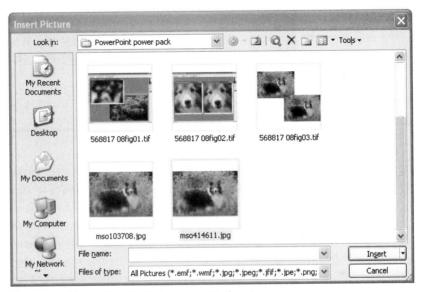

Figure 8-4: Choose the file that you want to insert.

3. Select the picture you want. Switch the view (by using the View button in the dialog box) to see thumbnails or details if either is effective in helping you determine which file is which.

4. Click Insert. Then within PowerPoint, edit the image (resize, move, and so on) as you would any other object.

TIP After importing an image, you may want to work with its properties to apply a border or shadow around it, to set it to a certain size, and so on. You can do this manually, but an add-in is available that will import batches of images at once and apply the same properties to all. Check out the Image Importer Wizard at www.mvps.org/skp/iiw.htm. You can also write a macro that will apply a series of formatting attributes to objects.

Linking to a Graphic File

If you're sharp-eyed you may have noticed that the Insert button in Figure 8-4 has a drop-down list associated with it. That list has two choices on it: the default Insert and Link to File.

Use Link to File whenever you want a pointer to the graphic file to be inserted in the presentation rather than the entire original graphic file. When the presentation opens, it pulls in the graphic file from the disk. If the graphic is not available, it displays an empty frame with a red X in the corner in the graphic's place.

Using Link to File keeps the size of the original PowerPoint file very small because it doesn't actually contain the graphics—only links to them. However, if the graphic file is moved, PowerPoint won't be able to find it anymore.

The important thing to know about this Link to File feature is that it is *not* the same thing as an OLE link (which you learned about in Chapter 6 with Excel data). This is not a dynamic link that you can manage with the Edit⇨Links command. It's a much simpler link and much less flexible. You can't change the file location to which it is linked, for example; if the location of the graphic changes, you must delete it from PowerPoint and reinsert it.

TIP If you are building a graphic-heavy presentation on an older computer, you might find that it takes a long time to move between slides and for each graphic to appear. You can take some of the hassle away by using Link to File rather than inserting the graphics. Then, temporarily move the graphic files to a subfolder so PowerPoint can't find them. It will display placeholders for the graphics on the appropriate slides, and the presentation file will be much faster to page through and edit. Then when you are ready to finish up, close PowerPoint and move the graphics files back to their original locations so PowerPoint will find them again when you reopen the presentation file.

If you chafe at the limitations of Link to File, like not being able to update the path of the link, you might prefer a real OLE link to the picture instead. Easy enough—it's basically just like linking to an entire Excel workbook, which you learned about in Chapter 6. Follow these steps:

1. Display the slide on which the picture should appear, and choose Insert⇨Object.

2. In the Insert Object dialog box, click Create from file. Then click Browse, locate the picture you want, and click OK to choose it.

3. Click the Link checkbox (see Figure 8-5).

4. Click OK.

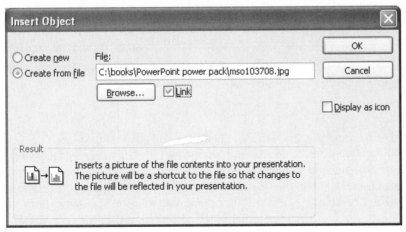

Figure 8-5: You can also link to a picture via an OLE link.

Now you have a real link, and you have access to its settings through the Edit⇨Links command as discussed in Chapter 6. Another advantage to the OLE link method is that if the original is not available, the last saved version will appear in the presentation, rather than an empty placeholder. The disadvantage to an OLE link to the picture is that it basically obliterates the original advantage of the Link to File method, which was to keep the file size small for the PowerPoint file. Since it must store a static copy of the linked picture so that it will appear if the linked file is not available, there is no file-size savings with an OLE type of link (and in fact, an OLE link will make the file size much larger in most cases).

 Links are not updated in real time, so if the image changes during the show, your show will not reflect it. An add-in is available called LiveImage that will get around this, though, and will update your graphics during the presentation. Check out www.mvps.org/skp/liveimage.htm.

Acquiring Images Directly from a Scanner

If you have a compatible scanner attached to your PC, you can scan a picture directly onto a PowerPoint slide. Scanning directly into PowerPoint saves time because you do not have to run the scanning software and assign a separate file name to the image.

 The scanner's driver must be compatible with Windows Image Acquisition (WIA), which is a standard for allowing Windows XP to directly interact with a scanner. If you are not sure about your scanner, give it a try. The Hardware Compatibility List at www.microsoft.com/hcl can tell you definitively whether your scanner is directly compatible with Windows XP; if it is, then it will work within PowerPoint 2003. If not, check the scanner manufacturer's Web site to see whether an updated driver is available that will make it WIA-compatible. No luck? You can still use the scanner, but you will need to use its own software to scan the image and then import the image into PowerPoint as a file.

During the scanning process you can choose to add the image to the Clip Organizer for future use or not. You'll learn about the Clip Organizer in Chapter 9; it's a system of organizing graphic, sound, and video files. If you choose not to add the scanned image there, the image will not exist outside of this presentation, and you will not be able to use it in other presentations or other applications. If you do add it to the Clip Organizer, the image will be placed in a file in the My Documents\My Pictures\Microsoft Clip Organizer folder, in JPEG format. You can also drag the image from PowerPoint into the Clip Organizer to store a copy for future use, or copy and paste the image from this presentation into another one or into other applications.

To scan directly onto a slide, follow these steps:

1. Choose Insert➪Picture➪From Scanner or Camera. The Insert Picture from Scanner or Camera dialog box appears (see Figure 8-6).

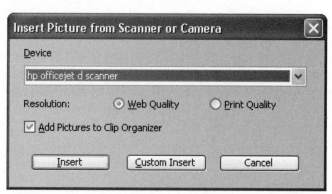

Figure 8-6: Scan an image from PowerPoint using the Windows scanner driver.

2. Choose the scanner from the Device list.

3. Choose a resolution: Web (low) or Print (high). Lower resolution means smaller file size and fewer pixels overall comprising the image. Low resolution is the best choice for on-screen presentations.

4. If you don't want to save the scanned picture in the Clip Organizer, clear the Add Pictures to Clip Organizer checkbox. Otherwise, leave it marked.

5. Click Insert to scan with the default settings, or click Custom Insert, make changes to the settings, and then click Scan.

6. Resize, move, or otherwise modify the graphic as needed.

The Custom Insert option opens the full controls for the scanner. They vary depending on the model; the box for my HP scanner is shown in Figure 8-7.

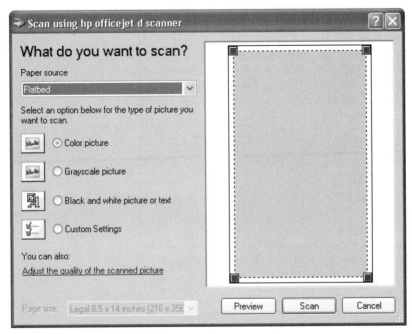

Figure 8-7: Custom Insert options.

Here are some of the things you can do there:

◆ *Choose a scanning mode*: Color picture, Grayscale picture, or Black and white picture or text. This choice determines the color depth. Color is full 24-bit color. Grayscale is 256 shades of gray (8-bit, single color). Black and white is single-bit scanning that produces an extremely small file similar to a fax.

◆ *Preview the scan*: Click the Preview button to do a test scan and then drag the black squares in the preview area to adjust what portion of the image will be saved when you do the "real scan" by clicking the Scan button.

◆ *Choose a paper source*: If your scanner has a document feeder (mine does), you'll have that choice on the Paper Source drop-down list in addition to Flatbed (the default).

◆ *Adjust the resolution, brightness, and contrast*: Click the Adjust the quality of the scanned picture hyperlink to open an Advanced Properties dialog box, as shown in Figure 8-8. From here you can drag the Brightness and Contrast sliders and choose a resolution setting (dots per inch). The default is 150 dpi.

Figure 8-8: Advanced Properties for the scanner enable you to change the resolution.

It is particularly important to choose an appropriate resolution when scanning directly into PowerPoint, since the image will not exist outside of PowerPoint, so you cannot edit it later in a third-party image-editing application to change its resolution. The default setting of 150 dpi is appropriate in most cases where you will be using the image at approximately the same size as the original, but if you are concerned about file size, you could reduce this to 100 dpi without noticeable loss of image quality on-screen. If you plan on using the image at a large size (like full-screen) and the image was originally a very small hard copy, scan at a higher resolution.

Acquiring Images Directly from a Digital Camera

There are lots of ways of transferring images from a digital camera under Windows XP. Most cameras can be connected to the PC via a USB port and treated as a removable drive, from which you can drag-and-drop pictures onto a folder on your hard disk. You can also remove the memory card from the camera and use a card reader, and in some cases you can even insert a memory card into a printer and print the images directly.

With all those methods available, inserting directly from the camera into the PowerPoint presentation is probably not your first choice. However, should you want to try it, use the same method as with the scanner: Insert⇨Picture⇨From Scanner or Camera. (Make sure the camera is connected to the computer first and turned on.) Then, just follow the prompts to select and insert the picture.

 When you hear digital cameras referred to as "megapixel" that means a million pixels in total—the height multiplied by the width. For example, a 1,152-by-864-pixel image would be approximately 1 megapixel (995,328 pixels, to be exact). High-end cameras are 5-megapixel or more these days, which is probably overkill for use in your PowerPoint show. Such cameras have settings you can change that control the image size, though, so you can reduce the image size on the camera itself.

Sizing and Cropping Photos

Here's something important to know: in and of itself, cropping and sizing a picture in PowerPoint does not reduce the overall size of the PowerPoint presentation file. When you insert a picture, PowerPoint stores the whole thing at its original size and continues to store it that way regardless of any manipulations you perform upon it within PowerPoint. That's why I have recommended throughout this chapter that you do any editing of the photo in a third-party image program, *before* you import it into PowerPoint.

There's a big "however," though, as of PowerPoint 2002. If you use the Compress Pictures option (from the Picture toolbar), it will discard any cropped portions of the images. That means that the file size will decrease with the cropping, and that you won't be able to reverse the cropping later.

Sizing a Photo

Sizing a photo is just like sizing any other object. Drag its selection handles. Drag a corner to maintain the aspect ratio, or drag a side to distort it. (Distorting a photo is seldom a good idea, though, unless you're after some weird funhouse effect.)

You can also specify an exact size for a photo the same as with drawn objects (see Chapter 7). Right-click the photo, choose Format Picture, and then specify a size on the Size tab, as shown in Figure 8-9.

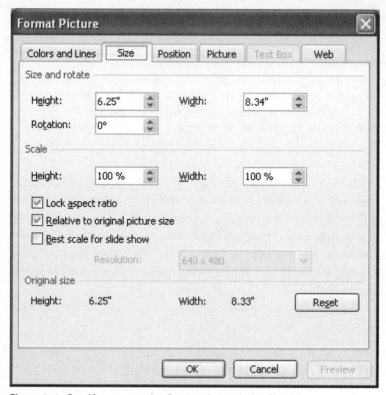

Figure 8-9: Specify an exact size for the photo on the Size tab.

The most straightforward way to specify the size is in inches in the Height and Width boxes. These measurements correspond to the markers on the on-screen ruler in Normal view. The size of a slide varies depending on how you have it set up (by using File⇨Page Setup), but an average slide size is 10 inches wide by 7.5 inches tall. You can also size the photo using the Scale controls, in which you adjust the size based on a percentage of the original size.

The Scale is based on the original size, not on the current size. So, for example, if you set the Height and Width to 50%, close the dialog box, then reopen it, and set them each to 75%, the net result will be 75% of the original, not 75% of the 50%. You can override this by deselecting the Relative to original picture size checkbox, however (see Figure 8-9).

If you are setting up a presentation for the primary purpose of showing full-screen graphics, you might want to use the Best scale for slide-show checkbox. This enables you to choose a screen resolution, such as 640 × 480 or 800 × 600, and size the pictures so that they will show to best advantage in that resolution. Choose the resolution that corresponds to the display setting on the PC on which you will show the presentation. To determine what the resolution is on a PC, right-click the Windows desktop, choose Properties, and then look on the Settings tab.

When possible, develop your presentation at the same Windows screen resolution as the PC on which you will present the show.

Cropping a Photo

Cropping is for those times when you want only a part of the image and not the whole thing. For example, you might have a great photo of a person or animal, but there is extraneous detail around it, as shown in Figure 8-10. You can crop out the important object in the image with the cropping tool.

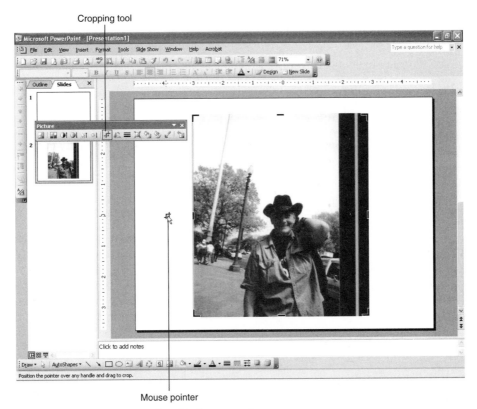

Figure 8-10: This picture can benefit from cropping.

Remember that cropping in PowerPoint does not reduce the file size, and does not really discard the cropped-out parts; it merely masks them (unless you use Compress Pictures). Therefore, if keeping the file size small is important, you'll want to crop the picture in an image-editing program rather than in PowerPoint.

You can crop two sides at once by cropping at the corner of the image, or crop each side individually by cropping at the sides. To crop an image, do the following:

1. Select the image.

2. Click the Crop tool on the Picture toolbar. Your mouse pointer changes to a cropping tool (see Figure 8-10).

If the Picture toolbar does not automatically appear when you click the picture, choose View ➪ Toolbars ➪ Picture. Or, you can right-click the picture and choose Show Picture Toolbar from the shortcut menu.

3. Position the pointer over a side handle of the image frame, on a side where you want to cut some of the image off.

4. Drag the handle inward toward the center of the image until only the part of the image on that side that you want to keep is in the dotted line.

5. Repeat steps 3 and 4 for each side. Then click the Cropping tool again, or press Esc to turn cropping off.

6. After cropping, move or resize the image as needed. Figure 8-11 shows the result of cropping the image from Figure 8-10.

To undo a crop, reenter cropping mode by clicking the Cropping tool again and then drag the side(s) back outward again. Or, you can simply reset the photo, as described in the following section.

You can also crop "by the numbers" with the Crop settings in the Format Picture dialog box (on the Picture tab). In Figure 8-12, for example, the picture is being cropped at the Left by 0.7″, top by 1.17″, right by 0.52″, and bottom by 0.03″.

Resetting a Photo

Once the picture is in PowerPoint, any manipulations you do to it are strictly on the surface. It changes how the picture appears on the slide, but it doesn't change how

Microsoft PowerPoint - [Presentation1]
File Edit View Insert Format Tools Slide Show Window Help Acrobat
Outline Slides
Picture
Click to add notes
Slide 2 of 2
Default Design

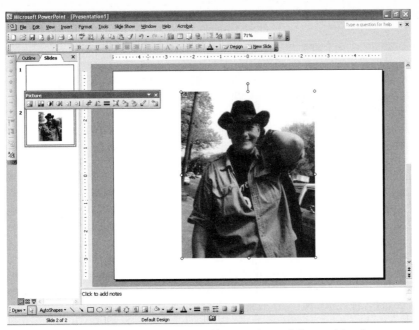

Figure 8-11: The picture has been improved by cropping and then resizing it.

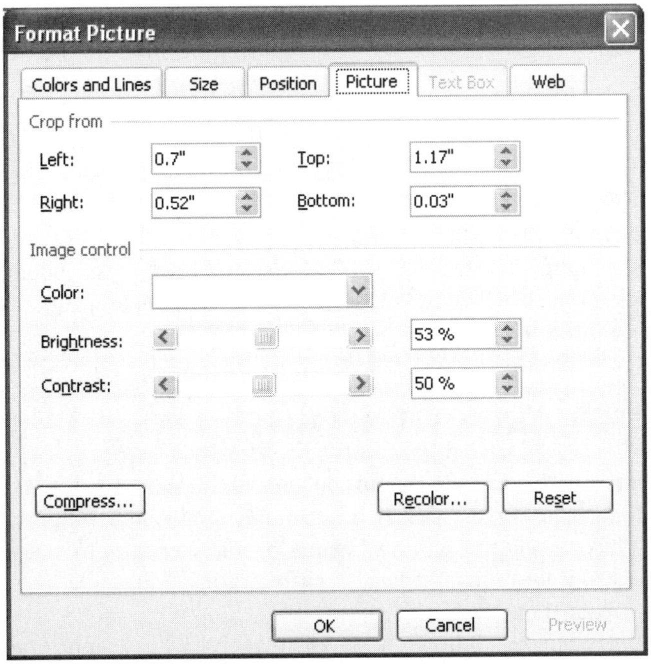

Format Picture
Colors and Lines
Size
Position
Picture
Text Box
Web
Crop from
Left: 0.7"
Top: 1.17"
Right: 0.52"
Bottom: 0.03"
Image control
Color:
Brightness: 53 %
Contrast: 50 %
Compress...
Recolor...
Reset
OK
Cancel
Preview

Figure 8-12: Pictures can be cropped by entering crop measurements on the Picture tab.

the picture is stored in PowerPoint. Consequently, you can reset the picture back to its original settings at any time. This resetting also clears any changes you have made to the image's size, contrast, and brightness (which are discussed in the next section).

Here are two ways to reset a picture:

♦ Select the photo and then click the Reset Picture button on the Picture toolbar.

♦ Double-click the picture—or right-click the picture and choose Format Picture—and then on the Picture tab, click the Reset button.

Adjusting Photo Contrast and Brightness

PowerPoint is not a very sophisticated photo editor, but it can do some very elementary things like increase or decrease a picture's brightness and contrast. The easiest way to access those controls is through the buttons on the Picture toolbar:

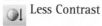 More Contrast

Less Contrast

More Brightness

 Less Brightness

Each time you click one of these buttons, it changes its setting by 3%. The default setting for each is 50%, so if you click once on More Contrast, for example, the contrast becomes set to 53%.

You can adjust the contrast and brightness more precisely through the Format Picture dialog box (refer to Figure 8-12). Drag the Contrast and Brightness sliders to the right or left to adjust as needed. Contrast and brightness settings are reset to 50% if you click the Reset button in the dialog box.

Setting a Transparent Color

The Transparent Color feature can be really useful, but not all pictures support it. It's available for bitmap images (including scans), and for some but not all clip art. For example, suppose you have a scanned photo of your CEO and you want to make the background transparent so it looks like his head is sitting right on the slide. This feature could help you out with that.

Why some clip-art images but not others? Well, an image can have only one color set to be transparent, and some clip art already has its background set to be transparent. That's why those clips won't work with the Set Transparent Color feature.

To check it out, first insert the picture on a slide. Then, select the clip. If the Set Transparent Color button is not grayed out on the Picture toolbar, you can set a transparent color by following these steps:

1. Select the picture.

2. Click the Set Transparent Color button on the Picture toolbar.

3. On the picture, click the color that you want to make transparent. If the results are not what you want, click the Undo button or press Ctrl+Z to undo, or repeat step 2 to choose a different color to be transparent.

If you set a color to transparent in PowerPoint, every instance of that color in the picture will become transparent. So, if you have a picture of a man with a white shirt on a white background and choose to make white the transparent color (trying to drop out the background), the guy's shirt will become transparent along with the background.

Conversely, what looks like one color in a photo is not usually just one color. Think of, for instance, a blue sky. It probably consists of at least two dozen different shades of blue. If you try to make one of those shades of blue transparent using PowerPoint's transparency tool, you'll probably just end up with splotches of transparent areas.

So what's the solution? The best way to go is to use alpha channels in a third-party image-editing program to create true transparency and save the image as TIF or PNG. (JPEG format does not support alpha channels.)

Using Special Image Modes

Most images can be displayed in any of four modes:

◆ *Automatic*: This is usually color if it is a color image. It's the image default appearance and is best for color presentations.

◆ *Grayscale*: This is a gray-shaded version of the original image, with shades of gray substituted for each color. Rather than separate values for red, green, and blue, each pixel is a numeric shade of gray from 0 (black) to 255 (white). This works well for presentations that you'll give in one color, such as with transparencies printed on a black-and-white printer.

◆ *Black and white*: The entire image consists of black and white. There is no shading; it's 1-bit color depth. Any colors are rounded to either black or white, whichever they are closest to. This results in a loss of image quality in an image that had any shading. It simulates what the picture will look like when faxed.

◆ *Washout*: This is a light background image of the original, like a watermark, suitable for placement behind text. Its effect can be subtle.

Figure 8-13 shows an image in each of the four modes. (You can't tell much difference between Automatic and Grayscale since this book is not in color, but you could immediately see the difference on your own screen.) To switch between the image modes, click the Color button on the Picture toolbar and choose from the menu that appears (see Figure 8-13).

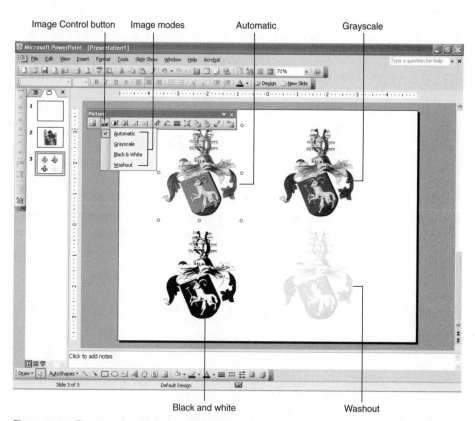

Figure 8-13: The same image in four different image modes.

You can also change the image mode from the Picture tab of the Format Picture dialog box (refer to Figure 8-12). Choose an image mode from the Color drop-down list there.

The Washout image setting gives you a fixed amount of washout. If you want to control the faintness of the image, try this instead. Create a rectangular AutoShape, and use Fill Effects to fill the rectangle with the picture. Remove its border. Then double-click the rectangle, and in the Format Autoshape dialog box, on the Colors and Lines tab, drag the Transparency slider to adjust the "washout" amount (which is actually transparency, not washout, but it gives a washout effect).

Compressing Images

Having an image that is too large (that is, too high a dpi) is not a problem quality-wise. You can resize it in PowerPoint to make it appear as small as you like; just drag its selection handles. There will be no loss of quality as it gets smaller. However, as I mentioned earlier, having a picture that is much larger than needed can increase the overall size of the PowerPoint file, which can become problematic if you plan to distribute the presentation on floppy disk or over the Internet.

To avoid problems with overly large graphic files, you can compress the images to reduce their resolution. You can do this from within PowerPoint or with a third-party utility.

 Here's a good tutorial for more information about working with graphics in PowerPoint: `www.powerpointbackgrounds.com/powerpointgraphics.htm`.

Reducing Resolution and Compressing Images in PowerPoint

PowerPoint offers an image compression utility that will compress all the images in the presentation in a single step and reduce their resolution to the amount needed for the type of output you specify (Web or Print).

To reduce resolution and compress images, do the following:

1. Click a picture, so that the Picture Toolbar appears. If it does not, right-click on the image and choose Show Picture Toolbar.

2. Click the Compress Pictures button. The Compress Pictures dialog box appears (see Figure 8-14).

3. Click All Pictures in Document (assuming you want to compress them all).

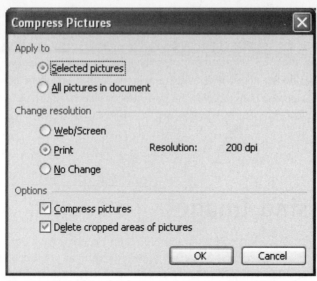

Figure 8-14: Compress the pictures here to make the PowerPoint file smaller.

4. Click Web/Screen if the presentation will be shown on-screen (to set each picture's resolution to 96 dpi), or click Print if it will be printed (to set each picture's resolution to 200 dpi).

5. The Compress Pictures checkbox is marked by default; leave it marked. All versions of PowerPoint (97 and higher) will open presentations that use compressed pictures.

6. The Delete Cropped Areas of Pictures checkbox is marked by default; leave it marked unless you plan on uncropping one or more of the images at some point.

7. Click OK to apply the settings.

The preceding steps accomplished several separate things, as you may have noticed. It enabled compression, it reduced the resolution, and it deleted cropped areas. Each of these decreases the file size in a different way; they work together to achieve maximum results.

Reducing Resolution with a Third-Party Utility

Working with resolution reduction from an image-editing program is somewhat of a trial-and-error process, and you must do each image separately.

You can approximate the correct resolution by simply "doing the math." For example, suppose you have a 10″ × 7.5″ slide. Your desktop display is set to 800 × 600. So your image needs to be 800 pixels wide to fill the slide. Your image is a 5″ × 3″

image, so if you set it to 200 dpi in an image-editing program, that gives you 1,000 pixels, which is a little larger than you need but in the ballpark.

Want something a little easier? There are a number of third-party image compression utilities specifically for PowerPoint. Check out these, both of which make your presentation file smaller by optimizing image sizes and resolutions and compressing images where possible:

◆ *RnR Presentation Optimizer*: www.rdpslides.com/pptools/ FAQ00013.htm

◆ *NXPowerLite*: www.nxpowerlite.com

Exporting a Photo from PowerPoint to a Separate File

What goes in must come out, right? Suppose you have a picture that exists only in PowerPoint, for whatever reason. Perhaps you scanned it directly into PowerPoint, or you no longer have access to the original graphic file.

There are two ways of getting a graphic out of PowerPoint and making it a separate file again: you can use the Save As Picture feature in PowerPoint, or you can do a simple copy-and-paste with the Windows Clipboard into a image-editing program.

Exporting a Graphic with Save As Picture

To save a picture separately from PowerPoint, do the following:

1. Right-click the picture in PowerPoint and choose Save As Picture.

2. In the Save As Picture dialog box, display the location where you want to save the file.

3. Open the Save As Type list and choose the graphic format you want. You can choose TIF, JPEG, or a variety of others. See the discussion of file formats earlier in this chapter for guidance.

4. Enter a name in the File name box.

5. Do one of the following:

   ■ To save the graphic as it currently appears in PowerPoint (including any cropping, different image mode settings, and so on), click Save.

   ■ To save the graphic as it was originally imported into PowerPoint (no cropping or other modifications), open the Save button's menu and choose Save Original (see Figure 8-15).

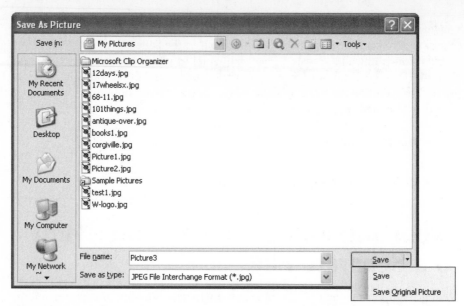

Figure 8-15: Save the graphic as it was originally imported into PowerPoint, or as it currently exists there.

Exporting a Graphic with the Clipboard

Copy-and-paste is a fast and simple way of transferring a graphic from PowerPoint into an image-editing program, and from there you can save it in any supported format. Select it in PowerPoint, copy it (Ctrl+C), open the graphics program, and paste it (Ctrl+V).

The main drawback to this method is that you don't have the opportunity to copy the file as it was originally inserted. The copy will reflect any modifications you made to it in PowerPoint, such as cropping or image mode change (grayscale, for example). If you wanted to copy the original version, you would need to reset the image in PowerPoint before copying it.

Exporting Entire PowerPoint Slides as Graphics

You can save entire slides—or all slides in the whole presentation—as graphics by simply choosing a graphic file format when doing a File ⇨ Save As. If you save the whole presentation as graphics, the files are placed in a folder.

Creating a Photo Album Layout

Most presentations in PowerPoint are text-based, with accompanying photographs. The default Blank Presentation template is biased in favor of text. Graphics, as you have seen throughout this book so far, require some extra effort.

However, the Photo Albums feature in PowerPoint creates a new presentation that is specifically designed as a carrier of pictures. It is useful when you need to create a presentation that is very heavy on photos, with little or no text except picture captions.

To start a new photo album, follow these steps:

1. Choose Insert⇨Picture⇨New Photo Album. The Photo Album dialog box opens.

2. To add a photo from a file, click the File/Disk button. The Insert New Pictures dialog box opens.

3. Select one or more pictures and then click Insert. (To select multiple pictures, hold down Ctrl or Shift as you click the ones you want.) The photos appear in the Photo Album dialog box, as shown in Figure 8-16.

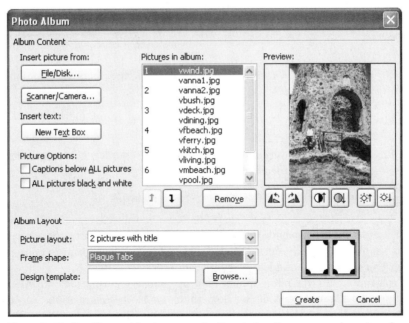

Figure 8-16: Specify graphics to appear in the photo album, a page layout, and a style of photo frame.

4. Repeat steps 2 and 3 as needed to insert all the photos from disk that you want.

5. (Optional) If you have any photos you need to scan or import from a digital camera, click the Scanner/Camera button, and then acquire those images has you learned earlier in this chapter.

6. For each image on the Pictures in Album list, select the picture and then apply any corrections needed with the buttons beneath the Preview pane. These are the same as on the Picture toolbar. You can rotate, adjust brightness, and adjust contrast.

7. Use the arrow buttons to move an image up or down in the order.

8. In the Album Layout section, open the Picture Layout box and choose the layout for the slides. For example, in Figure 8-16, 2 Pictures with Title has been chosen.

9. If available, choose a frame shape from the Frame Shape list. Some choices from step 8 do not permit a frame shape to be chosen.

You can create design templates specifically for photo albums and then use them here by choosing them from the Design Template list or clicking Browse to locate them.

10. (Optional) To add caption boxes for each picture, mark the Captions Below ALL Pictures checkbox.

11. (Optional) To show the pictures in black and white, mark the ALL Picture Black and White checkbox.

12. Click Create. PowerPoint creates a new presentation containing the photos and layout you specified.

13. Save the photo album (File➪Save) as a presentation.

Figure 8-17 shows a slide from a photo album. This particular album has no design template applied (in terms of any special fonts or backgrounds chosen); however, you could apply one just like with any other presentation.

You can modify the photo album later by choosing Format➪Photo Album. This reopens the Photo Album dialog box, the same as in Figure 8-16. You can also modify the slides in the presentation individually. These are just regular, editable slides, and you can add anything to them that you like, including text boxes, clip art, and so on. Think of it as an on-screen scrapbook.

The Photo Album puts your pictures in as AutoShape picture fills, not regular images, so you cannot crop them in PowerPoint.

Scenes from St. John, USVI

Notice the graphic accents on photo corners

Figure 8-17: A slide from the Photo Album presentation.

Summary

In this chapter you learned how to import and manipulate photographic images and other raster graphics in PowerPoint. Now you can include all the images you need in your presentation—without unduly increasing the size of the presentation file.

The next chapter continues the discussion of static graphics by looking at the clip art that comes with PowerPoint and the very powerful Clip Organizer utility for cataloging and organizing your artwork.

Chapter 9

Using and Organizing Artwork Libraries

IN THIS CHAPTER

◆ Inserting clip art

◆ Clip art search methods

◆ Modifying clip art

◆ Managing clips in the Clip Organizer

◆ Strategies for an effective artwork management system

◆ Tips for using clip art in presentations

CHAPTERS 7 AND 8 INTRODUCED you to two of the three major types of artwork you'll use in a presentation: drawn shapes and photographs. Here we'll look at the third type: clip art. You'll see how to find and insert clip art, how to modify it, and how to keep large collections of artwork organized with the Clip Organizer utility.

About the Clip Organizer

Clip art is vector artwork that comes with PowerPoint or that is available from other sources, such as through the Internet. Clip-art graphics are typically in Windows Metafile (WMF) or Enhanced Metafile (EMF) format. Since the clips are vector rather than raster, they can be resized freely without any degradation in image quality.

There are thousands of common images in PowerPoint's clip-art collection that you can use royalty-free in your work, without having to draw your own. For example, suppose you are creating a presentation about physician training. Rather than hiring an artist to draw a picture of a person in a white lab coat, you can use one of PowerPoint's stock drawings of medical professionals, like the ones in Figure 9-1, and save yourself a bundle.

The *Clip Organizer* is a utility program that helps you manage the large quantity of clip art that's available to you as a PowerPoint user. It also allows you to import your own clips, so you can use the Clip Organizer to organize your entire collection

Figure 9-1: Some examples of clip art available in PowerPoint.

of photographs, clip art, sound clips, and video clips in one handy place. There are many techniques for managing artwork libraries that don't have anything to do with PowerPoint, and if you have a system already in place—great. But if not, give the Clip Organizer a try, as described in this chapter, and see if it doesn't meet your needs. Figure 9-2 shows the Clip Organizer window. You'll learn a lot more about it as this chapter progresses.

There are several different "faces" to the Clip Organizer. One is the window you see in Figure 9-2, with a folder tree for all the folders on your hard disk that contain media clips (that is, graphics, sounds, or video clips). Another is the Clip Art task pane (shown on the right side of Figure 9-3), which you'll work with in the next section. The Clip Organizer can also be accessed through some special-purpose dialog boxes that appear at various times in PowerPoint, such as when choosing a graphical character for a bullet or when inserting clip art using a slide placeholder (as shown in Figure 9-3).

Inserting Clip Art

As with other object types, you can insert clip art either through a placeholder or manually with the Insert menu. There are some fairly significant differences between them, summarized in Table 9-1.

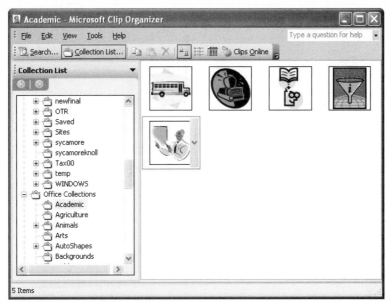

Figure 9-2: The Clip Organizer window.

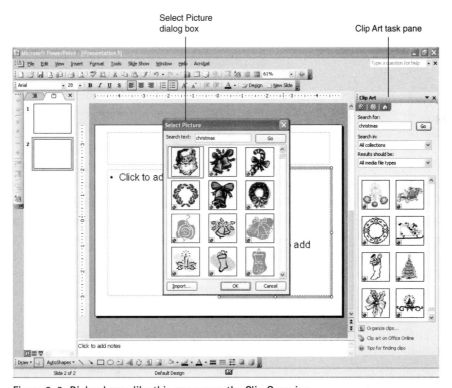

Figure 9-3: Dialog boxes like this one access the Clip Organizer.

TABLE 9-1 DIFFERENCES BETWEEN CLIP-ART PLACEHOLDERS AND MANUALLY INSERTED CLIP ART

	Placeholder	Manually Inserted
Insertion	A Select Picture dialog box appears.	The Clip Art task pane appears.
Layout Change	If new layout contains a clip-art placeholder, the clip moves to the specified new location. Otherwise, the clip moves to the far right edge of the slide and becomes "orphaned."	The layout change does not affect the clip art.
Deletion	The original placeholder reappears.	The clip's deletion does not affect the rest of the slide.

The most obvious difference between the two methods is that inserting with the placeholder opens the Select Picture dialog box, a considerably less powerful and user-friendly interface than the task pane that opens when you insert manually. Because of this, I tend to go with manually inserted clip art, whenever feasible.

 The first time you try to insert clip art, a dialog box appears prompting you to catalog the clips on your hard disk and associate keywords with the clips. This is useful because it enables you to access all the graphics on your hard disk from the Clip Organizer without your having to specifically add each clip to it. It does take a few minutes, however. Click the Now button to do it now or click Later to postpone the task.

Inserting Clip Art with a Placeholder

The main advantage to using a placeholder for clip art is that if you change the slide layout later, the clip art will move automatically to wherever the new layout specifies that the clip should be positioned. For example, if you switch from a layout where the clip is to the right of the bulleted list to one where it is to the left, it moves.

You can either use a layout that specifically calls for clip art, as shown in Figure 9-4, or use one of the multi-purpose graphic placeholders, as shown in Figure 9-5. The only difference is that with the specific clip-art placeholder, you must double-click, whereas with the multi-purpose placeholder you single-click the Clip Art icon.

These layouts are specific to clip art.

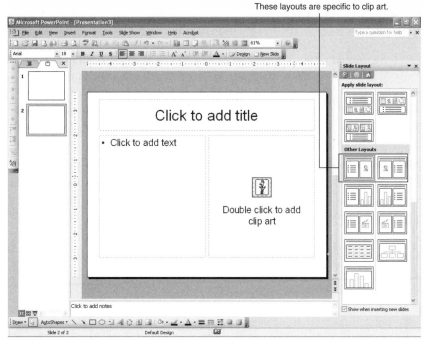

Figure 9-4: This slide layout calls specifically for clip art; no other object type will do.

Clip Art icon

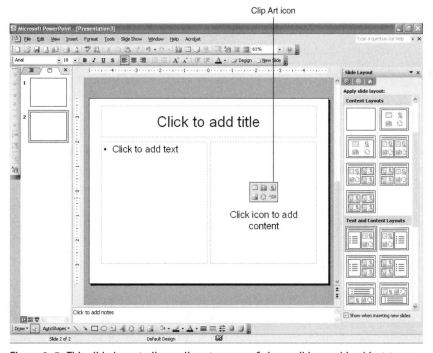

Figure 9-5: This slide layout allows clip art as one of six possible graphic object types.

Either way, when you click (or double-click) the icon, the Select Picture dialog box appears, as shown in Figure 9-3. From here you can do the following:

◆ Type a keyword in the Search text box and click Go to find all clips that have that keyword. Then, click the desired clip and click OK to insert it.

◆ Click the Import button to open the Add Clips to Organizer dialog box, from which you can select graphic files on your hard disk to add to the Clip Organizer. (I'll cover this procedure in greater detail later in the chapter.)

That's pretty much it! The Insert Picture dialog box is not particularly powerful or flexible. The manual method described in the next section has many more options.

Manually Inserting Clip Art

For complete access to the Clip Organizer's features, you will want to manually insert clip art via the Clip Art task pane or the Clip Organizer window.

You can use the manual method for clip art insertion even if you have a place-holder on a slide that you want to use. Simply select the placeholder frame before manually inserting, and PowerPoint will use that placeholder for the insertion.

To open the Clip Art task pane, do any of the following:

◆ Choose Insert ⇨ Picture ⇨ Clip Art.

◆ ☑ Click the Insert Clip Art button on the Drawing toolbar.

◆ Display any other task pane (View ⇨ Task Pane) and then open the drop-down list at the top of the task pane and choose Clip Art.

Then type one or more keywords in the Search for box (see Figure 9-6), refine the search in any additional ways desired (as explained in the following sections) and click Go. When you find the clip you want, click it to place it on the active slide. (You can change slides between doing the search and selecting the clip, if you find yourself on the wrong slide.)

Clip Art Search Methods

When searching for clips, you should be able to enter a single keyword, click Go, and get the clip you want, right? Well, in theory, it works that way, but not always in practice. Here are some tips for narrowing down your search enough that you don't get hundreds of duds, but not so much that you miss some good images.

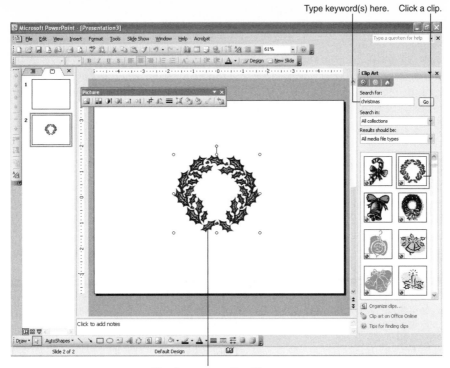

Figure 9-6: Search for clips from the Clip Art task pane.

Specify Which Collections to Search

Open the Search In list in the Clip Art task pane and mark or clear checkboxes to specify which collections you want to search. The default is All Collections, which searches everywhere.

The three main collections are as follows:

- *My Collections*: All the folders that the Clip Organizer is aware of on your local hard disks that contain usable graphics. When you used the Clip Art feature for the first time, it asked permission to catalog your clips; this is why.

- *Office Collections*: All the folders containing clips provided by Microsoft Office that are on your local hard disks.

- *Web Collections*: Pointers to all the locations on the Internet from which Office can pull Microsoft-sponsored clip art.

Eliminating some of the collections from the search can make the search results appear faster. For example, if you are not connected to the Web all the time, but the Web Collections are marked for searching, there will be a delay of up to a minute or two while PowerPoint unsuccessfully tries to locate those clip libraries. By eliminating them from the search process, you make the clips that you have available on your local PC appear faster.

Each of the main clip collections has a plus sign and a checkbox next to it. Click the checkbox to select or deselect an entire collection, or click the plus sign to expand the list of folders and then mark or clear the checkbox for individual folders as desired (see Figure 9-7).

Figure 9-7: Narrow down the search to only certain collections, if desired.

Specify Which Media File Types to Find

The default is to search for all media file types: vector graphics (clip art), raster graphics (such as photos), sounds, and videos. If you are sure you want only a certain type of file, you can eliminate the others to make the search go more quickly. For example, if you are searching for clip art, you probably don't want sound files!

To narrow down the list of file types, open the Results Should Be drop-down list and clear the checkboxes for one or more of the types.

Within each file type you can click the plus sign to further narrow down the types you want, by file extension. For example, you might exclude the PCX and TIF files from the Photographs category but keep the JPEG and GIF files in the search (see Figure 9-8).

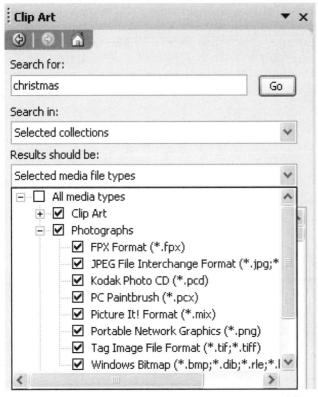

Figure 9-8: Narrow down the search to only certain types of files.

Use Multiple Keywords

When you enter multiple keywords, such as *green tree*, PowerPoint displays only the clips that have all the search words in as keywords. This helps narrow down the search results considerably, but may result in too few clips being displayed.

Use Wildcards

As with searches in Windows itself and in other applications, you can use an asterisk (*) as a wildcard. The asterisk * stands for any number of characters. So, for example, *aa** would find clips with keywords including *aardvark and Aaron*.

Find Clips by Similar Style

Among the Microsoft-provided clips are sets of artwork that are all created in the same style. Sometimes you might want to design a presentation around one of these sets, but how can you find all the images in a set, given that they probably have very different keywords?

The solution is to search by similar style. Right-click a clip in the Clip Art task pane and choose Find Similar Style (if available; it's not available for every clip). The search results display the other clips in that style (see Figure 9-9).

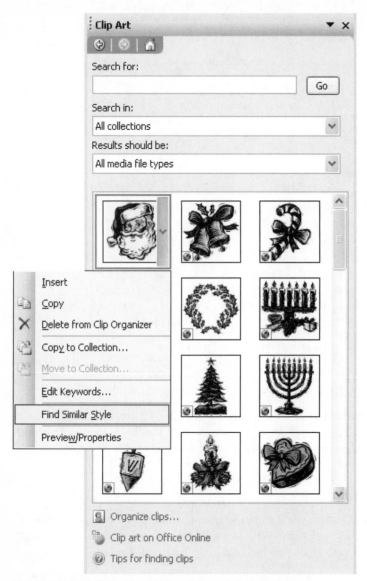

Figure 9-9: Find clips with a similar style to the selected one.

Find Clips by Browsing

Rather than searching by keyword, you can browse the available clip art by category. This requires the use of the Clip Organizer. Here's how to get started:

1. From the Clip Art task pane, click the Organize Clips hyperlink.

2. Click the plus sign next to a category in the folder tree to expand it, or click a minus sign to collapse a category.

3. Click the category you want to see, and its clips appear in the right pane (see Figure 9-10).

Figure 9-10: Browse the Clip Organizer to find a piece of clip art.

4. Once you've found the clip you want, copy it (Ctrl+C or right-click it and choose Copy).

5. Close or minimize the Clip Organizer window and paste it on your slide (Ctrl+V or Edit⇨Paste).

Notice that the Clip Organizer does not have a direct way of selecting a clip and inserting it on a slide. That's because the Clip Organizer is a separate application; it is not directly tied to the current presentation the way the Clip Art task pane is. You can copy and paste from it, but you can't simply click a clip to insert it the way you can with the task pane.

Browsing Clip Art Online

The complete collection of Microsoft clip art is available through PowerPoint automatically if you are connected to the Internet when you search for clips. Therefore, there is usually no reason to go to the Microsoft Office Online Web site to search for clip art.

However, if you want to browse using an attractive Web-based interface for available clips, you might check out Office Online. To do so, use any of these methods:

◆ From the Clip Art task pane, click the Clip Art on Office Online hyperlink at the bottom.

◆ From the Clip Organizer, click the Clips Online button on its toolbar.

◆ From the Clip Organizer, click the Search button and then click the Clip Art on Office Online hyperlink at the bottom of the search pane.

The Office Online Web site is constantly being changed and updated, so any steps I might provide for you here would likely be out of date before you read this. So, instead I'll just say *explore on your own*. Figure 9-11 shows it on the day I visited; as you can see it is fairly self-explanatory. You select clips you want to add to a "basket," and then you download the contents of your basket to your hard disk.

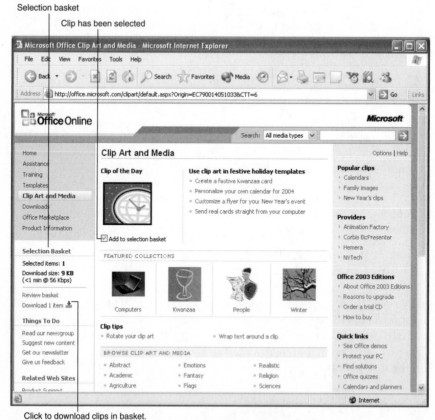

Figure 9-11: Browse clips at Microsoft's Web site through the Office Online interface.

The first time you download clips, you may be prompted to install an Office Template and Media Control utility. Follow the prompts to do so. Then, on subsequent times a page will display showing that it has already been done and prompting you to continue.

The file downloaded will be a Media Package File (MPF). You must open it to allow the clips to be extracted. Therefore, if you are prompted to save or open the file it is best to choose Open. This extracts the clips to the My Documents\Microsoft Clip Organizer folder, and then shows the clip in the Clip Organizer window in the Downloaded Clips category in the My Collections collection.

See *Managing the Clips in the Clip Organizer* later in the chapter for more information about working with clip collections.

Making a Clip Available Offline

In the preceding section you learned how to select and transfer Microsoft clip art from the Web to your own local PC. That method works for browsing the Web site, but what if you want to copy a clip to your hard disk that you located through the Clip Art task pane's search?

Easy enough—right-click the clip and choose Copy to Collection. Then, specify where you want it copied. To make it available when you are not connected to the Internet, save it in one of your My Collections folders.

Working with CIL or MPF Files

Occasionally you may encounter a file that claims to be clip art but it has a CIL or MPF extension. Both of these are clip art "package" formats that Microsoft has used to bundle and transfer clip art at one time or another. CIL is the older format, and MPF is the newer one.

When faced with one of these files, you can choose to run it rather than save it, or you can download it and then double-click it to extract the clip art from it.

Modifying Clip Art

Most of the modifications you learned about in Chapter 8 for photographs apply also to clip art. You can move, resize, increase or decrease brightness and contrast, rotate, and so on. But there are also some special modifications you can make that apply only to clip art and other vector images. The following sections explain them.

Recoloring an Image

One of the top complaints about clip art is that the colors are wrong. Maybe you've found the perfect drawing, but its colors clash with your presentation design? Not a problem. In most cases you can change any or all of its colors.

 You cannot recolor a raster graphic such as a scanned photo in PowerPoint. Recoloring works only on vector graphics like clip art. Some third-party image-editing applications allow you to replace one color with another in a raster graphic, however.

A piece of clip art consists of a series of lines and filled shapes, much like the AutoShapes from Chapter 7. Recoloring changes the colors of the lines and/or fills on a color-by-color basis.

To recolor a clip, do the following:

1. Select the clip that you want to recolor. If the Picture toolbar does not appear, display it.

2. On the Picture Toolbar, click the Recolor Picture button. The Recolor Picture dialog box appears showing all the colors used in the image (see Figure 9-12).

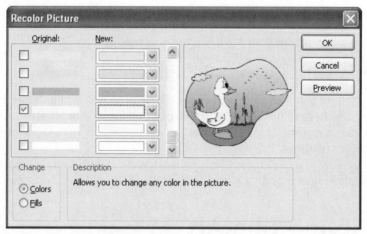

Figure 9-12: Choose the colors you want to change, and choose the colors you want to change them to.

3. Choose Colors or Fills at the bottom of the dialog box. Colors (the default) shows all the colors in the image, both the lines and the fills. The Fills option, on the other hand, shows only the fill colors.

4. Click the checkbox next to one of the Original colors. Then, open the New drop-down list next to it, and select a color to change it to.

5. The preview will update automatically. Drag the dialog box out of the way as needed so you can see the change in the image on the slide itself.

6. Repeat steps 4 and 5 for each of the colors you want to change. If you change your mind about a color, deselect its checkbox to retain the original.

7. Click OK to finish.

Deconstructing and Editing a Clip

Have you ever wished you could open a clip art image in an image-editing program and make some small change to it? Well, you can. And what's more, you can do it without leaving PowerPoint.

Since clip art is composed of vector graphic lines and fills, you can literally take it apart piece by piece. Not only can you replace certain colors (as in the preceding section), but you can choose individual lines and shapes out of it to recolor, move, or otherwise modify.

To deconstruct a piece of clip art:

1. Select the clip, and then on the Drawing toolbar, choose Draw ⇨ Ungroup. A warning message appears that this is an imported graphic, not a drawing, offering to convert it to a Microsoft Office drawing.

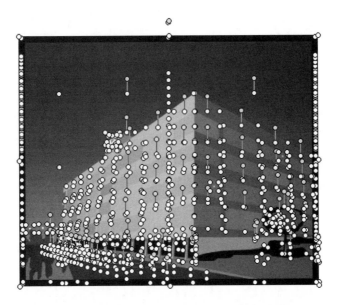

Figure 9-13: This clip comprises many tiny lines and shapes, each with its own round white selection handles and green rotation handle.

2. Click Yes to convert the clip to a Microsoft Office drawing. It will still be grouped at this point.

3. Choose Draw⇨Ungroup again. This time the drawing is broken apart into lines and shapes, with each one having its own selection handles (see Figure 9-13).

4. Click away from the clip to deselect all the selected pieces, and then click once on the piece you want to work with.

5. Move it, resize it, change its color, or do any other editing to it desired, as you learned in Chapter 7. For example, in Figure 9-14, I've recolored a few of the parallelograms that represent windows on the building so that it looks like the "lights" are on for a few of the offices on the top floor.

6. When you are finished editing the clip, regroup it. To do so, click any of the individual components on the clip and then choose Draw⇨Regroup.

Figure 9-14: I've changed the color of a few of the "windows" on the top floor.

Managing Clips in the Clip Organizer

There are probably images elsewhere on your PC that you would like to use in PowerPoint besides the Microsoft Office 2003 clip collection. For example, perhaps you have some scanned photos or some clip art you have downloaded from a Web site that offered free clips, or some clip art left over from an earlier version of Office.

If you need to use this "outside" art only once or twice, you can simply insert it with the Insert⇨Picture⇨From File command, covered in Chapter 8. But if you have a recurring need for the art, you might want to add it to the Clip Organizer.

 Remember, to open the Clip Organizer, click the Organize Clips hyperlink at the bottom of the Clip Art task pane.

You can include images of all image formats in the Clip Organizer, not just the default .wmf format that PowerPoint's clip art uses. The image formats that Power-Point supports include .emd, .wmf, .jpg, .png, .bmp, .pcx, .dib, .rle, .eps, .dxf, .pct, .cgm, .cdr, .drw, .tif, .tga, .pcd, .gif, .wpg, .fpx, and .mix. The Clip Organizer also accepts many sound and video formats as well. The Clip Organizer is not only for clip art, but also for scanned and digital camera photos, video clips, and sound clips.

Cataloging Clips from Other Sources

The first time you use clip art, PowerPoint offers to catalog the clips on your system. If you let it, you end up with a fairly complete "My Collections" group of folders in the Clip Organizer, containing every piece of usable artwork PowerPoint could find.

If you did not go through the cataloging process, or if you've added files to your hard disk after going through that process, you can recatalog your system at any time. You can also manually add an individual clip at any time.

 Any clips you add are placed in the My Collections collection. You cannot add clips to the Office Collections or Web Collections categories. This is true whether you add them automatically or manually.

ADDING CLIPS AUTOMATICALLY TO THE CLIP ORGANIZER

These steps repeat the process of cataloging the clips on your hard disk. It is not necessary to do this unless the content of your hard disk has changed since you originally cataloged it.

1. From the Clip Organizer, choose File⇨Add Clips to Organizer⇨Automatically.

2. (Optional) In the dialog box that appears, click the Options button to open the Auto Import Settings dialog box. You can then mark or clear checkboxes for various locations that you want to include in the automatic cataloging (see Figure 9-15). This might be useful for saving time if you know that the clips you want to catalog are all in a certain folder, for example.

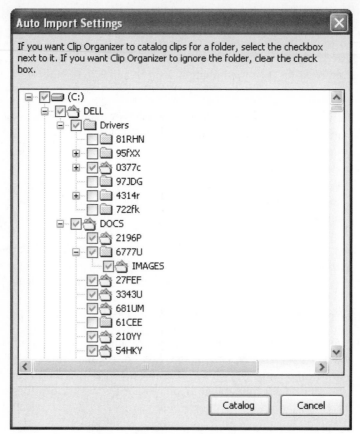

Figure 9-15: Specify the locations to catalog, if desired. By default, all locations are cataloged.

3. If you performed step 2, click Catalog to perform the search for clips. If you did not perform step 2, click OK to perform the search.

ADDING CLIPS MANUALLY TO THE CLIP ORGANIZER

Not all clips are picked up automatically during the cataloging process, so you might want to manually add some clips. For example, the automatic cataloging process looks for clips only on your local hard disk(s), and you might want to catalog the clips on a shared network drive at your place of business.

 Earlier versions of Office stored local collections of clip art in a different place. Office XP, for example, stored it in Program Files\Common Files\Microsoft Shared\Clipart\Cagcat50, and Publisher XP used Program Files\Microsoft Office\CLIPART\PUB60COR. The clip art in these old locations does not appear in the collections in Office 2003 applications by default. Neither is it picked up by the automatic cataloging process. The only way to get it into the Clip Organizer is by manually cataloging it, as described here.

To manually add one or more clips, do the following:

1. From the Clip Organizer window, choose File ⇨ Add Clips to Organizer ⇨ On My Own. The Add Clips to Organizer window appears.

2. Navigate to the clips you want to add. This can be on a local, network, or Internet location.

3. Select the clips. To select more than one clip, hold down the Shift key to select a contiguous group or the Ctrl key to select a non-contiguous group.

4. Click the Add To button. A list of the existing collections in the Clip Organizer appears (see Figure 9-16). (If you do not do this step, the clips are placed in the Unclassified Clips folder, and you can sort them out later.)

Figure 9-16: Select the clips to catalog and the collection in which to place them.

5. Select the collection in which you want to place the new clips, and click OK.
   or
   To create a new clip collection, click My Collections, and then click New. Type a name for a new collection, and click OK. Then select the new folder on the list, and click OK.

6. Click the Add button. The clips are added to the specified collection.

Removing Clips from the Clip Organizer

After the automatic cataloging process (or maybe after the manual one too), you might end up with some subcollections within My Collections that you don't want. The automatic cataloging process sometimes identifies artwork that is not really artwork—that is, little graphics that are part of some other application's operation. To remove these from your Clip Organizer, right-click the graphic and choose Delete. The same goes for entire folders—right-click and choose Delete.

For example, in Figure 9-17, notice that the Clip Organizer has cataloged a clip from the Windows\Help folder. I am right-clicking the Help folder in the folder tree and choosing Delete Help to get rid of it. This does not delete the picture or its folder from the hard disk; it simply removes its reference from the Clip Organizer.

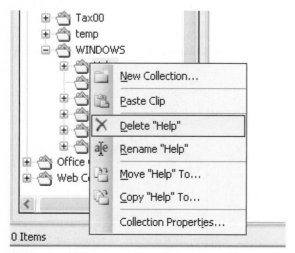

Figure 9-17: Remove a clip, or a category of clips, from the Clip Organizer.

Changing Clip Keywords

After creating an automatic catalog, you will probably end up with lots of clips in the Unclassified Clips collection. Some of these you might want to delete, having no use for them, but others you will want to keep. In order for these clips to show up when you do a search, you must assign keywords to them. You cannot modify the keywords for the clip art that comes with PowerPoint/Office 2003; you can modify them only for art you have imported.

Automatically cataloged clips will have several keywords pre-assigned based on the file name and location. For example, suppose that the clip Blue Hills.jpg has been cataloged from the `Documents and Settings\All Users\My Documents\My Pictures\Sample Pictures` folder. It will have the following keywords pre-assigned: Blue Hills, Documents and Settings, All Users, Documents, My Pictures, and Sample Pictures. These are not very helpful when trying to locate the clip by subject, however, so you will want to add some content-based keywords too.

To modify a clip's keywords, do the following:

1. From the Clip Organizer, right-click the clip (or click the down arrow next to it) and choose Edit Keywords.

2. The default caption for the clip is the file name. Change it to a more meaningful caption in the Caption box, if desired. This caption will appear in some views and anywhere that an application pulls a caption automatically.

3. To add a keyword for the clip, type the new keyword in the Keyword box and click Add (see Figure 9-18).

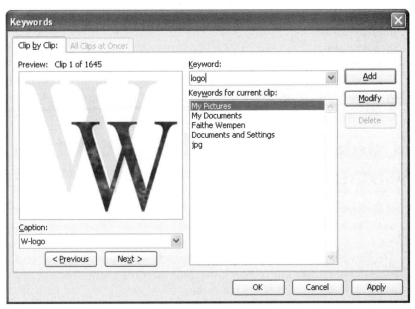

Figure 9-18: Add, delete, or modify the keywords for a clip.

4. To remove a keyword, select the keyword and click Delete.

5. When you are finished, click OK to close the dialog box, or click the Previous or Next button to move to another clip in the same folder.

You can modify multiple clips at once by selecting multiple clips before you right-click (step 1 in the preceding steps). When multiple clips are selected, the All Clips at Once tab becomes available in the Keywords dialog box. From there you can add keywords that will apply to all the selected clips.

Creating New Clip Collections

To add a new clip collection to the My Collections group, do the following:

1. Right-click My Collections and choose New Collection.

2. In the New Collection dialog box, type a name for the new collection.

3. Click OK.

Whatever folder you right-click in step 1 will be the parent folder for the new one, so you can nest folders several levels deep in the organizational structure. For example, you could create a Family folder and then within that have Aunts, Uncles, Cousins, and Siblings folders.

Moving and Copying Clips Between Collections

A clip can be in multiple collections at once without taking up double the space on the hard disk, so feel free to place a clip in as many different collections as are appropriate for it.

Drag-and-drop a clip onto a folder in the Collection List to copy it to that collection. Copying it to another collection does not remove it from its original location; if you want to move rather than copy, delete the original after copying it or use Move to Collection on the clip's menu in the Clip Organizer.

Strategies for an Effective Artwork Management System

The Clip Organizer can be a very useful tool, but the default settings aren't always the best. Here are some tips for making the most of the Clip Organizer:

◆ You aren't stuck with the folder structure shown on the Collection List. Within the My Collections group you can create any structure you want. You might even create a whole new set of categories, copy the appropriate clips into them, and then delete most or all of the automatically generated folders.

◆ Suppose, you have several clips with the same artwork style and you want to be able to locate them as a group in the future. Assign the same keyword to all of them. Establish a consistent naming system for sorting clips according to artwork style. For example, you might want to start the style-sorting keywords with "style" as in *style-line*, *style-block*, *style-sketch*, and so on.

Tips for Using Clip Art in Presentations

Don't just slap down any old image! You must never use clip art simply because you can; it must be a strategically calculated decision. Here are some reasons for using art and ways to make it look good:

◆ If your message is very serious, or you are conveying bad news, don't use clip art. It looks frivolous in such situations.

◆ Use cartoonish images only if you specifically want to impart a lighthearted, fun feel to your presentation.

◆ The clip art in Office has many styles of drawings, ranging from simple black-and-white shapes to very complex shaded color drawings. Try to stick with one type of image rather than bouncing among several drawing styles.

◆ Use only one piece of clip art per slide. Don't use clip art on every slide, or it gets overpowering.

◆ Don't repeat the same clip art on more than one slide in the presentation unless you have a specific reason to do so.

◆ If you can't find a clip that's exactly right for the slide, don't use a clip. It is better to have none than to have an inappropriate image.

◆ If clip art is important and Office doesn't have what you want, buy more. Don't try to struggle along with the clips that come with Office if they aren't meeting your needs; impressive clip art collections are available at reasonable prices at your local computer store, as well as online.

Summary

In this chapter you learned how to use clip art and the Microsoft Clip Organizer to select and manage artwork. Combined with what you learned in Chapters 7 and 8, you are now ready to tackle almost any kind of artwork! Well, almost. There are two special types of artwork in PowerPoint that we have not yet looked at: diagrams and charts. These will be the subjects of the next two chapters.

Chapter 10

Working with Diagrams and Org Charts

DIAGRAMS ARE A CROSS between graphics and tables. On one hand their graphical nature draws people in, and on the other they present text information. Whenever you have text to present and want something a little less ordinary, try a diagram. (If you have numbers to present, you might consider a graph, which I'll cover in Chapter 11.)

Diagram and Org Chart Basics

The term *diagram* in PowerPoint refers to a special class of vector graphic object that combines shapes, lines, and text. Diagrams are most often used to illustrate relationships between bits of text. For example, Figure 10-1 shows a simple diagram that shows the flow of a manufacturing process.

There are six diagram types available, and each kind is useful for displaying a different kind of data. One type—*organization chart*—is very different from the others, however. In this chapter I'll cover the five "easy" types first, and then focus on organization charts toward the end.

First, let's get a look at each of the diagram types in the following sections.

Cycle Diagram

Which came first, the chicken or the egg? Now you can represent this conundrum graphically. A cycle diagram is a flow chart that illustrates a repeating process with no start or finish. You can have as many different steps in the process as you like.

Manufacture Product

Release Product

Improve Product Design

Listen to Customer Feedback

Figure 10-1: This diagram shows a repeating process.

TIP By default, the shapes in a cycle diagram are arrows. In earlier versions of Microsoft Office, however, the default segment shape was a plain arch without arrows. You can change the shape of a segment by turning off AutoLayout (from the Diagram toolbar's Layout menu) and then making the change with the Draw ➪ Change AutoShape command.

Radial Diagram

A radial diagram shows relationships such that each item radiates from the center (hence the name "radial"). It is good for showing how multiple items feed into a center point, or the satellite offices of a central headquarters, as shown in Figure 10-2.

Pyramid Diagram

A pyramid diagram is just what it sounds like. It breaks up a triangle into horizontal slices and labels each slice. In Figure 10-3 it's used for staffing, for example.

Venn Diagram

Remember math class, when you learned about sets and subsets and how two sets can intersect? That's the basic idea behind a Venn diagram. It's a series of circles that overlap one another, as shown in Figure 10-4. It's useful when you need to show conceptually how different groups have some—but not all—members or characteristics in common.

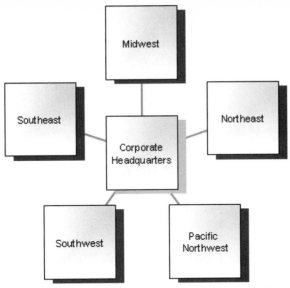

Figure 10-2: A radial diagram is like a simple organization chart that starts from the center rather than the top.

Figure 10-3: A pyramid diagram shows the progression from the base level (large) to the top level (small).

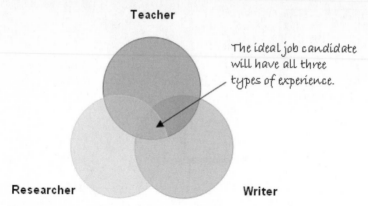

Figure 10-4: A Venn diagram overlaps circles to show groups and their commonalities.

TIP   In the previous versions of PowerPoint, the colors in Venn diagrams did not blend very well, so it was often better to create the diagram in an image-editing program and import it onto the slide. In PowerPoint 2003, however, the colors from the Venn diagrams blend automatically based on the colors applied to each circle. You can manipulate this somewhat by changing the transparency of the colors in the Format ⇨ AutoShape dialog.

Target Diagram

A target diagram shows progress toward a goal. Each layer moves closer to the end result at the center, as shown in Figure 10-5.

Figure 10-5: A target diagram is like a flowchart that flows from the outside to the center.

Organization Chart

An organization chart ("org chart") shows who reports to whom in a company's employment hierarchy. It's useful when describing how an organization functions and who is responsible for what, as shown in Figure 10-6. It can also be used to show match-ups for competitions as in a single-elimination or double-elimination tournament, so it'll come in handy when you're in charge of the office NCAA pool!

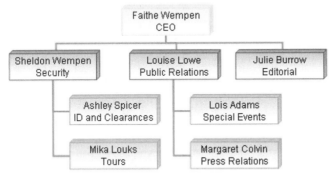

Figure 10-6: Show the chain of command in an organization with an org chart.

Org charts are also passably useful for flow charts for processes, although it's often better to use the flow-charting AutoShapes to manually draw flow charts or use a program like Visio, which is specifically designed for that type of thing.

This chapter covers organization charts last, because they're the most complicated type of diagram. (We'll work up to them.)

TIP Should you include your company's organization chart in your presentation? That's a question that depends on your main message. If your speech is about the organization, you should. If not, show the organization structure only if it serves a purpose to advance your speech. Many presenters have found that an organization chart makes an excellent backup slide. You can prepare it and have it ready in case a question arises about the organization. Another useful strategy is to include a printed organization chart as part of the handouts you distribute to the audience, without including the slide in the main presentation.

Inserting a Diagram

All diagrams start out the same way. You insert them on the slide as with any other type of content. That means you can use a diagram placeholder on a layout or you can insert the diagram manually.

To use a placeholder, start with a slide that contains a layout with a diagram placeholder, or change the current slide's layout to one that does, and then click the Diagram icon in the placeholder.

To insert the diagram manually, you can use either of these methods:

- ◆ Click the Diagram button on the Drawing toolbar.
- ◆ Choose Insert ⇨ Diagram.

Any way you start it, the Diagram Gallery dialog box opens, as shown in Figure 10-7. Select one of the six diagram types, click OK, and a diagram appears. From there it's just a matter of customizing.

Figure 10-7: Select the diagram type to insert.

When a diagram is selected, the Diagram toolbar appears. Some of the buttons are different depending on the diagram type; we'll look at the specifics in the following sections, where appropriate.

Working with Diagram Text

A diagram is basically just a group of text boxes, lines, and AutoShapes that have been grouped together in a special way. That means you can enter and edit text in its text boxes the same as you would anywhere else.

Click in any text box and type/edit. You can also select and format the text using regular text-formatting techniques such as changing the font, size, color, attributes, and alignment.

You do not need to manually insert text boxes in a diagram. When you insert new shapes (explained a bit later in the chapter), new text boxes are also inserted. For example, suppose you are creating a cycle diagram like the one shown in Figure 10-1. If you insert a new arrow AutoShape, a new text box appears too so that the ratio of text boxes to shapes remains 1:1. And with other diagram types the text actually appears within the AutoShape, so having a separate text box is not an issue.

Modifying Diagram Layout

There are two types of changes you can make to a diagram: those that affect the physical structure or layout, and those that are purely cosmetic formatting. I'll address them separately in this chapter.

The following sections explain the structural changes you can make to a diagram.

Adding or Deleting Shapes

The Diagram toolbar appears whenever the diagram is selected and includes an Insert Shape button. Use it to insert additional shapes. See Figure 10-8 for an example, but the button's picture varies depending on the diagram type. You do not get to choose the shape; it inserts whatever shape is appropriate for the chosen diagram.

Add shapes to the diagram

Figure 10-8: The Diagram toolbar when a pyramid diagram is selected; it is similar for other diagram types.

For some diagram types, it's important to select an existing shape that the new one should be inserted adjacent to (or subordinate to, in the case of charts that have hierarchical levels). For other types, it does not matter.

To delete a shape, click it to select it in the diagram. Gray circles appear around it with Xs in the centers, as shown in Figure 10-9. Press the Delete key on the keyboard.

 The gray circle selection handles with Xs indicate that the shape is selected but is grouped with other objects such that it cannot be individually moved or resized. However, it can be individually formatted and deleted. You can disable this grouping by choosing Layout ⇨ AutoLayout from the Diagram toolbar.

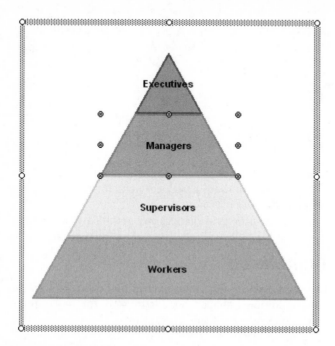

Figure 10-9: A selected shape has gray circle selection handles.

Changing the Layout Flow

Each diagram flows in a certain direction. A cycle diagram flows either clockwise or counterclockwise. A pyramid flows either up or down. A radial or target diagram flows from the outside in or from the inside out.

If you realize after typing all the text that you should have made the diagram flow in the other direction, you can change it by clicking the Reverse Diagram button on the Diagram toolbar. For example, in Figure 10-10, the diagram from Figure 10-9 has been reversed so that Executives are at the bottom of the pyramid and the workers are on top.

After reversing the flow of pyramid labels as shown in Figure 10-10, you might find that the labels run outside the top few slices. If this is a problem, you might be able to make the labels fit with a combination of line breaks (Shift+Enter) and font changes.

Figure 10-10: Reversing the diagram flow changes which labels are assigned to which shapes.

Rearranging Shapes

Not only can you reverse the overall flow of the diagram, but you can also move around individual shapes. For example, suppose you have a diagram that illustrates five steps in a process and you realize that steps 3 and 4 are out of order. You can move one of them without having to retype all the labels.

To move a shape, select it and then click the Move Shape Forward or Move Shape Backward button on the Diagram toolbar. These buttons look different depending on what kind of diagram you are working with, but they are always the second and third buttons on the Diagram toolbar (except for an org chart, which doesn't allow this kind of rearranging.) Figure 10-11 shows them for a Radial type diagram; compare to Figure 10-8, which showed the toolbar for a Pyramid diagram.

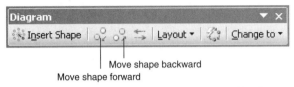

Figure 10-11: Move a shape forward or backward in the diagram structure with the Diagram toolbar.

Changing the Diagram Type

Except for the organization chart, you can change any diagram type to any other diagram type. To change the diagram type, click the Change To button on the

Diagram toolbar and choose the desired layout from the menu. (See Figure 10-12, where the current diagram type is the unavailable one—Target.)

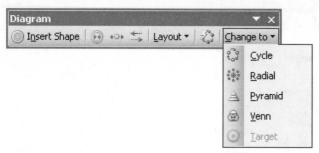

Figure 10-12: Switch to a different diagram type with the Change To button.

To change the diagram type as described in this section, you must have Auto-Format and AutoLayout both turned on. If they're not on, you'll be prompted to allow PowerPoint to turn them on. Note that this will sometimes affect color changes you might have made to the diagram, so it's better to decide on the appropriate diagram type before customizing.

Resizing a Diagram

There are two ways to resize a diagram frame. You can resize it so that the diagram itself does not change size—only its frame—or you can resize so that both the frame and the diagram inside change.

To resize the frame only, leaving the diagram at its default size, click Layout on the Diagram toolbar and choose Resize Diagram. Black line selection handles appear around the border, and you can drag them to resize the frame. You cannot resize the frame so small that the diagram will no longer fit, but you can make it as large as desired (see Figure 10-13). When you are finished resizing, press Esc to cancel the mode.

To reset the frame so that it is only as large as it needs to be for the diagram inside, open the Layout menu on the Diagram toolbar and choose Fit Diagram to Contents.

To resize the frame and the diagram as a whole, simply drag its regular white round selection handles. The entire diagram resizes along with the frame, as shown in Figure 10-14.

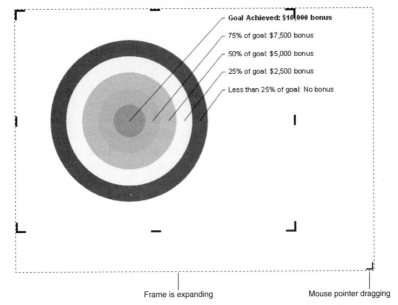

Figure 10-13: Resizing with Resize Diagram turned on resizes only the frame.

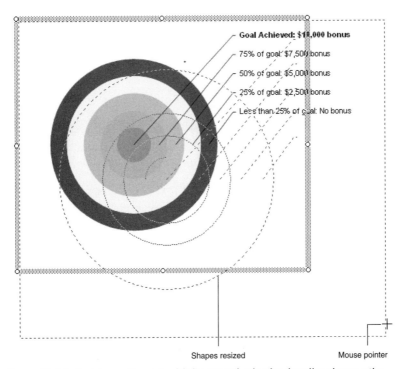

Figure 10-14: Resizing a diagram with its normal selection handles changes the size of everything in the frame as well as the frame itself.

Disabling AutoLayout

AutoLayout is turned on by default. It makes the entire diagram a single object that you move, resize, and otherwise manipulate as a whole. In most cases you will want to leave it turned on. However, sometimes some manual changes are necessary in a diagram, and these can be accomplished only after turning AutoLayout off.

To toggle AutoLayout on or off, choose it from the Layout menu on the Diagram toolbar.

The most obvious immediate consequence of disabling AutoLayout is that each part of the chart becomes a separate, free object with its own white circle selection handles. You can move parts of the chart around as if they were normal AutoShapes, format them, and do anything else you would like to do to them. See Figure 10-15 for an example.

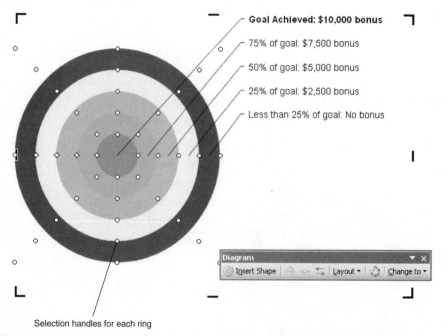

Figure 10-15: Turning off AutoLayout makes all kinds of manual changes possible for the layout.

Making Manual Layout Changes

Here are some things you can do to a diagram after turning off AutoLayout:

◆ Make any part larger or smaller by dragging its selection handles.

◆ Alter a shape, in some cases, by dragging the yellow diamond on it (as with AutoShapes in general). For example, you can make the circle segments in a Cycle diagram fatter, thinner, longer, or shorter.

◆ Change the shape to an entirely different AutoShape with the Draw ➪ Change AutoShape command.

◆ Reposition a shape by dragging it to a new location. For example, you can make the circles in a Venn diagram overlap less or more than the default, or make one of them not overlap at all with the others.

◆ Reposition a text by dragging it to a new location. For example, if you have too much text in a text box it might overlap with a shape in the diagram; you can scoot it over so it doesn't anymore. Or, you can intentionally place a text box on top of a shape.

◆ Add other objects to the diagram. For example, you can add extra text boxes with explanatory text. To do so, make sure the diagram frame is selected, and then use the Text Box tool in the Drawing toolbar to create a new text box. Or alternatively, copy one of the existing text boxes in the diagram by Ctrl+dragging it.

Modifying Diagram Formatting

You can format a diagram either automatically or manually. Automatically is the default, and many PowerPoint users don't even realize that manual formatting is a possibility. The following sections cover both.

Choosing an AutoFormat

Each diagram has a variety of AutoFormat choices you can apply to it. You choose one of these, and click the AutoFormat button on the Diagram toolbar. The Diagram Style Gallery dialog box opens (see Figure 10-16). Make your selection and click OK to apply it.

Disabling AutoFormat

To format the shapes on your own, you must disable AutoFormat. To do so, right-click the chart (anywhere on it), and choose Use AutoFormat to remove the checkbox next to that command. (It's a toggle.)

To reenable AutoFormat, choose the command again from the menu. It is also automatically reenabled if you select an AutoFormat from the Style Gallery as explained in the preceding section.

Making Manual Format Changes

If you want to separately format a certain shape, you must turn off AutoFormat. You may find it useful to turn off AutoLayout as well. It's a two-step process: you must be able to individually select a shape (which is easier when AutoLayout is off), and you must be able to individually format the shape (possible only when AutoFormat is off).

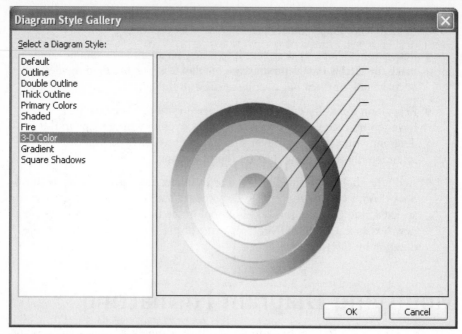

Figure 10-16: Select a different AutoFormat for the diagram.

You can then make any of the following types of changes:

◆ Change the line and/or fill color for a shape

◆ Add a border and/or fill to a text box

◆ Add a shadow

◆ Add a 3-D effect

◆ Change the text color, font, and size (although actually you can change these without turning off AutoFormat or AutoLayout)

Special Considerations for Organization Charts

As I said before, org charts are different from other diagrams because of their complexity. The relationships between the shapes are of a different nature than in other types: one box is subordinate to another box in a complex hierarchy.

Organization charts have their own toolbar, which is separate from the Diagram toolbar (although similar to it). Notice that it doesn't have Move Shape Forward, Move Shape Backward, or Change To buttons, and that the Insert Shape button has a drop-down list that it didn't have with other diagram types. Figure 10-17 shows the toolbar and I'll explain its buttons in the following sections.

Figure 10-17: The Organization Chart toolbar.

Inserting and Deleting Shapes

The main difference between an organization chart and other diagrams in inserting a shape is that each added shape must be in relation to another shape.

There are three kinds of relationships that the new shape can have to the existing selected one:

◆ *Subordinate*: Reports directly to that person

◆ *Coworker*: Is at the same level as that person, and reports to the same manager

◆ *Assistant*: Provides services to that person; may or may not directly report to him or her.

To get a new shape with the default subordinate relationship, you simply click the Insert Shape button, but to get a new shape with one of the other two relationships, you must open the drop-down list on the Insert Shape button and make your selection there (see Figure 10-18).

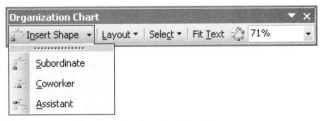

Figure 10-18: The Organization Chart toolbar.

 TIP Notice in Figure 10-18 that the Insert Shape menu has a handle—a row of small dots across the top, between the button and the menu. You can drag it to make the menu into a floating toolbar to keep its commands handy if that would be useful.

To delete a shape, select it and press the Delete key, as with any other diagram type.

Changing Supervisor Reporting

As the organization changes, you might need to change the chart so that people report to different supervisors. To do that, simply drag-and-drop a subordinate's box onto a different supervisor's box.

Switching to a Different Subordinate Layout

The subordinates for a supervisor can be arranged in any of several ways on the organization chart. The default is for each one to be shown horizontally beneath the supervisor, as shown in Figure 10-19.

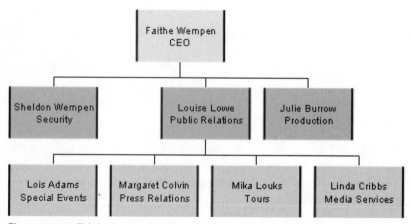

Figure 10-19: This is the standard layout for a branch of an organization chart.

In a large or complex organization chart, however, the diagram can quickly become too wide. Therefore, there are several "hanging" alternatives that make the chart more vertically oriented. The alternatives are Both Hanging, Left Hanging, and Right Hanging. They are just what their names sound like. Figure 10-20 shows examples of Right Hanging (the people reporting to the CEO) and Both Hanging (the Public Relations subordinates).

You can choose layouts for individual branches of the chart. Before selecting an alternative layout, you must click the supervisor box whose subordinates you want to change. Then on the Organization Chart toolbar, click the Layout button and choose one of the layouts from the menu (see Figure 10-21).

Selecting Multiple Shapes of a Common Type

When working with organization charts, it is often helpful to select all the boxes in a certain branch, or all the boxes at a certain level, before applying formatting.

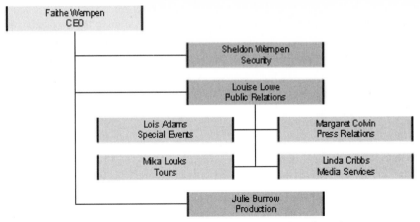

Figure 10-20: Hanging layouts make the chart more vertically oriented.

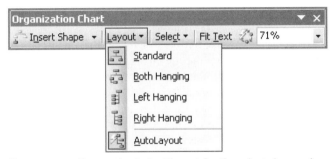

Figure 10-21: Choose the desired layout for the selected supervisor box.

For example, you might want to change the font color for all the boxes at a certain managerial level, or you might want to select all the connecting lines in the diagram so you can make them thicker or thinner.

The Organization Chart toolbar provides an easy way to make the selection. Select a box that belongs in the group you want to select. For example, to select all the managers of a certain level, select one such manager. Then click the Select button on the Organization Chart toolbar, opening a menu, and choose one of the following:

◆ *Level*: Selects all the boxes at the same level as the currently selected one.

◆ *Branch*: Selects all boxes in the same branch as this one.

◆ *All Assistants*: Selects all boxes with the Assistant type regardless of position.

◆ *All Connecting Lines*: Selects all connecting lines regardless of position.

TIP Many of the formatting changes you might want to make to the various boxes require you to turn off AutoFormat, AutoLayout, or both. If a certain formatting activity doesn't seem to work, try that. AutoLayout is on the Layout menu on the Organization Chart toolbar; to access AutoFormat, right-click anywhere on the chart.

Fitting Text

When you type more text into a box in an org chart than will fit, it hangs over the edges. Click the Fit Text button on the Organization Chart text box to automatically resize all text in the chart so that it does not overflow anymore. It makes all the text the same size on the whole chart, so it evaluates the needed size so that the largest amount of text will still fit.

Making Manual Layout Changes

You can turn off AutoLayout from the Layout button's menu on the Organization Chart toolbar, and once it's off you are free to drag the boxes and lines around. This enables you to change the positioning of individual boxes, and even to switch the chart to a left-to-right layout rather than a top-down one.

The connecting lines between boxes become somewhat twisted up if you start moving the boxes around dramatically. These are not just normal lines—they are a special class of AutoShape line called a connector. (You can choose connectors from the AutoShapes menu on the Drawing toolbar anytime, not just within an organization chart.) Notice when one is selected, there are little red balls on each end. The red indicates that the lines are successfully connected to boxes on both ends. If you drag a line so that it no longer connects at each end, that end's ball will turn green to warn you (see Figure 10-22).

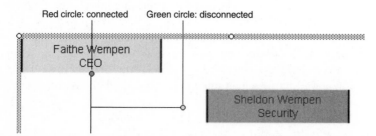

Figure 10-22: Connector lines show red when connected and green when disconnected.

As you move lines and boxes around, you might decide that a line should connect to a particular box on a different side of it than the default, to avoid having the line wrap around the box. To make that happen, do the following:

1. Click the line to select it.

2. Point the mouse pointer at the red circle to change, and hold down the left mouse button. The mouse pointer becomes a cross, and small blue markers appear on all four sides of the box, indicating the valid docking points.

3. Drag the red circle to one of the other docking points. When it is over a valid docking point, the mouse pointer will change to a square inside a crosshair, as shown in Figure 10-23.

4. Release the mouse button.

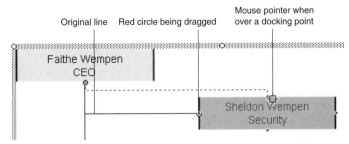

Figure 10-23: Changing the docking point of a connector line to a box.

Making Manual Formatting Changes

AutoFormat is turned on by default for the organization chart, just like with other diagram types. Right-click and choose Use AutoFormat to toggle it off. AutoFormat must be off in order to make manual formatting changes, and AutoLayout must be off in order to move boxes around.

 If you want the diagram to be based on an AutoFormat, make sure you apply the AutoFormat style you want first, before making any manual changes. If you later reapply a different AutoFormat, any manual changes you have made will be discarded.

When AutoFormat is off, you can format any shape on the org chart in any of the normal ways that you can format an AutoShape:

◆ Select a box and use the Fill Color, Line Color, and/or Text Color buttons on the Drawing toolbar to change any of those colors.

◆ Change the thickness of the shape border with the Line Style button on the Drawing toolbar.

◆ Make the shape border or any of the connector lines dotted or dashed with the Dash Style button on the Drawing toolbar.

◆ Right-click the box and choose Format AutoShape to make those same changes in the Format AutoShape dialog box instead, if you prefer.

◆ Apply a shadow or 3-D effect to the shape with the Shadow or 3-D buttons on the Drawing toolbar.

Figure 10-24 shows an example of some manual formatting applied to an organization chart.

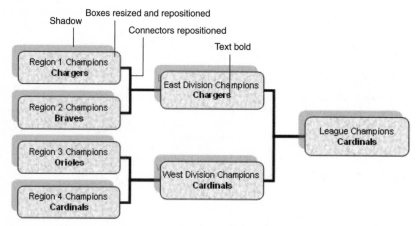

Figure 10-24: This organization chart has been manually formatted.

 You can make any of the shapes in an organization chart or diagram into a live hyperlink. Turn off AutoLayout and AutoFormat, then select the shape or text box, and choose Insert ➪ Hyperlink. Then create the hyperlink normally. I'll explain this more in Chapter 17.

Summary

In this chapter you learned to create and format various types of diagrams in Power-Point, including organization charts. There's one more major type of chart that we haven't talked about yet, though—graphs that show numeric data graphically as pie, bar, line, or area charts. That'll be the subject of Chapter 11.

Chapter 11

Using the Charting Tools

IN THIS CHAPTER

- ◆ Creating a chart in Microsoft Graph
- ◆ Working with chart data
- ◆ Changing the chart type
- ◆ Controlling chart options
- ◆ Formatting chart elements
- ◆ Using Excel charts

THE TERM "CHART" BY ITSELF IS FAIRLY GENERIC—lots of things can be considered charts, including diagrams, organization charts, and even tables. However, in this chapter, "chart" has a specific meaning: a graphical element that summarizes and presents numeric data, such as a pie chart or bar chart.

Some people prefer to use other charting tools, but the one that comes with PowerPoint is adequate for most needs. In this chapter you'll learn how to create charts using a utility called Microsoft Graph and how to manipulate and format them.

Which Charting Tool to Use?

Microsoft Graph is an integrated utility that comes with PowerPoint for creating charts. It is technically a separate application from PowerPoint, but it works so closely with PowerPoint that it seems like it is all one thing.

 Chart or Graph? In this chapter, the terms are synonymous. Microsoft itself even wavers as to the proper terminology. The utility for creating them is Microsoft Graph, but within Microsoft Graph the graphs are called charts. The Help system also uses "chart."

People who are familiar with the charting functionality of Excel will find Microsoft Graph familiar, as it's a somewhat stripped-down version of the same charting tools that Excel has. The "stripped down" aspect is mostly in the way the data is entered and selected; the formatting features are nearly identical between the two programs.

Here's the main difference. In Excel, you've got a big spreadsheet to work with, and you can pick and choose among the rows and columns to graph. You can also base graphs on cells that contain formulas that perform calculations on the contents of other cells. None of that is possible in Microsoft Graph. With Microsoft Graph there is a simple two-dimensional grid for the chart data, which must be contiguous. No formulas or functions are allowed.

If you need a simple chart based on a half-dozen or so rows and columns, Microsoft Graph is perfectly adequate. When more complex data manipulation is required than Microsoft Graph can handle, embedding an Excel chart can be a good solution. At the end of this chapter I'll explain how to do that.

Even Excel has its charting limitations. For scientific and technical presentations you may need a special science or math program such as MathCAD. These programs vary in their interoperability with PowerPoint, but most support Object Linking and Embedding (OLE) or at least the older Dynamic Data Exchange (DDE) technologies that enable you to copy-and-paste between programs. At the minimum all such programs should be able to output charts to graphic files, which you can then import as vector or raster graphics. You might also try embedding new objects from such programs on a PowerPoint slide using the Insert ⇨ Object command, as you did with Excel in Chapter 6.

Creating a Chart in Microsoft Graph

Microsoft Graph is fully integrated with PowerPoint, much like an embedded application, such that when you activate it, PowerPoint's regular menus and toolbars are replaced by Microsoft Graph's, but you remain in the PowerPoint application window. To return to normal PowerPoint menus and tools, simply click outside of the Microsoft Graph object's frame.

To start a new chart, display the slide on which you want to place it and then click the Insert Chart button on the Standard toolbar, or choose Insert ⇨ Chart. A new chart object appears on the slide, along with a floating datasheet window (see Figure 11-1).

Then edit the labels and values in the datasheet window to make the chart show the numbers and text you need. You can resize the datasheet window as needed to see more or less of it, and drag it around anywhere on the screen by its title bar.

 When you first start Microsoft Graph, it may move the Formatting toolbar up to the same line as the Standard one, even if you have set them to be on separate lines in PowerPoint. This is not the optimal arrangement because you can't see all the buttons. To move the Formatting toolbar back below the Standard one, just drag it down there, or click the down arrow at the right end of a toolbar and choose Show Buttons on Two Rows.

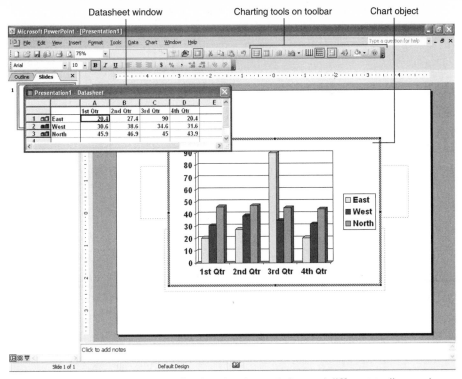

Figure 11-1: Microsoft Graph has a floating datasheet window and different toolbars and menus.

You can also start a new chart using a layout placeholder; Chart is one of the six on the multi-purpose layouts, and there is also a Title and Chart layout near the bottom of the list of layouts in the task pane.

Identifying Chart Elements

The sample chart shown in Figure 11-2 contains these elements:

◆ *Data series*: Each different bar color represents a different series: East, West, and North.

◆ *Legend*: Colored squares in the Legend box describe the correspondence of each color to a data series.

◆ *Categories*: The quarters listed along the bottom of the chart are the categories.

◆ *Category axis*: The horizontal line running across the bottom of the chart is the category axis, also called the X axis.

◆ *Value axis*: The vertical line running up the left side of the chart, with the numbers on it, is the value axis, also called the Y or Z axis.

◆ *Data points*: Each individual bar is a data point. The numeric value for that data point corresponds to the height of the bar, measured against the value axis.

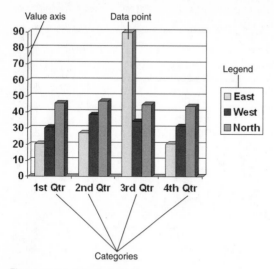

Figure 11-2: A typical chart.

 If you have taken geometry, you are probably used to calling the horizontal axis of the chart X and the vertical axis Y. However, on some 3-D charts, the vertical axis is called Z in some dialog boxes, and the axis that runs back-to-front is called Y. In most charts there is nothing plotted on the back-to-front axis, so you only deal with the vertical and horizontal axes (X and Z). Don't let the fact that the vertical one is called Z confuse you; it's really just your old familiar Y axis.

The data for the chart can come from anywhere—a PowerPoint or Word table, an Excel spreadsheet, or any other data source where there are delimited rows and columns. The data must be numeric, of course, except for a header row at the top and/or set of data labels in the leftmost column.

Basing a Chart on an Excel Worksheet

At first, it might seem counterintuitive to bring data from Excel into Microsoft Graph. After all, Excel's charting tools are superior to those of Microsoft Graph, so it would make more sense to make the chart in Excel and then copy the chart into PowerPoint. However, anytime you embed content from another program, you increase the file size, so using Microsoft Graph will keep the PowerPoint file size smaller.

To import data from Excel, do the following:

1. Insert a new Microsoft Graph chart, or display an existing chart. Double-click to make sure that Microsoft Graph is active.

2.  On the Standard toolbar click the Import File button. The Import File dialog box appears.

3. Select the file containing the data for the chart. It can be an Excel workbook or some other format where data is delimited. Then, click Open.

4. If you chose an Excel file that has more than one sheet, an Import Data Options dialog box appears prompting you to choose which sheet to use. You can also specify a certain range within that sheet (see Figure 11-3).

5. Make your selection and click OK. The data is imported into the datasheet for Microsoft Graph.

Figure 11-3: Select a worksheet to import data from, and optionally a range from it.

Basing a Chart on a PowerPoint Table

There isn't a really graceful way to convert a PowerPoint table to a chart; it's more of a manual cut-and-paste affair. Here's how:

1. In the table, select the cells that contain the data, plus any adjacent rows or columns that contain labels.

2. Start a new chart or double-click an existing one, displaying the data table.

3. Click in the datasheet in the cell where you want to begin pasting and press Ctrl+V or click the Paste button on the toolbar, or choose Edit⇨Paste.

If the copied table contained labels in the first row and the first column, you would want to paste into the top left cell in the datasheet (the unnumbered, unlettered one); otherwise, you would want to start pasting in A1 (which in the datasheet is actually the second row and second column because of the blank ones).

Working with Chart Data

First things first: does the chart contain the right data, presented in the right way? You've already seen how to type data into the datasheet or copy-and-paste data into it from some other source. Now let's look at some other things you can do that affect the chart data.

The datasheet should appear automatically whenever you open the chart for editing (by double-clicking it). If it does not appear, or if you accidentally close it, you can reopen it by clicking the View Datasheet button on the Standard toolbar.

Adding and Removing Data

The sample chart starts you out with four columns and three rows of data. You can have more or fewer just by typing them into the datasheet grid or deleting from there:

◆ *To add a row at the bottom*, simply type it in the first empty row. Type a label in the unlettered column at the left, and type the data in columns A, B, C, and so on. This adds a new category to the category axis of the chart.

◆ *To add a column at the right*, type it in the first empty column. Type a label in the unnumbered column at the top, and type the data in rows 1, 2, 3, and so on. This adds a new series to the legend and a new color of bar to the chart.

◆ *To add a row above an existing row, or add a column to the left of an existing column*, select the row or column that the new one should appear above or to the left of. To select it, click its number or letter. Then, choose Insert⇨Cells.

◆ *To delete a row or column*, select it and press the Delete key.

Including and Excluding Data

By default, all the data in the datasheet appears in the chart. You might occasionally want to exclude certain data without removing it from the datasheet, however. (For example, perhaps you want to make a different version of the chart for a certain audience.)

To exclude certain data, select that range of cells on the datasheet and then choose Data⇨Exclude Row/Col. If you selected an entire row or column, the exclusion occurs immediately; if you selected only certain cells, a dialog box appears prompting you to choose Rows or Columns. (You have to exclude entire rows or entire columns, not just individual cells.) When excluded, the selected row(s) or column(s) turn gray and no longer appear in the chart (see Figure 11-4).

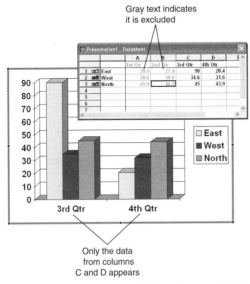

Figure 11-4: Columns A and B have been excluded.

You can also go the other way and include data that would not normally be included.

Plotting by Rows versus by Columns

The legend displays the different data series, with a colored square representing each series. By default, the rows of the datasheet form the data series, but if you want, you can switch that around so the columns form the series. Figures 11-5 and 11-6 show the same chart plotted both ways so you can see the difference.

To switch back and forth between plotting by rows and by columns, click the By Row or By Column buttons on the Standard toolbar.

A chart can carry a very different message when arranged by rows versus by columns. For example, in Figure 11-5, the chart compares the performance of the people against each other for each month. The message here is competition—which person did the best? Contrast this to Figure 11-6, where the series are the months. Here, you're invited to compare one month to another for each person. The overriding message here is time—which was each person's personal best month? It's easy to see how the same data can convey very different messages; make sure that you pick the arrangement that tells the story you want to tell in your presentation.

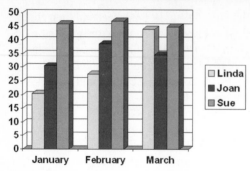

Figure 11-5: The data series are the people's names.

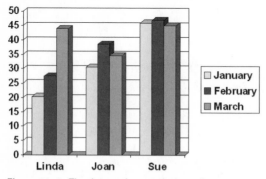

Figure 11-6: The data series are the months.

Changing the Chart Type

The default chart is a column chart, with vertical bars. There are lots of alternative chart types to choose from. Not all of them will be appropriate for your data, of course, but you may be surprised at the different spin on the message that a different chart type presents.

Many charts come in both 2-D and 3-D models. You choose which look is most appropriate for your presentation. Try to be consistent, however. It looks nicer to stick with all 2-D or all 3-D charts rather than mixing the types in a presentation.

Here are some of the types available:

◆ *Bar and column.* A column chart plots data with vertical columns. A bar chart is the same thing except the bars are horizontal.

◆ *Area and surface.* These charts convey the same information as column charts, but the area between the bars is filled in.

◆ *Line.* Line charts convey the same information as column charts, but instead of the bars, a line or ribbon runs where the tops of the bars would be.

◆ *3-D cones, cylinders, and pyramids.* These charts are just like columns except the bars have different, more interesting shapes.

◆ *Pie and doughnut.* These charts show how various parts relate to a whole, rather than showcasing individual number values. A pie shows a single data series, while a doughnut uses concentric rings to represent multiple series.

◆ *Bubble and scatter.* These charts show each bit of data as a point (or bubble) on a grid and are useful for spotting trends among lots of data points.

◆ *Radar.* This is a special-purpose chart that plots points on axes radiating from a center point. Most business presenters seldom use this type of chart.

Figures 11-7 through 11-9 show some examples of various chart types.

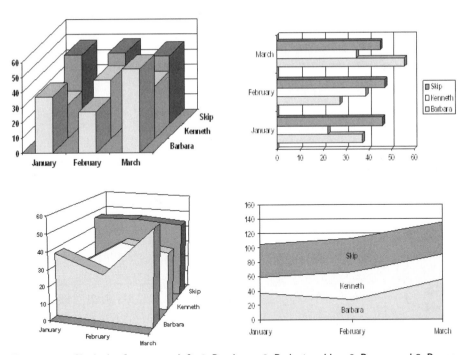

Figure 11-7: Clockwise from upper left: 3-D column, 3-D clustered bar, 2-D area, and 3-D area.

Choosing a Standard Chart Type

There are several ways to change the chart type. The easiest method is to use the drop-down Chart Type list on the Standard toolbar. It does not provide access to all of the types, but it can be handy if you happen to want one of the types it does provide (see Figure 11-10).

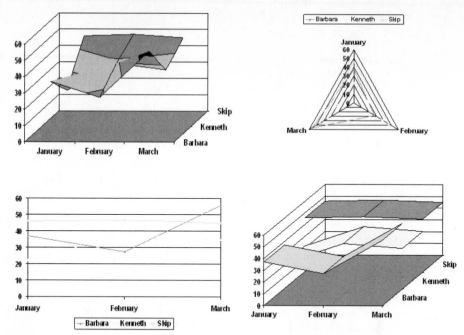

Figure 11-8: Clockwise from upper left: Surface, Radar, 3-D line, and 2-D line.

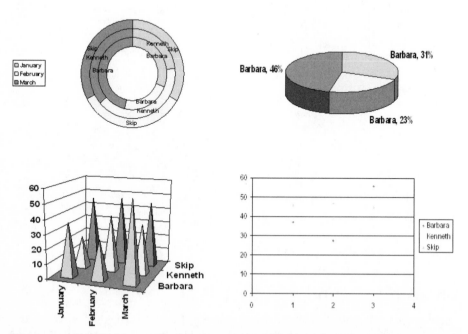

Figure 11-9: Clockwise from upper left: Doughnut, Pie, Scatter, and 3-D Pyramid.

Figure 11-10: Select a chart type from the Standard toolbar.

Another way to change the chart type is with the Chart Type dialog box. Follow these steps:

1. Choose Chart⇨Chart Type. This opens the Chart Type dialog box, shown in Figure 11-11.

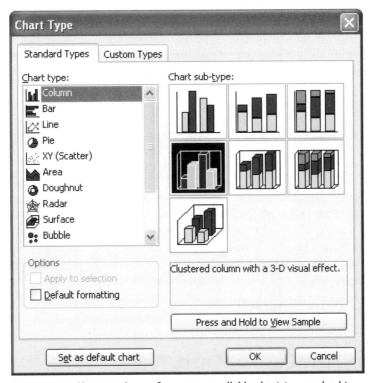

Figure 11-11: You can choose from every available chart type and subtype through this dialog box.

2. Click one of the chart types on the Chart Type list. The available subtypes appear in the pane to the right. For example, if you choose Column as shown in Figure 11-11, you can choose from among seven subtypes.

3. Click the subtype you want. If you want to see how the data will look with the chosen type, click and hold the Press and Hold to View Sample button.

4. When you are satisfied with your choice, click OK.

 The default chart type is Column. If you prefer a different chart type to be the default, make your selection in the Chart Types dialog box and then click the Set as Default Chart button before you click OK. This can save your time because you won't have to change the type of each chart that you create. This setting applies to your PC's installed copy of PowerPoint, not to the presentation file.

Choosing a Custom Chart Type

You may have noticed that there is a second tab in the Chart Type dialog box: Custom Types. When you click that tab (see Figure 11-12), a list of predesigned chart formats/types appears. You can select one of these custom types as a short-cut for choosing a particular chart type and formatting it in a certain way. For example, Figure 11-12 shows Blue Pie selected, and you can see an example of it in the Sample area. You could recreate this custom chart manually with a combi-nation of chart type and chart formatting commands, but it is much easier simply to apply the custom type from this list and then tweak it to create the look you want.

Making a selection on the Custom Types tab overrides any selection you have made on the Standard Types tab, and vice versa. Microsoft Graph goes with whatever you have most recently selected when you click OK.

 Applying a different chart type affects all data series by default, but you can also apply a different chart type to a particular data series. Select that series and then choose Chart ⇨ Chart Type. You can also format individual data series with dif-ferent styles of lines, bars, or whatever, through the Format Data Series dialog box for a particular series. This is covered later in the chapter in the *Controlling the Bar or Column Shape* section.

Creating New Custom Chart Types

If you frequently use the same formatting for charts, you can set up a chart just the way you want it in terms of type and formatting and then define that chart's design

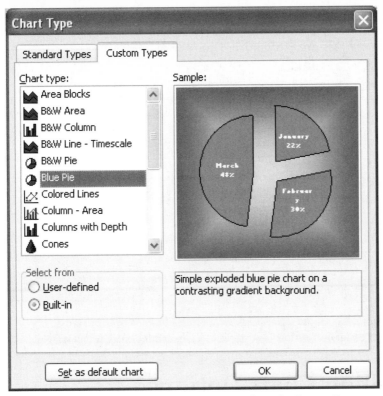

Figure 11-12: You can choose a custom chart type from the Custom Types dialog box.

as a custom chart. The custom chart will then be available from the Custom Types list (see Figure 11-12) when you select the User-Defined option button. (You learn more about chart formatting later in this chapter, so you may wish to skip this now and come back to it later.)

To create a custom chart type, perform the following steps:

1. Format any chart exactly the way you want it.

2. Choose Chart➪Chart Type, and display the Custom Types tab.

3. Click the User-Defined option button.

4. Click the Add button. The Add Custom Chart Type dialog box opens (see Figure 11-13).

5. Enter a name and description for the new chart type, and then click OK. The new chart appears on the list of user-defined custom charts.

This custom chart appears only on the PC on which you created it; it does not travel with the presentation if you move it to another PC.

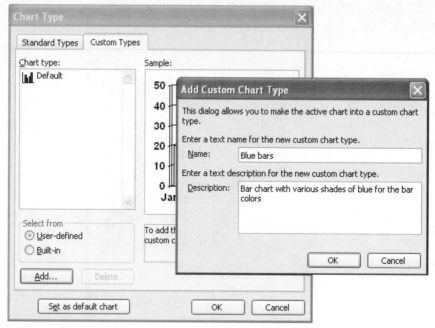

Figure 11-13: Create your own custom chart types using an existing chart as an example.

Controlling Chart Options

Chart type is just one of many options you can set for a chart. In the following sections I'll explain some of the elements you can display, hide, change, and reposition to change the way your data is presented.

Displaying and Positioning a Legend

The legend is the little box that sits to the side of the chart (or above or below it sometimes). It provides the key to what the different colors or patterns mean. Depending on the chart type and the labels in use, you may not find the legend useful.

If not, you can turn it off by clicking the Legend button on the Standard toolbar. Turning off the legend makes more room for the chart, and it grows to fill the available space (see Figure 11-14).

Hiding the legend is not a good idea if you have more than one series in your chart because the legend is instrumental in helping people decipher which series is which. However, if you have only one series, a legend is not necessary. It is also not necessary if you have some other indicators for the series, such as a data table or data labels that show the series.

Legend button

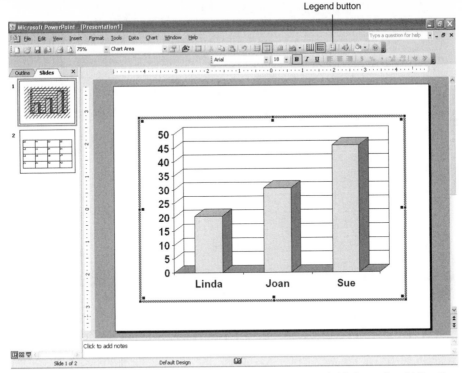

Figure 11-14: Hide the chart's legend if it doesn't provide any needed information; hiding it gives more room to the chart.

By default, the legend appears to the right of the chart, but you can place it somewhere else if you prefer. You can drag it anywhere you want it or change its position in the following way:

1. Choose Chart➪Chart Options.

2. Click the Legend tab. If the Show Legend checkbox is not already marked, mark it.

3. Select the option representing the desired position, for example, Top, Bottom, Right, and so on(see Figure 11-15). Then click OK.

 Don't worry if the text looks too big in the sample area or if some text is cut off, as shown in Figure 11-15. It will usually straighten itself out when you close the dialog box. And if it doesn't, you can always resize/reformat manually.

The controls on the Placement tab in Figure 11-15 refer to the legend's position in relation to the chart, not to the legend text's position within the legend box.

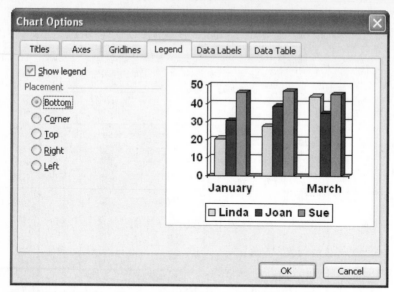

Figure 11-15: Position the legend in relation to the chart.

Some people find the above method preferable to dragging the legend to move it because it changes the shape of the legend box as needed to accommodate its new position. Notice in Figure 11-15, for example, that the legend box runs horizontally when under the chart, whereas it's vertically oriented when at the side.

You can also format the legend, just as you can format any other part of the chart. This is covered in detail later in the chapter, but if you want to experiment on your own, try dragging the selection handles for the legend's border to resize it and/or using the Font controls on the toolbar to change its font. You can also right-click it and choose Format Legend from the shortcut menu, or drag the legend where you want it.

Displaying Major and Minor Grid lines

Grid lines are the marks on the wall behind the chart that help your eyes track across and up from the category and value axes. In most cases the default gridlines are appropriate, but you may want to turn on the non-default gridlines if the chart is not easily readable.

If the audience needs to distinguish between two very similar values that are not adjacent on the chart, showing the minor gridlines can help the audience's eyes read the bars' positions better. For example, in Figure 11-16, the values of the bars are very similar, and it is difficult to tell exactly what value each bar represents. In Figure 11-17, with the minor gridlines turned on, it's easier to determine the value that each bar represents.

To control the display of major and minor gridlines, choose Chart ⇨ Chart Options, and on the Gridlines tab, mark or clear checkboxes for the various types of gridlines (see Figure 11-18).

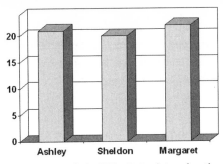

Figure 11-16: It is difficult to determine the exact values for these bars.

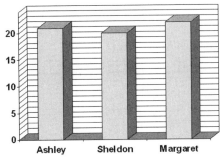

Figure 11-17: The minor gridlines make it obvious that the values for these bars are 21, 20, and 22.

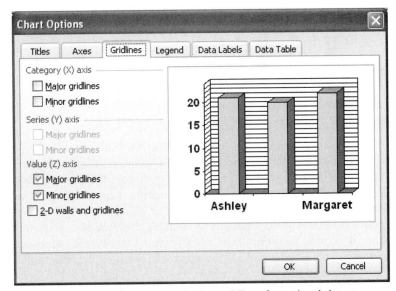

Figure 11-18: Turn on/off major and minor gridlines for each axis here.

Making the major and minor gridlines different thicknesses or line styles will often improve the readability of a chart. To format gridlines, choose Chart ⇨ Chart Options and then right-click the appropriate gridline and choose Format Gridlines. You can set the line thickness (weight), color, style, and scale there.

 If you just want to toggle the major horizontal and vertical gridlines on and off, there's an easier way: the Category Axis Gridlines and Value Axis Gridlines buttons on the Standard toolbar.

Changing the Axis Scale

When you have a situation like the one shown in Figure 11-17, where you have very similar values for all the bars, it can be difficult to discern the differences between the values even with the major and minor gridlines turned on.

It would be much easier to distinguish the values from one another if the scale were different. For example, in Figure 11-17, what if instead of the value (vertical) axis starting at 0 and ending at 25, it started at 19 and ended at 23? The differences between the values would be much more obvious then, as shown in Figure 11-19.

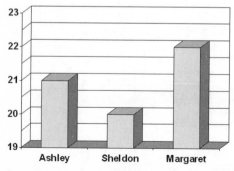

Figure 11-19: Change the value axis's scale to change the audience's perception of the differences between values.

You will probably never run into a case as dramatic as the difference between Figures 11-17 and 11-19 because Microsoft Graph has an Auto setting for the axis scale that's enabled by default. However, you may sometimes want to override the default scale for a special effect, such as to minimize or enhance the differences between data points. This is a good example of "making the data say what you want." If you wanted to make the point that the differences between the points are insignificant, you would use a larger scale. If you wanted to spotlight the importance of the differences, you would use a smaller scale.

Axis scale is adjusted in the Format Axis dialog box for each axis (see Figure 11-20). To display it, point the mouse at the axis, right-click, and choose

Format Axis. If there's no Format Axis command on the shortcut menu, you were not pointing at the right spot; try again.

 TIP   If you are having trouble selecting a part of the graph, use the drop-down list on the Standard toolbar to pinpoint it.

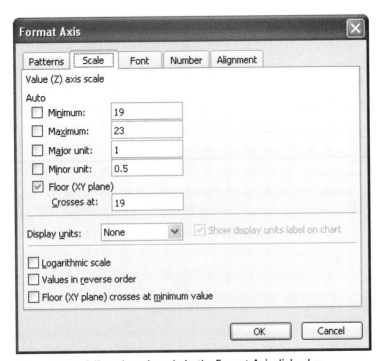

Figure 11-20: Adjust the axis scale in the Format Axis dialog box.

The Auto checkbox for each item sets it so that Microsoft Graph chooses the setting. If you do not want the automatic value, deselect the Auto checkbox for it and enter a number manually in its text box. The following lists what each value represents:

◆ *Minimum* is the starting number. The usual setting is 0, but in Figure 11-20 it starts at 19.

◆ *Maximum* is the top number. It is 23 in Figure 11-20.

◆ *Major unit* determines the axis labels (and also the major gridlines, if shown). On the chart in Figure 11-19, for example, notice that the numbers count by whole digits (19, 20, 21, 22, 23). That's because the Major Unit setting (as shown in Figure 11-20) is 1.

◆ *Minor unit* determines the placement of minor gridlines, if shown.

◆ *Floor (XY Plane)* or *Category (X) Axis* determines the place where the horizontal and vertical axes cross. This is normally the same as the Minimum value but could be different if you had a chart with values that descended below the horizontal axis line.

◆ *Logarithmic scale* is rarely used by ordinary folks. It recalculates the Minimum, Maximum, Major Unit, and Minor Unit according to a power of 10 for the value axis based on the range of data. (If that explanation doesn't make any sense to you, you're not the target audience for this feature.)

◆ *Values in reverse order* turns the scale backwards so the greater values are at the bottom or left.

◆ *Floor (XY plane) crosses at minimum value.* This sets the value of the Floor (XY plane) crosses at setting to the smallest value represented on the axis.

Figures 11-19 and 11-20 are for a 3-D chart. If it's a 2-D chart, instead of Floor (XY Plane) in the preceding options, you will see Category X instead. And depending on the chart type, you might have a "crosses at maximum value" option, which would run the X axis across the top instead of the bottom.

Changing the Axis Number Format

By default, the value axis shows plain numbers unless you have entered some type of special symbol such as dollar signs or percent signs in the data table along with your numbers.

To make the numbers on the value axis appear as currency, dates, or in some other special numeric format, right-click the axis and choose Format Axis, displaying the Format Axis dialog box (same as in the preceding section). Then, click the Number tab and choose a number format there (see Figure 11-21). These number formats are the same as the ones available in Excel.

Displaying Data Labels

Data labels announce the value, percentage, series, and so on for a bar, slice, or other value marker. They aren't appropriate for every chart, because they tend to crowd one another on charts with tightly packed bars or other data representations. The best place to use them is on a pie chart, where there's a fairly large expanse of area for each slice. Category and percentage data labels are shown in Figure 11-22. Notice that this figure doesn't contain a legend. It doesn't need one because the data labels convey the legend information.

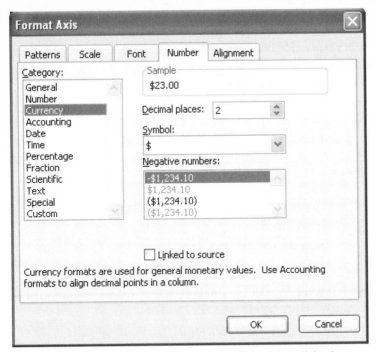

Figure 11-21: Adjust the number format in the Format Axis dialog box.

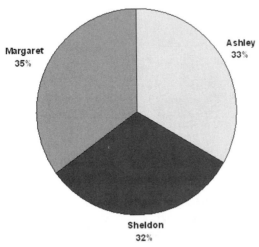

Figure 11-22: For some types of charts, data labels can help make the meaning clearer.

I have tinkered a bit with the formatting of the chart in Figure 11-22 to get it to look nicer. For example, I've made the data labels smaller in font size, and I've removed the black rectangular border around the plot area. If your chart is ugly, don't panic; you'll learn how to format it later in this chapter.

Data labels are controlled from the Chart Options dialog box (Chart➪Chart Options), on the Data Labels tab (see Figure 11-23). Mark the checkboxes there for each type of label you want. You can choose more than one, if desired:

◆ *Series name*: The names of the data series from the legend. If you use this one, you don't need the legend.

◆ *Category name*: The data from the category (X) axis.

◆ *Value*: The actual value from the cell on the datasheet.

◆ *Percentage*: What percentage of the whole each slice represents (not used on bar and column charts except for 100% stacked ones).

◆ *Bubble size*: Applicable only for bubble charts. Indicates what each size represents.

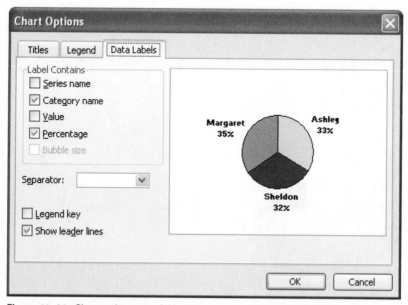

Figure 11-23: Choose the type of data labels you want to appear on your chart.

You can also indicate a separator character, which will appear between each label type if you choose more than one type.

The Legend Key checkbox turns on/off the block of color beside the data label that corresponds to the legend color for it. This can be useful on a stacked chart where the items are difficult to see because they're so small.

The Show Leader Lines checkbox enables/disables the use of callout lines that run between the labels and the corresponding slice or bar. On a simple chart, like in Figure 11-22, this is not necessary, but if you have a chart with many very thin pie slices it can help avoid confusion.

Adding Titles and Axis Labels

Most of the time, when you place a chart on a slide, that slide has its own title, so the chart itself does not need a separate title. However, if you have more on the slide than just the chart, it might be useful to have some text over the top of the chart to indicate why it's there. A title on the chart itself might also be useful if you plan to copy that chart into another application, such as Word.

Besides an overall title for the chart, you can also add labels to each axis to describe the unit of measurement it shows (for example, Millions or Salespeople). Figure 11-24 shows a chart with axis labels for both vertical and horizontal axes and a chart title.

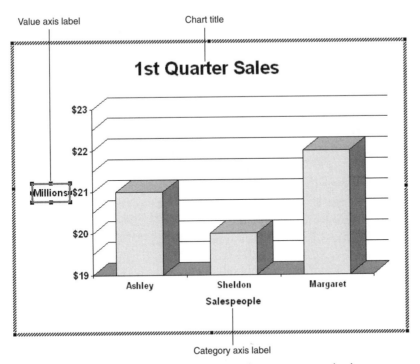

Figure 11-24: Axis labels can help explain a chart's message more clearly.

Titles and axis labels are set from the Chart Options dialog box (Chart⇨Chart Options), on the Titles tab (see Figure 11-25). Simply enter the text you want to appear in those locations and click OK. Each label appears in its own text box. Then format the text as you would any other text box (font, size, color, placement, and so on).

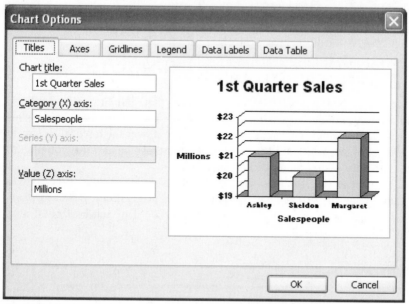

Figure 11-25: Enter the titles and labels you want to use.

 When you add titles, they take away from the available space for the plot area in the chart frame. The chart in the plot area appears smaller after you add titles because it has to shrink so that there will be room for the titles and labels to fit in the chart frame. One way to minimize the space taken up by these labels is to set them in a smaller font or, in the case of the vertical axis label, to rotate the text so it runs parallel to the axis. See *Formatting Titles and Labels* later in this chapter for more details.

Adding a Data Table

Sometimes the chart tells the full story that you want to tell, but other times the audience may benefit from seeing the actual numbers on which the chart is built. In those cases it's a good idea to include the data table with the chart. (The data table contains the same information that appears on the datasheet.)

To display the data table with a chart, click the Data Table button on the Standard toolbar (see Figure 11-26). If you don't see the Data Table button, make sure you have double-clicked the chart to activate it.

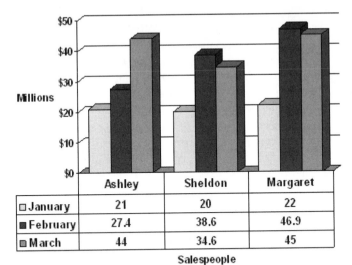

1st Quarter Sales

	Ashley	Sheldon	Margaret
□ January	21	20	22
■ February	27.4	38.6	46.9
▨ March	44	34.6	45

Salespeople

Figure 11-26: Use a data table to show the audience the numbers that formed the chart.

Sometimes Microsoft Graph doesn't do a very good job of appropriately sizing the fonts in the data table. If the text is too big, you can adjust it. Right-click the data table, choose Format Data Table, and then on the Font tab, choose a different font size. You can also control the gridline appearance for the data table from this same dialog box.

Formatting Chart Elements

As you have been working with the various chart elements so far in this chapter, perhaps you have been a bit disappointed in the look of some of the items. Now it's your chance to fix that. In the following sections, you learn about chart formatting. There is so much you can do to a chart that the subject could easily take up a whole chapter by itself. You can resize a chart, just like any other object, and you can also change fonts, colors, shading, background, 3-D angles, and much more.

Formatting the Plot Area and Chart Area

The *plot area* is a smaller frame within the larger chart frame. Almost everything in the chart frame is also within the plot area—only the chart title lies outside of it. (On some 2-D charts the legend also lies outside it.)

Depending on what type of chart it is and what you've done to it in the way of modifications, the plot area might not take up an appropriate amount of space within the chart frame. Fortunately, you can select and resize it the same as any other object with selection handles.

The plot area may or may not have a border around it. If it doesn't, you'll need to locate the plot area's border so you can click it to select it. One method is to move the mouse pointer from the vertical axis slowly out toward the edge of the chart frame until a ScreenTip appears that says Plot Area. Then, click to select the plot area's frame, as shown in Figure 11-27. You can also use the drop-down list on the Standard toolbar to select a chart element.

From there, you can use the selection handles to resize the plot area (which is limited by the outer frame of the chart area, of course.)

Once you've found the plot area, you can format it by adding a border and/or fill to it, the same as with any other object. (Use the Line and Fill tools on the Drawing toolbar, or right-click the plot area frame and choose Format Plot Area.) You can use fill effects, scheme colors, fixed colors, or any of the other line and fill options in PowerPoint.

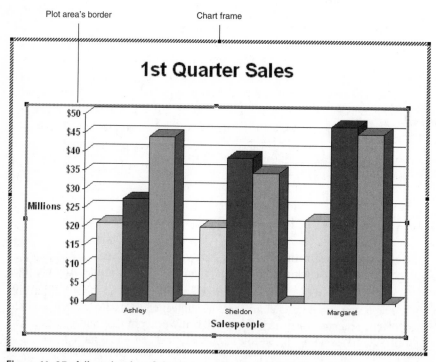

Figure 11-27: Adjust the size of the plot area inside the chart frame. You can also apply a border and/or fill to it, if desired.

Besides the plot area, there is also the chart area (that is, the space outside of the plot area but inside the chart frame). You can format it the same way as the plot area—with any fill and/or border desired. Selecting the chart area is handy for applying the same font formatting to all elements of a chart at once.

Formatting Walls and Gridlines

Any 3-D chart that can have gridlines can also have a wall. That includes Bar, Column, Area, Line, and so on, but not types like Pie or Doughnut. The *wall* is the area on which the gridlines appear. You can make the wall any color (or fill effect), or you can make it transparent so that the formatting of the plot area, chart area, or slide shows through.

The walls are formattable only on 3-D charts. To change the background behind a 2-D chart, apply the formatting to the plot area.

 The stacking order for a chart is this: Data point, wall, plot area, chart area, and slide background. If the first one is transparent, it'll display the color of the next one. If that one is transparent, it goes to the next one, and so on. Therefore, if you want the chart to appear to be sitting directly on the slide background, you would need to make the wall, the plot area, and the chart area all transparent (no fill).

To format a chart's wall, right-click the wall and choose Format Walls. There is only one tab in the Format Walls dialog box: Patterns. Select a border and shading for the wall.

 Try using a picture fill for a chart's wall or plot area that reflects something about that data. For example, look for some clip art with financial themes, or use the company's logo when plotting data specific to a certain company.

You saw earlier in the chapter how to turn major and minor gridlines on and off. You can format gridlines in the same way that you would format any other line-based objects. Just right-click a gridline and choose Format Gridline. Any changes you make affect all the gridlines of that type (for example, all horizontal major ones).

When you open the Format Gridlines dialog box, you see two tabs. One is for Scale, which is the same thing as the Scale settings for the axis that the gridline touches. Any changes made in one place are reflected in the other. The other is Patterns, and the controls there are the same as the controls for changing other chart parts. The only difference is that the None option is grayed out, because you can't turn gridlines off from here. You must turn them off through the Chart Options dialog box or with the gridlines buttons on the toolbar, or by right-clicking a gridline and choosing Clear.

Formatting Titles and Labels

As you learned earlier, you place titles and other labels on a chart through the Titles tab of the Chart Options dialog box (Chart⇨Chart Options).

Once you have the title or label on the chart, you can change its size, orientation, and font. Just right-click the title you want to format and choose Format Chart Title (or whatever kind of title it is; an axis's label is called Axis Title, for example). The Format dialog box appears for it.

There are three tabs in this dialog box: Patterns, Font, and Alignment. If you see only one tab (Font) in the dialog box, you have right-clicked the text itself rather than the text box. Close the dialog box and then click beside the text, rather than right on it, to select the text box. Then, right-click the text box's frame.

On the Patterns tab, shown in Figure 11-28, you can set a background color for the area behind the text. (Remember, all text sits in a text box on a slide, and each text box can have its own background formatting.) To place a border around the text box that contains the label, click the Custom option and then choose a line style, color, and weight. To use a background fill behind the text, click one of the colored squares in the Area part of the dialog box, or click the Fill Effects button to use fill effects such as gradients and textures.

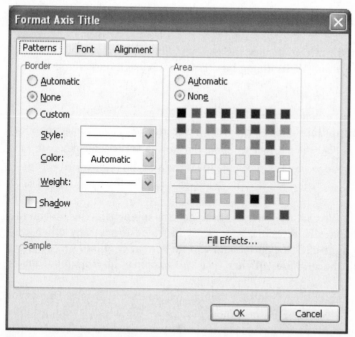

Figure 11-28: The Patterns tab controls the text box in which the title or label sits.

On the Font tab, you can use all the usual text effects that you learned about earlier in the book: font, size, font style, underline, color, and so on (see

Figure 11-29). You can also choose a background setting for your text in this box. If you set it to Transparent, whatever is behind the text box will show through as its background. If you choose Opaque, it will use its own color instead. The default is Opaque.

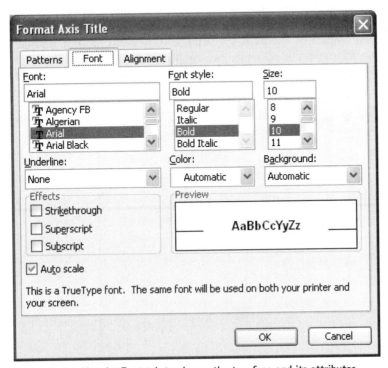

Figure 11-29: Use the Font tab to choose the typeface and its attributes.

The Auto Scale checkbox on the Font tab turns on/off the feature that resizes the text when you resize the text box or the chart area or plot area. It is on by default. You can turn this off if you want the text in the chart to be a certain size—for example, if you don't want the legend to automatically resize itself when you resize the plot area.

The text boxes that contain the chart title and axis titles are a little different from normal PowerPoint text boxes, in that they are not resizable. If you want a text box that is larger than it needs to be to accommodate this text, create a new text box on the chart by using the Text Box button on the Drawing toolbar instead of using Chart and Axis Titles. Using text boxes also allows you to insert line breaks if necessary, something that is not possible to control when using Chart and Axis Titles.

The Alignment tab controls the way the text is aligned in its text box. You can set both vertical and horizontal alignment, just like in table cells. However, vertical and horizontal alignments are usually a non-issue in a short label or title text box. The text box is exactly the right size to hold the text, so there is no way for the text to be aligned other than the way it is. Therefore, no matter what vertical and horizontal alignment you choose, the text looks pretty much the same. The only exception might be in a box with a long string of text.

The more useful alignment feature is the Orientation control. With it, you can rotate the text to any angle. For example, you can rotate the label for the vertical axis to run parallel to that axis (see Figure 11-30).

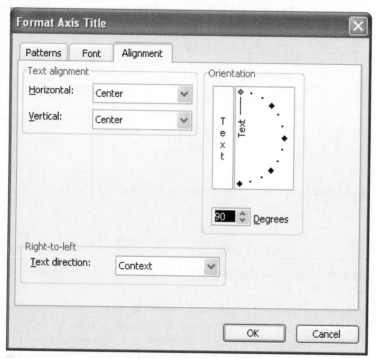

Figure 11-30: Change the text alignment and orientation on the Alignment tab.

By default, all text starts out formatted horizontally, at 0 degrees of tilt. (Exception: some Y-axis titles default to vertical.) But it doesn't have to stay that way; you can rotate it to any number of degrees from 1 to 359. (360 is a full circle, so 360 is the same as 0.) To rotate the text, drag the red diamond up or down in the Orientation area. The word Text rotates as you drag it. In Figure 11-30, it is dragged all the way to the top, resulting in text that runs straight up. You can also type an angle measurement (for example, 90) in the Degrees text box instead of dragging the red diamond, if you prefer.

Formatting the Legend

With a multi-series chart, the value of the legend is obvious—it tells you what colors represent which series. Without it, your audience won't know what the various bars or lines mean.

You can do all the same formatting for a legend that you can for other chart elements. Just right-click the legend, choose Format Legend, and then use the tabs in the Format Legend dialog box to make any of these modifications:

♦ *Change the background.* Use the Area controls on the Patterns tab.

♦ *Change the border around the legend.* Use the Border controls on the Patterns tab.

♦ *Change the font, font size, and attributes.* Use the controls on the Font tab or use the drop-down lists and buttons on the Formatting toolbar.

If you select one of the individual keys in the legend and change its color, the color on the data series in the chart itself will change to match. This can be useful with stacked charts, especially where it's sometimes difficult to select the data series you want.

Changing Data Series and Data Point Options

The individual bars, pie slices, lines, or whatever shape you have chosen can be formatted on a chart too. Before we get started with that, however, it's important that you understand the distinction between a data series and a data point.

A *data series* is all the bars, columns, and so on of a certain color. For example, in Figure 11-31 there are three data series, one for each person listed in the legend. Each data series consists of three bars. A *data point* is an individual piece of data, represented by an individual bar in Figure 11-31.

You can format either a data series or a data point. When you click once on a bar, the entire data series becomes selected. You can tell because a small square appears on each bar in the series (for a 2-D chart) or the bar becomes highlighted at the corners (for a 3-D chart), and if you right-click, a Format Data Series command will appear on the shortcut menu. If you click again on one of the bars in the selected data series, that individual bar will become selected, and the right-click menu will have a Format Data Point command instead.

So select whichever you want, and then right-click and choose the Format command. In the dialog box that appears, choose the colors, shapes, and other settings as desired. The following sections explain the individual settings available for a data series; the options for an individual data point are similar.

CHOOSING SERIES PATTERNS AND COLORS

On the Patterns tab of the Format Data Series dialog box, you can choose a color or pattern for all the bars in that series. This is virtually identical to the Patterns tab

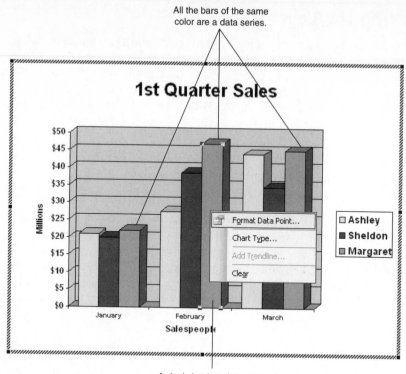

A single bar is a data point.

Figure 11-31: Understand the difference between a data series and a data point.

you saw in Figure 11-28; the only difference is an Invert If Negative checkbox. This swaps the foreground and background colors if the number represented by the data point is negative. It applies to bars and columns.

The colors you choose here apply only to the particular data series you right-clicked if there is more than one series in your chart. That's because you will want to select the color for each series separately rather than having them all appear in the same color.

 You can also choose a different color/pattern for an individual data point, but beware: in a multi-series chart, if you change the color of a bar, the audience will not be able to match it up with any of the items in the legend.

CONTROLLING THE BAR OR COLUMN SHAPE

On the Shape tab (see Figure 11-32), you can choose which shape you want the bars or columns to be. Why settle for an ordinary bar? Have some fun. Don't forget, however, that you don't want anything to distract from your message. Don't make each series in the chart a different bar shape, for example.

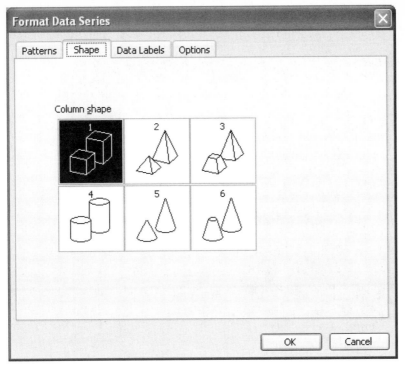

Figure 11-32: One the Shape tab, you can choose from among several bar and column shapes.

One of the coolest shapes is the sawed-off pyramid (number 3 in Figure 11-32). The highest data point is a full pyramid, but the shorter one looks like its top has been sawed off. Number 6 is the same effect but with a cone.

TIP To apply a different shape only to a certain series, select that series first. To apply it only to one point, select that point first.

CONTROLLING DATA SERIES LABELS FOR AN INDIVIDUAL SERIES OR POINT

The Data Labels tab in the Format Series dialog box contains the same controls as the Data Labels tab in the Chart Options dialog box, except that they apply only to the one selected series or data point. You could use these, for example, to add data labels only for the series that you want to spotlight.

SETTING THE GAP AND DEPTH ON A BAR OR COLUMN CHART

The Options tab in the Format Data Series dialog box is different for different chart types. It contains options specific to that type. For example, Figure 11-33 shows the options for a 3-D column chart. You can set the gap size between bars and the overall chart depth.

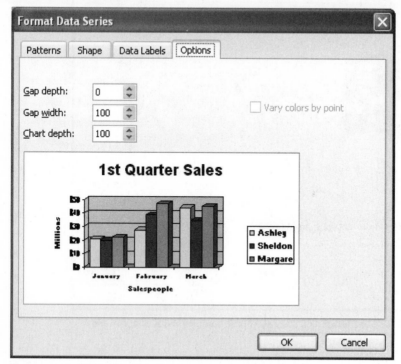

Figure 11-33: The Options tab for column and bar charts enables you to set the gaps between bars.

SETTING THE ROTATION OF THE FIRST SLICE ON A PIE CHART

Figure 11-34 shows the Options tab for a pie chart. Here you can set the angle of the first slide, effectively rotating the slices so that any slice is in any position you want. This can be very handy if the data labels are all bunched up on a pie chart. By modifying the position of the first slice, you can rotate the pie so that the large slices are at the top or bottom, where there is less room for labels, and the smaller slices are on the sides, where there is more room.

There is also a Vary Colors by Slice checkbox on the Options tab for pie charts. Leave this checked. If you deselect it, all the slices will be the same color, and you won't be able to tell them apart without data labels.

Changing 3-D Effect Settings

Not all charts in Microsoft Graph turn out perfectly right away. The application can't anticipate how your data is going to look in the chart, so sometimes in a 3-D chart some of the data bars or lines are obscured by other, taller ones in front of them. For example, in Figure 11-35, the middle row's values are not visible because the front

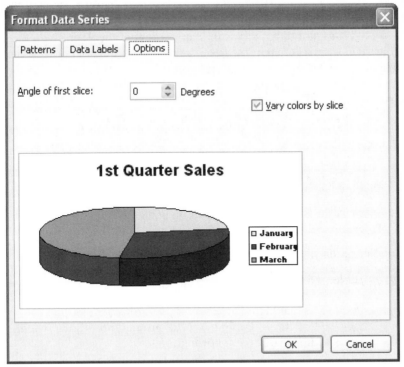

Figure 11-34: The Options tab for pie charts enables you to specify the angle of the first slice.

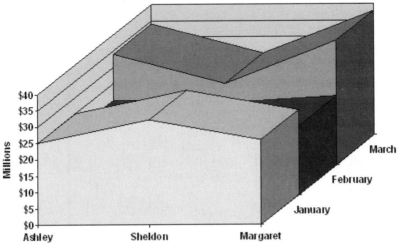

Figure 11-35: This chart could benefit from some 3-D setting changes to make the back rows more readable.

row is too tall. Modifying the 3-D settings makes the chart appear at a different angle and brings the obscured data points into view.

A quick way to tilt a chart differently is to drag a corner of the floor. To do this, point the mouse pointer at a corner of the floor so that a pop-up reads Corner. Then click and hold down the mouse button. The chart turns into a wireframe view of the chart. Drag, continuing to hold down the mouse button, to change the angle. Then release the mouse button to redisplay the chart.

You can also change the 3-D view with a dialog box, like this:

1. Choose Chart⇨3-D View.

2. In the 3-D View dialog box, click the buttons to change the view and then click Apply to try out the following settings:

   - *Elevation buttons*: Click to tilt the chart up and down, or enter a value in the Elevation text box.

   - *Rotation buttons*: Click to rotate the chart, or enter a value in the Rotation text box. When you rotate the chart so much that the walls are in the way, the walls move to the opposite side.

   - *Auto Scaling*: This maintains the aspect ratio of the chart, so when one dimension changes, the others do too. After turning this off, the Height box becomes available (see the following).

   - *Right Angle Axes*: This is similar to Auto Scaling; it forces the axes to remain at right angles to one another. Turning it off enables the Height box too, and it also brings the Perspective controls into view, shown in Figure 11-36.

   - *Perspective buttons*: Click these to tilt the 3-D perspective up or down, or enter a value in the Perspective text box.

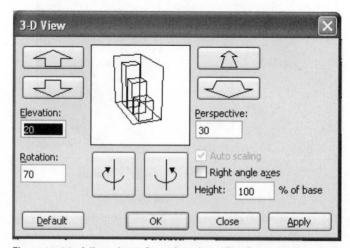

Figure 11-36: Adjust the 3-D settings here. The Perspective controls appear only when the Right Angle Axes checkbox is unmarked.

- *Height*: Enter a percentage of the base width to represent the height of the chart. The default is 100. A setting of less than 100 makes a short, squat chart, whereas a setting of more than 100 makes a taller, thinner chart. This is especially useful for 3-D pie charts that appear too thick.

3. Click OK. Figure 11-37 shows the chart from Figure 11-35 with 3-D settings applied to improve its readability.

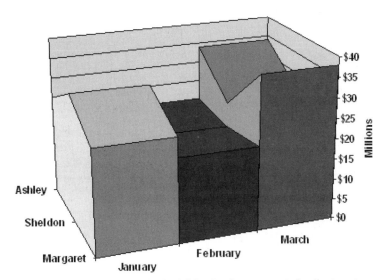

Figure 11-37: Now each series is visible, thanks to some 3-D adjustments.

Using Excel Charts

Throughout this chapter I've assumed that you're going to be using Microsoft Graph, but in reality, you may find it more helpful to create a chart in Excel and then bring it over into PowerPoint. Excel's charting tools are more feature-rich, and you can base your chart on the results of formulas and functions.

There are several ways to get an Excel chart into PowerPoint:

◆ Create the chart in Excel and then use Copy and Paste to bring it into Excel. This results in a static, embedded copy of the chart that PowerPoint that can be edited with Excel's tools.

◆ Paste the chart with Paste Special and specify Picture (Enhanced Metafile) as the file format, or place the chart on the Office Clipboard (Clipboard task pane) and paste it from there into PowerPoint. This results in a static copy of the chart that PowerPoint treats as a graphic.

◆ Paste the chart with Paste Special and specify a link to use OLE to link the original chart to your PowerPoint presentation. See *Linking and Embedding Excel Data* in Chapter 6 for details. If the chart changes in Excel, it will change in PowerPoint too. (You'd edit the chart in the original Excel file.)

◆ Embed a new Excel chart on the slide. This process is similar to the one described in Chapter 6 for embedding a new Excel datasheet. When you double-click the embedded chart, Excel's tools open for you to edit it. This is my favorite method in terms of convenience, but it can make the PowerPoint file much larger.

Here's a quick review of the process for embedding a new Excel chart:

1. Display the slide on which you want to place it, and then choose Insert Object.

2. Click Create New, select Microsoft Excel Chart, and click OK. A default chart appears.

3. Click the Sheet1 tab at the bottom of the chart window to switch to the datasheet, and replace the sample data with your own data.

4. Click back to the Chart1 tab and view the results. Then use the Excel menus and toolbars to format and edit the chart. Your primary tools will be the Chart toolbar (floating) and the Chart menu's commands.

5. When you're done, click the PowerPoint slide away from the chart to return to PowerPoint.

The embedded Excel chart appears as a graphic object on the slide, and you can move and resize it like any other graphic. To reenter it for editing with Excel, double-click it.

Embedded/linked charts created in earlier versions of PowerPoint (prior to 2000 SR-1) may appear flipped when opened in PowerPoint 2002 or 2003. If you still have access to the earlier version, open the file in that version, modify the object, save the file, and then open it in PowerPoint 2003. If you don't have the earlier version anymore, try the add-in available here: www.mvps.org/skp/unflip.htm. Note that it only works for PowerPoint files in 2000 or earlier format; if you save the presentation in 2002/2003 format, the add-in won't be able to help.

Summary

In this chapter you learned all about Microsoft Graph, including how to create, edit, and format charts in it. This concludes the section of the book that covers still images. In Chapter 12, we'll start a whole new topic—multimedia—beginning with a look at sounds and narration.

Part IV

Motion Images and Effects

Chapter 12

Sound Effects, Soundtracks, and Narration

IN THIS CHAPTER

◆ Understanding sound files

◆ Placing a sound icon on a slide

◆ Fine-tuning sound play settings

◆ Applying a sound effect to an object

◆ Associating CD tracks as soundtracks

◆ Sequencing sound clips with the advanced timeline

◆ Recording sounds and narration

HAVE YOU EVER WATCHED A MOVIE with the sound turned off? It's not the same, is it? Sounds, speech, and music make an enormous difference in the audience's understanding of the message. In this chapter, I'll explain when and how to employ sounds, music, and narration in a PowerPoint presentation.

Because It's There...

Let's get something straight: "because it's possible" is not a good reason for using sound in a presentation. Nobody in the audience is going to think you are clever for figuring out how to insert gratuitous sound effects into your show. Sounds should serve the purpose of the presentation.

That said, there are many legitimate reasons for using sounds in a presentation. Just make sure you are clear on what your reasons are before you start working with them. Here are some ideas:

◆ You can assign a recognizable sound, such as a beep or a bell, to each slide, so that when your audience hears the sound, they know to look up and read the new slide.

◆ You can record a short voice-over message from a CEO or some other important person who couldn't be there in person.

315

◆ You can punctuate important points with sounds or use sounds to add occasional humorous touches.

However, if you are trying to pack a lot of information into a short presentation, you should avoid sounds as they take up time playing. You should also avoid sounds and other whimsical touches if you are delivering very serious news. You may also want to avoid sounds if you will be using a very old and slow computer to present because any kind of media clip will slow such a system down even more, both when loading the presentation and when presenting it.

Keeping all this in mind, there are several ways to include a sound in a presentation:

◆ You can place a sound icon on the slide so that the sound plays whenever anyone points to or clicks the icon. This is useful in an interactive presentation because it gives the audience a choice of whether to play the sound.

◆ You can associate the sound with an object, such as a graphic, so that the sound plays when anyone points to or clicks that object. This is another good one for interactive presentations.

◆ You can associate a sound with an animation effect so that the sound plays when the animation effect occurs.

◆ You can associate a sound with a slide transition so that the sound plays when the next slide appears.

◆ You can insert a sound that plays automatically in the background as the presentation progresses, like a soundtrack. This can either be a sound clip or a track from an audio CD.

◆ You can record voice-over narration that explains the slides to the audience as they watch them. This is good for stand-alone presentations without a live speaker.

For more on how to associate a sound with an animation effect, see Chapter 14. Turn to Chapter 13 for how to associate a sound with a slide transition.

Understanding Sound Files

Computer sound files come in many different formats, but there are two broad categories: wave and MIDI.

The term *wave* can refer to a specific file format that has a .wav extension, but it can also refer generically to any sound file that has an analog origin. For example, when you record sound using a microphone, the resulting file is a wave file in a generic sense of the word because it was originally a "sound wave" in the air that the microphone captured. The tracks on an audio CD can also be considered wave files because at some point, presumably, a person went into a recording studio and made music with voice or instruments that was recorded. Similarly, the very popular MP3 music format is a wave format. Other wave formats include .rmi, .au, .aif, .wma, and .aifc. Wave files are very realistic sounding because they are basically recordings of real-life sounds. The drawback to wave files is that the file size is typically large. It's important to remember that "wave" in a generic sense is different from WAV the file format. Many of the Windows and Office sound effects are in WAV format, and WAV format is the only sound format that can be embedded in a PowerPoint presentation. WAV is far from the only wave type of sound, however.

The other category is Multi-Instrument Digital Interface (MIDI), which refers to the interface between a computer and a digital instrument such as an electric keyboard. When you make a MIDI recording, there is no analog source—it is purely digital. For example, you press a key on a keyboard, and that key press is translated into an instruction and written in a computer file. There is no microphone and no sound waves in the air. The sound it makes is completely up to the software.

MIDI files usually have a .mid extension. They are smaller in size than wave files. Several minutes of recording typically takes up much less than 1MB of space. The drawback to MIDI music is that it can sound rather artificial and computer-like. A computer emulating a saxophone is not the same thing as a real saxophone, after all.

It's important to understand the difference between wave and MIDI so you can choose the right format when recording sounds for your presentation or when choosing recorded music. Keep in mind that whenever you use a wave file in a presentation, you may be adding considerable bulk to the presentation's file size (unless you link to an external wave file, in which case you would have to make sure the file continued to be available). Also, keep in mind that when you choose MIDI, you get a different type of music, one that is more artificial-sounding.

The sounds that come with Microsoft Office are royalty-free, so you can use them freely in your presentation without paying an extra fee. If you download sounds from the Internet or acquire them from other sources, however, you must be careful not to violate any copyright laws. Sounds recorded from television, radio, and audio CDs are protected by copyright law, and you or your company might face serious legal action if you use them in a presentation without the permission of the copyright holder.

Placing a Sound Icon on a Slide

The most elementary way to use a sound file in a presentation is to place the sound clip directly on the slide as an object. An icon appears for it, and you can click the icon to play the sound during the presentation, or you can set it up to play automatically.

 TIP To "hide" the sound icon, drag it off the edge of the slide. The sound will still work, but the audience won't see the icon. Of course, you won't be able to click it during the presentation, so you'll need to set it up to play automatically.

You can either place a sound from the Clip Organizer or insert a sound file from your computer, the same as with clip art (see Chapter 9). However, many experts recommend that you not use the Clip Organizer for organizing and inserting sounds because the path where Clip Organizer files are stored is typically several levels deep on the hard disk (or on the Internet), which makes it awkward for the sound file to be linked. (And remember, unless it's a WAV file, it's always linked rather than embedded.)

Working with Sounds in the Clip Organizer

Everything you learned in Chapter 9 about the Clip Organizer applies to sound files as well as artwork. Choose Insert⇨Movies and Sounds⇨Sound from Clip Organizer to display the Clip Art pane with the file type set for Sounds (see Figure 12-1). Notice that when you access the Clip Organizer this way, the Results Should Be setting is automatically set to Sounds only. If you access the Clip Organizer in some other way, you would need to manually change this setting to find only the sound clips. You can enter keywords to narrow down the choices the same as you do with artwork.

 NOTE The icon for the sound clips in the Clip Organizer pane may vary depending on what application is configured as the default player for wave files on your PC. On my PC the default is the Apple iTunes player, for example.

With clip art, you see previews of the clips before you insert them, but with sound files, the icon is generic for all sounds. Therefore, you will probably want to preview various clips before selecting one. To do so, right-click a clip and choose Preview/Properties. In the Preview/Properties dialog box that appears, play the clip (click the Play button if the clip does not play automatically). To preview other clips without closing the dialog box each time, click the Next Clip button (see Figure 12-2).

One thing that's different for sounds versus images is that a dialog box appears asking when you want the sound to play: Automatically or When Clicked (see Figure 12-3). If you choose Automatically, the sound will play automatically when the slide appears. Otherwise, it will play as specified by its animation settings.

Figure 12-1: Search the Clip Organizer for sounds from your hard disk and from Microsoft's Office and Web collections.

Setting a sound clip to play automatically sets up a custom animation for it that makes the sound play After Previous, where the previous event is the appearance of the slide itself. That makes it seem like the sound is playing automatically when the slide appears, but those are actually two separate events. In Chapter 14 you will learn about fine-tuning custom animations.

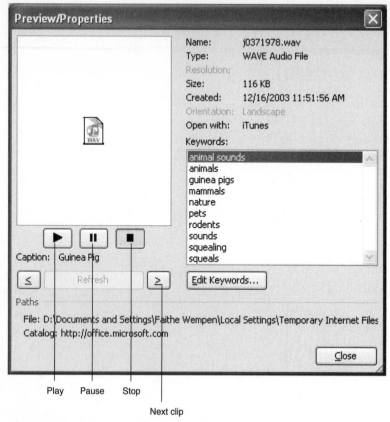

Play   Pause   Stop

Next clip

Figure 12-2: Preview a clip in the Preview/Properties box.

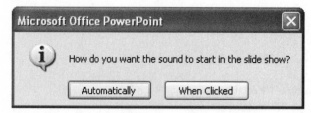

Figure 12-3: Specify when the sound should play.

Inserting a Sound from a File

As you learned in Chapter 9, you can insert your own clips into the Clip Organizer to make them accessible from there, but if you're just going to use the clip once, it makes more sense to insert it from a file instead.

To insert from a file, choose Insert⇨Movies and Sounds⇨Sound from File. Then, select and insert the sound the same as you would any other file (a picture, for example, as in Chapter 8). You see the same dialog box as shown in Figure 12-3, prompting you to indicate whether the sound should play automatically or when clicked.

Embedding or Linking Sound Files

When you insert a sound using the Insert⇨Movies and Sounds⇨Sound from File command, or use the Clip Organizer, WAV files smaller than a certain size will be embedded, while sounds larger than that specified size will be linked. This is automatic; you can't directly choose which files to link and which to embed.

However, you can change the cutoff point for the file size. To do so, follow these steps:

1. Choose Tools⇨Options.

2. Click the General tab.

3. Enter a file size in the Link sound files greater than __ kb box.

4. Click OK.

So which is better—embedded or linked? It all depends on your priorities. Embedded sound files travel automatically with the presentation file, so you do not have to worry about copying them separately if you copy the presentation file. However, they do add to the size of the PowerPoint file. Linked sound files take up virtually no space in the presentation file, but they must be available whenever the presentation is shown.

 If you plan on a sound file being linked, place it in the same folder as the presentation file before inserting it. This will ensure a relative reference to the link, so that when you move the files to another location the link will retain its integrity.

Sources of Sound Files

There are sound collections available all over the Internet, just like there are clip art collections. You can also buy sound collections on CD. If you find yourself putting together lots of presentations, or searching the Internet for hours to find specific sounds for this or that purpose, you might find it more cost-effective to simply buy a good collection of sounds.

Here are some Web sites where you can find some sounds:

◆ A1 Free Sound Effects (www.a1freesoundeffects.com/noflash.htm). Lots of free sounds for non-commercial use. You can also buy them for commercial use quite cheaply.

◆ Microsoft (`http://office.microsoft.com/downloads/2002/ Sounds .aspx`). Microsoft offers a nice collection of free sounds to work with Office versions 2000 and higher. Add them to the Clip Organizer for easy retrieval later.

◆ Partners in Rhyme (`www.musicloops.com`). Sound and music collections are for sale, plus some free ones for download. Their background music clips are cool because they are set up for perfect looping—that is, continuous play without a noticeable break between the end and the beginning.

The Microsoft Clip Organizer (see Chapter 9) can also be a source of sounds from Microsoft's collection of clips. Although the collection of sounds is not as extensive as that of clip art, you may be able to find something of use. The Clip Organizer searches `http://dgl.microsoft.com`.

Fine-Tuning Sound Play Settings

When you insert a sound, as you saw earlier in the chapter, you choose Automatically or When Clicked as the trigger. The following sections explain how to fine-tune those settings.

Mouse Click and Mouse Over

Any object in PowerPoint can be set up to do something when the mouse clicks it, when the mouse points at it, both, or neither. "Something" can be anything from playing itself (if it's a playable object like a sound or video), running an application, exiting the presentation, or just about anything else.

In the case of a sound file, if you chose When Clicked as the trigger when inserting it, PowerPoint sets it to be triggered by the Mouse Click action setting. To see this, do the following:

1. Right-click the sound file and choose Action Settings.

2. Check the setting on the Mouse Click tab. If you chose When Clicked when you inserted the sound, the Object Action will be set to Play, as shown in Figure 12-4. If you chose Automatically when you inserted the sound, None will be chosen here instead.

You can also set the sound to play when the mouse pointer moves over the icon, on the Mouse Over tab. This tab's buttons and controls are identical to those on the Mouse Click tab. You can have separate settings for the mouse click and mouse over actions, and one does not preclude the other. For example, you can specify that the sound play both on mouse click and mouse over.

Figure 12-4: The Action Settings dialog box specifies that a sound should play when clicked.

Adjusting the Sound Play Settings for Custom Animation

When you choose Automatically as the setting when inserting the sound, it sets it up to play at the exact moment that the sound icon appears on-screen, with no delay. You can change this so that there is a delay, you can mix the sound icon in with other custom animation sequences, or you can turn it off so that the sound does not play automatically at all.

As mentioned earlier, the Automatically setting configures a custom animation event for the sound clip. To see those settings, choose Slide Show⇨Custom Animation. The Custom Animation task pane appears. The clip will have an After Previous designation and appear at the top of the list (see Figure 12-5).

Notice in Figure 12-5 the following points:

◆ There is a 0 next to the sound icon and also next to its entry in the task pane. Numbering for custom animation starts with 0, and this is the first (and only) custom animation set up for this particular slide.

◆ The clock icon next to the clip in the task pane indicates that it is set to play automatically. If it were set to play on mouse click, it would be a mouse icon instead.

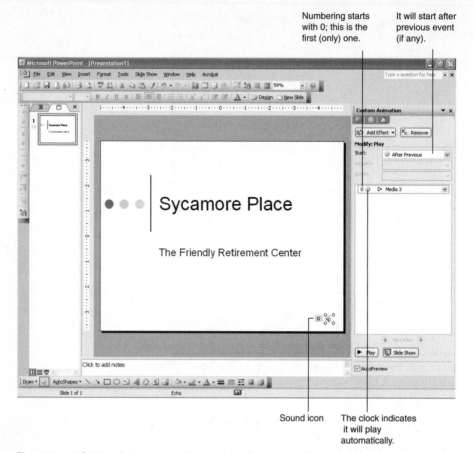

Figure 12-5: Custom Animation settings let you fine-tune when a sound will play.

◆ The Start setting is After Previous, which means that the event will occur when the previous event has finished. In this case it is the first event on the slide, so there is no previous event. Therefore, the appearance of the slide itself is the previous event, and the sound will play immediately after the slide appears.

TURNING AUTOMATIC PLAY ON/OFF

To turn off the automatic play for the clip, open the Start drop-down list and choose Start on Click. This will make the sound play only when a mouse click occurs (see Figure 12-6). If you want to disable it from playing completely, delete it from the Custom Animation task pane entirely by selecting it there and pressing Delete.

It's important to note that the mouse click described above is *not* the same mouse click event as the On Click action from the Action Settings dialog box (see Figure 12-4). The On Click event in the Action Settings box refers specifically to clicking the sound icon. The Start On Click action in the Custom Animation task pane refers to any click when the mouse is pointing anywhere on the slide.

Figure 12-6: Choose when the sound should begin to play.

DELAYING OR REPEATING THE SOUND

Depending on the situation it may be useful to have the sound play after a short delay, or to repeat it more than once. In Chapter 14 you will learn more about setting animation options, but here's a quick set of steps specifically for sounds:

1. Display the Custom Animation task pane if it does not already appear.

2. On the slide, select the icon for the sound. A gray box appears around its name in the task pane.

3. Click the down arrow next to the clip's name on the task pane and choose Timing. The Play Sound dialog box appears with the Timing tab displayed.

4. Enter a number of seconds in the Delay box. The delay will be between the time the previous event happens (such as the slide appearing initially) and the sound begins.

5. Open the Repeat list and choose a number of times that the sound should repeat (2, 3, 4, 5, 10, Until Next Click, or Until Next Slide). You can also type in a number if you want some other number than the one shown.

6. (Optional) Click the Triggers button to open the additional controls, as shown in Figure 12-7.

7. If you chose On Click for the start, do one of the following:

   a. If the sound should play when any click occurs, choose Animate as part of click sequence.

   b. If the sound should play when a specific object is clicked (and this can be the sound icon itself but does not necessarily need to be), choose Start effect on click of and then choose the object from the drop-down list.

8. Click OK.

Figure 12-7: Use the Timing controls to set a delay for when the sound will play.

 TIP If you don't want the sound icon to appear on the slide but you want to be able to click something in particular to make it play, drag the slide icon off the slide and then set the Start effect on click of setting in step 7 to some other visible element on the slide, such as the title text box.

SPECIFYING START AND STOP POINTS

There might be times when you'll want to start the clip from some point other than the beginning. For example, maybe you recorded a really good sound clip except that the first five seconds are garbled or contain something inappropriate for your use.

Professionals typically edit sounds in a third-party editing program rather than trying to edit them in PowerPoint, as you get much more precise controls. However, the following will serve to set up rough start and stop points.

To control the starting point for a clip, do the following:

1. From the Custom Animation task pane, open the menu for the sound clip (click the down arrow next to it) and choose Effect Options. The Play Sound dialog box opens with the Effect tab displayed, as shown in Figure 12-8.

Figure 12-8: Specify at what point the clip will start and stop.

2. In the Start Playing area, choose one of these options:

   From beginning to use the default play mode.

   From last position if you want it to pick up where you left off when you stopped it earlier.

   From time, and then enter the number of seconds into the clip that the clip should begin playing.

3. In the Stop Playing area, choose one of these options:

   On click to stop the sound with the next mouse click.

   After current slide to stop the sound when the slide is replaced by another on-screen or when the clip finishes playing the specified number of times, whichever comes first.

   After_slides and then enter a number of slides.

4. Click OK.

You might have also noticed the Enhancements section in Figure 12-8. For a sound clip, the only thing you can do is specify what happens to the icon after animation. The default is Don't Dim, which is basically "do nothing." You can choose to dim the icon, hide it, or make it a different color after it executes.

SPECIFYING THE SOUND VOLUME

When you give your presentation, you can specify an overall volume for it through the computer's volume control in Windows. However, sometimes you might want one sound to be more or less loud in comparison to the others.

To change the volume for a specific sound, right-click its icon and choose Edit Sound Object. The Sound Options dialog box opens. Click the speaker icon button in the dialog box to display a volume slider, and then drag it up or down (see Figure 12-9).

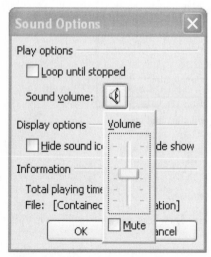

Figure 12–9: Adjust the volume for an individual sound in comparison to the baseline volume for the entire presentation.

The sound will play at a consistent volume throughout the duration of the clip; you can't make it play louder or softer at different points. If you need that capability, use a sound-editing program on the clip before inserting it in PowerPoint.

 The volume control in the Sound Options dialog box works for only certain audio formats, even though the controls for it appear regardless of the clip's format. The sound volume setting works for AIF, AIFF, AIFC, AU, M3U, SND, and WMA formats, but is ignored for CD audio, WAV, MIDI, MP2, MP3, MPA, and RMI formats. For those latter formats, you'll need to set the volume in a sound-editing program before inserting them into PowerPoint.

An add-in is available that gives you more control over volume, including during a presentation. You can set a separate volume level for each slide, create a mute control for use during a presentation, and more. See `http://officeone .mvps.org/volctrl/volctrl.html`.

Applying a Sound Effect to an Object

Many presenters prefer to assign sounds to clip art or other objects on the slide rather than to use a separate sound icon. That way they still have precise control over when the sound plays, but they don't have to deal with having the icon on the slide.

Although you can assign a sound to any object, including text boxes, most people assign their sounds to graphics. For example, you might attach a sound file of a greeting from your CEO to the CEO's picture.

To assign a sound to an object, use the Action Settings for that object, as follows:

1. Right-click the object and choose Action Settings. The Action Settings dialog box appears. This is the same one you saw back in Figure 12-4.

2. Click either the Mouse Click or Mouse Over tab, depending on what you want. Mouse Click will play the sound when you click the object; Mouse Over will play the sound when you point to it with the mouse.

3. Select the Play Sound checkbox. Then, open the drop-down list (see Figure 12-10) and choose a sound, or choose Other Sound to open the Add Sound dialog box and pick a sound from any location. There are a variety of sounds in C:\Windows\Media, for example.

4. Click OK to close the dialog box.

The first time you select a sound from the Play Sound list, you may be prompted to reinsert your Office or PowerPoint CD so PowerPoint can install the needed sound files. Just follow the prompts.

Figure 12-10: Choose a sound to assign to an object.

Associating CD tracks as Soundtracks

Adding a CD audio clip to a slide is much like adding a regular sound clip. You place the clip on the slide, and a little CD icon appears that lets you activate the clip. Then you can set properties for the clip to make it play exactly the way you want. It's different, however, in that the audio track is not stored with the presentation file. (It's too big!) Therefore, the audio CD must be in the CD drive of the computer that you're using to present the show. You can't use CD audio tracks in presentations that you plan to distribute on self-running data CDs or over the Internet because the computers on which it will run will not have the audio CD.

If you need to include audio from a CD in a presentation that will be shown on a PC without access to the original audio CD, you can record a part of the CD track as a WAV file using Windows Sound Recorder or some other audio-recording utility. Keep in mind, however, that wave files can be extremely large, taking up many megabytes for less than a minute of sound. To keep the size smaller, consider instead using Window Media Player to copy the track from the CD to your hard disk as a Windows Media Audio (wma) format file, or using MP3 or ASF format through some other third-party audio-ripping program. And as always, make sure you are not violating any copyright laws.

To play a CD track for a slide, you must place an icon for it on the slide (or drag the icon off to the side of that slide). You can actually place a range of tracks, such as 1 through 4 from a CD, using a single icon.

Placing a CD Soundtrack on a Slide

To place a CD icon on a slide, follow these steps:

1. Choose Insert⇨Movies and Sounds⇨Play CD Audio Track. The Insert CD Audio dialog box appears.

2. Enter the starting track number in the Start at Track box under Clip Selection (see Figure 12-11). The default is 1.

3. Enter the ending track number in the End at Track box. The default is the last track on the CD.

Figure 12-11: Specify the starting and ending track, and optionally, a time within those tracks.

If you want to play only a single track, the Start at Track and End Track numbers should be the same. If you want a range of tracks, make the range inclusive of the last track; for example, if you want 1, 2, and 3, put track 3 as the ending track (as opposed to track 4).

If the End at Track appears as 1 with a time of 00:00 seconds, PowerPoint is not correctly reading your CD. You will be able to place the CD icon on the slide, but the CD tracks will not play during the presentation. Try removing and reinserting the CD in the drive. Or, if you have two CD drives in your computer, try putting the CD in the other one. On some systems PowerPoint will only see the CD drive with the lower drive letter. For example, if the CD drives are D and E, it will only see D.

4. If you want to begin the starting track at a particular spot (other than the beginning), enter that spot's time in the Time box for that line. For example, if you want to start the track 50 seconds into the song, enter 00:50.

5. The end time that appears for the End at Track is the total number of seconds from the starting point to the end of the specified track. If you want to end the ending track earlier than that, decrease that number of seconds.

6. Click OK. A message appears asking whether you want it to play Automatically or When Clicked. Make your selection.

7. The CD icon now appears in the center of the slide. Drag it elsewhere if needed, or drag it off the slide completely (provided you do not need to click it to play it). You can also resize its icon as you would any graphic.

Making a CD Soundtrack Continue Across Multiple Slides

By default, a CD soundtrack plays only when the slide on which its icon appears is displayed on-screen. If you want the CD to continue playing across multiple slides, do the following:

1. Right-click the CD icon and choose Custom Animation. The Custom Animation task pane opens.

2. In the task pane open the menu for the CD clip and choose Effect Options. The Play CD Audio dialog box appears with the Effect tab on top.

3. Enter 999 in the box for Stop Playing After_slides (see Figure 12-12). Then click OK.

Figure 12-12: To play across multiple slides, set the Stop setting to 999 slides.

TIP I always use 999 as the setting in step 3 to head off any possible problems. When another track plays, the first one will stop. For example, suppose you have a 30-slide presentation, and you want to play tracks 2, 4, and 6 from your CD, each for 10 slides. On slide 1, you would insert track 2 and set its custom animation to stop playing after 999 slides. Then you would do the same thing for track 4 on slide 11 and track 6 on slide 21. Don't worry about the tracks playing over the top of each other—they won't. (However, file-based sound files, such as WAV, do play on top of each other, so you would not typically layer them in this way.)

You can play any number of tracks from a single CD using a single icon, as long as they are contiguous and you play them in their default order. If you need non-contiguous tracks from the CD or in a different order, or you just want certain segments of some of the clips, you must place each one individually on the slide and then control their order with Custom Animation. If you don't want the icons to appear on the slide, drag them off the edge.

See Chapter 13 for help with custom animation.

Using a Soundrack in a Web Presentation

In a Web presentation, you can't use CD audio (obviously, because your audience won't have that CD). Instead, you must use a music file in a digital format like Windows Media Audio (WMA). Copy that music file to the same Web location as the rest of the HTML files for the presentation.

One glitch with a soundtrack in an HTML presentation is that the music plays only on the first slide; then it stops. To make it play throughout all slides, you must edit fullscreen.html.

When you save a presentation in HTML, one of the files that is created is called fullscreen.html. Edit this file with an HTML editor (or plain-text editor), to add the following line between the ⟨html⟩ and ⟨head⟩ tags at the beginning:

```
<bgsound src="music.wma" loop=infinite>
```

Substitute the actual name of the music file for music.wma.

Sequencing Sound Clips with the Advanced Timeline

The Advanced Timeline is turned off by default. When you turn it on, a timeline appears at the bottom of the Custom Animation task pane, and indicators appear next to each clip that show how long each clip will take to play and at what point each one starts. This can be useful when you are trying to coordinate several sound and/or video clips to play sequentially with a certain amount of space between them. It saves you from having to do a lot of math to calculate their starting and ending times in relation to the initial appearance of the slide.

To use the Advanced Timeline, follow these steps:

1. Display the Custom Animation task pane if it doesn't already appear (Slide Show⇨Custom Animation).

2. Open the menu for any of the items on the list in the task pane and choose Show Advanced Timeline.

3. (Optional) Widen the task pane by dragging its left border, so you will have more room. You might also want to click the word Seconds at the bottom of the task pane, opening a menu, and then choose Zoom In or Zoom Out to change the zoom on the timeline.

4. Click a clip on the list. A red right-pointing arrow appears next to it. The arrow appears at the spot that corresponds to the place on the timeline where the clip is currently set to begin. Figure 12-13 shows several clips, each beginning at a different point.

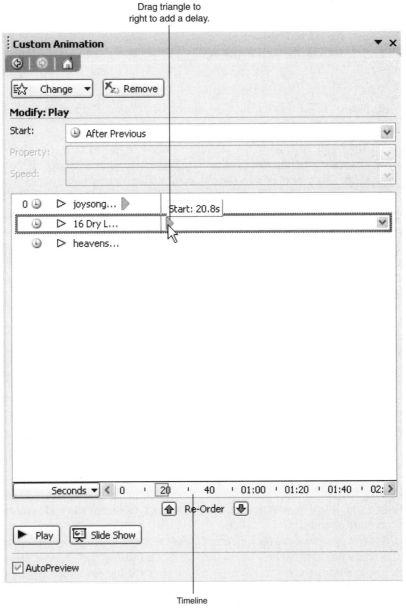

Figure 12-13: You can use a timeline to set the timing between clips on a slide in a graphical way.

5. For each clip, change the Start setting to With Previous or After Previous, depending on how you want it to relate to the earlier clip.

 If there is more than one sound clip set to After Previous, a vertical line appears where the first clip will finish. If a clip is set to After Previous, it cannot start before the clip that precedes it. Therefore, any delay that you set up for a subsequent clip will be in relation to the end of the preceding clip. If the clip is set to With Previous, the two can overlap.

6. (Optional) To reorder the clips on the list, click a clip and then click the up or down Reorder arrow at the bottom of the task pane.

7. (Optional) To change the amount of delay assigned to a clip, drag the red arrow next to it to the right or left. This is the same as changing the number in the Delay text box in the clip's animation timing properties.

You can use custom animation to create complex systems of sounds that play, pause, and stop in relationship to other animated objects on the slide. See Chapter 14 for the full details, but here's a quick explanation of it: add a sound to the Custom Animation task pane by clicking Add Effect and then choosing Sound Actions and finally Play, Pause, or Stop. In this way you can create separate actions for the same clip to start, pause, or stop at various points.

Recording Sounds and Narration

Most PCs have a microphone jack on the sound card where you can plug in any of a variety of small microphones. If you have a microphone for your PC, you can record your own sounds to include in the presentation. This can be short, simple sound effects and comments, or full-blown voice-over narration.

Recording Sounds

To record a short sound effect or blurb, use the Record Sound feature in PowerPoint. This is a simple utility with few options, but it serves nicely when all you need is a few seconds of audio.

Display the slide on which it should appear, and then choose Insert⇨Movies and Sounds⇨Record Sound. In the Record Sound dialog box, type a name in the Name box, ready your microphone, and then click the Record button (the red circle). When you are finished recording, click the Stop button (the black square) (see Figure 12-14). You may want to play the sound back to make sure it's okay; to do so, click the Play button (the black triangle). When you are satisfied, click OK to place the sound on the slide.

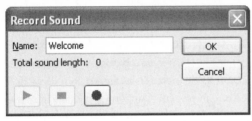

Figure 12-14: Record your own sounds using your PC's microphone.

 TIP You can add your recorded sound to the Clip Organizer if you like, for easy reuse. To do so, display the Clip Organizer window (from the Clip Art task pane, click Organize Clips) and then display the category in which you want to place it. Then, tile that window with the PowerPoint application window and drag-and-drop the recorded clip from the active slide into the Clip Organizer.

Recording Voice-Over Narration

Voice-over narration is a somewhat specialized thing. You normally wouldn't want it for a presentation that you would give "live" because you would be there yourself to narrate it. And most presentations you would distribute via the Web should be self-sufficient enough that the audience would immediately understand them even if they can't hear the audio, as a courtesy to people who may be Web-surfing without sound support. Therefore, think carefully before you rely on voice-over narration as a presentation tool.

In some cases, however, voice-over narration is the perfect choice. For example, suppose you are creating a self-running show that consists of scanned images of works of art. Almost the entire slide is taken up by each scan, so there is no room for a lengthy text block listing the artist, date, title, and description. In cases like that, recording a voice-over narration might make a lot of sense to relieve the slides from carrying the entire burden of information conveyance.

Bad narration is almost worse than none at all, and the recording equipment makes a big difference. Get the best audio recording equipment you can afford. Get a high-quality microphone (these are relatively inexpensive at your local computer store) and plug it into a high-quality sound card on the recording PC. If your PC is not up to the job, borrow someone else's.

Then, set the recording quality to the desired level. CD quality is usually not important for narration, so going with a lower quality may be preferable. Audio recording uses up an obscene amount of disk space: CD-quality (the highest quality) audio consumes about 10MB per minute of recording. That means, to fully narrate a 20-minute show at high quality, you need over 200MB of disk space. And with an inexpensive microphone and sound card, you won't be able to get dramatically better results between the highest and lowest recording qualities.

If you need to transfer the presentation to another PC for the show and you must transfer it using a floppy disk, transfer it first and then record the narration on the show PC (if the show PC has a sound card that you can hook a microphone to, that is). If you record the narration first, the presentation file will be so large that it won't fit on your floppy disk. You can store the narration separately from the main presentation, but even so the narration file may be too big to fit on a floppy. If you can't avoid recording the presentation narration before transferring it to the show machine and you don't have any means of transfer besides a floppy disk, you might try e-mailing the presentation to yourself. Send the e-mail on the machine containing the presentation file, and then receive it using the show machine. (Warning: sending and receiving the e-mail may take a long time, especially with a slow connection.) You could also upload it to a network drive, Web site, or FTP site for transfer.

The controls for recording narration are much more feature-rich than those for recording sounds, as you will see in the following sections.

ADJUSTING THE MICROPHONE RECORDING LEVEL

The first time you use narration recording with a certain microphone/sound card combination, you will need to set the microphone level appropriately. To do so, follow these steps:

1. Choose Slide Show⇨Record Narration. The Record Narration dialog box appears.

2. Click the Set Microphone Level button. The Microphone Check dialog box appears.

3. Read into the microphone, enabling PowerPoint to set the optimum recording level (see Figure 12-15). You can also set the recording level by manually dragging the slide bar shown in Figure 12-15, but this is not recommended because you do not know which setting to use without testing the microphone.

4. Click OK to return to the Record Narration dialog box.

From this point you can change other settings in the dialog box, click OK to begin recording with the current settings, or click Cancel to close the dialog box without recording anything right now.

CHOOSING A RECORDING QUALITY

As I mentioned earlier, recording quality has a direct relationship to file size: the higher the quality, the larger the file.

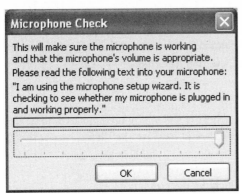

Figure 12-15: Read the text shown in the dialog box to allow PowerPoint to adjust the recording level as needed.

The three preset qualities are Telephone (low), Radio (medium), and CD (high). You can also create your own custom quality settings by choosing a certain format and attributes.

The default quality is Low, but it may appear as [untitled] in the Record Narration dialog box. To choose a recording quality, perform the following steps:

1. Choose Slide Show⇨Record Narration if the Record Narration dialog box is not already open from the preceding steps.

2. Observe the Quality setting in the Current recording quality section of the dialog box. If needed, click Change Quality.

3. In the Sound Selection dialog box, open the Name list and choose one of the presets. Or, if you want the recording in a certain format or with certain attributes, choose them from the Format and/or Attributes lists (see Figure 12-16).

4. Click OK to close the Sound Selection dialog box.

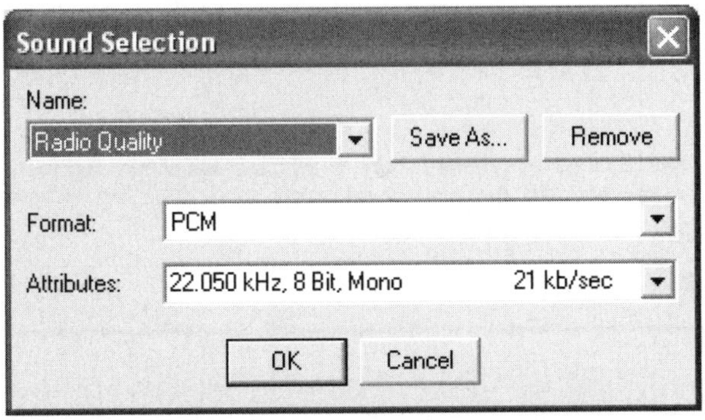

Figure 12-16: Choose a recording quality or set one up on your own.

Beginners should choose one of the preset quality settings. If you chose your own combination of format and attributes in step 3, you can click the Save As button and enter a name for a new quality setting, if desired.

From this point you can change other settings in the dialog box, click OK to begin recording with the current settings, or click Cancel to close the dialog box without recording anything right now.

CHOOSING LINKED OR EMBEDDED NARRATION

By default, narration is embedded in the PowerPoint file. As discussed earlier, this has pros and cons to it. It makes the file much larger, but it also makes it more conveniently portable because you do not have to worry about associated files and keeping them all in the right locations. On the other hand, linking the narrations gives you the opportunity to edit the narration sound files in sound-editing software after inserting them in PowerPoint and having the updated versions appear through PowerPoint.

If you want to link rather than embed the narration, mark the Link narrations in checkbox in the Record Narration dialog box (see Figure 12-17). Then, click the Browse button to select a location in which to store the narration. Try to store the narration file in the same folder as the PowerPoint file itself if possible; this makes the path to it relative, so if you move both files to another location the link will still work.

Record Narration

Current recording quality

Quality:	Radio Quality
Disk use:	21 kb/second
Free disk space:	16811 MB (on D:\)
Max record time:	13324 minutes

OK

Cancel

Set Microphone Level...

Change Quality...

Tip

Adjust quality settings to achieve desired sound quality and disk usage. Higher recording quality uses more disk space. Large narrations should be linked for better performance.

☑ Link narrations in: D:\...\Faithe Wempen\My Documents\   Browse...

Mark this checkbox to store
narrations separately.

Figure 12-17: Link the narration file, if desired.

RECORDING NARRATION FOR THE ENTIRE PRESENTATION

After performing any setup required from the preceding sections, you are now ready to do the recording. In the Record Narration dialog box (shown in Figure 12-17), click OK to begin.

If the first slide of the presentation was selected when you opened the dialog box, the first slide appears immediately in Slide Show view, and you're off and running; simply speak into the microphone and click to advance the presentation. Keep going till the end of the presentation.

However, if any other slide was selected when you opened the dialog box, you will be prompted to choose whether you want to begin recording with the Current Slide or the First Slide. Click First Slide to begin.

When you get to the last slide, the screen goes black, and a message appears prompting you to press Esc.

After you press Esc, a dialog box appears reminding you that the narrations have been saved with each slide—the box will also ask whether you want to save the timings. Timings are automatic transitions between slides that make the slides automatically advance just as you advanced them when you were narrating. Usually the answer here is Yes, but itdepends on your specific needs.

Then, test your show by displaying it in Slide Show view from start to finish and listening to your narration.

RECORDING NARRATION FOR AN INDIVIDUAL SLIDE

Nobody's perfect, and it can be difficult to record the narration perfectly for an entire presentation at once. Therefore, you may want to go back and change the narration for individual slides. To do so, select the slide that you want to rerecord and choose Slide Show⇨Record Narration. Change any settings and then click OK. When the dialog box asks you to choose between Current Slide and First Slide, click Current Slide. When you are finished recording the narration for that slide, press Esc.

DELETING THE NARRATION FOR A SLIDE

After you add the narration to slides, a little speaker icon appears at the bottom of each one. You can double-click this icon to preview the narration at any time. To remove the narration from a slide, delete this icon.

Summary

In this chapter you learned how to insert sounds in a presentation as stand-alone objects or as effects that accompany other objects. You also learned how to use CD soundtracks, how to record your own sounds, and how to record narration.

The next two lessons deal with transitions and animations, which are ways of making the static content of your slides move around on-screen—usually on its way in or on its way out. Chapter 13 introduces the topic by covering basic transitions and preset animations, while Chapter 14 gets into the nitty-gritty details of custom animation effects.

Chapter 13

Using Transitions and Animation Effects

ALTHOUGH POWERPOINT PRESENTATIONS are more like slide shows than full-motion movies, that doesn't mean you're stuck with boring static slides like on an old 35mm slide projector. There are many ways to add movement to your slides through transitions between slides and animation within each slide.

In this chapter you'll learn the difference between transitions and animations, and how to set up automatic transitions between slides. Then, we'll delve deep into the complex topic of animation, starting with the very basic preset animations and moving into timings, layering, custom motion paths, and chart animation.

Automatic versus Manual Transitions

A *transition* happens whenever the presentation moves from one slide to another. There can be a fancy flourish of some type associated with the event or not. I'll explain later in the chapter how to assign such flourishes. For now, however, your first big decision is whether the transitions between slides will occur automatically or manually.

Generally speaking, if there will be a live person controlling and presenting the show, transitions should be manual. With manual transitions, the presenter must click the mouse to move to the next slide, just like clicking the button on a 35mm slide projector. This might sound like a pain, but it helps the speaker maintain control of the show. If someone in the audience asks a question or wants to make a comment, the show does not continue on blindly but pauses to accommodate the delay.

However, if you are preparing a self-running presentation, such as for a kiosk, automatic transitions are a virtual necessity. You learned in Chapter 12 how to record narration and set timings for a presentation, and those timings represent the length of time between one slide and the next. You can also set automatic timings for the slides without recording any narration.

Setting Up Automatic Transition Timings

The default is manual transition, so you must specifically set up automatic timings if you want them. For automatic timings, you can either assign the same transition time to all or assign individual times for each slide. Rehearsing the timings (which is covered in the next section) is the most effective method of assigning individual times per slide.

You will probably want to assign automatic transitions to all slides in the presentation or none—but not a mixture of the two. It can get confusing if some of the slides automatically advance and others don't. However, you are free to assign different timings and effects to the various slides' transitions.

To assign an automatic transition to an individual slide, display the Slide Transition task pane (by choosing Slide Show ⇨ Slide Transition), display or select the slide, and then mark the Automatically After checkbox and enter a number of seconds in its text box (see Figure 13-1). Then, to apply that same setting to all the slides in the presentation, click the Apply to All Slides button.

It is perfectly okay to leave the On Mouse Click checkbox marked even if you choose automatic transitions. In fact, it's a good idea. There may be times when you want to manually advance to the next slide before the automatic transition time has elapsed, and leaving On Mouse Click turned on allows you to do so when needed.

It does not matter what transition is selected in the Apply to Selected Slides list; even if it is set to No Transition, transitions will still occur. There will simply be no special transition effect with that setting.

Transition timings appear beneath each slide in Slide Sorter view, as shown in Figure 13-2.

Figure 13-1: Set a slide to advance automatically after a certain number of seconds.

Rehearsing and Recording Timings

The trouble with automatic timings set as a whole for all slides is that not all slides deserve or need equal time on-screen. Some slides have more text than others, or more complex concepts to grasp.

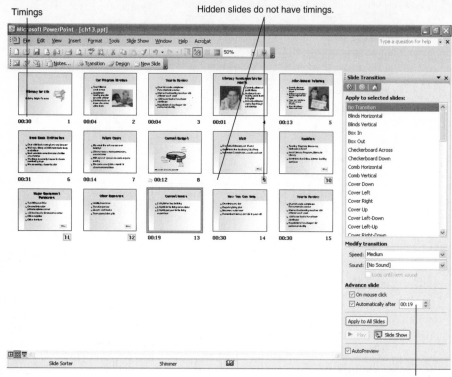

Figure 13-2: The numbers beneath and to the left of each slide represent the timings set for them.

To allow for the differences, you can manually set the timings for each slide as in the preceding section, but there's another way. Use the Rehearse Timings feature in PowerPoint to run through your presentation in real time, and then let PowerPoint set the timings for you based on that rehearsal.

 When you set timings with Rehearse Timings, any hidden slide is ignored. If you later unhide that slide, it will not be set to advance automatically. You will need to individually assign it an Automatically After transition, as in the preceding section.

To set transition timings with the Rehearse Timings feature, choose Slide Show ⇨ Rehearse Timings. The slide show begins, with a floating Rehearsal box as shown in Figure 13-3.

   Wait until you think it is time for the next slide to appear; then click the Next button, click the mouse, or press Page Down.

Current slide timing   Total so far for the presentation

Figure 13-3: The Rehearsal box helps you set timings for moving from slide to slide.

TIP If you want a fairly long time for a slide, such as 30 seconds or more, you might find it faster to enter the desired time in the Current Slide Timing box on the Rehearsal toolbar rather than waiting the full amount of time before advancing. Click in that box to move the cursor there, and then enter the desired time and press Tab. After entering the desired time, make sure you do press Tab and don't simply click the Next button, or it won't take.

It may help when setting timings to read the text on the slide out loud, rather slowly, to simulate how an audience member who reads slowly would proceed. When you have read all the text on the slide, pause 1 or 2 more seconds and then advance.

If you need to pause the rehearsal at any time, click the Pause button. When you are ready to resume, click it again.

If you make a mistake on the timing for a slide, click the Repeat button to begin timing that slide again from 00:00.

When you reach the last slide, a dialog box appears telling you the total time for the show. If you want to preserve the timings, click Yes. Otherwise, click No and choose Slide Show ➪ Rehearse Timings again to try again.

After setting the timings, test them by viewing the show normally (select Slide Show ⇨ View Show). If any of the timings are off, return to Normal view and adjust them with the Slide Transition task pane.

Choosing Transition Effects

Back in the old slide projector days, there was only one kind of transition: the old slide got pushed out, and the new slide plunked into place. With a computerized presentation, you can choose from all kinds of fun transitions, including wipes, blinds, and much more.

The transition effect for a slide refers to how the slide enters, not how it exits. So if you want to assign a particular transition to occur while moving from slide 1 to slide 2, for example, you would assign the transition effect to slide 2.

The looks of the individual transitions are hard to explain on paper; it's best if you just view them on-screen to understand what each one is. Try out as many of them as you can before making your final selections.

 Transitions add a nice little flourish to your presentation, but you don't want them to distract unduly from your message. It's usually best to stick to a single transition effect used consistently across the entire presentation unless you are consciously striving for a whimsical touch.

To apply a transition, simply select the slide, and then choose one of the transitions in the Slide Transition task pane. (If it does not already appear, choose Slide Show ⇨ Slide Transition.) If AutoPreview is on (and it is by default, there's a checkbox for it at the bottom of the task pane), the effect previews immediately for the active slide.

After choosing the desired transition effect, you can fine-tune it with the settings in the Modify Transition section of the task pane. For example, you can choose a speed and associate a sound with the effect (see Figure 13-4). After perfecting the transition settings, click Apply to All Slides if you want to copy the settings to all the other slides in the presentation.

You learned about sounds in Chapter 12, and the sound option for the transition has a lot in common with those other sound settings. Instead of being attached to an object, though, the sound is attached to the transition event. Choose one of the sounds on the Sound list or choose Other Sound to browse for a sound file (see Figure 13-5).

 Only WAV files can be used for the sounds associated with slide transitions.

Figure 13-4: Set up transition effects, including the basic effect, the speed, and an associated sound (optional).

Working with Preset Animations

PowerPoint includes over 30 animation schemes that you can apply to slides. *Animation schemes* are preset combinations of animation effects for the entry and exit of the slide's content. Most of these schemes involve making one part of the slide appear before another part. The title might appear first, and then the bullets, for

Figure 13-5: Associate a WAV format sound file with the transition, if desired.

example, or each bullet point might appear individually each time you click the mouse. There might also be separate entry and exit animations. Some of the preset animations also include sound effects.

An animation scheme provides an easy way to get started with animations. You can then customize the animation (covered later in this chapter) as you gain more proficiency with the feature. For example, you might choose a scheme that fades letters in quickly on the slide and then modify it later so that they fade in a little more slowly.

Be careful not to overuse special effects such as animation. The audience can quickly turn from thinking "what a cool effect!" to "what a silly show off!" if you use too many effects or use effects too frequently.

You can apply an animation scheme either from Normal or Slide Sorter view. It doesn't make much difference; both work equally well. However, for custom animation, Normal is your only choice.

PowerPoint groups animation schemes into three categories: Subtle, Moderate, and Exciting. These refer to the amount of activity involved in each one and provide a guide for which one might be appropriate. For example, you might want one of the Exciting schemes on the first or last slide, and one of the Moderate schemes on some of the important slides in between. A Subtle scheme might work well for an "ordinary" slide.

To apply an animation scheme, select the slide on which you want to apply it, and choose Slide Show⇨Animation Schemes. The Slide Design task pane appears showing the animation schemes as shown in Figure 13-6. From there, simply click the desired scheme. It will preview automatically on the slide. If you miss it, you can click the Play button to replay it.

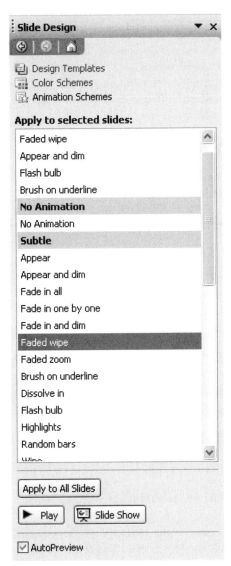

Figure 13-6: Select an animation scheme for the selected slide.

If you select an animation effect and the task pane immediately reverts back to No Animation being selected, then the effect is not available for the content on the selected slide.

Some problems with anti-aliasing have been reported with animated text on some backgrounds. Here's an article that sums up the findings: www.powerpointanswers.com/researchsummary.html.

As with transition effects, you can apply an Animation Scheme to all the slides by clicking Apply to All Slides, if desired. However, animation schemes implement themselves differently on slides with different kinds of content, so you will want to make sure you watch the entire presentation after applying an animation scheme globally to make sure the effects work appropriately on each slide.

Creating Your Own Preset Animations

Ever wonder where the preset animation schemes come from? They're provided by Microsoft, of course, but what you might not know is that they're stored in a file called quikanim.ppt, stored in Program Files\Microsoft Office\Office 11\1033, and you can edit it.

Here's what to do:

1. Make a backup copy of quikanim.ppt first, from a file management window. If the original is read-only, remove that attribute in the file's Properties.

2. In PowerPoint, move to the end of the presentation and insert a new slide. Apply the Title Slide layout to it.

3. Enter the category name in the Title placeholder (such as User Defined) and enter the desired name for the new scheme in the Sub Title placeholder.

4. Right-click on the Title placeholder, select Custom Animation, and add whatever effects you want to it. Repeat the process for the subtitle.

5. Choose Insert ⇨ Duplicate Slide and apply the Title & Text layout to it. Apply custom animation to it as desired.

6. Save and exit.

7. If you turned off the read-only attribute for quikanim.ppt, turn it back on.

You can also use this same technique to change the category of the existing custom animations (Subtle, Moderate, Exciting, and so on). Just change the category in the Title placeholder for the desired slide.

Applying Custom Animation

Preset animation is a useful method of creating an animation initially, but it isn't very flexible. Fortunately, however, you can take what you created through preset animation and use it as a starting point for custom animation. (You can also create new custom animation from scratch, if you prefer.)

Custom animation is pretty amazing in its feature set. You can control how and when each individual object enters and exits, and you can even make objects dance around and make noise while they are just sitting there on the slide.

To work with custom animation, display the Custom Animation task pane (choose Slide Show⇨Custom Animation). Any animation that you set up earlier with preset animation appears there on the list, ready for your fine-tuning.

When you print slides, the full content of the slide prints, not each animated build. (This ability disappeared as of PowerPoint 2002, unfortunately.) However, an add-in is available that will capture snapshots of the presentation slides as you present with each animation event as a separate shot, and then you can print them as images. See `www.mvps.org/skp/cshow.htm`.

Dissecting a Preset Animation Scheme

A good way to learn about custom animation is to play around with the settings from a preset, so do the following if you want to try it out:

1. Display a slide that has a title and at least two bullet points on it.

2. Apply the Bounce preset animation to it from the Animation Schemes task pane.

3. Switch to the Custom Animation task pane. The animations used in the Bounce scheme appear on the list there, as shown in Figure 13-7.

If the animation was applied to all slides, the animation is on the Slide Master, so you will need to click one of the grayed-out options and click Copy Effects to Slide to transfer them to the individual slide before you can dissect it for this exercise.

Here are some things to notice:

◆ The selected animation's Start setting is With Previous. That means it will begin simultaneously with the previous animation event. Since it is the first one on the list, the previous animation event is the transition to this slide from the one before it.

◆ The selected animation's speed is Medium. There are other choices available on the Speed drop-down list.

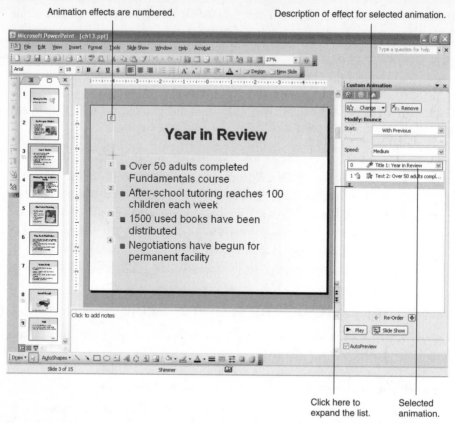

Figure 13-7: Here's one of the animation schemes when viewed in the Custom Animation task pane.

◆ Notice the grayed-out Property drop-down list. Some animations have some special property you can set, and it appears in that space. For example, some entrance and exit effects specify a direction. The selected effect does not happen to have that.

◆ Each animated item is numbered starting with 0. They will execute in numeric order. That means the title will appear before the bullets, as shown in Figure 13-7.

◆ Each bullet is individually numbered, but only the first one appears on the task pane's list. However, if you click the down arrow below the first one, a list will expand to show each one individually, as shown in Figure 13-8. This is by design. If you apply a change to the first one while the others are collapsed, the change will apply to all of them; if you apply a change to the first one (or any of them) while the list is expanded, it will apply only to that individual bullet point.

◆ The mouse icons next to the bulleted list items indicate that each bulleted list item will appear one-by-one each time you click the mouse button.

Figure 13-8: Expanding the list of animations shows the animations for items 2 through 4 (the other bullets on the bulleted list in Figure 13-7).

◆ The Re-Order up and down arrows at the bottom can be used to change the order in which items are animated on the slide.

◆ Although it's not obvious from the black-and-white photo in Figure 13-7, the star symbols next to each item are green, which indicates an entrance effect (green means "entrance" in PowerPoint). That's the most common kind but not the only kind, as I'll explain next.

Applying a Custom Animation Effect

There are four types of animation effects possible on a slide, and each has a different color icon as follows:

◆ *Entrance (green)*: The item appears on the slide separately from the slide itself. Either it does not appear right away, or it appears in some unusual way (like flying in), or both.

◆ *Emphasis (yellow)*: An item that is already on the slide moves or changes in some way. For example, perhaps it spins around, grows, or changes color.

◆ *Exit (red)*: The item disappears from the slide before the slide itself disappears, and (optionally) it does so in some animated way.

◆ *Motion paths (gray)*: The item moves on the slide according to a preset path you specify, like a toy train running on a track you have designed. Motion paths are covered later in the chapter.

Entrance and exit effects usually involve some type of motion. Emphasis effects can involve motion but not necessarily; there are also emphasis effects for changing color, changing font, growing/shrinking, and so on.

There are many effect choices in each category. Different effects may have different icons, but the colors always match up with the category.

To apply a custom animation effect, follow these steps:

1. Select the object to be animated in Normal view.

2. In the Custom Animation task pane, click Add Effect. A menu appears with the four types listed previously. Point to the one you want, and a submenu appears.

3. Choose a recently used effect from the submenu (see Figure 13-9), or choose More Effects to open a dialog box (see Figure 13-10).

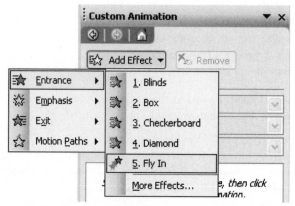

Figure 13-9: Choose a recently used effect from the menu, or choose More Effects.

4. If you opened the dialog box, make your selection. A preview of the effect appears behind the dialog box. Then, click OK to apply it.

 Effects are broken down into categories within the dialog box (refer to Figure 13-10), such as Basic, Subtle, Moderate, and Exciting (just like preset animation!). As long as the Preview Effect checkbox is marked at the bottom of the box, you can click an effect on the list and see it demonstrated on the slide behind the dialog box. You might need to drag the dialog box to the side.

5. After applying the effect, use the Start drop-down list at the top of the Custom Animation task pane to set its start event (On Click, With Previous, or After Previous).

Figure 13-10: The Add Effect dialog box (the exact name varies) shows the full list of available effects of the chosen type.

6. If there is a property or setting in the middle drop-down list in the task pane, set it. For example, for an entrance or exit effect, there may be a Direction setting (Top, Bottom, and so on).

7. Open the Speed drop-down list in the task pane and select the speed at which the animation should occur (Very Fast, Fast, Medium, and so on).

8. Test the animation by clicking the Play button at the bottom of the task pane, or click the Slide Show button there to preview it full-screen. (If you do the latter, press Esc to return to Normal view afterwards.)

Applying Multiple Effects to the Same Object

An object can have many effects applied to it. It can have separate entrance and exit effects, for example, plus emphasis effects that execute at various times in relation to the other activities. Select the object and click Add Effect, just like you do normally.

Changing to a Different Effect

To change to a different animation effect, select the animation effect for that object in the Custom Animation pane and click the Change button. The same menus/dialog boxes appear as when you initially applied the effect (refer to Figures 13-9 and 13-10). Now you can make a different choice.

Removing an Animation Effect

You can remove the animation for one specific object or remove all animation from an entire slide. When an object is not animated, it simply appears when the slide itself appears with no delay. The net result is that unanimated objects display first on the slide, followed by objects that have entrance animation effects.

To remove the animation for a specific object, start in the Custom Animation task pane. If the object is part of a group, such as a bulleted list, expand or collapse the list depending on what you want. To remove an effect from an entire text box, collapse it first. To remove an effect from only a single paragraph, expand the list first. Then, select the animation effect in the task pane, and click the Remove button. The animation is removed, and any remaining animation effects on the slide are renumbered.

To remove all animation for the whole slide, go back to the Animation Schemes controls (select Slide Show⇨Animation Schemes), and choose No Animation in the task pane. This works even if you did not use an animation scheme to set up the animation initially.

 There are actually several ways of displaying the Animation Schemes list besides using the Slide Show menu. You can click the task pane's title to open a list of available task panes, for example, or you can click the Slide Design button on the toolbar, and then click the Animation Schemes hyperlink.

Reordering Animation Effects

Animation effects occur in the order in which they are listed in the Custom Animation task pane. To reorder them, drag-and-drop them up or down on the list, or use the Re-Order up/down arrow buttons at the bottom of the task pane.

Text Animation Options

When animating multiple paragraphs in a single text box, extra animation options are available that enable you to specify in what order and with what grouping the items will animate.

One way to change the order in which a bulleted list was animated would be to expand the animation list in the Custom Animation task pane, and then drag-and-drop or use the Re-Order arrows to put them in a different order, as described in the preceding section. However, if you just want them reversed in order (for example, bottom-to-top), you might find it easier to set the special Reverse option for the animation instead.

You can also choose the grouping for the animation. For example, suppose you have three levels of bullets in the text box, and you want a different second-level bullet to appear each time you click the mouse. You can specify the second level as the animation grouping, and all third-level bullets will appear as a whole along with their associated second-level bullet.

To access the text options for an animation effect, do the following:

1. In the Custom Animation task pane, make sure that the list is collapsed so that a single item represents the entire text box. Then, right-click that animation effect on the list and choose Effect Options.

2. Click the Text Animation tab (see Figure 13-11).

3. Open the Group Text list and choose how you want the animation grouped. The default is By 1st level paragraphs.

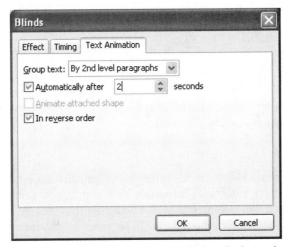

Figure 13-11: Control how the text within a single text box is animated.

 If you choose By Letter or By Word in step 3, an additional text box appears beneath the box. Enter the percentage delay between letters or words, if desired.

4. (Optional) If you want the next bullet point to appear automatically without having to click again after each one, mark the Automatically after checkbox and enter a number of seconds of delay between them.

5. (Optional) Mark the In reverse order checkbox if you want the list built from the bottom up.

6. Click OK.

Specifying When an Animation Begins

An animation's start can be triggered in any of these ways:

◆ *With Previous*: The animation begins simultaneously with any previous animations on the slide. For example, you can set up two different objects to animate at the same time by setting the second of the two to With Previous. If there is no previous animation event on the slide, the animation will occur concurrently with the slide itself appearing.

◆ *After Previous*: The animation begins immediately after the previous animation finishes on the slide. If there is no previous animation, it occurs immediately after the slide itself appears.

◆ *On Click*: The animation occurs when the mouse is clicked. This is useful when you want to build a slide item-by-item with each click, or for an exit effect.

When you set an animation to On Click, the "click" being referred to is *any* click. The mouse does not need to be pointing at anything in particular. Pressing a key on the keyboard will serve the same purpose.

In addition to these three normal sequence triggers, you can also set up an effect to trigger only when you click something in particular. For example, suppose you have three bullet points on a list and three photos. You would like each bullet point to appear when you click its corresponding photo. To set that up, you animate each bullet point's entrance effect with the graphic object as its trigger.

There's one little hitch to the preceding example: you can have only one trigger per object, and in this case "object" means the entire text placeholder. There-fore, if you want to animate bullet points separately with separate custom trig-gers, you need to place each bullet point in a separate text box.

To set when an animation starts, do the following:

1. In the Custom Animation task pane, right-click the effect and choose Timing. A dialog box for the effect appears with the Timing tab on top. We will look at the options on this tab in the next section of the chapter.

2. Click the Triggers button, expanding the dialog box controls to show additional controls at the bottom (see Figure 13-12).

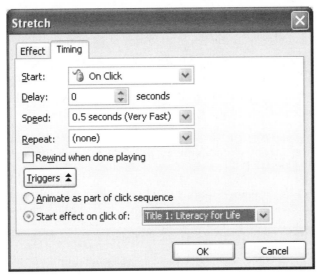

Figure 13-12: The Timing tab with the Triggers controls expanded.

3. Click Start Effect on Click Of, and then open the drop-down list and select an object. All objects on the current slide appear on this list. (You cannot set the start of an animation to depend on an object on a different slide.)

4. Click OK.

Setting Custom Animation Timings

Each animation has timing settings that control the speed at which the animation occurs and the delay between the preceding event and the beginning of the animation. You can also specify whether an animation should repeat, and if so, how many times.

At the most basic level, you can set the timing from the Speed drop-down list in the Custom Animation task pane, as you saw earlier in the chapter. For most animations you can choose from Very Fast, Fast, Medium, Slow, and Very Slow.

For more control, you can work with the Timing tab (see Figure 13-12) by right-clicking the animation effect in the task pane and choosing Timing. From the Timing tab, you can set the following options:

◆ *Start*: This is the same as the Start drop-down list in the task pane. See the preceding section.

◆ *Delay*: The amount of pause between the event start from the Start setting and the execution of the animation. For example, if the animation effect is set for After Previous, the delay is the number of seconds between the *end* of the previous event and the beginning of the animation. If the Start setting is With Previous, the delay is the number of seconds between the *beginning* of the previous event and the beginning of the animation. Delay is set to 0 by default.

◆ *Speed*: This is the same as the Speed drop-down list in the task pane.

◆ *Repeat*: The number of times the animation should repeat. The default is None. You would rarely set an animation to repeat because it makes the slide harder for the audience to read. However, it can be useful when you want a graphic to flash until the end of the slide, for example.

◆ *Rewind when done playing*: This setting applies mostly to video clips; it is available for animation effects, but you will not see much difference between on and off.

◆ *Triggers*: Click this button to display extra controls that enable you to set an animation to occur when a particular object is clicked, as opposed to a click in general. See the preceding section.

You can also use the Advanced Timeline to sequence animations, just as you did with sounds in Chapter 12. To turn on the timeline, right-click any animation and choose Show Advanced Timeline. The timeline is useful because it can give you a feel for the total time involved in all the animations you have set up on a slide, including any delays you have built in (see Figure 13-13).

 The Advanced Timeline is most useful for With Previous and After Previous animations; for On Click it is not particularly helpful.

Notice in Figure 13-13 that there are two pieces to each bullet point's timing bar—a colored part and a transparent part. The colored part represents the time required for the basic animation. For example, each of these is set to Medium speed for the animation, which takes 2 seconds, so each of the colored portions of the bars represents 2 seconds. The transparent portions of the bars are there because these bullet points happen to have been set up (in the Effect Options dialog box, on the Effect tab) to display the text "by letter," which takes longer than the base effect would normally take. The extra portion of the time bar represents that extra time is required. If I were to change the setting on the Effect tab to "All at Once," the timing bars would change here to be just the solid parts, and they would be much shorter.

You can use the timeline to create additional delays between animations and increase the durations of individual animations. To increase or decrease the duration of an item, drag the *right* side of the colored bar. To create a delay or an overlap between animations, drag the *left* side of the bar.

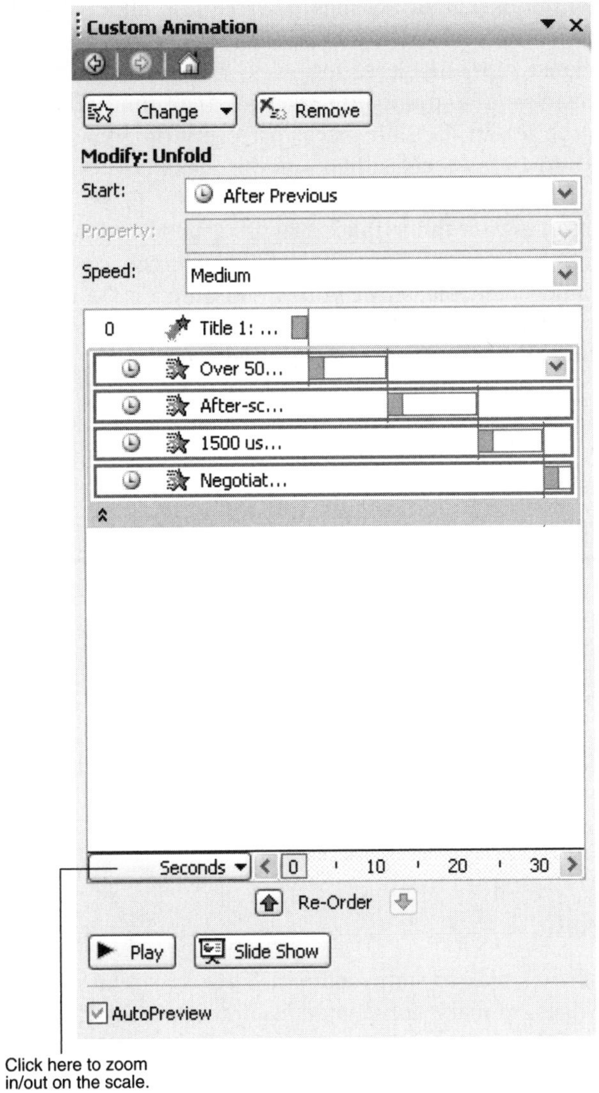

Click here to zoom
in/out on the scale.

Figure 13-13: The Advanced Timeline shows the amount of
time that your animations will take up.

Dragging a bar for an item that is set to After Previous will move the other bars
too to allow the timing for the entire sequence to change. When you drag a bar for
an item set to With Previous, however, overlap is allowed.

Applying Sounds to Animation Effects

In Chapter 12 you learned about sounds and how to apply them to objects so that
the sound would play when the object was clicked or pointed to.

There's a subtle distinction (but an important one) between that kind of sound assignment and the kind we're going to talk about in this chapter: assigning a sound to the animation effect associated with an object.

An example may make this clearer. Suppose you associate the sound of a telephone ringing to a piece of clip art on the slide, such that every time that clip is clicked, the telephone sound plays. This is not animation; this is just an "On Click" action setting.

On the other hand, suppose you want the telephone ringing sound to play automatically when the clip art appears on the slide, and you want the clip to appear when you click the mouse (anywhere). To do this you would animate the clip art with an entrance effect set to On Click as the Start setting and then set the effect options for the animation so that the sound was associated with the effect.

See the difference? When you assign a sound to an animation event that is triggered on mouse click, you click *anywhere* to trigger the event and the sound plays as part of that event. When you assign a sound to an On Click action setting for an object, the sound plays only when you click *on that object*.

Now that we've got that straightened out, here's how to associate a sound with an animation effect:

1. Right-click the effect in the Custom Animation task pane, and choose Effect Options.

2. On the Effect tab, open the Sound drop-down list and choose a sound, or choose Other Sound to pick from another location. (It's the same deal as in Chapter 12.) Or, to make the previously playing sound stop when this animation occurs, choose Stop Previous Sound.

3. Click OK.

Triggering an Event

There's more animation than the standard start methods. You can set up *triggers* that enable the click of one object to make the animation of another object begin. This is a very powerful feature! Here are some things you can do with it:

◆ Toggle a video between playing and pausing by clicking buttons you create.

◆ Drag a sound icon off the slide, and then trigger its play with a click to some other object on the slide.

◆ Create user-interactive slides where different things happen based on what the user clicks. For example, a multiple-choice question might animate a certain text box to appear with a right answer.

To set up a trigger, create the custom animation for the object as normal, and then do the following in the Custom Animation task pane:

1. Open the drop-down menu for the item and choose Effect Options.

2. Click the Timing tab and then the Triggers button to display the trigger controls.

3. Open the Start effect on click of list and choose the object that should be clicked to start this animation (see Figure 13-14).

4. Click OK.

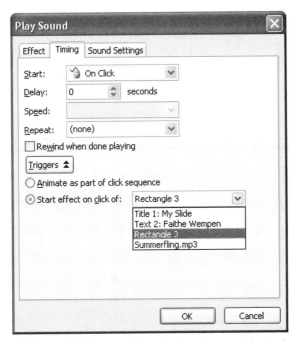

Figure 13-14: Create a trigger that makes one object animate when another is clicked.

Dimming or Hiding After Animation

What happens after an animation effect has finished? Usually nothing in particular. Other effects may execute, but the animated object just sits there after it has finished doing its thing.

However, if desired, you can set up one of the following to occur for an object after it has finished animating:

◆ *Change color*: You can choose a scheme color or a fixed color. This is called *dimming*, because usually the color you would choose would be less contrasting to the background than the original, giving the appearance that the object had dimmed in brightness. (However, actually you are free to choose any color to change to, including a brighter one than the original.) As you might expect, this works best on text rather than graphics; a graphic usually becomes a shapeless mono-color blob if you apply a color change to it.

◆ *Hide*: The object can disappear entirely from the slide, either after the animation or after the next mouse click.

TIP   You can also create change-of-color effects using emphasis animation, and hide animations using exit animation.

To choose an after-animation effect, right-click the animation effect in the Custom Animation task pane and choose Effect Options. On the Effect tab, set the After Animation setting to the desired color or effect (see Figure 13-15).

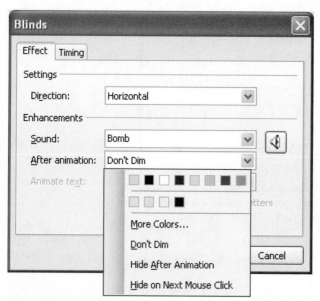

Figure 13–15: Specify a color change or disappearance for an object after its animation.

TIP   To make bullet points appear one at a time, with the preceding bullet point disappearing as the next one enters, set each bullet point's After Animation setting to Hide on Next Mouse Click.

Using Motion Paths

Have you ever played with model trains where you can lay down sections of track with curves, twists, and straight segments where you want them? That's the basic principle behind motion paths. You set up a track, and the object runs along that track as its animation effect.

Perhaps you are thinking, "Cool, but when would I ever use that, really?" You might be surprised. For example, suppose you are showing a map on a slide, and you want to graphically illustrate the route being taken when traveling. You could create a little square, circle, or even a tiny piece of clip art of a car or airplane, and then set a custom motion path for it that would trace the route on the map along certain highways.

PowerPoint comes with dozens of motion paths in every shape you can imagine, and you can also create your own (for example, for situations like the aforementioned map).

Applying a Preset Motion Path

Let's start with something easy: a preset motion path. To apply a motion path, choose it just like you would choose an entrance or exit effect:

1. Display the Custom Animation task pane.

2. Select the object, click Add Effect, point to Motion Paths, and then click one of the paths on the list (see Figure 13-16). You can also opt to click More Motion Paths or Draw Custom Path (which I'll explain later).

3. If you choose More Motion Paths, choose the path from the Add Motion Path dialog box (see Figure 13-17). Then, click OK.

The motion path appears on the slide, adjacent to the animated object. A green arrow shows where the object will begin, and a dotted line shows the path it will take (see Figure 13-18). To change the starting point for the path, drag the green arrow. The motion path in Figure 13-18 is a closed shape, which means that the starting and ending points are the same. The object will travel along the motion path and end up back where it started.

If you have selected a motion path that is a line rather than a shape, it will have both a start and an end point. The start point is a green arrow, and the end point is a red arrow with a line at its point (see Figure 13-19).

You can change to a different motion path by selecting the animation in the task pane and clicking the Change button on the task pane, the same as with changing any other type of custom animation.

Modifying a Preset Motion Path

Motion paths are editable objects, much like AutoShapes. You can click one to place round white selection handles around it, and then drag those selection handles to

Figure 13-16: Choose one of the common motion paths from the menu or choose More Motion Paths for a more complete set.

Figure 13-17: The Add Motion Path dialog box provides a large set of motion paths from which to choose.

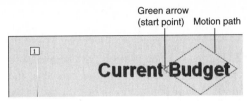

Figure 13-18: The motion path appears on the slide. The green arrow is the starting point and shows the direction of the flow.

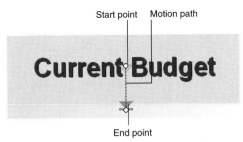

Figure 13-19: Line motion paths have starting and ending points.

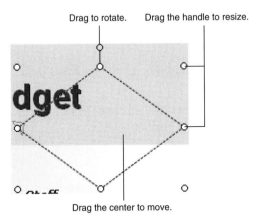

Figure 13-20: A motion path is an object on the slide that can be moved, resized, and/or rotated like any other object.

resize it, either proportionally or in one dimension only. You can also drag the green rotation handle to rotate a motion path (see Figure 13-20).

But wait—there's a lot more you can do to modify a motion path. For starters, you can reverse the direction by switching the starting and ending points. To do so, right-click the motion path and choose Reverse Direction.

On a closed shape like the one in Figure 13-20, you can disconnect the starting and ending points so you have a separate red end-point marker. To do so, right-click the motion path and choose Open Path.

You can also reshape the motion path. Right-click the motion path and choose Edit Points to allow this; black squares appear on the path, and you can drag the black squares to change the shape of the path. And if you have opened the path (see the previous example), you can also drag the ending and starting points to further modify the shape (see Figure 13-21).

Mouse pointer dragging end point

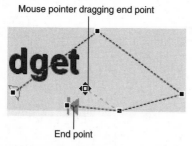

End point

Figure 13-21: Right-click and choose Edit Points to make all the points that make up the path draggable.

Creating a Custom Motion Path from Scratch

You saw in the preceding section how to modify an existing motion path, but what about creating your own from scratch, like for the aforementioned map example? Easy enough. Follow these steps:

1. Display the Custom Animation task pane, and select the object to be animated.

2. Choose Add Effect ⇨ Motion Paths ⇨ Draw Custom Path, and then choose the type of path you want: Line, Curve, Freeform, or Scribble.

3. Drag to draw on the slide the path you want.

Here are some tips for creating your motion path:

◆ For a line, where you begin will be the start point and where you end will be the end point. However, you can always reverse this later, if desired (by right-clicking and choosing Reverse Direction).

◆ For a Curve, click at the beginning of the line, then move the mouse a little, and click again to anchor the next point. Keep going like that until you have completely defined the curve. Don't draw the entire curve before you click! You need to create interim anchor points along the way. Double-click when finished.

◆ For a Freeform path, click for each anchor point you want; straight lines will appear between them. Double-click when finished.

◆ For a Scribble, the pointer changes to a pencil. Draw on the slide with the mouse button held down the whole time. Single or double-click when finished, or just release the mouse button and pause for a second.

You can modify these motion paths just as you can with the path shapes supplied by PowerPoint.

Locking and Unlocking Motion Paths

Open the Path drop-down list on the Custom Animation task pane for your motion path, and you'll find Locked and Unlocked settings. The default is Unlocked. Locking it locks the path into place so that if you move the object to which the path is applied, the path will remain in its own spot. Unlocked allows the path to move along with the object.

Layering Animated Objects

Part of the "art" of custom animation is in thinking about which objects should appear and disappear and in what order. Theoretically, you could layer all the objects for every slide in the entire presentation on a single slide and use custom animation to make them appear and disappear on cue.

 If you are thinking about creating complex layers of animation where some objects disappear and are replaced by other objects on the same slide, first take a step back and consider whether it would be easier to simply use two or more separate slides. When there is no delay or animation defined in the transition between two slides (if their content is identical or very similar), the effect is virtually identical to that of layered animated objects—with much less time and effort to set up.

Layering can be useful when you want part of a slide to change while the rest of it remains static. For example, you could create your own animated series of illustrations by stacking several photos and then animating them so that first the bottom one appears, then the next one on top of it, and so on. This can provide a rough simulation of motion video from stills, much like flipping through illustrations in the corners of a stack of pages. Set the animation speeds and delays between clips as needed to achieve the desired effect.

When objects are stacked, the new object placed over the top of the old obscures the old one, so it is not necessary to include an exit action for the item beneath.

However, if the item being placed on top is smaller than the one beneath, you will want to set up an exit effect for the one beneath and have it occur concurrently (that is, With Previous) with the entrance of the new one.

An example may make this clearer. Suppose, you want to place a photo on the right side of a slide and some explanatory text for it at the left, and then you want it to be replaced by a different photo and different text (see Figure 13-22).

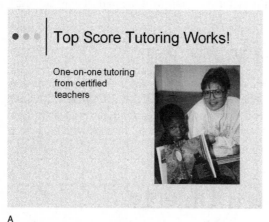

A

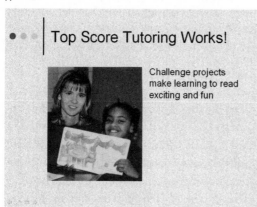

B

Figure 13-22: First the slide should appear as shown at top, and then it should change to show the content shown at bottom.

To set this up to occur all on the same slide, you would first place the content that should appear first, and then apply exit effects to the content, as shown in Figure 13-23. Notice that the picture is set to On Click for its exit effect, which will make the picture disappear when you click. The accompanying text box is set for With Previous, which means that it will disappear at the same time that the picture disappears.

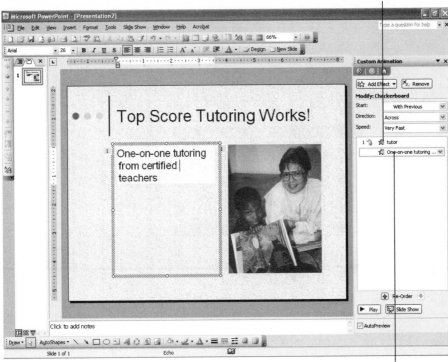

The picture exits on a click.

The text box exits when the picture exits.

Figure 13-23: Place the "bottom" layer object first and animate the objects with exit effects.

Next, I'll place the other text box and other picture over the top of the first items. The new photo obscures the old text box.

Then, I'll animate the new text box, and the new picture with entrance effects that are set to With Previous, so that both will appear at the same time that the other two items are exiting (see Figure 13-24). Notice that they all have the same animation number, 1, because they all occur simultaneously.

It's always a good idea to preview animation effects in Slide Show view after creating them. Click the Slide Show View icon in the bottom left corner of the screen to preview the active slide, then press Esc to return to PowerPoint.

Animating Charts

If you have a chart created with Microsoft Graph (see Chapter 11), you can introduce the chart all at once or you can set up some animation effects for it. You can make the chart appear by series (that is, broken down by legend entries), by category (broken down by X-axis points), or by individual elements in a series or category. Figures 13-25 and 13-26 show progressions based on series and category so you can see the difference.

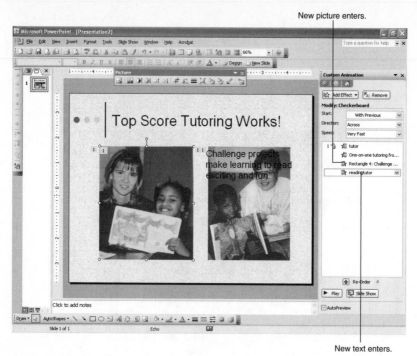

New picture enters.

New text enters.

Figure 13-24: Place the next layer of objects on the slide, and animate their entrances to be With Previous.

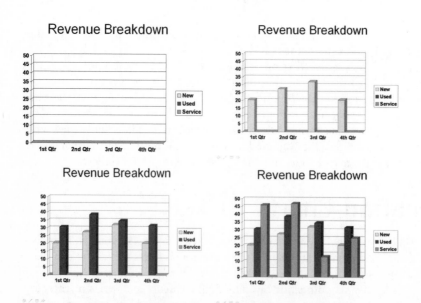

Figure 13-25: In this progression, the chart is appearing by series.

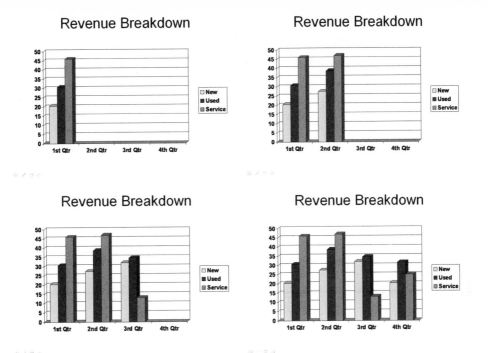

Figure 13-26: In this progression, the chart is appearing by category.

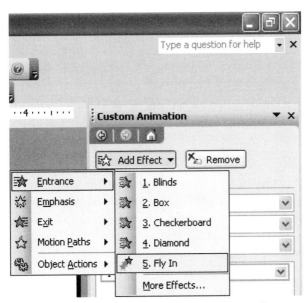

Figure 13-27: Apply a custom animation entrance effect to the chart as a whole.

To animate a chart, follow these steps:

1. Display the slide containing the chart in Normal view, and display the Custom Animation task pane.

2. Animate the chart with an entrance effect (your choice). See Figure 13-27.

3. In the task pane, click the Chart animation, open its menu, and choose Effect Options.

4. Click the Chart Animation tab.

5. Open the Group Chart drop-down list and choose how you want the chart animated (see Figure 13-28).

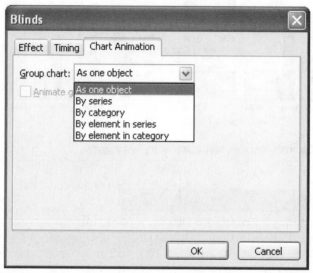

Figure 13-28: Animate a chart by series, by category, or by individual data points.

 Some effects cannot be used to animate the parts of a chart separately; if that's the case for the effect you chose in step 2, you will not have any options except As One Object on the Group Chart list in step 5. If that happens, go back to step 2 and choose a different effect.

6. Click OK. Then, in the task pane click the double down-pointing arrow to expand the listing of animated elements. Notice that each part of the chart (each category or series, depending on your earlier choice) is its own entry in the list of animations (see Figure 13-29).

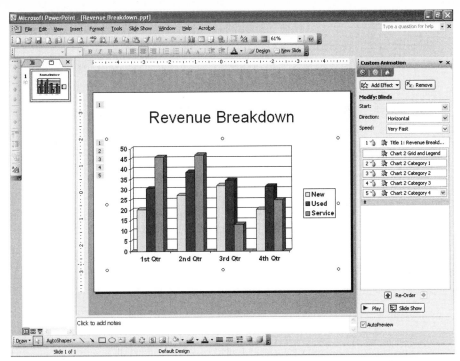

Figure 13-29: Each animated segment of the chart appears separately in the task pane.

Summary

In this chapter you learned how to add action to your static slides with transitions, animation schemes, and custom animations, and how to set sequencing and timings between them. Use these skills to get really creative and innovative with your presentation designs.

Animation effects can simulate motion video, but they are nowhere near as realistic and sophisticated as real video. In Chapter 14 you will learn how to capture and integrate real motion video into your presentations.

Chapter 14

Incorporating Motion Video

IN THE PRECEDING CHAPTER YOU LEARNED how to use animation and transition effects to make a presentation appear to be moving—well, *almost*. While animation does provide some movement in a presentation, few would mistake it for a real video clip. This chapter rounds out this section of the book on movement by showing how you can integrate various types of motion video clips in a PowerPoint presentation, for the ultimate in moving content.

Where Do Videos Come from?

Let's begin at an obvious starting point: figuring out how you are going to get a hold of the videos you need.

Not all videos are live-action recordings; some are digitally created cartoons (either 2-D or 3-D). PowerPoint can show both kinds. The difference is not that important once you get them into PowerPoint, but when you are determining how you will acquire clips, it's helpful to make the distinction.

The following sections discuss the types of videos that PowerPoint supports.

Animated GIFs

When is a video not *really* a video? When it's an animated GIF.

As you may already know, GIF is a file format for static graphic files. One of the advantages of it over other graphic file formats is that you can create animated

379

versions. These are not really videos in the traditional sense; they are a collection of still graphic images stored in a single file under one name. When the file is displayed—on a presentation slide, a Web page, or some other place—it cycles through the still graphics at a certain speed, making a very rudimentary animation. The animation of an animated GIF cannot be controlled through PowerPoint, nor can it be set up to repeat a certain number of times. That information is contained within the GIF file itself. PowerPoint simply reads that information and plays the GIF accordingly.

PowerPoint's Clip Organizer comes with many animated GIFs that have simple conceptual plots, like time passing, gears turning, and computers passing data between them. They are more like animated clip art than real movies or even real animated clips, but they do add an active element to an otherwise static slide.

TIP It is possible to convert an animated GIF to a "true" video format, such as AVI. However, you can't do it using PowerPoint alone; you'll need a conversion utility. Paint Shop Pro comes with an Animation Shop utility that will do this (www.jasc.com), as do many GIF-editing programs.

A few of the animation clips from the Clip Organizer are actually AVI files, rather than animated GIF. This is significant because you have more options when working with an AVI than with a GIF. For example, when you click on an AVI during a slide show, it pauses, but clicking on a GIF has no effect. To determine the format of a clip from the Clip Organizer, point at it in the Clip Art task pane; a ScreenTip appears showing its keywords, and one of them will be either GIF or AVI.

Most of what you will learn in this chapter about working with videos will not apply to animated GIFs. The reason I include them in this discussion is that the Clip Organizer refers to them as "movies," and unless you understand that they're really GIFs, it can be confusing.

Live-Action Videos

Now, we get into the "real videos." Recorded videos have a live origin. Someone went out with a video camera and pointed it at something in the world (see Figure 14-1). You can get live-action video from the Internet, but in most cases for business presentations, you will want to record it yourself with a camera to suit your purpose. You might use recorded video to present a message from someone who could not be present in person, show how a product functions, or provide a tour of a facility, for example.

There are two kinds of video cameras: digital and non-digital. It's important to know which kind you have, because they hook up to the PC differently to transfer the video. A digital video camera hooks up directly to the PC via a USB or FireWire interface port, whereas a regular (analog) video camera requires a conversion box or an adapter card that will convert analog video to digital video.

Figure 14-1: Live-action video is video that was filmed from "real life."

If you are not sure what type of video camera you have, look at how it stores the video. If it stores it on a VHS or mini-tape, it's analog. If it stores it on a disk or cartridge that says "digital" on it, it's digital. Also, look at its interfaces. If it's digital, it will have either a USB or a FireWire port. (However, don't look for a plug with the same shape and size as the USB or FireWire plug that fits into your PC; the end of the cable that fits into the video camera will be smaller and more square.)

You will probably not import videos directly from the camera into PowerPoint because they will be too rough and may contain extraneous footage, unwanted sounds, or awkward jerks or transitions. Instead, you'll want to polish up your videos in a video-editing program. Windows Movie Maker, which comes with Windows Me and Windows XP, is a decent low-end choice. If you bought an analog-to-digital video converter box or card, it may have come with video-editing software as well. Video editing can be very time-consuming, so allow plenty of time to do this work before assembling your presentation in PowerPoint.

 TIP Don't assume that you have to record every bit of live-action footage with your own camera. As long as you are diligent about obeying copyright restrictions, you can safely download tons of great footage from the Internet. For example, the Internet Archive at www.archive.org contains links to huge repositories of footage on all subjects, mostly pre-1964 material on which the copyright has expired. Warning—you can easily get sucked in here and waste several days browsing!

 TIP If you spend a lot of time working with video in PowerPoint, try out Microsoft Producer 2003, an add-in for PowerPoint that helps you capture, synchronize, and publish audio, video, slides, and images, and publish them in online format. It is free to licensed users of PowerPoint 2002 and 2003. It makes it easy to capture audio and video from VHS, DVD, and Beta SP. It also enables you to export to HTML using a library of templates based on cascading style sheets. See `www.microsoft.com/office/powerpoint/producer/prodinfo/default.mspx`.

Digital Animation

Animation does not have a live origin—it's a simulation of life. Simple animations appear cartoonish, but there are animation applications that, in the right hands, can create extremely realistic 3-D simulations. Digital animation is useful when showing things that either don't exist yet or are unavailable for live filming. For example, you could demonstrate how a planned product will be built or how it will work after it is manufactured. Simple cartoons can also add a whimsical touch or lighten the mood in a presentation. Figure 14-2 shows a frame from a digital animation that explains how the PCI slot on a motherboard works, for example.

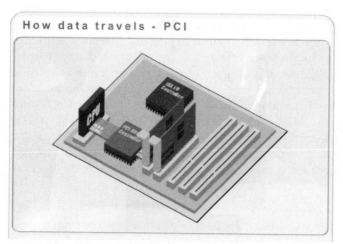

Figure 14-2: Digital animation consists of a sequence of computer-generated drawings.

To create your own animations, turn to a separate animation application; Power-Point doesn't have any capability for doing it. If you want high-end, high-quality 3-D animation, you'll want a professional-quality application like Adobe After Effects.

Video File Formats

The video-capture-/-editing program you use to create or acquire your video clips will determine the file's format and specifications. PowerPoint can accept videos with the following file formats:

◆ Audio Video Interleave (.avi)

◆ QuickTime (.mov or .qt) versions 1 and 2.x

Versions of QuickTime 3 and higher will not work as an inserted movie in PowerPoint. You would need to either insert a later-format QuickTime file as an object (choose Insert ➪ Object) or convert it to a supported format, such as AVI using a third-party utility. Here's an excellent article about it: www.indezine.com/products/powerpoint/ppquicktime.html.

◆ Motion Picture Experts Group (.mpg, .mpeg, .m1v, .mp2, .mpa, and .mpe)

◆ Microsoft streaming format (.asf and .asx)

◆ Microsoft movie format (.wmv)

You may not have a choice in the settings used for recording live video or the file format. If you do have a choice, AVI is among the best formats for use in PowerPoint because of its near-universal compatibility. There may be compatibility issues with video in some MPEG variants, such as MPEG-2 and MPEG-4, such that you might need to install a separate DVD-playing utility or a specific codec to handle those formats. (See the *Clip Won't Play in PowerPoint* section later in the chapter for more information.)

On the theory that Microsoft-to-Microsoft always works, the Windows Media Video (.wmv) format is also a good choice. Since Windows Movie Maker creates its movies in this format by default, it's a good bet that it will work well in PowerPoint.

If you have a choice in quality, balance file size against quality, usually measured in frames per second (fps), which will be anywhere from 15 (low) to 30 (high), or in kilobits per second, which will be anywhere from 38kbps to 2.1mbps. You might experiment with different settings to find one with acceptable quality for the task at hand with the minimum of file size. With Windows Movie Maker, for example, there are a wide variety of quality settings available.

What's the difference between a movie and a video? There really isn't any. PowerPoint uses the terms interchangeably.

If you would like to know more about video editing and digital video formats and issues, check out the *PC Magazine Guide to Digital Video* by Jan Ozer (Wiley Publishing, Inc., 2004).

Incorporating Video Clips

Your first step is to place the movie clip on the slide. After that you can worry about the position, size, and playing options. Just as with audio clips, you can place the clip from a file or from the Clip Organizer. (Of course, it has to already be in the Clip Organizer to use that method; you can add video clips to the Clip Organizer the same as you added artwork in Chapter 9.)

Video clips are linked, not embedded, in the presentation. If you move the presentation file to another location, make sure you move the movie clips too. For this reason, inserting videos from the Clip Organizer may not be a good idea; it's linked from the original location and difficult to move if you move the presentation.

Animated GIFs are different; they are embedded like normal graphics (select Insert ⇨ Picture ⇨ From File).

Inserting a Video Clip from the Clip Organizer

Just as with sounds and graphics, you can organize movie files with the Clip Organizer. Most of the clips that are in the Clip Organizer are animated GIFs, but a few are AVI format instead, offering more options. You won't find any live-action video clips in the Clip Organizer unless they were cataloged from content that was already on your hard disk. (However, you can catalog such clips to make them appear there, as you learned in Chapter 9.)

To insert a movie from the Clip Organizer, choose Insert ⇨ Movies and Sounds ⇨ Movie from Clip Organizer. The Clip Organizer task pane appears with the file type set to show only movies. All the available clips in the specified location(s) appear by default; you can filter the list with keywords just like with clip art (see Figure 14-3). Click the clip you want, and it appears on the slide. The only difference from clip art is that a box appears asking whether you want it to play Automatically or When Clicked (just like with sounds as discussed in Chapter 12).

The Clip Organizer shows real movies mixed up together with animated GIFs in the search results. Check a clip's properties if you're in doubt as to its type.

Unlike normal clip art, most videos and animated GIFs lose quality when you resize them. Try to use a movie clip at as close to its original size as possible.

Star indicates an animated clip.

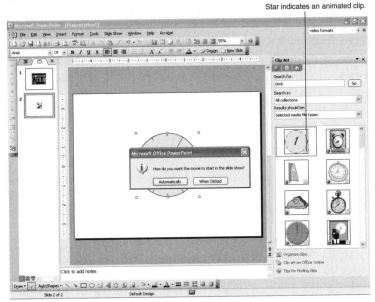

Figure 14-3: Insert movies from the Clip Organizer.

If you find some movies or animated GIFs that you would like to have available later, you might want to add them to the local collection of clips on your hard disk. That way if your Internet connection is not available later, you can still access them.

 See Chapter 9 for information about the Clip Organizer and making clips available offline.

Inserting a Movie from a File

If the movie is not in the Clip Organizer and you don't want to bother with placing it there, you can place it directly just like any other content. Use the Insert⇨Movies and Sounds⇨Movie from File command if you want it to play from within Power-Point (recommended, if possible), or use Insert⇨Object to insert it to play with some external player for that type of content.

Setting Movie Options

Video clips are a lot like sounds in terms of what you can do with them. You can specify that they should play when you point at them or click them (with their Action Settings), or you can make them play, pause, and stop at a certain time (with Custom Animation).

Animated GIFs always play the number of times specified in their header. That could be infinite looping (0), or it could be a specified number of times. You can't control it. (You can, however, delay its appearance with custom animation.) Other movies, such as your own recorded video clips, have more settings you can control.

Playing on Mouse Click or Mouse Over

When you insert a clip, its default play setting depends on the choice you made in the dialog box, as shown in Figure 14-3. It will either be set up to play on mouse click (if you chose On Click), or it will be set up through Custom Animation to play automatically after the slide begins (if you chose Automatically).

In addition, just like with sounds, you can change the Action Settings, if desired, to adjust the clip's Mouse Over and Mouse Click settings. To do so, right-click the clip and choose Action Settings. Then, on the Mouse Click and Mouse Over tabs make your selections, as you did with sounds in Chapter 12. Many of the options will not be available; mostly you will be choosing between None and Object Action: Play (see Figure 14-4).

Figure 14-4: Control a clip's Mouse Over and/or Mouse Click settings in its Action Settings dialog box.

Controlling a Clip's Volume and Appearance

If you are working with a real video clip (not an animated GIF), you can also edit the movie object controls. These controls enable you to specify whether the video plays in a continuous loop or not, and which frame of the movie remains on the screen when it is finished (the first or the last). You can also control whether any clip controls appear on the slide.

To check them out, right-click the movie clip on the slide and choose Edit Movie Object. The Movie Options dialog box appears (see Figure 14-5). From here you can do the following:

◆ Mark the Loop until stopped checkbox if desired, to make the clip repeat until you move to the next slide or until you click it to pause it.

◆ Mark the Rewind movie when done playing checkbox if you want the first frame of the clip to appear on-screen after the clip has finished; otherwise the last frame will appear there.

◆ Set the sound volume for the clip in relation to the overall sound for the presentation by clicking the Sound volume icon and then dragging the slider. This works just like it did for sounds in Chapter 12.

◆ Mark the Hide while not playing checkbox if desired, to make the clip go away when it is not playing. Do this only if the clip will play automatically, because if you set it to On Click and it's hidden, you won't be able to find it to click it.

◆ Mark the Zoom to full screen checkbox if you want the clip to play in full-screen size. (This is not such a great idea if the clip is low-resolution and you have a large monitor, because it will look all grainy.)

Figure 14-5: You can control some play options from this dialog box for movie files.

Understanding Custom Animation Play Options for Video

When you place a movie clip on a slide and set it to play automatically, the Custom Animation task pane (choose Slide Show⇨Custom Animation) will have two entries for it by default: Play and Pause. For example, in Figure 14-6, it's set to play automatically when the slide appears and to pause when clicked. If you set it to play When Clicked when you insert it, you'll only have the Pause trigger.

Figure 14-6: These two entries represent a single movie clip. The top one starts it playing automatically, and the second one pauses the clip when you click it.

Before setting the custom animation properties for the clip, it's important to select carefully. If you click the clip on the slide, both of the animation triggers for that object become selected at once (there'll be a gray box around each of them). If you then open the menu for either clip and choose Timing or Effect Options, the Effect Options dialog box appears, with settings that refer to all instances of custom animation for the clip. However, if you select only one of the animation triggers and then right-click and choose Timing or Effect Options, either a Play Movie or Pause Movie dialog box will appear, and those settings refer only to that instance of animation.

Controlling When the Video Will Play

You can control the play timing for real video clips (not animated GIFs) through the Custom Animation box. These settings enable you to specify whether the video should play automatically when the slide appears and whether there should be a delay before it, much like with sound clips (as discussed in Chapter 12).

These controls are accessed from the Custom Animation task pane (choose Slide Show ⇨ Custom Animation). After selecting the appropriate item, right-click it and choose Timing. A dialog box opens with the Timing tab on top. Depending on what you selected, the dialog box may be called Effect Options, Play Movie, or Pause Movie.

Here are the settings that all three of those dialog boxes have in common:

◆ *Start*: Your choices are On Click, With Previous, or After Previous.

◆ *Delay*: This is the delay in seconds between the Start event described previously and the clip playing.

In addition, the Play Movie dialog box has these additional items:

◆ *Repeat*: Choose how many times you want the clip to repeat before it stops.

◆ *Rewind when done playing*: If you want the last frame of the movie to remain on-screen after it completes, leave this checkbox unmarked. If you want the first frame to reappear, mark this checkbox.

All of these dialog boxes have a Triggers button that displays or hides the extra trigger options, just like with sounds in Chapter 12. Triggers specify when the action should occur. They enable you to trigger an event as a result of clicking the event object itself or on something else. For example, you can place a movie on the slide and have it play when someone clicks a button that you create with AutoShapes. You could also create a Pause AutoShape that would trigger a pause event, or you can leave the settings as they are. A pause trigger that allows you to pause the movie by clicking on it is inserted by default when you insert the movie.

Specifying Where a Clip Will Begin

Just like with sounds, you can specify that a video clip should play from some point other than the beginning and should continue through a certain number of slides and then stop. Because you probably would not want a video clip to continue to play after you have moved past its slide, the stopping portion is less useful for videos than for sounds. However, the Start feature can be very helpful in trimming off any portion of the beginning of the clip that you don't want.

To set the start point for the clip, you must have the Play event of the custom animation selected—not the Pause event or the clip itself. (See the description in the preceding section.)

Open the Play Movie dialog box by right-clicking the Play event and choosing Effect Options. If you get the Pause Movie dialog box when you do this, *you are in the wrong place*; try again.

From there, in the Start Playing section of the Effect tab (see Figure 14-7), choose the desired starting point:

Figure 14-7: Specify the starting and stopping points for the clip.

◆ *From beginning*: The default starting point.

◆ *From last position*: The starting point will be at whatever point it was paused or stopped earlier. If it was not paused or stopped earlier, the starting point is the beginning.

◆ *From time*: The starting point will be a certain number of seconds into the clip. (You specify the number of seconds.)

Then, in the Stop Playing section, if desired, set up the video to stop either on a click, after the current slide, or after a specified number of slides.

Sizing the Video Clip Window

You can resize a video clip's window just like any other object. Simply drag its selection handles. Be careful, however, that you do not distort the image by resizing in only one dimension. Make sure you drag a corner selection handle, not one on a single side of the object.

Be aware that when you enlarge a video clip's window, the quality of the clip suffers. If you make the clip too large and are unhappy with its quality, you can reset it to its original size: right-click the clip and choose Format Picture, and on the Size tab, click Reset.

Balancing Video Impact with File Size and Performance

When you are recording your own video clips with a video camera or other device, it is easy to overshoot. Video clips take up a huge amount of disk space.

Movie files are linked to the PowerPoint file, rather than embedded, so they do not dramatically increase the size of the PowerPoint file itself. However, since the linked movie file is required when you show the presentation, having a movie does greatly increase the amount of disk space required for storing the whole presentation package.

Depending on the amount of space available on your computer's hard disk, and whether you need to transfer your PowerPoint file to another PC, you may want to keep the number of seconds of recorded video to a minimum to ensure that the file size stays manageable. On the other hand, if you have a powerful computer with plenty of hard disk space and lots of cool video clips to show, go for it!

Playing Flash Content in PowerPoint

The easiest way to insert Flash content is to use the Flash Movie tool, which is part of Shyam's toolbox, on the CD that comes with this book.

 The Flash object will always remain on top in the presentation. You can't layer it or place anything on top of it.

You can also set it up manually, but it's a bit complicated. Before you start, make sure you have the Shockwave Flash ActiveX Object installed. If you have ever visited a Web site that uses Flash and downloaded the control when prompted, then you already have it.

Then follow these steps:

1. Display the Control Toolbox toolbar.

2. Click More Controls.

3. Choose Shockwave Flash Object. Draw a box where you want the content to be placed.

4. Right-click the box and choose Properties. This will open a Visual Basic code window.

5. In the Movie property, in the Value box, type the full path to the file. Make sure the Playing property is set to True.

6. Return to PowerPoint and save it. Then, try running it.

The preceding steps, by the way, are based on an excellent article found at www.flashgeek.com/index.htm. If you need more detail, check out that original article.

If you get a red X instead of the object, check the version of the Shockwave component and the version of the Flash movie. The Flash ActiveX component must be at least as high a number as the Flash movie. If you are creating the Flash movie yourself, save it as Flash 3 so it will run on any machine.

TIP To make a Flash movie rewind automatically, get the FlashBack add-in, available at www.mvps.org/skp/flashback.htm.

Playing Macromedia Director Content in PowerPoint

Macromedia Director content does not import directly into PowerPoint, but you can insert it as an ActiveX control. Here's how to do it:

1. Update your Director control at www.macromedia.com/shockwave/download/index.cgi? P1-Prod-Version=Shockwave.

2. In Director, output the file in DCR format, in the same folder as the Power-Point presentation file.

3. In PowerPoint, display the Control Toolbox toolbar.

4. Click More Controls.

5. Choose Shockwave ActiveX. Draw a box where you want the content to be placed.

6. Right-click the box and choose Properties.

7. In the SC box, type the name of the DCR file. (It's an absolute path so you will need to update it later if you move the presentation.)

TIP

Need to go the other way and put PowerPoint content into director? Warning: it's not easy.

Director version 6.5 and higher has an Xtra (add-in) that imports PowerPoint files into Director. However, it accepts only PowerPoint version 4.0 files, and Power-Point 2003 does not save to that format. Therefore you have to save in Pow-erPoint 97 format, then open the file in a copy of PowerPoint 97 and save to PowerPoint 4.0 format.

You can also set up a script in your Director file that runs the PowerPoint viewer and uses it to run a presentation in a separate space. You could cre-ate a Director front-end that runs multiple presentations interactively as the user clicks them. Here is an article that provides more information, by Adam Crowley and Geetesh Bajaj: www.indezine.com/products/powerpoint/ppdirector2.html.

Troubleshooting

Any time you are working with multimedia clips like video, you are likely to run into compatibility and performance issues because not all computers support multimedia equally well. It can take up quite a bit of CPU time and memory to do a good job, and not all PCs are up to it. In addition, not all PCs have the needed software and codecs installed to handle all types of clips.

Clip Won't Play in PowerPoint

If you can't get a certain clip to play within PowerPoint, but you have some other media player that it will play in, use Insert➪Object to insert the video clip instead of inserting it with Insert➪Movies and Sounds➪Movie from File. The clip will then play using whatever player is defined as the default for that file type. However, it will not be eligible for any PowerPoint animation or timing settings; you will need to use the external player's controls for it.

To set up a default player for a certain file type, do the following:

1. From a Windows file management window, such as My Computer, choose Tools⇨Folder Options.

2. On the File Types tab, locate the desired extension, select it, and then click the Change button.

3. Choose the desired application to associate with that extension and click OK.

If the clip will not play anywhere—not in PowerPoint or in any of your players—then perhaps your system does not have the needed codec. A *codec* is a compression/decompression driver, and different formats need different ones.

When you play a video clip in Windows Media Player 9 for which you do not have a codec, it will try to connect to Microsoft's servers to download one automatically. If it fails, you can try manually searching the Web for a suitable codec for that file format. You can also try downloading the latest official set of codecs for Windows Media Player from www.microsoft.com/windows/windowsmedia/format/codecdownload.aspx.

DVD movie clips are a special case. Windows Media Player may attempt to play them but fail, and you'll get an unhelpful generic error message. This is usually caused by not having a DVD hardware or software-based encoder/decoder. If your PC plays DVD movies, then you already have one. If not, there are many good ones. You might give WinDVD a try; a free trial is available at www.intervideo.com. You can then use Insert⇨Object to insert the clip and let it play with WinDVD (or whatever player you are using.)

If you record video with your own video camera, and it won't play in PowerPoint, it is probably because your camera uses a proprietary codec. Use the software that comes with the camera to rerender it using a more common codec. Some of the most popular standard codecs are Cinepak and Indeo Video Codec (R3.1, R3.2, 5.04). A utility called *gspot*, available at www.headbands.com/gspot, can identify what codecs are being used in your video files.

This may seem hard to believe, but it's true. If you get an error message when you try to drag-and-drop an AVI video clip into your presentation, or if you try to insert it and PowerPoint simply ignores you, try renaming the file extension from .avi to .mpg. This often will fix it.

Playback Quality Is Poor

Be aware that slower, older computers, especially those with less than 64MB to 128MB of RAM, may not present your video clip to its best advantage. The sound may not match the video, the video may be jerky, and a host of other little annoying performance glitches may occur if your PC is not powerful enough. On such PCs, it is best to limit the live-action video that you use, and rely more on animated GIFs, simple AVI animations, and other less system-taxing video clips.

When constructing a presentation, keep in mind that you may be showing it on a lesser computer than the one on which you are creating it, and therefore performance problems may crop up during the presentation that you did not anticipate when creating it. Here are some ideas for at least partially remedying the situation:

◆ Copy the entire presentation and all its support files to the fastest hard disk on the system, rather than running it from a CD. Hard disks have much faster access time than removable disks. Use Package for CD to copy the needed files rather than simply copying through the file management interface in Windows, to ensure you get all the files.

◆ Run the entire presentation on the playback PC from start to finish beforehand. If there are delays, jerks, and lack of synchronization, just let it play itself out. Then try the whole presentation again, and it will usually be much better the second time. This happens because the system caches some of the data, and it's faster reading it from the cache than from the disk.

◆ Make sure the playback PC is in the best shape it can be in. If it is feasible to upgrade its RAM, do so. Run Disk Defragmenter and Disk Cleanup on it, and make sure its video driver is updated.

◆ Work with the original media clips to decrease their complexity, and then reimport them into PowerPoint. For example, use video-editing software to lower the frames per second of video clips, and use image-editing software to lower the dots per inch of any large graphics.

◆ If possible, spread out the more complex slides in the presentation so they are not adjacent to one another. Have an intervening slide that is just simple text.

◆ If all else fails, copy the presentation to videotape or digital video from the original PC (where presumably it plays correctly). See the following section for tips on that.

◆ Make sure you test the presentation on the actual computer on which you are going to show it, especially if you are using a non-standard codec.

Copying a Presentation to Videotape

While not normally considered an optimal presentation method, sometimes VHS video is the only format that will do for a presentation, for one reason or another.

If you have a video card with TV/video out capability, such as an ATI All-In-Wonder card, the process is very easy. Hook the video card to your VCR with a compatible cable (S-Video if possible, because it's the best quality), press *Record* on the VCR, and start the presentation on the PC. It doesn't get much easier than that.

If you don't have a video card with TV/video out, consider buying one; they're not that expensive, and you will be saving yourself a tremendous amount of grief and headache. Otherwise, you will need to buy a scan converter, which is an external box that converts between PC and TV/VCR, and a decent one of those will be around $150, which is probably more than you would spend on a basic video card with TV/video out.

If you are determined not to buy a video card with TV/video out, see the excellent tutorial produced by the PowerPoint 2000 MVP team at www.soniacoleman .com/Tutorials/PowerPoint/recordvhs.htm, providing much more thorough coverage of the topic than I have presented here.

But wait—you'll want to do some testing before recording your presentation to VHS in its entirety. TV screens, especially the old-time picture tube types (not so much with the newer plasma ones), show colors and shapes differently than PC monitors, and what looks good on the PC may not look so hot on a TV. Before doing the final recording, hook up a television to the VCR and do a test recording. You may decide you need to adjust some colors in the presentation, for example, or change the slide dimensions.

Summary

In this chapter you learned about the various types of video footage that PowerPoint can accept, and how to place such clips on slides and control how they start, play, and stop.

At this point, your presentation is probably just about ready content-wise, right? So it's time to turn the attention to the equally important topic of figuring out the nuts-and-bolts of preparing and presenting a show, such as managing the Slide Show play settings, preparing handouts, and adding navigational controls to a presentation to make it user-interactive.

Part V

Preparing and Presenting a Show

Chapter 15

Managing the Presentation Process

IT'S A NO-BRAINER TO CLICK THE MOUSE to move from slide to slide, right? But Power-Point offers much more in the way of tools for the presenter. You can skip around, jump to hidden slides, branch off into custom mini-shows, and even draw annotations on slides and save those annotations for later use. In this chapter, you'll learn about some of those tools and features that can take your presentation skills to the next level.

Presentation Basics: A Quick Review

I'm assuming that you already know how to start a presentation, right? Just switch to Slide Show view. Then, click the mouse to move to the next slide or activate the next animation. Depending on how you switch to Slide Show view, however, you'll start in a different spot.

◆ If you use the View ➪ Slide Show or Slide Show ➪ View Show commands, or press F5, you'll start at the beginning.

◆ If you click the Slide Show view icon in the bottom left corner of the screen, or press Shift+F5, you'll start with whatever slide was active when you did it.

This is by design; the latter method enables you to quickly check a single slide in Slide Show view without paging through all the others.

399

If you want the slide show to start in Slide Show view when you double-click it from a file management window, rather than opening in Normal view in Power-Point, rename the file so that its extension is .pps instead of the regular .ppt.

The following sections briefly review the basics of presentation navigation.

Displaying the Controls

In Slide Show view, the mouse pointer and show controls are hidden. To make the mouse pointer and the controls appear, move the mouse.

Moving the mouse makes four icons appear in the bottom left corner of the slide. They are rather faint, so they don't distract from the main presentation, but they're obvious if you're looking for them—see Figure 15-1. If you want to hide them again after displaying them, type A or =, or press Ctrl+H.

Back Pen Slide Forward

Figure 15-1: Presentation controls in the bottom left corner in Slide Show view.

 Pressing A or = is not a true toggle; it cycles between three states each time you press one of those keys. The three states are On, Off, and Flash, which makes the items appear briefly on-screen.

Displaying the Slides Menu

Those two middle icons at the bottom left corner of the screen both open menus. The one that looks like a pencil opens the Pen menu, which we'll talk about later in the chapter. The Slides icon—the one that looks like a rectangle—opens the Slides menu, as shown in Figure 15-2. I'll explain the specifics of this menu later in the chapter.

You can also open this same exact Slide Show menu by right-clicking anywhere on the slide. There's no difference. Therefore, that icon doesn't get much real-life use because why would you take the trouble to click directly on a little icon if you could right-click *anywhere* to get the same thing?

Going Forward and Backward

The arrow buttons are Back and Forward—obvious, right? Back moves you to the previous slide or animation, and Forward moves you to the next one.

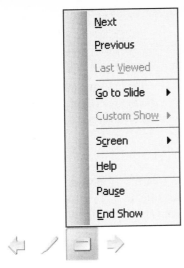

Figure 15-2: Click the Slides icon, or right-click anywhere, to open the Slides menu during the presentation.

 Reread that last sentence above, because there's something important there you may have missed: "*to the previous slide or animation.*" The arrow buttons do not necessarily move you to the next slide; they simply advance or go back one step in the presentation. If, for example, there are six animated events on a slide, the arrow buttons would go to the next event or take back the previous one, all on the same slide.

Most people never use those arrow buttons on-screen because there are so many faster and easier ways to go forward and backward in a presentation as follows:

◆ *To go forward*: N, spacebar, right arrow, down arrow, Enter, Page Down, or left-click, or open the Slides menu and choose Next.

◆ *To go backward*: P, Backspace, left arrow, up arrow, or Page Up, or open the Slides menu and choose Previous.

Notice that the left mouse button takes you forward, but the right mouse button does *not* take you backward. That's because the right mouse button is used to display the Slides menu. (But see the following tip.)

 If you would prefer that the right mouse button take you backward rather than popping up the Slides menu, return to Normal view, choose Tools ⇨ Options, and clear the Popup menu on right mouse click checkbox. If you did this, you would then have to rely on clicking the Slides icon in the bottom left corner in Slide Show view to get to the Slides menu.

You can also go to the last slide viewed. This is usually the same thing as the previous slide, but if you've been jumping around (see the next section), it may not be. To revisit the last slide viewed, display the Slides menu and choose Last Viewed.

Jumping to Specific Slides

There are several ways to jump to a particular slide. One of the easiest is to select the slide from the Slides menu. Choose Go to Slide, and then click the slide you want to go to. Hidden slides (see the next section) appear with their slide numbers in parentheses. The currently displayed slide appears with a check mark next to it (see Figure 15-3).

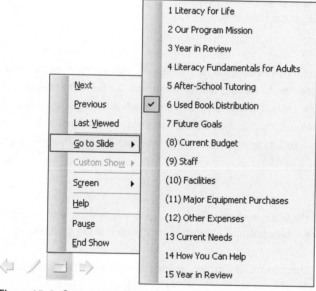

Figure 15-3: Go to a specific slide from the Go to Slide command on the Slides menu.

You can also jump to a certain slide number, if you happen to know the number, by typing that number and pressing Enter.

One more way—you can press Ctrl+S to open the All Slides dialog box, and then make your selection there and click OK (see Figure 15-4).

TIP If you have custom shows defined (these are covered later in this chapter), you can open the Show drop-down list in the All Slides dialog box and choose a particular show; this filters the list of slides to show only the ones in that show. If you have a huge presentation with lots of slides in it and several custom shows, this could potentially be a time-saver; otherwise, you probably won't want to bother with it.

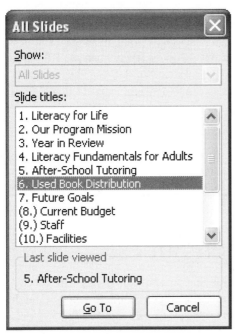

Figure 15-4: Select the slide to display from the All Slides dialog box.

To go back to the beginning of the presentation, you can either type 1 and press Enter, or hold down the left and right mouse buttons together for two seconds.

Blanking the Screen

Sometimes during a live presentation there may be a delay. Whether it's a chatty audience member with a complicated question, a fire drill, or just a potty break, you'll want to pause your show.

Assuming that you have the slides set for manual transition, the show isn't going anywhere. However, whatever slide you stopped on will remain on the screen until you get going again, and perhaps you don't want that. (It can be distracting to the audience, especially if the pause is to let someone get up and speak at a podium in front of the projection screen.)

The solution: turn the screen into a blank black or white expanse. To do so, type W or a comma (for white), or B or a period (for black). To return to the presentation do the same again, or press any key on the keyboard, or click either the right or left mouse button.

While the screen is plain black or plain white, you can draw on it with the Pen tool (which I'll discuss later in the chapter), so it makes a nice quickie "scratch pad." However, there are a couple of quirks with it. First, you must select the pen *before* blanking the screen, because there is no way to open the Pen menu from a blank screen unless a pen pointer is already selected. (When the pen pointer is selected first and then the screen is blanked, the Pen icon is available at the bottom left corner of the screen for changing pen colors.) Second, any annotations you make with the pen while on the blank screen will not be saved; when you resume the presentation, they're gone forever.

Getting Help

Don't feel like you have to remember all the shortcut keys I've been bombarding you with; help is available. In Slide Show view, right-click to display the Slides menu and choose Help to open the Slide Show Help dialog box shown in Figure 15-5, listing all the important shortcut keys.

Working with Hidden Slides

You may not always want to show every slide that you have prepared. Often it pays to prepare extra data in anticipation of a question that you think someone might ask, or to hold back certain data unless someone specifically requests it.

By hiding a slide, you keep it in reserve without making it a part of the main show. Then, at any time during the presentation when (or if) it becomes appropriate, you can call that slide to the forefront to be displayed. Hiding refers only to whether the slide is a part of the main presentation's flow; it has no effect in any view other than Slide Show.

If you have only a handful of slides to hide, go ahead and hide them, but if you have a large group of related slides to hide, consider creating a custom show for them instead, as discussed later in this chapter.

The easiest way to hide and unhide slides is in Slide Sorter view because an indicator appears underneath each slide to show whether it is hidden. That way you can easily tell which slides are hidden and which aren't. Alternatively, you can select the desired slides (in Normal or Slide Sorter view) and then right-click them and choose Hide Slide.

To hide a single slide or a group, select it (or them) and then click the Hide Slide button on the Slide Sorter toolbar. Repeat to unhide. (It's a toggle.) See Figure 15-6. You can also use the Slide Show⇨Hide Slide command if you prefer. That command

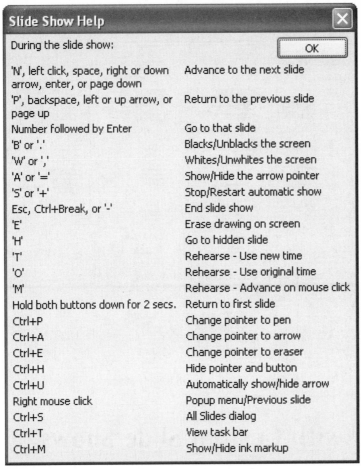

Figure 15-5: Jog your memory regarding keyboard shortcuts by displaying the Slide Show Help dialog box.

works in Normal view too, whereas the Hide Slide button on the toolbar is available only in Slide Sorter view.

To show a hidden slide during the presentation, jump to it using either the Go to Slides command or the All Slides dialog box, covered under *Jumping to Specific Slides* earlier in the chapter. The hidden slides will have parentheses around their numbers.

If you already know the number of the hidden slide, you can simply type the number and press Enter to jump to it. This also works with slides that aren't hidden.

Once you have displayed a hidden slide, you can easily go back to it. When you move backwards through the presentation (using Backspace or one of the other shortcuts), any hidden slides that were displayed previously will be included as you scroll back through. However, if you start moving forward again through the presentation, the hidden slide does not reappear, regardless of its previous viewing.

Hide slide button

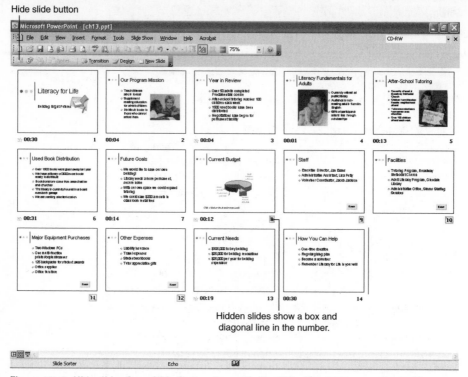

Hidden slides show a box and
diagonal line in the number.

Figure 15-6: Hide slides from Slide Sorter view with the Hide Slide button on the toolbar.
Slides 8 through 12 are hidden.

Working with Custom Slide Shows

Most slide shows have a linear flow: first slide one, then slide two, and so on. This format is suitable for situations where you are presenting clear-cut information with few variables, but if the situation becomes more complex, a single-path slide show may not suffice.

For example, suppose your show's purpose is to convince a group of managers to buy your product. You will sell your product based on three of its qualities. If you encounter any skepticism to your claims about any of these three topics, you want to be prepared to show a set of backup slides presenting the technical facts behind your assertions. Therefore, you will need to prepare three custom shows and keep those custom shows as backups in reserve for those situations. Figure 15-7 shows an example.

You might also use a custom show to set aside a group of slides for a specific audience. For example, you might need to present essentially the same information to employees at two different sites. You could create custom shows within the main show that include the slides that both shows have in common plus slides that are appropriate for only one audience or the other. This is better than creating

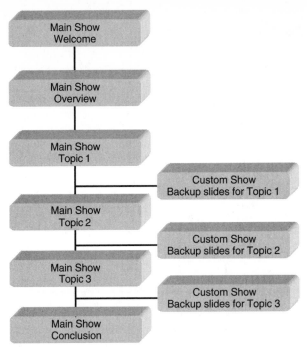

Figure 15-7: You can use custom shows to hide related groups of backup slides.

two separate presentation files because if the common slides need to change, you can make the changes only once, and they will appear in both custom shows. Figure 15-8 shows an example.

Notice in Figure 15-8 that some of the slides in the two custom shows are the same, yet they're repeated in each custom show rather than jumping back to the main presentation. That's because it's much easier to jump to a custom show once and stay there than it is to keep jumping into and out of the show.

Slides in a custom show remain a part of the main presentation. Placing a slide in a custom show does not exclude it from the regular flow. However, you may decide that you don't want to show the main presentation in its entirety anymore; you may just want to use it as a resource pool from which to select the slides for the various custom shows you create in it. You can then create a slide at the beginning of the presentation with buttons that you can click to jump to one custom show or another.

Chapter 17 explains how to create action buttons.

Figure 15-8: Custom shows can allow the same basic presentation to be used for multiple audiences with some of the same slides and some different ones.

Here are some ideas to get you started thinking about how and why you might want to include custom shows in your presentation files:

◆ *Managing change.* By creating a single presentation file with custom shows, you make it easy to manage changes. If any changes occur in your company that affect any of the common slides, making the change once in your presentation file makes the change to each of the custom shows automatically.

◆ *Avoiding duplication.* If you have several shows that use about 50 percent of the same slides and 50 percent different ones, you can create all of the shows as custom shows within a single presentation. That way the presentations can share those 50 percent of the slides that they have in common. (Beware file size, though, if that's an issue for you.)

◆ *Overcoming objections.* As I mentioned earlier, you can anticipate client objections to your sales pitch and prepare several custom shows, each of which addresses a particular objection. Then whatever reason your potential customer gives for not buying your product, you have countermeasures.

◆ *Covering your backside.* If you think that you may be asked for specific figures or other information during a presentation to your bosses, you can have that information ready in a custom show (or on a few simple hidden slides, if there is not much of it) to whip out, if needed.

Creating and Editing a Custom Show

The custom show itself contains no slides per se—it is just a playlist of slides that gets pulled from the main presentation at large when you run the custom show. Therefore, you must create all the slides for the custom show(s) ahead of time, and then define the show. To create a custom show, follow these steps:

1. Choose Slide Show➪Custom Shows. The Custom Shows dialog box opens.

2. Click the New button. The Define Custom Show dialog box appears.

3. Enter a name for your custom show in the Slide Show Name text box.

4. In the Slides in presentation pane, click the first slide that you want to appear in the custom show.

 TIP You can select multiple slides in step 4 by holding down the Ctrl key as you click the ones you want. However, be aware that if you do this, the slides move to the Slides in Custom Show pane in the order that they originally appeared in that selection group. If you want them in a different order, copy each slide over separately in the order that you want them, or rearrange the order when you get to step 7.

5. Click the Add button to copy the slide(s) to the Slides in Custom Show pane (see Figure 15-9).

6. Repeat steps 4 and 5 as needed to add more slides.

7. If you need to rearrange the slides, click the slide and then click the Up or Down arrow buttons.

8. Click OK. The new show appears in the Custom Shows dialog box.

9. (Optional) To test your custom show, click the Show button. Otherwise, click Close to close the dialog box.

To edit a custom show, choose Slide Show➪Custom Shows again to open the Custom Shows dialog box (see Figure 15-10). Select the custom show, click Edit to reopen the Define Custom Show dialog box (refer to Figure 15-9), and make your changes. Removing a slide from a custom show does not remove it from the presentation at large.

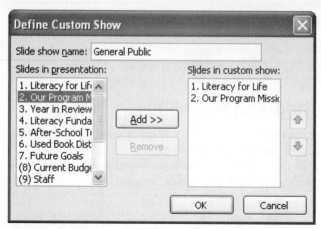

Figure 15-9: Use the Add button to copy slides from the main presentation into the custom show.

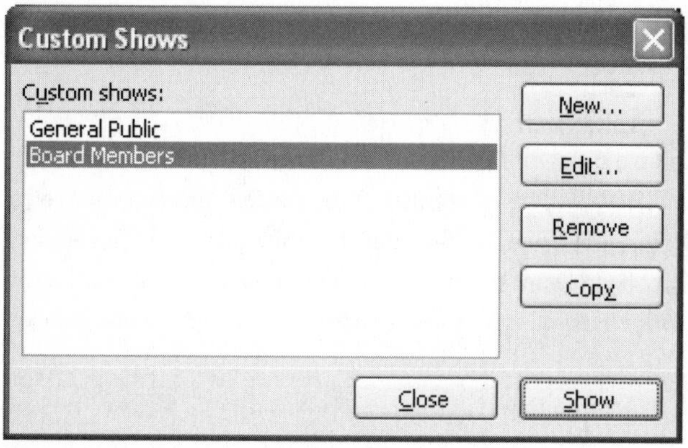

Figure 15-10: Manage your custom shows here.

You may find that you want to create several very similar custom shows; if so, use the Copy button in the Custom Shows dialog box (see Figure 15-10) to create a copy of a show and then edit it (using the Edit button). You can also delete custom shows from the Custom Shows dialog box (using the Remove button).

Displaying a Custom Show During a Presentation

From the Slides menu in Slide Show view, choose Custom Show to open a submenu listing the available custom shows, and then pick the custom show you want.

When you start a custom show, you are no longer in the main presentation. To test this for yourself, open the Slides menu again, point to Go to Slide, and check out the list of slides. The list will include only the slides from the custom show.

To get back to the main show, press Ctrl+S to open the All Slides dialog box, and then from the Show drop-down list choose All Slides. This will give you a full list of all slides in the presentation. Then, simply select a slide you want to go to and click the Go To button (see Figure 15-11).

Figure 15-11: Return to the full presentation from the All Slides dialog box.

Annotating with the Pen Tools

Have you ever seen a coach drawing out football plays on a chalkboard? Well, you can do the same thing in PowerPoint. You can have impromptu discussions of concepts illustrated on slides and punctuate the discussion with your own circles, arrows, and squiggles. (It's a lot easier if you have a Tablet PC, or at least something with a touch-sensitive screen, but it's not impossible to do with an ordinary mouse or trackball.)

The Pen icon in Slide Show view opens a Pen menu, from which you can select your ink color and pen type. The pen types are Ballpoint (a thin line), Felt Tip Pen (a thicker line), and Highlighter (a thick, semi-transparent line). See Figure 15-12. You can also turn on the default pen type (Ballpoint) by pressing Ctrl+P at any time.

The pen stays a pen when you advance from slide to slide. (In earlier versions of PowerPoint, it didn't.) To go back to a regular arrow (no pen), select Arrow, press Ctrl+A, or press Esc.

 The on-screen buttons in the slide show do continue to work while you have the pen enabled, but you have to click them twice to get them to work—once to tell PowerPoint to switch out of Pen mode temporarily and then again to open the menu.

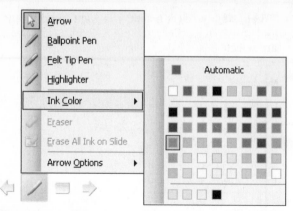

Figure 15-12: Choose a pen color and type.

After enabling a pen, just drag-and-draw on the slide to make your mark. It takes awhile to get good at it with a mouse. Figure 15-13 shows my rather crude attempt.

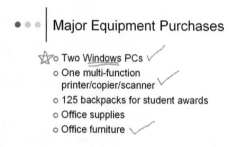

Figure 15-13: Draw on the slide with the pen tools.

TIP As you can see in Figure 15-13, the on-screen pen doesn't produce very attractive results. If you know in advance that you will want to emphasize certain points, build the emphasis into the presentation by making the text larger, bolder, a different color, or animated, or use AutoShapes to put a circle or line on it.

To erase your markings, press *E* (for Erase), or open the Pen menu and choose Erase All Ink on Slide. To erase just a part of the ink, open the Pen menu, choose Erase, and then use the mouse pointer like an eraser.

Annotations stay with the slide even when you move away from it (unlike in earlier versions of PowerPoint).

When you exit Slide Show view after drawing on one or more slides, a dialog box appears asking whether you want to Keep or Discard your annotations. If you choose

Keep, the annotations become drawn objects on the slides, which you can then move, format, or delete just like any other AutoShape. For example, in Figure 15-14 my annotations from Figure 15-13 are selected in Normal view.

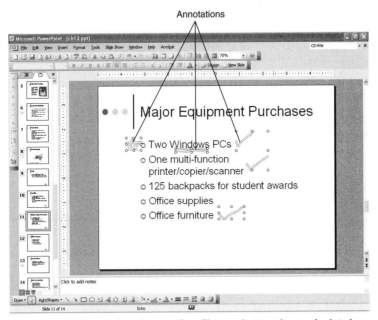

Figure 15-14: Annotations become AutoShapes that can be manipulated as graphics.

 The annotations in Figure 15-14 appear outlined because they are selected. If I were to click away from them to deselect them, they would go back to looking normal (non-outlined).

Viewing Speaker Notes

You will probably want to print out any speaker notes that go along with the presentation (see Chapter 16), but Murphy's Law says that when you need your notes, they will be nowhere to be found. Rather than fumbling around, you may want to refer to the notes on-screen.

Not only can you view notes during a presentation, but you can take more notes. To access your notes pages during a presentation, display the Slides menu and choose Screen➪Speaker Notes. A Speaker Notes box appears (see Figure 15-15). You can just view the notes, or you can make changes to them. When you're finished, close the window.

Literacy for Life

Building Bright Futures

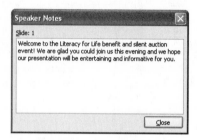

Figure 15-15: View speaker notes on-screen during the presentation.

TIP If you need to refer frequently to your speaker notes as you present, consider using a multi-monitor configuration as described in the next section. That way you can leave the notes box on-screen for yourself without the audience seeing it.

Presenting with a Multi-Monitor Configuration

If you have two monitors—either your notebook PC screen and an external monitor, or two external monitors hooked up to the same PC—you can display the presentation on one of them and your own notes on the other. Very handy!

CAUTION If you create a presentation CD using the Package for CD feature (covered later in the chapter), you can show that presentation on any PC using the built-in PowerPoint viewer. However, you won't be able to use a multi-monitor setup unless PowerPoint is installed on the PC on which you are presenting the show.

Configuring the Display Hardware

First, you need to prepare your display hardware. On a notebook PC, that means enabling both the built-in and the external monitor ports and connecting an external monitor. Some notebook PCs toggle between internal, external, and dual monitors with an Fn key combination; check your documentation.

On a desktop PC, you'll need to install a second video card and monitor, and then set them up in the Display Properties in Windows (on the Settings tab).

Confused? Okay then, here are some specific steps:

1. After you install the second video card and hook up a monitor to it (with the power off, of course), you'll restart the PC, and Windows will recognize the new video card and install any drivers for it, as needed. If it doesn't, you may need to run a Setup utility that came with the video card.

2. Right-click the desktop and choose Properties. In the Display Properties dialog box that appears, click the Settings tab. There should be two monitors shown in the Sample area, as shown in Figure 15-16. If there are not, Windows is not seeing one of the video cards; troubleshoot using the Device Manager (from the System properties in the Control Panel.)

3. Assuming you see two monitors on the Settings tab, the monitor that you use most of the time should be 1 and the other one should be 2. To determine which is which, click the Identify button, and large numbers will briefly appear on each screen.

4. If you need to swap the monitor numbering, click the one that should be the primary monitor and mark the Use This Device as the Primary Monitor checkbox. (It will be unavailable if the monitor is already the primary one.)

5. Select the secondary monitor (by clicking its picture in the sample area) and then click Extend My Windows Desktop Onto This Monitor checkbox.

6. (Optional) If the monitors are not arranged in the Sample area in the way that they are physically positioned on your desk, drag the boxes for the monitors in the sample area to match your physical arrangement. This is not essential, but it does make it easier for you to remember which is which.

7. (Optional) Click a monitor in the sample area and adjust its display settings, if needed. You can change the screen resolution and color quality from the Settings tab. You do not have to have the same resolution for both monitors.

TIP   You can also adjust the refresh rate for each monitor. To do so, make sure you have selected the video card to which the monitor is attached and then click the Advanced button. On the Monitor tab in the dialog box that appears, change the refresh rate. A higher refresh rate makes the screen more flicker-free, but if you exceed the monitor's maximum supported rate, the display may appear distorted and the monitor may be damaged.

Figure 15-16: Set up the monitors in the Display Properties box in Windows.

Now, close all open dialog boxes (click OK), and you're ready to go. You can drag things from your primary monitor to your secondary one. This can be great fun outside of PowerPoint as well as inside. For example, you can have two applications open at once, each in its own full monitor window.

Configuring the Presentation for Two Screens

Next, you'll set up the presentation in PowerPoint to take advantage of the second screen.

Open the presentation and choose Slide Show➪Set Up Show to display the Set Up Show dialog box. In the Multiple Monitors section, open the Display Slide Show On list and choose the monitor that the audience will see. Then, mark the Presenter View checkbox (see Figure 15-17) and click OK.

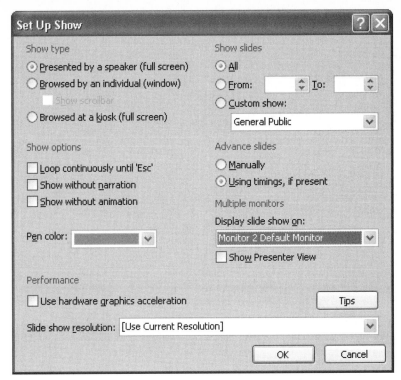

Figure 15-17: Configure the presentation to use a two-monitor setup.

Using Presenter View

Now when you enter Slide Show view, you'll get two very different displays. On the monitor you chose in the Set Up Show dialog box, the presentation will appear in Slide Show view. On the other monitor, Presenter View will display, which is sort of like a modified Normal view. It displays your speaker notes if any, along with thumbnails of the presentation slides and some buttons for controlling the action (see Figure 15-18).

Presenter View doesn't have a lot of bells and whistles. For example, it doesn't have a pen, and it can only black the screen, not "white" it. However, don't forget that the audience's monitor is still active and available for your use! Because you extended the desktop onto the second monitor, you can simply move the mouse pointer onto the audience's display and then use the buttons in its bottom left corner (or right-click for the Slides menu) as you normally can.

After giving your presentation in Presenter view, you might need to reset the primary display monitor in the Windows display settings, especially if the second monitor is going to be disconnected.

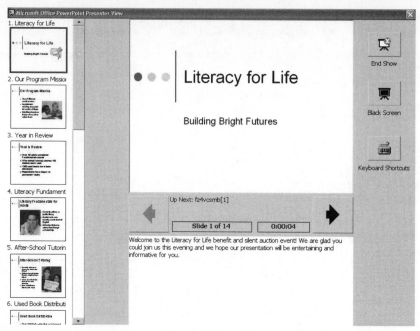

Figure 15-18: Presenter View provides tools for helping you manage your slideshow from a second monitor.

Packaging a Presentation

Many times the PC that you use to create a presentation is not the same one that you use to show it, especially if it's a desktop PC. Therefore, the issue of transferring files from one PC to another is a very real concern.

One way to transfer a presentation to another computer is simply to copy the PowerPoint file (the file with the .ppt extension) using a floppy disk, writeable CD, network, or other medium from one computer's hard drive to another. However, this method is imperfect because it assumes that the other PC has PowerPoint or the PowerPoint Viewer and all the needed fonts, sounds, graphics (if any are linked), music files, and other elements needed for every part of the show. This can be a dangerous assumption.

A better way to ensure that you are getting everything you need is to use the Package for CD feature in PowerPoint. It reads all the linked files and associated objects and makes sure that they are transferred along with the main presentation. You don't even have to have a writeable CD drive—you can send the package to any folder on any drive.

Packaged versions of presentations do not include comments, revisions, or ink annotations. If you want a version that includes those items to be transferred to the destination PC, you will need to copy it there manually.

If you have a CD-R or CD-RW drive, copying the presentation to CD-R is an attractive choice. It produces a self-running disc that contains a PowerPoint Viewer application, the presentation file, and any linked files needed for the show.

You can copy many presentation files to a single CD—not just the currently active one. The only limit is the capacity of the disc (usually 650 to 700MB). Further, you can set them up to run automatically one after the other, or you can specify that a menu will appear so the user can choose each time the CD is inserted.

Windows XP has a built-in CD writing utility that PowerPoint hooks into to make the CD, but earlier versions of Windows do not. Therefore, if you are using Windows 2000, you will package the presentation to a folder on your hard disk and then use a separate CD writing application to create the CD.

 CD-R stands for Compact Disc Recordable; it's a standard for writeable discs that can be written to only once. CD-RW is Compact Disc ReWriteable—the standard for writeable discs that can be written to multiple times. Modern writeable CD drives usually support both, but some older drives support only CD-R. PowerPoint can use either type of blank but will overwrite anything that was previously on a CD-RW disc.

Here's the basic procedure, assuming you have a writeable CD and Windows XP:

1. Place a blank CD-R in your writeable CD drive, or a CD-RW that is either blank or contains nothing you want to keep.

2. Open the presentation in PowerPoint to review it to make sure it is exactly the way you want it. CD-R discs are not rewriteable, so if you make a mistake you will have wasted the disc. (For this reason, it's often better to package to a folder and then burn those files to a CD after testing.)

3. Choose File⇨Package for CD. The Package for CD dialog box opens (see Figure 15-19).

4. Type a name for the CD; this is like a volume label for the disc.

5. (Optional) Add more files to the CD layout, if desired. See *Including Multiple Presentations* later in the chapter for details.

6. (Optional) Set any other options as desired. See *Setting Copy Options* later in the chapter for details.

7. Click the Copy to CD button and wait for the CD to be written. It may take several minutes, depending on the size of the files, the speed of your computer, and the speed of the CD drive's writing capabilities.

8. A message appears when the files are successfully copied to CD, asking whether you want to copy the same files to another CD. Click Yes or No. If you choose No, click Close to close the Package for CD dialog box.

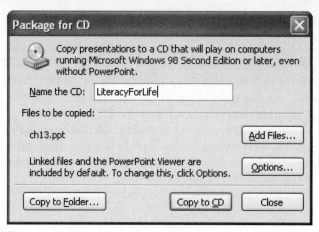

Figure 15-19: Use Package for CD to place all the needed files for the presentation on a CD (or in some other location).

 If you are packaging a Web presentation (.mht file) that PowerPoint originally saved in that format, PowerPoint will convert it back to PowerPoint format when it copies it to the CD. However, standard .mht files that PowerPoint did not generate will remain .mht files.

COPYING TO OTHER LOCATIONS

If you don't have Windows XP, you won't be able to directly write to the CD as in the preceding steps. Instead, you will need to package to a folder on a drive that Windows can directly write to, such as a hard disk, floppy disk, or network location, and then use a third-party CD writing program to make the CD. (You probably have a program that came with your CD writer; popular programs include Roxio Easy CD Creator and Nero Burning ROM.)

 If you are burning a CD using a third-party application, include on that CD only the contents of the folder in which you packaged the presentation, not the folder itself.

Even if you do have Windows XP and a CD writer, you might still want to some-times package to some other location. For example, if you are transferring a pre-sentation from your desktop PC to a notebook computer via a network connection, you could send it directly to the notebook PC's hard disk.

To change the package location from the CD to somewhere else, in the Package for CD dialog box, click the Copy to Folder button. A Copy to Folder dialog box appears (see Figure 15-20). Enter a name for the new folder to be created, and enter a path for it in the Choose Location box. Then, click OK and continue packaging normally.

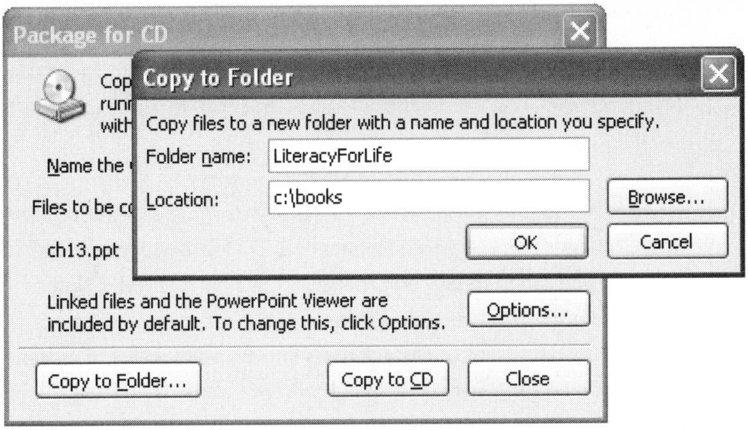

Figure 15-20: Package the presentation files to some other location if appropriate.

INCLUDING MULTIPLE PRESENTATIONS

By default, the active presentation will be included on the CD, but you can also add others, up to the capacity of the disc. For example, perhaps you have several versions of the same presentation for different audiences; a single CD can contain all of them.

As you prepare to copy using the Package for CD dialog box, click the Add Files button. An Add Files dialog box opens. Select the additional files to include (hold down Ctrl to select multiple files), and click Add to return to the Package for CD dialog box. The list of files appears as shown in Figure 15-21, with extra controls.

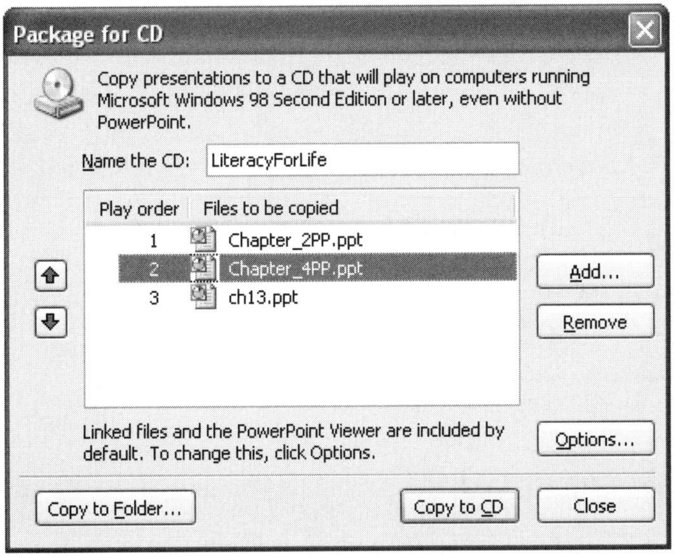

Figure 15-21: You can specify multiple presentations to include on the CD and set the order in which they should play.

If you set up the CD to play the presentations automatically (which is one of the options I'll cover in the next section), the order in which they appear on the list becomes significant. Rearrange the list, if desired, by clicking the Up or Down arrow buttons to the left of the list. Use the Remove button to remove any that aren't needed. Then, continue packaging normally.

If you make a mistake about the order, or want to include more or fewer presentations, you are out of luck if you wrote directly to a CD. However, if you wrote to a hard disk folder, you can manually edit the `playlist.txt` file with Notepad to modify the list of presentations that will play and the order in which they will execute. `Playlist.txt` is a plain-text file that contains a simple list of presentation files, each one on a separate line. You can remove or rearrange these, and you can add other presentations to the list. (If you do that, however, those presentations must be manually copied to the folder, along with any necessary support files.) You cannot repackage to the same folder if you want to redo it through PowerPoint; you must repackage to a different folder name.

SETTING COPY OPTIONS

From the Package for CD dialog box, you can click Options to display a dialog box of additional choices, as shown in Figure 15-22.

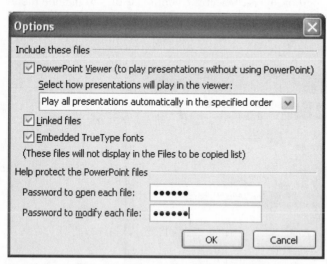

Figure 15-22: Set options for copying the presentation(s) to CD.

Here are the options you can set:

◆ *PowerPoint Viewer.* The PowerPoint Viewer is included by default. It is needed if the destination PC does not have PowerPoint 2002 or 2003 or the

PowerPoint 2003 Viewer installed. Usually it's a good idea to include it, but if you are certain that the destination PC has the needed application and you need the extra space on the CD for more presentation files, omit it by clearing the PowerPoint Viewer checkbox.

◆ *Presentation Play.* Open the Select how presentations will play in the viewer drop-down list and choose one of these:

   ■ *Play all presentations automatically in the specified order.* If you choose this, the order in which the presentations appear on the list becomes significant (see the preceding section).

   ■ *Play only the first presentation automatically.* Again, this makes the order significant. The first presentation, by default, is the one that is active when you opened the dialog box.

   ■ *Let the user select which presentation to view.* This shows a menu when the CD is inserted. A nice feature if you want the user to be able to select each time.

   ■ *Do nothing.* This completely turns off the Autorun for the disc.

◆ *Linked Files.* The Linked Files checkbox is marked by default; it includes the full copies of all linked files. If you clear it, a static copy of the linked data will remain in the presentation, but the link will not work. That's fine for text and graphics, but it doesn't work for sounds and movies. Therefore, it is important to leave the checkbox marked if you have sounds or multimedia files in your presentation, as these are always linked (with the exception of some WAV files).

◆ *TrueType Fonts.* The Embedded TrueType Fonts checkbox is cleared by default. If you think the destination PC might not contain all the fonts used in the presentation, mark it. This makes the presentation file slightly larger. Not all fonts can be embedded; it depends on the level of embedding allowed by the font manufacturer.

◆ *Passwords.* If you want to add password protection to the presentation, do so in the Help protect the PowerPoint Files area. There are separate boxes for read and modify passwords. The passwords apply to the packaged version only; they do not apply to the original presentation file.

Using the PowerPoint Viewer

The PowerPoint Viewer is a utility that shows PowerPoint presentations but cannot edit them. It's kind of like being in Slide Show view permanently. If the PC on which you will show the presentation does not have PowerPoint 2003 installed, the PowerPoint Viewer will be necessary to view the presentation there.

PowerPoint 2003's PowerPoint Viewer is very different and much improved from the version supplied with earlier versions of PowerPoint. Earlier versions often did not play properly. The 2003 PowerPoint Viewer, however, is virtually flawless in its playback abilities. Therefore, if the PC on which you are planning to show the presentation has an earlier version of the PowerPoint Viewer installed, it's best to bring along a copy of the newer Viewer.

Playing a Presentation with the PowerPoint Viewer

To use a self-running presentation CD that you've created with the Package for CD feature, just insert the CD. Assuming the PC has Autorun set up for the CD drive, the presentation will start automatically. If it does not, double-click the CD icon in My Computer.

If you have placed multiple presentations on the CD and specified that a menu should appear for them, a menu (actually a modified Open dialog box) appears when you insert the CD. Select the desired presentation and click Open. This dialog box reappears when the presentation has completed; click Cancel if you're finished.

You can also play presentations with the PowerPoint Viewer independently from any package. Simply double-click the executable file for the viewer (pptview.exe), and a dialog box will prompt you to choose the presentation file to open.

Making the PowerPoint Viewer Available Separately

The PowerPoint Viewer must be packaged with a set of dynamic link library (.dll) files in order to work. When you use the Package for CD feature, it automatically includes those support files.

Here are the files that need to stay together when distributing the PowerPoint Viewer:

- ◆ pptview.exe
- ◆ gdiplus.dll
- ◆ intldate.dll
- ◆ ppvwintl.dll
- ◆ saext.dll
- ◆ unicows.dll

Here's an easy way to make a disk or folder containing these six files:

1. Create a blank presentation, and save it as `Deleteme.ppt`. Then package it for CD, but package it to a folder on your hard disk rather than to a CD.

2. Open that folder in a file management window, such as My Computer, and delete the following files: `Deleteme.ppt`, `Autorun.inf`, `Playlist.txt`, and `Play.bat`. You can keep `pvreadme.htm` if you want; it's optional.

3. (Optional) If you want to make the set of files available to others via e-mail or Web, use a zipping program (or Windows XP's built-in right-click Send To⇨Compressed (zipped) Folder command) to create a ZIP file containing the files.

Add-Ins that Help Show Presentations

Here's a quick roundup of some of the most useful add-ins on the market that extend PowerPoint's ability to present live shows.

◆ *PowerShow* allows you to show multiple presentations on different monitors (`http://officeone.mvps.org/powershow/powershow.html`).

◆ *PPT-Timer* adds a real-timer to Slide Show view so you can keep an eye on how long a presentation is taking (`www.tushar-mehta.com/powerpoint/index.htm`).

◆ *Randomizer* randomizes the order in which slides are shown (`www.tushar-mehta.com/powerpoint/randomslideshow`).

◆ *Kiosk Assistant.* In PowerPoint 2000, kiosk shows used to reset to the first slide after a period of inactivity. You can have that feature back in PowerPoint 2002 and 2003 with this add-in (`http://officeone.mvps.org/kioskassist/kioskassist.html`).

◆ *ShowPlus* lets you view two different shows side-by-side on a single monitor (`http://officeone.mvps.org/showplus/showplus.html`).

◆ *No* Esc lets you disable the Esc key for escaping out of a presentation. Be careful with this because in Kiosk mode Esc is the only way out. Once the Esc key is disabled, you'll need to create an invisible object on the slide and set it to exit the show when clicked (`www.mvps.org/skp/noesc.htm`).

◆ *SundayStar* allows you to start multiple slide shows on a monitor simultaneously and switch between them with keyboard shortcuts (`http://officeone.mvps.org/sundaystar/sundaystar.html`).

◆ *Word/Phrase Search* lets you search for a word or phrase not only from Normal view but also from Slide Show view, so you don' have to leave the show to perform the search (`www.mvps.org/skp/wordsearch.htm`).

Summary

In this chapter you learned many strategies for taking charge of the presentation delivery process, including using the on-screen controls, working with multiple monitors, and packaging a presentation for delivery on some other computer.

But what appears on the screen is only half the picture in a live-action presentation, right? The other half are the handouts that the audience receives. Often the handouts will make a more lasting impression than the live show, since people will take them home and keep them on file. In the next chapter, you'll learn some advanced techniques for maximizing the effectiveness of your printed support materials.

Chapter 16

Attractive Handouts and Speaker Notes

IN THIS CHAPTER

◆ Creating handouts

◆ Using the Handout Master

◆ Creating speaker notes

◆ Modifying handouts and notes pages with Microsoft Word

SO FAR IN THIS BOOK IT'S BEEN ALL ABOUT THE SLIDES, but the slides you show on-screen are actually only part of the equation. For a fully successful live presentation experience, the audience needs something to take home with them. In this chapter you'll review the basic procedure for creating audience handouts and speaker notes pages, look at some printing options, and find out how to edit the Handout Master and Notes Master layouts. Then, we'll end up by exporting these handouts to Microsoft Word for some really serious formatting changes that PowerPoint can't do by itself.

Creating Handouts

As you may already know, a simple set of handouts is as easy to create as File ⇨ Print. Just decide on a layout (the number of slides per page) and then choose that layout from the Print dialog box when you go to print as follows:

1. Select the slides you want to include on the handouts if you don't want them all.

2. Choose File ⇨ Print, and in the Print dialog box, change the Print What setting to Handouts. The Handouts area of the dialog box becomes available, as shown in Figure 16-1.

3. Choose the number of handouts you want from the Slides per page drop-down list.

4. Depending on the number you choose, the Order controls may be available or not; if they are, choose Vertical or Horizontal.

5. Click OK. A set of handouts prints on your default printer.

427

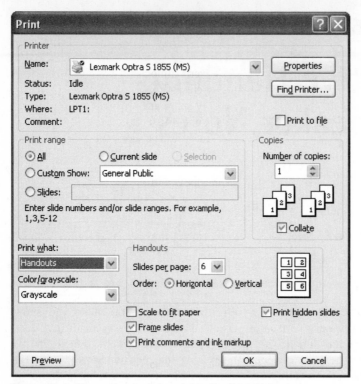

Figure 16-1: Choose Handouts to print in the Print dialog box.

 The Order in step 4 refers to the order on which the slides are arranged on the page. Horizontal places them by rows, Vertical by columns. This ordering has nothing to do with the orientation of the paper (portrait vs. landscape); you would set the paper orientation in the Page Setup dialog box (File ⇨ Page Setup).

Now, let's look at some of the options that go with that.

Choosing an Appropriate Color/Grayscale Setting

The Color/Grayscale drop-down list in the Print dialog box has three available choices: Color, Grayscale, and Pure Black and White. Sounds pretty basic, doesn't it? But there are some little things associated with that choice that you might not have considered:

◆ *Color*: Choosing Color creates handouts that look as much like the original slides as possible. Both the background and the text are the original colors. If you print on a black-and-white printer using the Color setting, you'll get various shades of gray that reproduce the original contrast as closely as they can.

◆ *Grayscale*: Not only does Grayscale convert all colors to shades of gray (obviously), but it also removes the background color and makes all text black.

◆ *Pure Black and White*: This setting converts almost all color and grayscale to either black or white, whichever it is closest to, but it also hides most shadows and patterns, resulting in a very spare and clean-looking printout. This setting is good when creating handouts for faxes and overhead transparencies. It does leave a few select item types in grayscale; see Table 16-1.

Curious about exactly what is changed and removed in Grayscale and Pure Black and White? Consult Table 16-1.

TABLE 16-1 CHANGES TO A SLIDE WHEN PRINTED IN GRAYSCALE OR PURE BLACK AND WHITE

Item	Grayscale	Pure Black and White
Text	Black	Black
Text Shadows	Grayscale	None
Embossing	Grayscale	None
Fill	Grayscale	White
Frame	Black	Black
Pattern Fill	Grayscale	White
Lines	Black	Black
Object Shadows	Grayscale	Black
Bitmap Images	Grayscale	Grayscale
Clip Art	Grayscale	Grayscale
Slide Backgrounds	White	White
Charts	Grayscale	Grayscale

Here's a little-known but very handy option. Each slide and even each object can have its own custom behavior set for Grayscale and Pure Black and White printing modes.

To check this out, choose View➪Color/Grayscale➪Grayscale. The Grayscale View toolbar appears and the slide appears as it would look if printed with Grayscale chosen in the Print dialog box. To fine-tune that, open the Settings drop-down list and choose a different mode (see Figure 16-2).

You can do the same thing with individual objects on the slide. Select the object and then use that same Settings menu to apply a custom grayscale setting to it. Or,

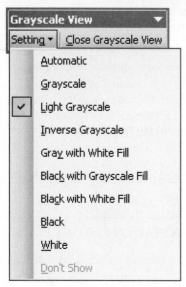

Figure 16-2: Select a Grayscale mode for each slide.

you can right-click the object and choose Grayscale Setting, and then choose one of the modes from the shortcut menu. (It's the same set of modes as on the Settings menu.)

You can move to other slides and preview/change their grayscale settings too; click Close Grayscale View when finished.

 It's important to note that you are *not* changing the object's default appearance here. The settings you are applying will take effect *only* when the slide is printed using Grayscale the Color/grayscale setting in the Print dialog box.

Then, you can repeat this process to customize the settings for the slide(s) when they are printed with Pure Black and White selected from the Print dialog box's Color/grayscale drop-down list. Choose View➪Color/Grayscale➪Pure Black and White and then make your selections.

It is possible to choose a grayscale setting for an object or slide for Pure Black and White mode, and vice versa. Those are just names of modes, not absolute rules as to how each object will appear. (Remember, in Table 16-1 there were some items that printed in grayscale by default even when in Pure Black and White mode.)

Setting Other Handout Print Options

Here are some of the other options you can set for handout printing in the Print dialog box:

◆ *Name*: Choose among the available printers from this list (if you're lucky enough to have more than one).

 The Find Printer button in the Print dialog box lets you search (on a network, for example) for printers with a certain name or that have certain features. This can be useful on a large corporate network when you need to find a printer with features that your own personal printer lacks, such as two-sided printing or color printing. Its use requires Active Directory (which is implemented on almost all corporate networks that use Microsoft Windows 2000 or higher servers).

◆ *Print Range*: The default is All. Current slide prints only the active slide. If you selected more than one slide before you opened the dialog box, Selection will also be a choice. You can also choose a custom show (if you have any set up), or enter a range of slide numbers.

◆ *Number of copies*: The default is 1. The Collate checkbox enables you to specify how multiple copies should print. Collated printing will print in sets, while uncollated printing will print all the copies of page 1, then all the copies of page 2, and so on.

◆ *Scale to Fit Paper*: This enlarges the slides to the maximum size they can be and still fit on the paper when you print one slide per page.

◆ *Frame Slides*: This places a black border around each slide. This is useful for slides that have white backgrounds because otherwise how will you distinguish between the white paper and the white slide?

◆ *Print Comments*: This prints any comments that have been inserted with the Comments feature. This option is not available if you don't have any comments.

◆ *Print Hidden Slides*: This includes hidden slides in the printout (see Chapter 15). This option is not available if you don't have any hidden slides.

Setting Printer-Specific Options

In addition to the controls in the Print dialog box, there are controls you can set for the individual printer you have chosen. These vary greatly depending on the printer, as they are supplied with the printer's driver rather than by PowerPoint. To access them, click the Properties button next to the printer name in the Print dialog box. (You can also access them from outside of PowerPoint through the Control Panel.)

These settings affect how the printer behaves in all Windows-based programs, not just in PowerPoint, so you need to be careful not to change anything that you don't want globally changed.

Here are some of the options you may see:

◆ *Paper Size*: The default is Letter.

◆ *Paper Source*: If the printer has more than one paper tray, you may be able to select a particular tray to pull from.

◆ *Copies*: This sets the default number of copies for the printer. Beware: this is a multiplier. If you set two copies here and then set two copies in the Print dialog box in PowerPoint, you get four copies.

◆ *Graphics resolution*: If your printer has a range of resolutions, you may be able to choose between them. Higher resolutions take longer to print, and on an inkjet printer anything higher than 720dpi usually requires special glossy paper.

◆ *Graphic dithering*: On some printers you can set the type of dithering that makes up images. Dithering is a method of creating shades of gray from black ink by using tiny crosshatch patterns. The choices may include Coarse, Fine, or None.

◆ *Image intensity*: On some printers there is a light/dark slider bar for darkness. Turn it darker if you are running out of toner on a laser printer to eke out a few extra usable copies.

◆ *Orientation*: You can choose between Portrait and Landscape. I don't recommend changing this setting here, though; make such changes in the Page Setup dialog box in PowerPoint instead. Otherwise you may get the wrong orientation on a printout in other programs.

◆ *Page order*: You may be able to choose the order in which the pages of a print job print.

Using the Handout Master

Just as your slide layout is controlled by the Slide Master (see Chapter 3), your handout layout is controlled by the Handout Master. There are actually separate handout masters for each number of slides that you can choose from the Print dialog box, but they are all accessed from the same interface.

To view the Handout Master, choose View⇨Master⇨Handout Master. It has much in common with the Slide Master, as you can see in Figure 16-3.

Notice that the Handout Master View toolbar (see Figure 16-4) has buttons with different numbers of rectangles on them. These represent the different handout layouts that you can choose from the Slides per page drop-down list in the Print dialog box (refer to Figure 16-1). Click a button to view that layout.

Common Handout-Formatting Activities

You can do almost exactly the same things with the Handout Master that you can with the Slide Master. Here are some ideas:

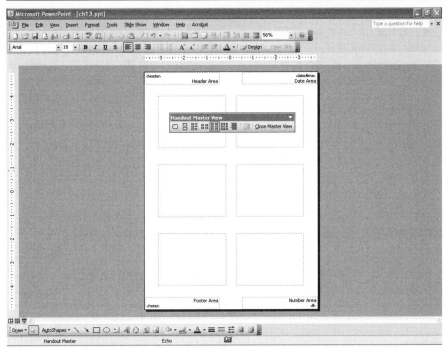

Figure 16-3: The Handout Master defines the layout for each handout type.

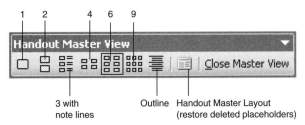

Figure 16-4: Choose a handout layout to work with.

◆ *Change fonts.* The text placeholder areas (Header Area, Date Area, Footer Area, and Number Area) can all be formatted with a different font, size, color, and text attribute, and their text alignment can be changed.

◆ *Delete placeholder areas.* The four aforementioned text placeholder areas can each be deleted from the layout (select and press *Delete*). To restore one after it has been deleted, click the Handout Master Layout button to open a dialog box where you can reselect deleted items for redisplay.

◆ *Move placeholder areas.* Drag any of the text placeholder frames to a different location on the layout, if desired.

◆ *Apply a different color scheme.* If you have a color printer, right-click the handout area and choose Slide Design; from there, click Color Schemes in the task pane, and then choose a color scheme, just like for regular slides.

◆ *Change the background.* Right-click the handout area, choose Handout Background, and then choose a background. Be aware, however, that a patterned or colored background may distract from the slides' message and use a lot of ink when printed. It will also not print to the edge of the paper on most printers, so there will be a plain white border around the outside of each printout.

One thing you *can't* do is to resize or move the placeholder boxes for the slides on the Handout Master. These are fixed, as are the page margins for the handouts. If you want to change those features, consider exporting the handouts to Word and working on them there. I'll explain this in detail later in the chapter.

Controlling the Display of Headers and Footers

You don't have to delete text placeholders on the handouts to suppress them; just turn them off or leave them blank. Those methods have the advantage of allowing you to keep any custom positioning or formatting you have set up for them while still temporarily suppressing them.

 Suppressing header/footer elements for handouts also does the same for any speaker notes you print (discussed later in the chapter). A single set of settings applies to both.

You can adjust these settings either from Handout Master view or from anywhere else. Choose View ➪ Header and Footer, and click the Notes and Handouts tab (see Figure 16-5). Then adjust any of the settings discussed in the following sections.

DATE AND TIME
To suppress whatever is in the Date Area text placeholder, clear the Date and Time checkbox. However, it is not really necessary to do this because the default setting is Fixed and there is nothing in the Fixed text box by default. Therefore, the end result is that nothing appears in the Date Area.

If you do want a date/time to appear, either type something in the Fixed text box, or choose Update Automatically and then choose a date/time format from the drop-down list (see Figure 16-5).

HEADER AND FOOTER
The Header and Footer placeholders are enabled by default, but there is nothing in them by default so the end result is that nothing prints in those areas.

You can type text in the Header and Footer dialog box to create header and footer text if desired, or you can delete the bracketed codes that appear on the Handout Master View in those areas and replace them with your own text.

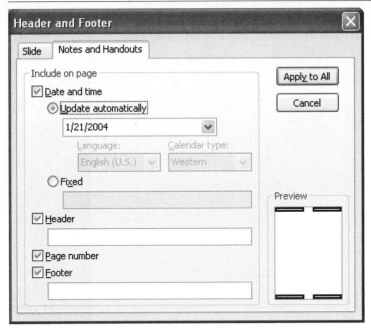

Figure 16-5: Control the header and footer display for handouts and speaker notes.

PAGE NUMBER

By default, the pages are numbered. Clear the Page Number checkbox if you don't want this. However, page numbering is usually a good idea (unless you have only one page in the print job).

Creating Speaker Notes

Speaker notes are like handouts, but they're for the speaker. Only one printout format is available for them, consisting of a slide on the top half (the same size as in the two-slides-per-page handout) with the blank space below it for the speaker notes.

Speaker notes printed in PowerPoint are better than traditional note cards for several reasons. For one thing, you can type your notes right into the computer and print them out on regular paper. There's no need to jam a note card into a typewriter. The other benefit is that each note page contains a picture of the slide so it's not as easy to lose your place while speaking.

Entering Speaker Notes in PowerPoint

You can type your notes for a slide in Normal view in the notes pane, or in Notes Page view. To switch to Notes Page view, choose View ⇨ Notes page (see Figure 16-6).

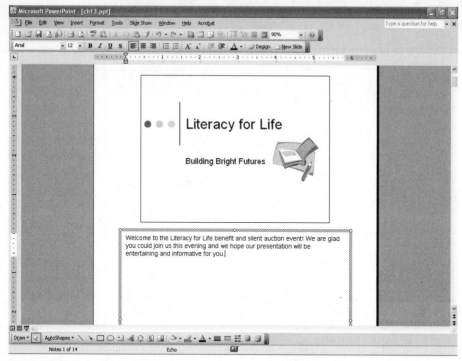

Figure 16–6: Notes Page view lets you type your notes in a big text box and see how each notes page will look when printed.

Working with the Notes Master

The Notes Master is like the other masters except it applies to the Notes Pages print-out. It's more flexible than the Handout Master in that you can resize and reposition the slide placeholder and the text box.

Choose View⇨Master⇨Notes Master, and then edit the layout as you have learned with the other masters (see Figure 16-7). Here are some ideas:

◆ Resize and reposition the slide placeholder if desired. It has normal round white selection handles, just like any other object.

◆ Resize and reposition the text box placeholder, if desired. For example, if you have so many notes that some of them won't fit on a single page, enlarging the box may help.

◆ Add clip art or some other graphic to the background or border.

◆ Add a colored, textured, or patterned background to the page. (Remember though that it will take more ink to print it.)

◆ Delete or move the header and footer placeholders, as you did with the Handout Master earlier in the chapter.

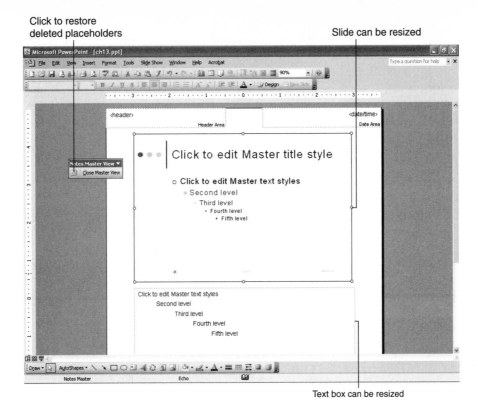

Figure 16-7: Edit the layout of notes pages in Notes Master view.

Modifying Handouts and Notes Pages with Microsoft Word

If you are frustrated with the lack of flexibility in customizing handouts and notes pages (especially handouts), don't give up just yet. There's a whole new world of formatting awaiting you if you send your handouts over to Microsoft Word and format them there.

Sending Handouts or Notes Pages to Word

Assuming you have Word installed, your first step is to send the slides from PowerPoint into Word in a specific handout or notes page format.

Follow these steps:

1. Choose File ⇨ Send To ⇨ Microsoft Office Word. The Send to Microsoft Office Word dialog box appears.

2. Choose one of the formats (see Figure 16-8).

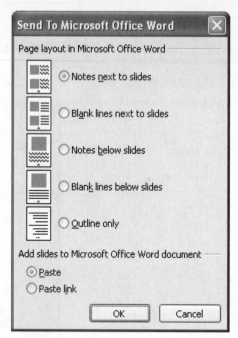

Figure 16-8: Choose a format for sending the presentation to Word.

3. Choose either Paste or Paste Link. The latter maintains a link between PowerPoint and the Word document so that if you make changes in PowerPoint, the Word document will update too so you can reprint a fresh set of handouts. I don't usually recommend using linking, but in this case I do. One limitation: if you add, rearrange, or delete slides, the Send to Word link will ignore those changes.

4. Click OK. Word opens, and the slides appear in the format you chose.

Editing Handouts or Notes Pages in Word

The slides appear in Word as a table (see Figure 16-9). You can do anything to this table that you can do to other Word tables.

 If you don't see the table gridlines as shown in Figure 16-9, but want to, choose Table ➪ Show Gridlines.

"Like what?" you might be asking. Well okay, here is a sampler of some of the things you can do to your handouts in Word.

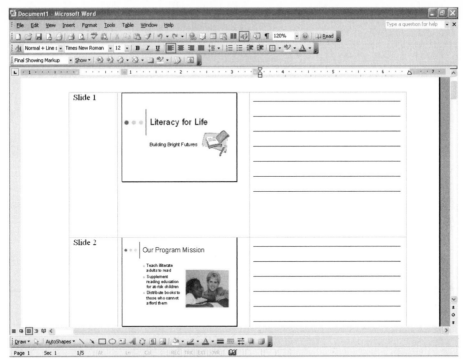

Figure 16-9: Format handouts in Word.

CHANGE THE MARGINS

One benefit of exporting handouts to Word is being able to change the margins. Choose File⇨Page Setup, and on the Margins tab, enter new values for the Left, Right, Top, and Bottom margins (see Figure 16-10).

Note, however, that changing the page margins does not resize the table. If you change the left margin, the table may start at a different place in relation to the left margin (because the table is left-aligned), but if you want to increase the margins so that you can increase the table width, those are two separate activities.

You can also set internal margins for a row, columns, or cell. To do so, click inside the cell and choose Table⇨Format Table. Click the Cell tab, then click the Options button, and in the dialog box that appears you can set margins within that cell. This can be used to create "padding" between two cells.

CHANGE THE TABLE ALIGNMENT

The table itself has a default alignment in relationship to the page: top/left. If you prefer the look of a centered table, you may want to switch this to middle/ center.

First, select the table as a whole. To do this, click the square above and to the left of the table with the four-headed arrow in it (see Figure 16-11). Then click the Center button on the Formatting toolbar to center the table horizontally on the page.

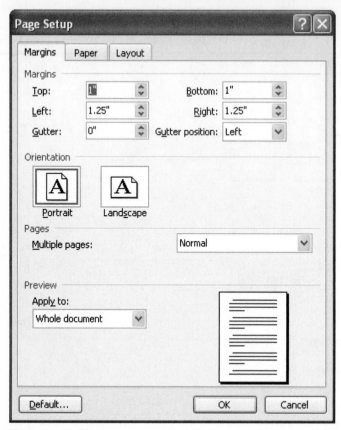

Figure 16-10: Change page margins in Word.

Centering the table vertically requires you to set the entire document (or document section) to center alignment. To do so, choose File⇔Page Setup, click the Layout tab, and set the Vertical Alignment setting to Center.

CHANGE ALIGNMENT WITHIN A CELL

To center the content within a cell horizontally, click in that cell and use the Center button on the toolbar. To center within a cell vertically, click in the cell and choose Table⇔Table Properties. Then, on the Cell tab choose a vertical alignment.

Alternatively, you can display the Tables and Borders toolbar (View⇔ Toolbars⇔Tables and Borders) and use the Alignment drop-down list to choose both vertical and horizontal alignments at once for the selected cell(s) (see Figure 16-12).

RESIZE ROWS AND COLUMNS

To resize a column, drag the border between that column and the one to its right. To resize a row, drag the border between that row and the one beneath it. Alternatively, you can specify an exact size by right-clicking and choosing Format Table and then entering a preferred size on the Row or Column tab.

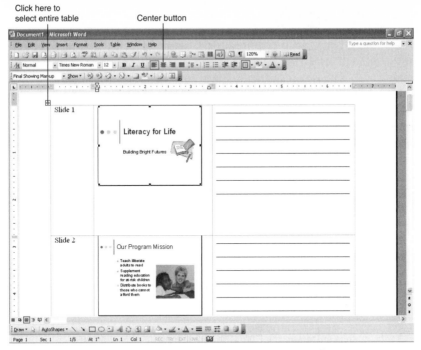

Figure 16-11: Select the whole table and then center it horizontally.

Figure 16-12: The Tables and Borders toolbar offers a
convenient menu for choosing both vertical and horizontal
alignment at once.

To make all rows or all columns the same size, select them as a group and then
right-click and choose Distribute Rows Evenly or Distribute Columns Evenly.

You will not be able to resize a row or column such that its text content no longer
fits. (And the lines for the audience to write on arecomprised of underline characters, which are considered text.) Therefore, you may find yourself needing to
resize the content or even delete some of it. For example, if you use a layout that
includes blank lines, you'll get several blank lines in some of the cells. To make
these cells narrower, you would need to decrease the length of the lines first. To
make these cells shorter, you might have to delete one or more of the lines.

TURN ON/OFF CELL BORDERS

By default, all borders are turned off for all cells in the table. You can turn them on in a variety of ways, but perhaps the easiest is to select the cell(s) and then use the Border button on the Formatting toolbar to select a border for one or more sides of it (see Figure 16-13). Choose the button that has no borders (all dotted lines) to turn all borders off again.

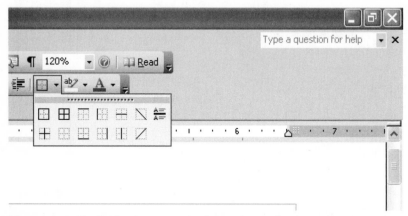

Figure 16-13: The Borders button on the Formatting toolbar has a drop-down list of border sides to turn on/off.

To get fancier with borders, select some cells, choose Format⇨Borders and Shading, and then click the Border tab.

 One thing to note about these borders is that whatever you choose applies to the selected range, not to the individual cells. For example, suppose you chose a range of cells containing three rows and applied a bottom border. The border would be applied only to the bottom of the bottom row of cells.

APPLY A BACKGROUND

To apply a background to the entire page, choose Format⇨Background. A palette of colors appears. The choices are much the same as in PowerPoint except there aren't scheme colors (since Word doesn't use color schemes).

To apply a background to only certain cells, select the cells and then choose Format⇨Borders and Shading. Choose a shading on the Shading tab. This is a lot like applying shading to an object such as an AutoShape in PowerPoint.

RESIZE THE GRAPHIC IMAGES

Resizing the slide images is one of the most common reasons why people export their PowerPoint handouts to Word. Each image is resizable individually, so they need not necessarily be all the same size (although it usually looks better if they are).

If you would like to make the slides larger, you will probably need to first increase the column width for the column in which they reside. Then drag the selection handles on the slide thumbnail to resize. Or, if you want a precise size, choose Format⇨Object and change the size on the Size tab of the dialog box that appears.

If you want to resize all the slide images and you want them all to be the same size, use the Format ⇨ Object method and enter a precise size for each one. Unfortunately, you cannot do them as a batch; each must be resized individually. However, if you have a lot of them to do, you can save yourself some time by writing a macro that resizes to a certain size. Then, just select an image and run the macro. Or go on, and then select the next image and use Edit ⇨ Repeat (Ctrl+Y or F4).

REMOVE A COLUMN OR ROW

You can remove rows and columns as with any other table. For example, perhaps you don't want the leftmost column from Figure 16-9 that had Slide 1, Slide 2, and so on in it.

To delete a column, point to the top border of the top cell. The mouse pointer turns into a down-pointing black arrow. Then, click to select the entire column and cut it with Ctrl+X or Edit⇨Cut.

Another method is to click anywhere within that column and then choose Table⇨Delete⇨Columns.

This works with rows too except you point to the left border of the leftmost cell until you see a right-pointing black arrow. Then click to select the entire row and press Ctrl+X. Or choose Table⇨Delete⇨Rows.

ADD A COLUMN OR ROW

To add a column or row, click in an existing column or row and then choose Table⇨Insert and then Columns to the Left, Columns to the Right, Rows Above, or Rows Below. To insert more than one at once, select more than one before issuing the command.

To extract embedded PowerPoint slides from a Word document and save them as presentation, go to www.mvps.org/skp/pptxp010.htm, copy the macro you find there, and run it in Word.

Add-Ins for Working with Handouts

Here are a few useful add-ins for enhancing your printed materials, all from www.mvps.org:

◆ *Handout Wizard for PowerPoint* creates handouts in presentation format and lets you use layout templates and create your own layouts (www.mvps.org/skp/how/).

◆ *Print-Only Handouts* replaces the standard Print dialog box with a custom Print dialog box that allows only handouts to be printed. This is useful if you find yourself accidentally printing slides one-per-page instead of handouts, or if others are doing that on the computers you control (www.mvps.org/skp/savetree.htm).

◆ *Print Custom Show* prints a custom show, complete with correctly numbered pages (www.mvps.org/skp/customprn.htm).

Summary

In this chapter you learned how to create hard copy to support your presentation, including handouts and speaker notes, and how to fine-tune them with the editing capabilities of Word if PowerPoint's offerings are not adequate for your situation.

So far we've been proceeding as if you were going to give a live presentation, but the next chapter looks at other possibilities: self-running and user-interactive shows. These can be extremely cost-effective to deliver to large groups compared to live presentations, but they have some special challenges in making sure they are user-friendly and usable.

Chapter 17

User-Interactive and Web-Based Shows

IN THIS CHAPTER

◆ An introduction to user-interactivity

◆ Navigational control basics

◆ Creating text hyperlinks and action buttons

◆ Setting up a user-interactive kiosk

◆ Creating a Web-based presentation

◆ Transferring a presentation to a Web server

◆ Creating a Web interface

WHEN USING A LIVE SPEAKER ISN'T PRACTICAL for one reason or another, one compelling alternative is to make the show user-interactive so individuals can move through it at their own pace. Many people actually prefer a user-interactive show, because they have more control and can pause, back up, or even start over as their individual needs dictate. In this chapter I'll review the tools for making a show interactive and for posting it publicly.

User-Interactivity: Letting the Audience Drive

It can be scary letting the audience take control. If you aren't forcing people to go at a certain pace and view all the slides, what's to guarantee that they don't skim through quickly or quit halfway through?

Well, there are no guarantees. Even in a show with a live speaker, though, you can't control whether people pay attention or not. The best you can do is put together a compelling presentation and hope that people want to view it. The same goes for a user-interactive presentation. People are either going to watch and absorb it or they're not. There's no point in treating the audience like children. On the contrary, they will likely respond much better if you give them options and let them decide what content they need.

445

Navigational Controls

Navigational controls are the main thing that separates user-interactive presentations from normal ones. You have to provide an idiot-proof way for people to move from slide to slide. Okay, technically yes, they could use the same navigational controls that you use when presenting a show (see Chapter 15), but those controls aren't always obvious. Moving forward is a no-brainer (click the mouse), but what about moving backward? Would you have guessed "P" for Previous if you hadn't already known? Probably not. And what if they want to end the show early? In the first half of this chapter I'll show you various techniques for creating navigational controls.

Here are some ideas for ways to use navigational controls.

◆ *Web resource listings.* Include a slide that lists Web page addresses that users can visit for more information about various topics covered in your presentation. You can also include Web cross-references throughout the presentation at the bottom of pertinent slides.

◆ *Product information.* Create a basic presentation describing your products, with For More Information buttons for each product. Then, create hidden slides with the detailed information about each product and hyperlink those hidden slides to the For More Information buttons. Don't forget to put a Return button on each hidden slide so users can easily return to the main presentation.

◆ *Access to custom shows.* If you have created custom shows, set up action buttons or hyperlinks that jump the users to them on request.

◆ *Quizzes.* Create a presentation with a series of multiple-choice questions. Create custom action buttons for each answer. Depending on which answer the user clicks, set it up to jump either to a "Congratulations, You're Right!" slide or a "Sorry, Try Again" slide. From each, include a Return button to go on with the quiz.

◆ *Troubleshooting information.* Ask the user a series of questions and include action buttons or hyperlinks for the answers. Set them up to jump to the slides that further narrow down the problem based on their answers until they finally arrive at a slide that explains the exact problem and proposes a solution.

◆ *Directories.* Include a company directory with e-mail hyperlinks for various people or departments so that anyone reading the presentation can easily make contact.

Distribution Methods

Besides navigational controls, the other big consideration with a user-interactive show is distribution. How will you distribute the presentation to your audience?

Some of the methods you've already learned about in this book will serve well here, such as packaging a presentation on CD (see Chapter 15). Or, you may choose instead to set up a user kiosk in a public location, e-mail the presentation file to others, or make it available on the Web. In the second half of this chapter I'll help you weigh the pros and cons of each distribution method and show you how to set each one up.

 The Secure Pack add-in allows you to package one or multiple presentations as a stand-alone, non-editable executable file. You can use password protection, and you can limit the number of times it runs. See `www.mvps.org/skp/securepack/index.htm`.

Navigational Control Basics

All navigational controls that you create on slides are *hyperlinks*. You're probably already familiar with hyperlinks from using the Web; they're underlined bits of text or specially enabled graphics that take you to a different page or site when clicked. In the case of your PowerPoint presentation, the hyperlinks will take users to the next or previous slide, a hidden slide, a custom slide show, or perhaps some external object, such as a Web site or data file.

Types of Navigational Controls

Even though they are all hyperlinks (so they all work the same underneath) on the surface, the various types of navigational controls can look very different. You can have "bare" hyperlinks where the actual address appears, hyperlinks where the text is different from the address, action button graphics, or graphics you create or import yourself. In addition, a navigational control can have pop-up helper text in a Screen-Tip. Figure 17-1 shows various types of navigational controls on a sample slide.

 Most people associate the word hyperlink with the Internet. However, a hyperlink is simply a link to somewhere else; it does not necessarily refer to an Internet location. You can hyperlink to another slide in the same presentation, for example, or to a different presentation, or even to some unrelated data file in another application like Word or Excel.

Notice the directions at the bottom of Figure 17-1. This is necessary because it's not obvious that the gears are a hyperlink, and users would not normally think to try clicking them. Notice also the ScreenTip associated with the second text hyperlink. This is useful because the text itself does not provide the address, and the user may want to know the address before clicking the hyperlink. For example, if the PC

Figure 17-1: A sampler of the various navigational control types available in PowerPoint.

does not have Internet access, the user would not want to click on a hyperlink that pointed to a Web page.

The action buttons in the bottom right corner of the screen in Figure 17-1 are typical of the action buttons that PowerPoint provides. They are just AutoShapes with pre-assigned action settings for On Click. You can create your own, but the preset ones are awfully handy.

Evaluating Your Audience's Needs

Before you dive into building an interactive presentation, you must decide how the audience will navigate from slide to slide. There is no one best way; the right decision depends on the audience's comfort level with computers and hyperlinks. Consider these points:

◆ Is the audience technically savvy enough to know that they should press a key or click the mouse to advance the slide, or do you need to provide that instruction?

◆ Does your audience understand that the arrow action buttons mean Forward and Back, or do you need to explain that?

◆ Does your audience understand hyperlinks and Web addresses? If they see underlined text, will they know that they can click it to jump elsewhere?

◆ Is it enough to include some instructions on a slide at the beginning of the show, or do you need to repeat the instructions on every slide?

Think about your audience's needs and come up with a plan. Here are some sample plans:

◆ *For a beginner-level audience*: Begin the presentation with an instructional slide explaining how to navigate. Place action buttons on the same place on each slide (using the Slide Master) to help them move backward and forward, and include a Help button that they can click to get more detailed instructions.

◆ *For an intermediate-level audience*: Place action buttons on the same place on each slide, along with a brief note on the first slide explaining their presence.

◆ *For an advanced audience*: Include other action buttons on the slide that allow the user to jump around freely in the presentation—go to the beginning, to the end, to a certain section, and so on. Advanced users understand and can take advantage of a more sophisticated navigation system.

In the next few sections, I'll show you how to create all the types of navigational controls shown in Figure 17-1.

Creating Text Hyperlinks

The most common type of hyperlink is underlined text. Hyperlink text is typically underlined and a different color than the rest of the text on-screen. In addition, followed links may be a different color from ones that you have not yet checked out, depending on the program and how the link was set up.

 If you want a hyperlink that never changes its color, one way is to alter the color scheme in PowerPoint so that the colors for followed and unfollowed links are the same. (Refer back to Chapter 2.) Another way is to place a transparent object over the text, such as a rectangle, and apply the hyperlink to that object rather than to the text. The user will think he is clicking the text, but he will actually be clicking the rectangle. You can also assign a hyperlink to a whole text box (manual text boxes only, not placeholders) as opposed to the text within it.

Creating Bare Hyperlinks

When you type an Internet-style address directly into a text box, PowerPoint automatically converts it to a live hyperlink. This works with the following:

◆ *Web addresses*: Anything that begins with http:// or www.

◆ *E-mail addresses*: Any string of characters with no spaces and an @ sign in the middle somewhere.

◆ *FTP addresses*: Anything that begins with ftp://.

 FTP stands for File Transfer Protocol. It's a method of transferring files via the Internet. Up until a few years ago, FTP was a totally separate functionality from the Web, but nowadays most Web browsers have built-in FTP capabilities.

I call these "bare" because you can see what's underneath them—the actual addresses. There is no friendly "click here" text that the link hides behind. For example, the text *support@microsoft.com* is a hyperlink that sends e-mail to that address. In contrast, a link that reads *Click here to send e-mail to tech support* contains the same hyperlink address but is not bare because you do not see the address directly.

You do not have to do anything special to create bare hyperlinks. Just type the text and press Enter or the spacebar. You know the conversion has taken place because the text becomes underlined and is in a different color.

 If PowerPoint does not automatically create hyperlinks, the feature may be disabled. Choose Tools ➪ AutoCorrect Options. Click the AutoFormat As You Type tab, and make sure the Internet and network paths with hyperlinks checkbox is marked.

Creating Friendly Text Hyperlinks

A "friendly" hyperlink is a hyperlink comprising text but not just the bare address. For example, in Figure 17-1, "customer satisfaction surveys" is a friendly hyperlink. ("Friendly" is not an industry-standard technical term; it's just one I find convenient for discussion in this book.)

You can select already-entered text and make it a hyperlink, or you can enter new text. In the following steps I'll outline the general process, then, in the next few sections I'll explain the specifics for various types of hyperlink addresses.

1. To use existing text, select the text or its text box. Otherwise just position the insertion point where you want the hyperlink.

2. Choose Insert⇨Hyperlink, press Ctrl+K, or click the Hyperlink button on the Standard toolbar. The Insert Hyperlink dialog box opens (see Figure 17-2).

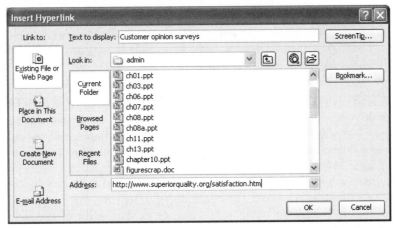

Figure 17-2: Insert a hyperlink by typing the text to display and choosing the address to jump to.

3. In the Text to display box, type or edit the text. This text is what will appear underlined on the slide. Any text you've selected in step 1 will appear here by default; changing it here changes it on the slide as well.

4. Enter the hyperlink address or select it from one of the available lists. See the following sections to learn about the options here.

5. (Optional) Click the ScreenTip button and enter the text that should appear when the user points at the hyperlink. Then click OK.

6. Click OK to accept the hyperlink settings.

TIP   Ideally, the combination of the hyperlink text and the ScreenTip should provide both the actual address and some friendly explanation of it. If the bare address appears as the hyperlink text, use friendly text describing the link location as the ScreenTip. If friendly text appears as the hyperlink text, use the actual address as the ScreenTip.

I purposely glossed over the options in step 4 for selecting the address because this is a rather complex topic. I'll show you the various options in the next few sections.

CREATING A LINK TO A WEB SITE OR FTP SITE

If you want to link to a Web or FTP site, you can simply type the address directly into the Address box in the Insert Hyperlink dialog box (see Figure 17-2). There's no trick to it at all.

If you don't know the address, you can browse for it in one of these ways:

◆ Click the Browsed Pages button and then choose from recently viewed pages.

◆ Click the Browse button (globe with a magnifying glass) to open Internet Explorer and navigate to the page you want; then return to PowerPoint, and it will be filled in automatically.

CREATING A HYPERLINK TO A SLIDE IN THE SAME PRESENTATION

The most common kind of hyperlink is to another slide in the same presentation. There are lots of uses for this link type; you might, for example, hide several backup slides and then create hyperlinks on certain key slides that allow people to jump to one of those hidden slides for more information.

To create a hyperlink to another slide, start the hyperlink normally (choose Insert⇨Hyperlink). In the Insert Hyperlink dialog box, click the Place in This Document button. The dialog box controls change to show a list of the slides in the presentation (see Figure 17-3). Select the slide or custom show you want and click OK.

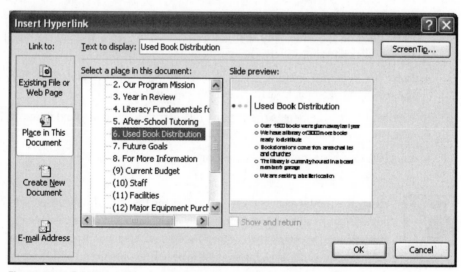

Figure 17-3: Select the slide that the hyperlink should jump to.

 If you are choosing a custom show and you want the presentation to continue from the original spot after showing this custom show, mark the Show and return checkbox (see Figure 17-3). This checkbox is not available for individual slides. For an individual slide, put a Return action button on it to return to the previously viewed slide. See *Creating Action Buttons* later in the chapter.

CREATING A HYPERLINK TO A FILE ON YOUR HARD DISK OR LAN

You can also create a hyperlink to any file available on your PC's hard disk or on your Local Area Network (LAN). This can be a PowerPoint file or a data file for any other program, such as a Word document or an Excel spreadsheet. Or, if you don't want a particular data file, you can hyperlink to the program file itself, so that the application simply opens. (But see the following section for an alternate way to do that.)

For example, perhaps you have some detailed documentation for your product in Adobe Acrobat format (PDF). This type of document requires the Adobe Acrobat Reader; it can't be displayed from within PowerPoint. So, you could create a hyperlink with the text "Click here to read the documentation" and link to the appropriate file. When someone watching the presentation clicks that link, Adobe Acrobat Reader opens and the documentation displays.

 Remember that not everyone has the same applications installed that you do. For example, although Adobe Acrobat Reader is free, many people don't have it installed yet. You might want to add another hyperlink or button to your slide that users can click to download a free viewer for that application's data from the Web, if needed.

To link to a data file, start the hyperlink normally (choose Insert ⇨ Hyperlink) and click on Existing File or Web Page if it is not already selected. Then, do one of the following:

◆ Click Current Folder to display a file management interface (as shown in Figure 17-2) from which you can select any folder or drive on your system. Then navigate to the location containing the file and select it.

◆ Click Recent Files to display a list of the files you have recently opened on the PC (all types), as shown in Figure 17-4, and click the file you want from the list.

◆ Complete the hyperlink normally from that point.

You are not limited to only the folders on your local hard drives if you choose Current folder; you can open the Look In list and choose My Network Places to browse the network. However, make sure that the PC on which the presentation will be displayed will also have access to this same network location.

CREATING A LINK TO AN APPLICATION FOR CREATING A NEW DOCUMENT

Perhaps you want the audience to be able to create a new document by clicking the hyperlink. For example, perhaps you would like them to be able to provide

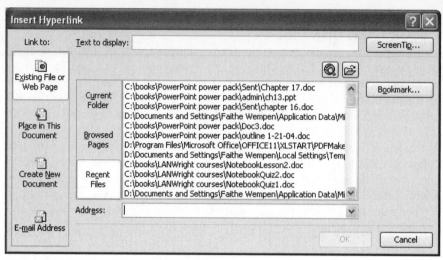

Figure 17-4: Browse a list of recently used files.

information about their experience with your Customer Service department. One way to do this is to let them create a new document using a program they have on their system, such as a word processor.

To create a link to a new document, start the hyperlink normally. Click the Create New Document button, and the controls in the Insert Hyperlink dialog box change to those shown in Figure 17-5.

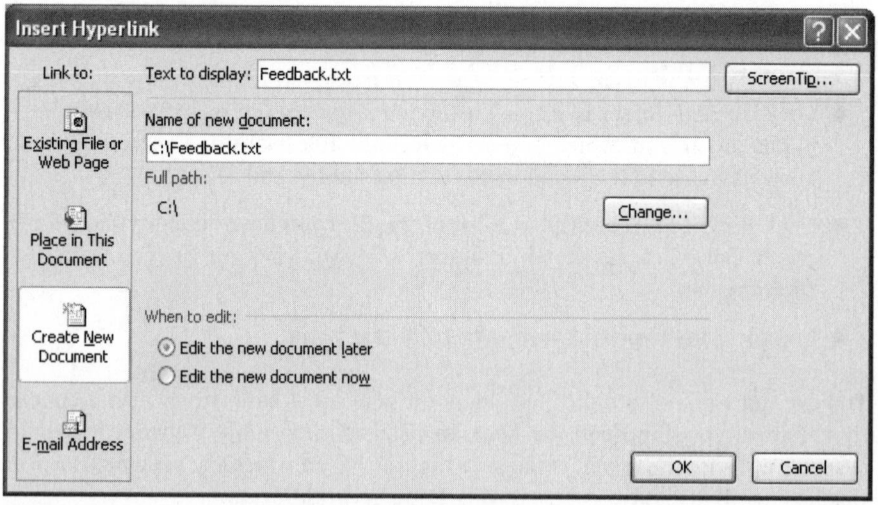

Figure 17-5: Enter the new document name and location.

Enter the name of the new document that you want to create. The type of document depends on the extension you include. See Table 17-1 for common extensions. If the path where it should be stored is not correct in the Full Path area, click the Change button, navigate to the desired location, and click OK. Then click Edit the new document later and finish up normally.

 If you provide this presentation to multiple users, each one will use the same file name for the new document. This can be a problem because one file may over-write another. It might be easier and less trouble-free to collect information from multiple users using an E-Mail Address hyperlink instead (see the next section).

The most important thing about this type of hyperlink is to make sure that you use an extension that corresponds to a program that users have on their PCs. When a program is installed, it registers its file extension (the three-character code after the period in the file's name) in the Windows Registry, so that any data files with that extension are associated with that program. For example, when you install Microsoft Word, it registers the extension .DOC for itself. PowerPoint registers .PPT for its own use. Table 17-1 lists some of the more common file types and their registered extensions on most PCs. Also, make sure that the location you specify for the Full Path will always be accessible whenever the presentation is run.

TABLE 17-1 COMMONLY USED FILE EXTENSIONS

Extension	Associated Application
DOC	Microsoft Word, or WordPad if Word is not installed. Use this for documents if you are not sure whether your audience has Word but you are sure they all have Windows 95 or higher.
WRI	Write, the predecessor to WordPad. WordPad and Word also open these if Write is not installed. This is safest to use for documents if you do are not sure that all audience members will have at least Windows 95.
TXT	Notepad, a plain-text editor. This creates text files without any formatting—not my first choice for documents unless you specifically need them to be without formatting.
WPD	WordPerfect, a competitor to Word.
BMP	Microsoft Paint, which comes free with Windows, or some other more sophisticated graphics program, if one is installed.
MDB	Microsoft Access, a database program.
MPP	Microsoft Project, a project management program.
XLS	Microsoft Excel, a spreadsheet program.

CREATING A LINK TO AN E-MAIL ADDRESS

You can also create a link that opens the user's e-mail program and addresses an e-mail to a certain recipient. For example, perhaps you would like the user to e-mail feedback to you about how he liked your presentation or send you requests for product brochures.

 For an e-mail hyperlink to work, the person viewing the presentation must have an e-mail application installed on his or her PC and at least one e-mail account configured for sending e-mail through it. Web-based e-mail does not count. This isn't always a given, but it's probably a safer bet than assuming a particular application is installed, as in the preceding section.

To create an e-mail hyperlink, either type the e-mail address directly into the text box (for a bare hyperlink) or start a hyperlink normally with Insert⇨Hyperlink. Then click the E-mail address button and fill in the e-mail address and a subject line, if desired. PowerPoint will automatically add `mailto:` in front of the address; you don't have to type it (see Figure 17-6). Then complete the hyperlink normally.

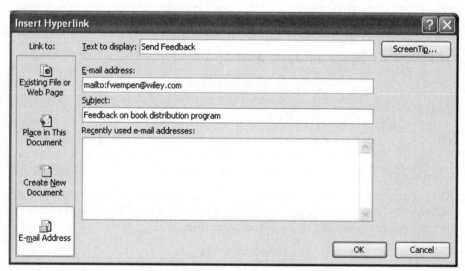

Figure 17-6: Fill in the recipient and subject of the mail-to link.

Editing or Removing a Hyperlink

If you need to change the displayed text for a hyperlink, simply edit it just as you do any text on any slide. Move the insertion point into it, and press Backspace or Delete to remove characters; then retype new ones.

If you need to change the address or the ScreenTip, open the Edit Hyperlink dialog box. To do so, right-click the hyperlink and choose Edit Hyperlink. The Edit Hyperlink dialog box appears, which is identical to the Add Hyperlink dialog box except for the name. From there you can change any properties of the link, just like you did when you created it initially.

To remove a hyperlink, you can either delete it completely (select it and press Delete) or just remove its hyperlink, leaving the text intact. To do the latter, right-click it and choose Remove Hyperlink.

Creating Action Buttons

Action buttons are button-shaped AutoShapes that you can easily insert on slides for use as graphical hyperlinks. Many of them have default actions preassigned to them for added convenience. For example, the one that looks like a right-pointing arrow has a preassigned hyperlink that goes to the next slide in the presentation.

The action buttons that come with PowerPoint are shown in Table 17-2, along with their preset hyperlinks. As you can see, some of them are ready to go; others require you to specify where they jump. You can change the hyperlink on any of the preset buttons, if desired.

At first glance it may seem like there would be little reason to use action buttons that simply move to the next or previous slide. After all, isn't it just as easy to use the keyboard shortcuts? Well yes, but if you use Kiosk mode, described later in the chapter, you cannot move from slide to slide using any of the conventional keyboard or mouse methods. The only thing the mouse can do is click on action buttons and hyperlinks.

Placing an Action Button on a Slide

You can either place an action button on an individual slide or place it on the Slide Master (see Chapter 3). Some action buttons are well-suited to the Slide Master, such as Next and Previous; others, such as Return, are more for special individual use.

To place an action button, choose Slide Show⇨Action Buttons. A palette of buttons appears, corresponding to the buttons from Table 17-2.

You can drag the Action Buttons palette off the Slide Show menu, making it into a floating toolbar.

TABLE 17-2 ACTION BUTTONS

Button	Name	Default Hyperlink
□	None	Nothing, by default. You can add text or fills to the button to create custom buttons.
🏠	Home	First slide in the presentation. (Home is where you get started, and it's a picture of a house, get it?)
?	Help	Nothing, by default, but you can point it toward a slide containing Help or a Help file from an application (usually has a .HLP extension).
ⓘ	Information	Nothing, by default, but you can point it to a slide or document containing information.
◁	Back or Previous	Previous slide in the presentation (not necessarily the last slide viewed; compare to Return).
▷	Forward or Next	Next slide in the presentation.
◁|	Beginning	First slide in the presentation.
▷|	End	Last slide in the presentation.
↩	Return	Last slide viewed, regardless of normal order. This is useful to place on a hidden slide that the audience will jump to with another link—it will help them return to the main presentation when they are finished.
🗎	Document	Nothing, by default, but you can set it to run a program that you specify.
🔊	Sound	Plays a sound you specify. If you don't choose a sound, it plays the first sound on PowerPoint's list of standard sounds (Applause).
🎞	Movie	Nothing by default, but you can set it to play a movie that you specify.

Click the button you want to place. Your mouse pointer turns into a crosshair. Then, do one of the following:

◆ Drag on the slide where you want the button to create a specific size.

◆ Click once on the slide to place a button of a default size.

TIP If you are going to place several buttons and you want them all to be the same size, place each at the default size to begin with. Then, later you can select them as a group and resize. That way they will all be the same.

After you place the button, the Action Settings dialog box appears with the Mouse Click tab on top (see Figure 17-7). Confirm or change the hyperlink set up there as described in the following and then click OK to finish up the button.

Figure 17-7: Check the action setting for the button and make a change if needed.

◆ If the action button should display a slide, file, or Web page, make the appropriate selection from the Hyperlink to drop-down list (see Table 17-3).

◆ If the action button should run a program, choose Run Program and enter the program's name and path, or click Browse to locate it. For example, to run Internet Explorer, the file would be iexplore.exe.

◆ If the action button should play a sound, click None in the Action On Click section and mark the Play Sound checkbox. Then choose the sound from its drop-down list or choose Other Sound to select from a dialog box.

TABLE 17-3 "HYPERLINK TO" OPTIONS IN THE ACTION SETTINGS DIALOG BOX

Setting	Result
Previous Slide Next Slide First Slide Last Slide Last Slide Viewed	These choices all do just what their names say. These are the default actions assigned to certain buttons you learned about in Table 17-2.
End Show	Sets the button to stop the show when clicked.
Custom Show . . .	Opens a Link to Custom Show dialog box, where you can choose a custom show to jump to when the button is clicked.
Slide . . .	Opens a Hyperlink to Slide dialog box, where you can choose any slide in the current presentation to jump to when the button is clicked.
URL . . .	Opens the Hyperlink to URL dialog box, where you can enter a Web address to jump to when the button is clicked.
Other PowerPoint Presentation . . .	Opens a Hyperlink to Other PowerPoint Presentation dialog box, where you can choose another PowerPoint presentation to display when the button is clicked.
Other File . . .	Opens a Hyperlink to Other File dialog box, where you can choose any file to open when the button is clicked. If the file requires a certain application, that application will open. (If you want to run an application without opening a specific data file, use the Run Program option instead of Hyperlink to.)

TIP You can also run macros with action buttons. This is not all that common, however, because most of the macros you record in PowerPoint are for building a presentation, not showing one. For example, you might have a macro that formats text in a certain way (see Chapter 19). You would almost never need to format text while a presentation was being shown to an audience.

Try out an action button in Slide Show view after its creation to make sure it works as intended. You can reopen the Action Settings dialog box at any time by right-clicking the button and choosing Action Settings.

Inserting Text in a Blank Action Button

Action buttons are basically the same as AutoShapes, so you can add text to them just like with an AutoShape. In fact, that's the main purpose of the blank action button—to provide a clean slate in which you can type your own button text.

To type text into a blank button, right-click it and choose Add Text, or just select it and start typing. An insertion point appears in it. Type your text, and format it as you would any other text. When finished, click outside the button.

Formatting an Action Button

Action buttons can have all the same types of formatting as AutoShapes (see Chapter 7). You can resize them, change their color, rotate them, and all the usual stuff.

Most of the time if there is more than one action button on a slide you will want them all to have the same formatting. Select them all before applying any formatting changes to make it apply to them all as a group. Or, format one the way you want it and then use Format Painter to copy its formatting to the others.

Creating Your Own Action Buttons

You can create an action button out of any object on your slide—an AutoShape, a piece of clip art, a photograph, a text box—anything. To do so, just right-click the object and choose Action Settings. Then set it to Hyperlink to, Run Program, or Play Sound, just as you do when you are checking/changing the settings for a preset action button.

Make sure you clearly label the object that you are using as an action button so that users will know what they are getting when they click it. You can add text to the object directly (for example, with an AutoShape) or add a text box next to it that explains its function. If you add a regular hyperlink to an item, you can use a ScreenTip with it.

Creating Other Graphical Hyperlinks

There are two ways to create a graphics-based hyperlink. Both involve skills that you have already learned in this chapter. Both work equally well, but you may find that you prefer one method or the other. The Action Settings method is a bit simpler, but the Insert Hyperlink method allows you to browse for Web addresses more easily.

Creating a Graphical Hyperlink with Action Settings

I just described this under *Creating Your Own Action Buttons*. A graphics-based hyperlink is really no more than a graphic with an action setting attached to it. Simply place the graphic, then right-click it, and choose Action Settings. Choose

Hyperlink to, and then from the drop-down list, choose URL and enter an Internet address or use one of the other options described in Table 17-3.

Creating a Graphical Hyperlink with the Insert Hyperlink Command

If you would like to take advantage of the superior address-browsing capabilities of the Insert Hyperlink dialog box when setting up a graphical hyperlink, and the ability to use ScreenTips, select the graphic and then choose Insert ⇨ Hyperlink. Then create a hyperlink for it normally, as you learned earlier in the chapter.

Setting Up a User-Interactive Kiosk

There are many ways of distributing a user-interactive presentation. One of them is to set up a computer in a public place and allow people to view the presentation on that computer. This is called a *kiosk*.

Security is an issue with a kiosk because you don't want people to steal the computer, shut down the presentation, alter the presentation, or do any other mischief. Therefore, you may want to use PowerPoint's special Kiosk Mode when running such presentations, to give yourself more control over what the audience can and can't do.

Specifically, here's what happens when you use Kiosk Mode:

◆ The keyboard does not work except for the Esc key (which exits the presentation).

◆ The mouse can be used to click action buttons and hyperlinks, but clicking in general does not do anything.

◆ The control buttons do not appear in the bottom left corner of the display, and you cannot right-click to open a menu. Right-clicking does nothing.

To turn on Kiosk Mode, choose Slide Show ⇨ Set Up Show. In the Set Up Show dialog box, choose Browsed at a kiosk (full screen) and click OK (see Figure 17-8).

If you turn on Kiosk Mode, you must use action buttons or hyperlinks in your presentation, or set slides to auto-advance. Otherwise users will never get past the first slide.

A kiosk is only as good as its physical security, however. You will need to hide the keyboard at the kiosk (otherwise people will be able to press Esc to shut it down), and you will probably want to hide the system unit too (so people will not be able to press its power button to restart). Leave only the monitor and mouse available for public use; lock the rest of the equipment up in a secure cabinet.

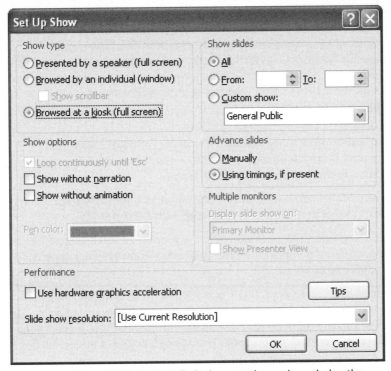

Figure 17-8: Set up Kiosk Mode to limit the control users have during the show.

The No Esc add-in lets you disable the Esc key for escaping out of a presentation. Be careful with this because in Kiosk mode, Esc is the only way out. Create an invisible object on the slide and set it to exit the show when clicked. Check out www.mvps.org/skp/noesc.htm for more details.

Here's an article about creating a trade show loop: www.powerpointanswers.com/article1034.html.

Creating a Web-Based Presentation

PowerPoint is probably not your best choice for building a general-purpose Web site. There are other, better tools, such as Microsoft FrontPage or Macromedia Dreamweaver. You can even use Microsoft Word or Microsoft Publisher.

Even though you probably won't create a lot of stand-alone Web pages with PowerPoint, you may want to publish a presentation on an existing Web site. You can do this in either of two ways: PowerPoint format or HTML format.

A presentation delivered on the Web has the same overall goal as any other presentation. You want the audience to see it, appreciate it, and buy into it, but the means for accomplishing this over the Web are slightly different.

A successful presentation over the Web is:

◆ *Universally accessible to the intended audience.* You must know your audience and their Web browser versions so you can save your presentation in the best format for their needs.

◆ *Friendly and interactive.* That means you should include directions, hyperlinks, and action buttons to help users move around.

◆ *Quick to download.* That means keeping the file size as small as possible without sacrificing the important things. Don't use unnecessary sounds, graphics, videos, or photos.

◆ *Not heavily reliant on sound.* Don't make sound an integral part of a presentation for the Web because you can't assume that everyone who views it will have a PC with sound support. Further, consider making the sounds that you do include optional, perhaps by clicking a button on the slide rather than playing automatically.

You may find that you have to compromise one or more of these goals to meet another. For example, there is a way of ensuring compatibility with multiple browsers when saving in Web format, but it results in larger file sizes. I'll tell you more about that shortly.

Choosing PowerPoint versus Web Format

Will you save the presentation in Web format and publish it like a Web page, or will you make it available for online download in PowerPoint format? Both have their pros and cons.

PowerPoint format ensures that the audience sees the presentation exactly as you created it, including any embedded sounds, transitions, and animations. However, only people who own a copy of PowerPoint or who have downloaded the PowerPoint Viewer can see it. Therefore, most people who don't already have either one are likely to conclude that it's too much work to see your presentation, and you may turn off potential viewers.

With Web format, anyone with a Web browser can view the presentation without any extra software. It makes your presentation widely accessible. However, certain special effects in the presentation might not be visible to all users, depending on the effect you used and the browsers the individual audience members have.

TIP Microsoft provides an add-in that allows you to view PowerPoint 2002 and 2003 HTML-format presentations that contain animation in Internet Explorer 5.0 or later. See `www.microsoft.com/downloads/details.aspx?Family ID=4033A84A-24C7-40B2-8783-D80ADA33CFF8&displaylang=EN`.

Web format provides some nice extra navigational aids for users that make action buttons unnecessary. Notice in Figure 17-9 that users can use arrow buttons at the bottom of the window to move forward and back or click a slide in the Contents pane to jump to that slide.

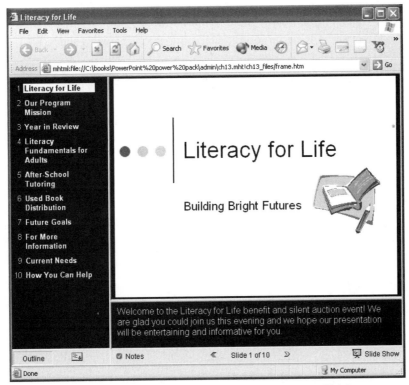

Figure 17-9: A presentation saved in Web format and shown in a Web browser.

If you choose Web format there are a few PowerPoint features that don't work correctly. It's good to know about these up front so you can avoid using them in a presentation destined for the Web. Here are some examples:

◆ If you set a sound or music clip to continue to play for a certain number of slides, it will stop when you advance past the initial slide.

TIP If you need to make a music clip play through multiple slides, you might be interested in this article: `www.powerpointanswers.com/article1018.html`. You can also doctor the HTML file itself in a text editor, as I mentioned in Chapter 12. After saving in Web format, open fullscreen.html in Notepad and add the following line between the <html> and the <head> tags at the top (where *your-song* is the name of the music clip and the actual file extension of that clip is substituted for *wma*): `<bgsound src="yoursong.wma" loop=infinite>`.

◆ If you set up the text on an AutoShape to have a different animation than its AutoShape, it will lose the special animation and be animated together with the AutoShape.

◆ If the presentation is set up for automatic transitions between slides, all mouse-click animations behave as automatic animations.

◆ Sounds attached to objects that are hyperlinks (for example, action buttons) don't play.

◆ If a hyperlink on the Slide Master is covered by a placeholder, even if that placeholder is transparent, the hyperlink is unavailable on the individual slides.

◆ Shadow and Embossed text effects are not supported; the text appears as normal text.

You may also find other features that will not work correctly on Web page presentations, such as certain animation effects that don't work properly.

CAUTION Don't assume that a presentation will look the same in all Web browsers. At a minimum, try your Web presentation in both Internet Explorer and Netscape Navigator and note any differences.

Choosing Traditional HTML versus Single File Web Page

If you decide to go with Web format, you have another decision to make: a Single File Web Page or a traditional HTML file.

The Single File Web Page creates a single file with an .MHT extension that contains everything needed for the entire presentation. No support files or folder is needed. This is very convenient; the entire presentation is encapsulated in a single file so you can e-mail that file, upload it, or do anything else with it. However, the file size is slightly larger than the combined file size of the traditional HTML file plus all its support files. Also, some older Web browsers do not support the use of MHT files, so some audience members may not be able to see it.

 PowerPoint 2002 called the Single File Web Page a Web Archive. It is also known as an MHTML file (which stands for MIME-encapsulated HTML). The most common use for this format is to e-mail Web pages.

Traditional HTML creates a single text-based HTML file and a support folder containing all the graphics and helper files needed to turn it into a Web presentation. An HTML presentation consists of many files. PowerPoint creates a home page (an entry point) with the same name as the original presentation. This is the file you name when you save. For example, if the presentation file is named Literacy.ppt, the home page is named literacy.htm. Then, PowerPoint creates a folder names presentation name Files (for example, Literacy Files) that contains all the other HTML, graphics, and other files needed to display it.

This type of file is easy to import into a larger Web site (in FrontPage, for example), and you can edit the HTML file in any application that supports text editing. That means you don't have to go back to PowerPoint every time you need to make a change. However, working with a support folder can be unwieldy, and you might forget to copy the folder when you are moving the presentation to a server.

Choosing a Level of Browser Compatibility

The final decision you must make is which Web browsers you will support. This is applicable to both HTML and MHT formats.

The higher the Web browser format you support, the more of PowerPoint's bells and whistles will transfer flawlessly to the Web version, and the better the quality of the multimedia content (sound, video, and so forth). You basically get a nicer show with the higher version support.

However, by choosing higher version support, you potentially exclude a portion of your audience. Anyone who does not have that version or higher will not be able to see the show—either not at all or not as you intended.

The third piece of the equation is file size. The lower the version you support, the smaller the file size. An exception to this is the option to save for multi-browser compatibility (covered later); doing this accomplishes both near-universal support and inclusion of all the features, but at the expense of a much greater file size.

The default browser support is Internet Explorer 4.0 or later, and this works well in most cases. Internet Explorer 4.0 is now several years old, and 6.0 is the current version. Chances are good that almost everyone will have at least 4.0.

If you decide to go with a lower setting, and support Internet Explorer 3.0 and Netscape Navigator 3.0 or later, here are the consequences:

◆ Animation and transition will not work.

- ◆ Animated GIFs will not play if the presentation is saved with a screen size of 640 × 480 or less.

- ◆ Sounds and movies will not play.

- ◆ Some graphics will appear degraded in quality.

- ◆ The slide is not scaled to fit the browser window. It runs at a fixed size based on the screen size setting you select when you publish the presentation.

- ◆ You cannot view the presentation full-screen.

- ◆ You cannot open or close frames.

- ◆ The active slide does not appear highlighted in the outline pane.

- ◆ The mouse cannot be used to highlight items in the outline pane.

If you save the presentation to support IE 4.0 or later but people try to view the presentation with an earlier version or with Netscape Navigator, they will still be able to see it, but the following will occur:

- ◆ The presentation outline will appear permanently expanded.

- ◆ No notes or additional frames will appear.

- ◆ Hyperlinks will not be operational.

- ◆ Clicking a slide title in the outline pane will not jump to that slide.

- ◆ The default browser colors will be used to display the presentation text color and background color. (Exception: the colors do appear correctly in IE 3.0.)

- ◆ Sounds and movies will not play.

You can also further fine-tune the version number by choosing compatibility for Internet Explorer 5.0 or 6.0. If you choose either of these, PowerPoint will use VML (Vector Markup Language) for graphics, to speed up their loading. The graphics are then not viewable with any earlier browser versions.

If you choose Internet Explorer 6.0 compatibility, PowerPoint will allow the use of PNG graphics (a graphic format that is an improved version of GIF) in the presentation. Earlier browser versions will not be able to see those graphics.

Now that you know the pros and cons of your myriad options, let's get down to some of them.

Saving a Presentation in Web Format

If you go with the default settings, saving a presentation as a Web page is almost as easy as saving it normally.

When you save as a Web page, the resulting HTML or MHT presentation remains open in PowerPoint and on-screen. If you make additional edits to it, and then save, those edits will not apply to the original PowerPoint version, but only to the Web version. After saving your work on the Web version, make sure you use File ⇨ Save As to resave your work in PowerPoint format too if you want all copies to stay synchronized.

Choose File⇨Save as Web Page to display the Save As dialog box. Single File Web Page is the default file format, and the default file name is the presentation name (see Figure 17-10). Change either of these, if desired. You can also change them permanently (choose Tools⇨Options, General tab, Web Options button).

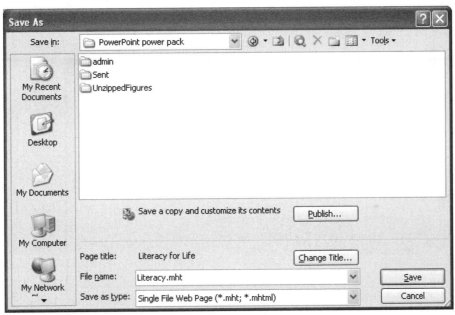

Figure 17-10: The Save as Web Page command displays a slightly different Save As dialog box than normal.

PowerPoint takes the default page title (that is, the words that will appear in the Web browser title bar when the page displays) from the title of the first slide. If you want a different title, click the Change Title button, type a different title, and click OK.

If you want to save in a different location, navigate to the drive or folder you want. I'll explain later in the chapter how to save files directly to a Web or FTP server.

After completing the save, you will probably want to check your work by opening the file in your own Web browser and checking to make sure the slides appear as you intended. To do so, browse to the save location from My Computer and double-click the HTML file to open it.

 When you view a Web presentation in the default Web view, as was shown in Figure 17-9, many of the animations, transitions, and so on will not work. To take full advantage of them you must switch to Slide Show view by clicking the Slide Show button in the bottom right corner (see Figure 17-9).

Web Format Options

The process described in the preceding section gives you very little control over how PowerPoint translates the presentation to Web format. For more control, click the Publish button in the Save As dialog box to display the Publish as Web Page dialog box, as shown in Figure 17-11.

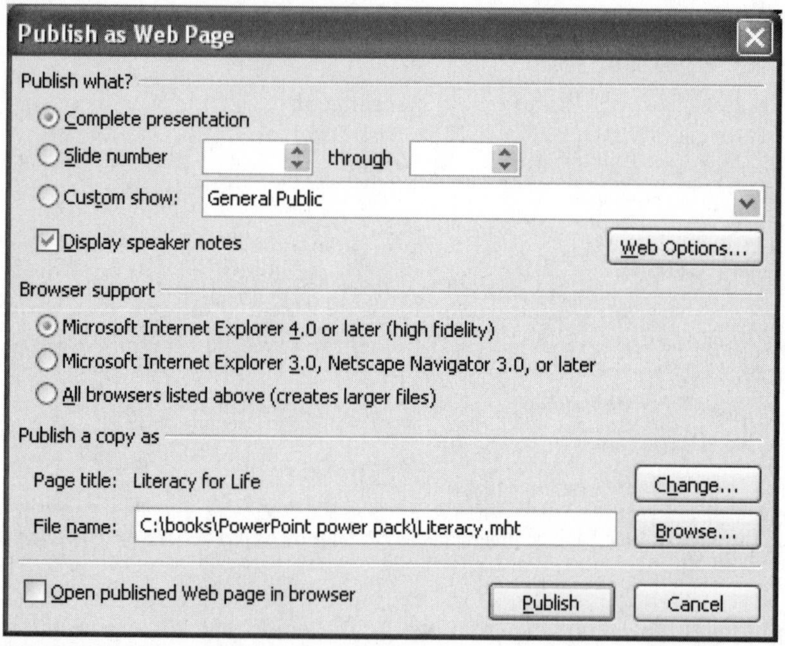

Publish as Web Page [X]

Publish what?
- ( ) Complete presentation
- ( ) Slide number [   ] through [   ]
- ( ) Custom show: [General Public   ▼]
- [✓] Display speaker notes   [Web Options...]

Browser support
- ( ) Microsoft Internet Explorer 4.0 or later (high fidelity)
- ( ) Microsoft Internet Explorer 3.0, Netscape Navigator 3.0, or later
- ( ) All browsers listed above (creates larger files)

Publish a copy as
- Page title: Literacy for Life   [Change...]
- File name: [C:\books\PowerPoint power pack\Literacy.mht]   [Browse...]

[ ] Open published Web page in browser   [Publish]   [Cancel]

Figure 17-11: Use this dialog box to provide more input on how PowerPoint converts your work to Web format.

After displaying this dialog box, you use it as a replacement for the Save As dialog box for the rest of the saving process. Here are the options you can set:

◆ *Publish what?* The default is Complete Presentation, but you can choose a range of slides or a custom show.

◆ *Display speaker notes.* The default is yes, so that an icon on each page enables your readers to jump to that page's notes, and a notes page pane appears at the bottom (as shown in Figure 17-9).

◆ *Browser support.* The default is Microsoft Internet Explorer 4.0 or later. This format takes advantage of these versions' capability to process certain codes and run certain mini-applications. If you think some of your audience may not have this browser, choose one of the other following options instead:

◆ *Microsoft Internet Explorer 3.0, Netscape Navigator 3.0, or later.* This option results in many of the animated features of the presentation not being saved, but it also makes for a smaller file size and greater compatibility with a variety of browsers.

◆ *All browsers listed above (creates larger files).* This option is for maximum compatibility. It essentially saves two versions of the presentation in the same file—one for IE 4.0 and higher and one for everything else. That way there is no sacrifice of features in order to ensure compatibility. However, it does increase the file size.

◆ *Publish a copy as.* These are the same controls as the ones in the Save As dialog box (see Figure 17-10). You can change the page title with the Change button, or type a different name and/or location in the File name box.

◆ *Open published Web page in browser.* If you leave this checkbox marked, PowerPoint opens Internet Explorer and displays your presentation's first page automatically after the save. This is a good way to check your work.

Notice the Web Options button in Figure 17-11. Click it to display the Web Options dialog box, where you have even more choices regarding the presentation's conversion. The following sections summarize those options.

GENERAL
On the General tab, you can set the following:

◆ *Add slide navigation controls.* This is turned on by default. It results in the left-hand pane shown in Figure 17-9 that lists the names of the slides. Users can click a slide's name to jump to it.

◆ *Colors.* Notice in Figure 17-9 that the aforementioned navigation area is black with white lettering. You can choose a different color scheme from the Colors list. Choices include Browser Colors (whatever the default colors are set in the user's Web browser), Presentation Colors (text color or accent color) taken from the presentation, or Black Text on White.

◆ *Show slide animation while browsing.* If you have any slide animations and you want them to be part of the Web version, mark this checkbox. It is unmarked by default because Web users may find animations annoying, rather than clever, because of their Internet connection speed.

◆ *Resize graphics to fit browser window.* This option is marked by default so that if users are running their browsers at less than full-screen size or using a different screen resolution, your content will not be cut off, but rather resized so that it fits their screen.

BROWSERS

Have you been wondering exactly what the differences are when saving with compatibility for one browser versus another? You'll find some answers on the Browsers tab, as shown in Figure 17-12.

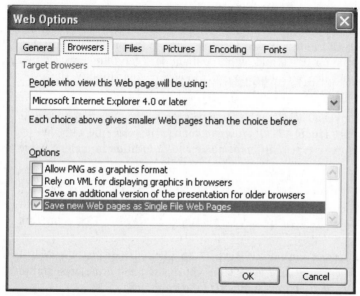

Figure 17-12: Customize the presentation's save for a specific browser version.

Choose a browser version from the drop-down list, and the checkboxes in the Options section are automatically marked or cleared for that version based on its capabilities. You can also manually mark or clear any of these checkboxes. The lower the version you choose, the fewer features will be enabled and the smaller the file(s) will be.

The four checkboxes are as follows:

◆ *Allow PNG as a graphics format.* PNG is an improved version of the GIF format. IE 6.0 supports it fully; earlier versions might not. If your presentation contains PNG files and this option is not marked, they will be converted to a supported format when you save.

◆ *Rely on VML for displaying graphics in browsers.* VML stands for Vector Markup Language. It's a way of making graphics appear more quickly in Web pages. You must have at least IE 5.0 to see graphics that rely on VML; people with older browsers will not see the graphics.

◆ *Save an additional version of the presentation for older browsers.* This checkbox is turned off by default no matter which version you select. Marking it will insert the needed codes for backward compatibility but will increase the file size.

◆ *Save new Web pages as Single File Web Pages.* This option enables or disables MHT as the default format. To view a single file Web page, users must have at least IE 4.0.

FILES

On the Files tab you can control how your files are saved, organized, and updated:

◆ *Organize supporting files in a folder.* This option is the default when you save as traditional HTML. PowerPoint saves the needed files in a folder with the same name as the presentation home page. If you deselect this option, the supporting files will be placed in the same folder as the home page itself.

◆ *Use long file names whenever possible.* This option preserves the Windows 95 and higher long file names, which are usually more descriptive than the shorter eight-character names in DOS and Windows 3.1. If you need to transfer the presentation to a server that does not support long file names, deselect this option.

◆ *Update links on save.* With this option marked, every time you save your presentation in Web format through PowerPoint, all links are updated.

◆ *Default editor.* Unmark the single checkbox in this section if you want to use a third-party editing program (non-Office) as the default for editing Web pages and you don't want a warning to appear each time you open the file in that third-party program.

PICTURES

There is only one control on the Pictures tab: Target Monitor. In most cases the default of 800 × 600 is a good choice.

The presentation can run at several screen resolutions. The smallest is 640 × 480. (The numbers refer to the number of pixels, or individual dots, that make up the display.) Most people run Windows at 800 × 600 or higher (that's the minimum for Windows XP), but people with older systems may still be using 640 × 480. If you choose a higher setting for the presentation than a user has on his screen, he will have to scroll in the Web browser window to see everything.

ENCODING

On the Encoding tab are a couple of settings that only multilingual offices will use:

♦ *Save this document as.* Choose a language character set here. The default for the United States is US-ASCII, which is fine in most cases. A more general setting for any English-speaking country or for languages that use the same alphabet as English is Western European (ISO).

♦ *Always save Web pages in the default encoding.* If you want PowerPoint to always rely on Windows' information about what kind of alphabet you are using, mark this checkbox, and you never have to worry about the character set again.

FONTS

The Fonts tab enables you to select a character set to encode with the Web presentation. This is mostly an issue when you are creating a presentation in a non-English language. The default is English/Western European/Other Latin Script.

 What's all this about character sets? To see a demonstration, open Microsoft Word and choose Insert ➪ Symbol. Then open the Subset drop-down list. Notice all the different subsets within that font? Each of those is a character set. Each character set has a unique four-digit hexadecimal code—that's over 65,000 possible codes. So there's much more flexibility to a given font than just the handful of characters you can generate by typing on your keyboard normally.

You can also select a font for any text in the Web presentation that does not have a specific font assigned to it. Actually, you select two fonts: one proportional and the other fixed-width (monospace). Leaving these set at their defaults is a good idea because the defaults (Times New Roman and Courier New) are available on almost every PC.

Transferring a Presentation to a Web Server

Publishing a presentation to the Web means transferring it to a server or other computer that has a direct, full-time Web connection. If you are an individual or small business user, that server probably belongs to your local Internet service provider (ISP). If you work for a large company that has its own full-scale Web site, there may be a server in-house that you should transfer your files to. Consult your company's network administrator or Webmaster to find out what you need to do.

Following are several ways of getting your presentation onto a Web server:

◆ You can save it to the server through PowerPoint with a Web address, using the Save As dialog box.

◆ You can save it directly to the Web site through FTP within PowerPoint, again using the Save As dialog box.

◆ You can save it to your hard disk first, check it, and then upload it to the Web server using a third-party utility.

I recommend that you always save first to your hard disk and check your work. After that, however, you can resave within PowerPoint using either of the first two methods or you can go with a separate FTP utility—it's your choice. This chapter does not cover the third-party utility method because each one is different. One popular utility is WS_FTP, available from most shareware Web sites, such as www.tucows.com. Another good one is called Bulletproof FTP.

These methods all work no matter which format you are using. You can save a file in native PowerPoint format to a Web server just as easily as a presentation in Web format.

TIP Every Web location has two addresses: its FTP address and its Web address. They both point to the same location; it's just a matter of how you access that location. Some ISPs prefer that you upload Web pages via the FTP protocol using an FTP address; others allow you to upload them using the HTTP protocol and a Web address. You need to use a different address when uploading using FTP than when saving to a Web location. Your ISP will tell you what address to use.

Saving to the Web

The easiest way of publishing a Web presentation is to save it directly to the Web site. This may not work in every case, though, because the company that owns the server might not allow it for some reason.

To publish to the Web directly, you need a user name and password for the Web server. Otherwise anyone could upload to your Web site. You can get these from your ISP. They might or might not be the same as your normal logon name and password for the Internet.

Choose File ⇨ Save as Web Page, and then in the File name box, type the full Web site address to which you want to publish, including the file name. For example, if the file name is literacy.mht, the full address might be www.mysite.com/literacy.mht. Then click Save and PowerPoint attempts to connect to the Web site. A login box prompts you for that user name and password, and the save proceeds as if it were a normal save.

The first time you do this for a particular Web location, a shortcut is created in My Network Places. The next time you save as a Web page to that same location, you can click the My Network Places icon in the Save As dialog box and select the address from the shortcuts stored there.

Saving to an FTP Location

If you can't save to the Web location directly, you might be able to save to an FTP address. As mentioned earlier, this address is a "back door" to the Web server. You will need to know the FTP address to use, as well as have the user name and password for access.

The first time you save to a particular FTP location, you must set up that location. In subsequent saves, that FTP site will appear on the Save in drop-down list, and you can simply select it from there and save normally.

To set up an FTP location, follow these steps:

1. Start the save normally (choose File ⇨ Save as Web Page).

2. Open the Save in list and choose Add/Modify FTP Locations.

3. In the Add/Modify FTP Locations dialog box (see Figure 17-13), enter the FTP site's address and your user name and password.

4. Click Add, then OK. The available FTP locations appear in the Save As dialog box.

5. Double-click the location you just created. The top level of folders at the FTP site you specified appear. Navigate through them to the spot where you are instructed to save Web files. Then, click Save.

Copying Files to a Web Server via Windows XP

You can transfer the presentation files to a Web server via a third-party FTP utility, or you can use Windows itself (if you have Windows XP) by doing the following:

1. Create a Network Place shortcut to the Web or FTP address. If you saved the file directly to the server using either of the preceding methods, this has already been done.

2. Open that network location in a Windows file management window. (Hint: double-click it from My Network Places). If a prompt appears for a user name and password, enter them and click OK.

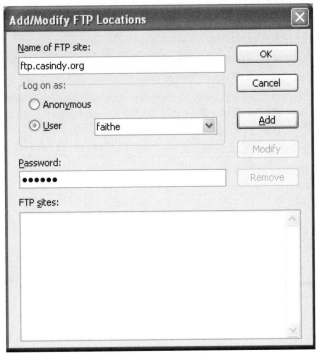

Figure 17-13: Enter a name and address for the FTP location you want to add.

3. Open a My Computer window for your local hard disk and navigate to the folder containing the files you have prepared for uploading to the server.

4. Drag-and-drop the files to the network window to copy them there.

Making the PowerPoint Viewer Available Online

If you plan to distribute your presentation as a regular PowerPoint file via a Web site, you probably cannot safely assume that everyone who might want to view it will have a copy of PowerPoint. Therefore you must make the PowerPoint Viewer available for download. See *Making the PowerPoint Viewer Available Separately* in Chapter 15 to learn what files you need to make available; then create a compressed archive (ZIP) file that contains them and make that file available for download from your Web site. Or, alternatively, add a hyperlink that points people to the Microsoft Web site where they can download the PowerPoint Viewer on their own: www.microsoft.com/downloads/details.aspx?FamilyID=428d5727-43ab-4f24-90b7-a94784af71a4&DisplayLang=en.

Making a ZIP file is very simple in Windows XP because Windows XP includes built-in support for the ZIP format. Here's how to do it:

1. In Windows, create a folder that contains all the files needed for the Power-Point Viewer (see Chapter 15's listing.)

2. Select all the files (Ctrl+A), and then right-click the selection and choose Send To⇨Compressed (Zipped) Folder. A ZIP file is created with the same name as the first file in the group.

3. Rename the ZIP file with a more meaningful name, such as `pptviewer .zip`. To rename, right-click and choose Rename, then type the new name and press Enter.

 Should you type the .ZIP extension on the end when renaming the ZIP file? It depends on whether you have Windows set up to show the file extensions for known file types or not. If the file had .ZIP on the end before renaming it, then yes, include it. If it did not, then don't.

Depending on your needs, you might choose to zip up the presentation file itself with the viewer, or keep them separate. If you are distributing several PowerPoint presentations, separate may be the way to go.

If you don't have Windows XP, you will need to use a third-party program to create ZIP files. One of the best known is WinZip (www.winzip.com), a shareware program that works with Windows very well.

 One of the advantages of WinZip over the zipping tool in Windows is that it can be used to create a self-extracting compressed archive. This is an executable file that unzips its contents when you run it. If you distribute the presentation and the viewer in this format, users will not need an unzipping utility or Windows XP in order to unpack it.

Creating a Web Interface

In most cases you won't just post a Web presentation on a Web site "raw," without any kind of introduction. You will want to introduce the presentation on a more traditional Web page and provide a link to the presentation.

Perhaps you already have an existing Web page from which you will link, and if so, that's great—just edit the page to include a link to the presentation—but if not, you can create a very basic one in PowerPoint.

Start a new presentation with a single slide in it (the Title and Text layout would be a good one for it, with the bullets turned off), and save it as a Web page. Then, create instructions and hyperlinks on it to access the presentation. You know how to make hyperlinks from earlier in this chapter. Figure 17-14 shows an example that makes both a Web version and a native PowerPoint version available, as well as the PowerPoint viewer.

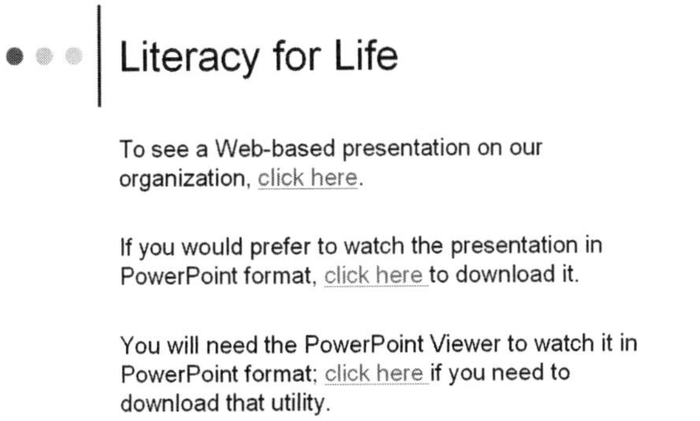

● ● ● | ## Literacy for Life

To see a Web-based presentation on our organization, click here.

If you would prefer to watch the presentation in PowerPoint format, click here to download it.

You will need the PowerPoint Viewer to watch it in PowerPoint format; click here if you need to download that utility.

Figure 17-14: An instruction page like this one provides hyperlinks to the various files that visitors to the Web site may want to access.

TIP   To make the HTML presentation start in full-screen view, see this article www.oldfco.ca/tutorial.

Summary

In this chapter you learned how to make presentations interactive by adding various types of hyperlinks, including action buttons. You also learned about the many options available for saving a presentation in Web format, and some techniques for transferring presentation files to a Web server.

At this point, your presentation is probably complete. Congratulations! But this book is not quite finished yet. The next part of the book provides some techniques for helping you customize and extend PowerPoint to get the most out of your PowerPoint experience in the future.

Part VI

Extending PowerPoint

CHAPTER 18
Custom Work Environments: Menus
and Toolbars

CHAPTER 19
Working with Macros and Add-Ins

Chapter 18

Custom Work Environments: Menus and Toolbars

IN THIS CHAPTER

◆ Customizing menus and toolbars

◆ Creating new toolbars and menus

◆ Setting program options

POWERPOINT WORKS GREAT RIGHT OUT OF THE BOX, as you've seen so far in this book, but it may work even better for you with a few tweaks. In this chapter you'll learn how to customize the PowerPoint interface to produce exactly the work environment you want.

Customizing Menus and Toolbars

The toolbars and menus in PowerPoint change depending on what you're doing and on what settings you use. For example, when you're working with Slide Sorter view, you get a different set of toolbar buttons than in Normal view, and when you're working on a chart, different menus and commands appear.

You can also manually change toolbars and menus, in the following number of ways:

◆ You can display or hide various toolbars and menu bars.

◆ You can add or remove commands to toolbars and menu bars.

◆ You can change the look of the commands and buttons by setting them to show text, graphics, or both.

◆ You can change the hotkeys for menu commands.

◆ You can create your own toolbars and menu bars.

It might seem on the surface that toolbars and menu bars are two different things, but they are actually just two different manifestations of the same basic element.

With a toolbar, the commands appear as graphic in a single-level organization. With a menu bar, the commands appear as text in a multi-level nesting. In this chapter I'll treat them all as one element as much as possible to avoid duplication, but I'll try to show you examples of each type.

Moving Toolbars

Toolbars can be dragged around anywhere on-screen. If you drag them to the top, bottom, left, or right, they become "docked" there. If you drag them toward the center, they become free-floating windows. Some toolbars are free-floaters by default, such as the Picture toolbar, but you can make any of them appear anywhere you like.

If a toolbar is already docked, drag it by its handle. The "handle" is the set of four dots at the left end. If a toolbar is floating, drag it by its title bar. You do not have to enter Edit Mode (see the next section) in order to move toolbars around.

Placing Menus and Toolbars in Edit Mode

Toolbars and menus can be customized only when the Customize dialog box is open (select Tools⇨Customize, or right-click any menu bar or toolbar and choose Customize).

When the Customize dialog box is open, the menus and toolbars cease to work normally. Instead they are placed in a special editing mode, where you can make changes to them.

When you click a button or menu while in this special editing mode, instead of a command executing, the button or menu becomes selected, with a black box around it. You can then do all sorts of things to edit it—things I'll describe in the upcoming sections (see Figure 18-1).

The Undo commanddoesn't work when the Customize dialog box is open. Ctrl+Z does nothing, and of course the toolbar and menu methods of undoing don't function either.

Moving and Deleting Commands and Buttons

With the Customize dialog box open, simply drag-and-drop buttons to move them to different places on a toolbar or to other toolbars. To get rid of a button entirely, drag it down into the slide area, away from the toolbars, and then drop it when its icon looks like an X (see Figure 18-2).

All of the Microsoft-supplied menus and toolbars are reset-able. If you make a mistake and want to go back to the original arrangement, select the menu or toolbar from the Toolbars tab of the Customize dialog box and then click the Reset button.

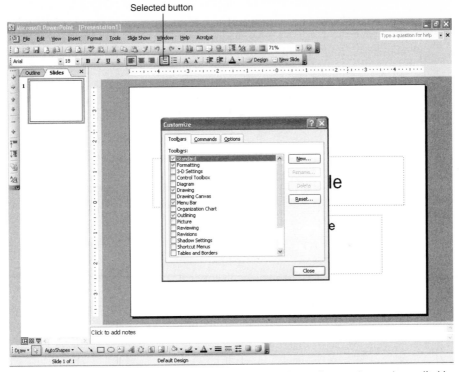

Figure 18-1: Open the Customize dialog box in order to make toolbars and menu bars editable.

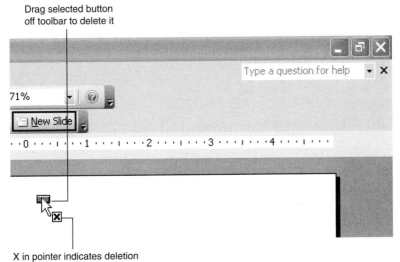

Figure 18-2: Delete a button by dragging it off the toolbar.

The same goes for menus. You can edit menus at the top level (that is, the names of the menus themselves, such as "File" or "Edit"), and you can also edit the individual commands on each menu.

To remove an entire menu off the menu bar, drag-and-drop it down below the menus and toolbars. To rearrange the top-level menus, drag them to the left or right.

Working with commands on individual menus is similar. Click a menu name on the menu bar to open the menu, and then work with the commands there (drag them up or down to rearrange them on the menu, or drag them away from the menu system to delete them.) See Figure 18-3.

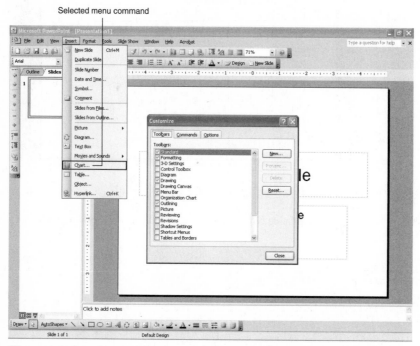

Figure 18-3: Rearrange or delete menu commands by opening the menu and then dragging the commands.

Adding Commands to Menus and Toolbars

If there's a certain command you use frequently from the menu system that does not have a toolbar button, you might want to add it to a toolbar for easier access. One example is the Slide Layout command on the Format menu; I'll use that one for the example shown.

To add a command to a toolbar, do the following:

1. In the Customize dialog box, switch to the Commands tab.

2. Scroll through the list of commands, broken down by menu, and find the one you want. For example, in Figure 18-4, I've found the Slide Layout

command by clicking Format in the left pane and then scrolling through the right pane.

3. Drag the command from the right pane onto the desired toolbar, in the spot where you want it. When it is in a valid spot, the mouse pointer will show a plus sign, as shown in Figure 18-4.

4. Release the mouse button to drop it there. A button for the command appears.

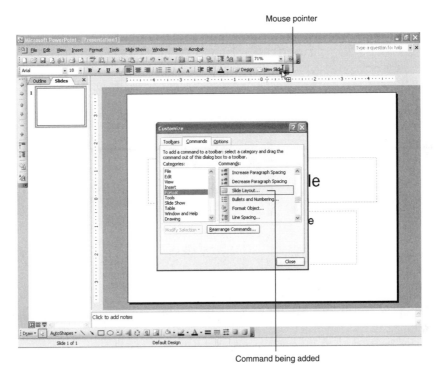

Figure 18-4: Add a command to a toolbar or menu by dragging it from the Commands tab.

To add a command to a menu, do the same thing except drag the command onto the menu name and pause—without releasing the mouse button—until the menu opens. Then, you can drag it onto the menu.

Adding commands to a menu is much less common than adding them to a toolbar because the menu system is already pretty complete. The main reason you might add a command to a menu is if you create a brand-new menu and want to populate it with commands. I'll explain creating menus later in the chapter.

Editing Button and Command Properties

Each menu item and each toolbar button has its own set of properties. To set them, right-click the button or command, and use the shortcut menu that appears (see Figure 18-5). You can also click a button or command to select it and then click the Modify Selection button in the Customize dialog box. (Doing so opens basically the same menu as the right-click method.)

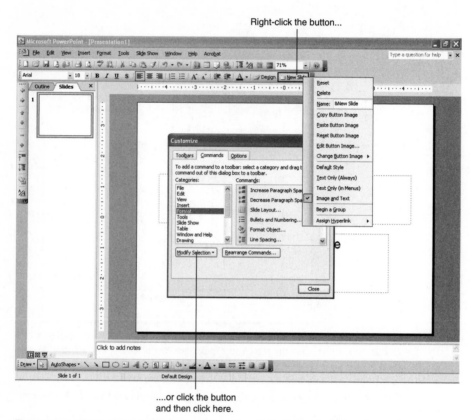

Figure 18-5: Right-click a button or menu command to display its Properties menu.

Here are the properties you can set:

◆ *Reset*: Reverts the button or command back to its original settings as specified by Microsoft.

◆ *Delete*: Removes the button or command from the menu or toolbar. It's the same as deleting it with drag-and-drop.

◆ *Name*: If text appears for the button or menu item, the name is that text. An ampersand sign (&) before a character makes that character the hot key (in menus only).

◆ *Button image commands*: I'll address these later in the chapter; they have to do with editing the button image.

 Hot keys are used in conjunction with Alt to open menus. Once a menu is open, you can type the hot key for a command on that menu (without Alt) to select that command. Hot keys used to be very important back in the days when the keyboard was king, but nowadays most people use the mouse so it is not as big a deal to have hot keys for all commands on all menus.

◆ *Image/Text setting*: This is what determines whether a picture appears (as in a toolbar button), the Name text appears, or both. The choices are as follows:

  ■ *Default Style*: Appears however that particular command has been set up to appear by default. Usually, this is as text on a menu and as an image on a toolbar, but some commands are exceptions to that.

  ■ *Text Only (Always)*: Appears as text, no image, whether it is on a menu or a toolbar.

  ■ *Text Only (in Menus)*: Appears as text when on a menu, but as an image when on a toolbar.

  ■ *Image and Text*: Appears as text when on a menu, but as both an image and text when on a toolbar.

◆ *Begin a Group*: This places a divider between this button or command and the one(s) above or to its left. You can see examples of such dividers on the default toolbars and menus; for example, there's one to the left of the Print button on the Standard toolbar, and above the Save command on the File menu. This is a toggle setting; choose it again to turn the group divider off.

◆ *Assign Hyperlink*: This enables you to set up a hyperlink to open when the button or command is clicked. Your choices are Open or Insert Picture. Both choices display the Insert Hyperlink dialog box, from which you make your selection. If you assign a hyperlink to a button or command, it ceases to have its normal functionality when clicked, and instead executes the hyperlink. After setting up a hyperlink, a Remove Hyperlink command appears in the Assign Hyperlink submenu for easy removal of it.

Editing a Button's Image

Most commands have a button image pre-created, so that when you place them on a toolbar, there's a unique button image there. However, you might sometimes run into cases where there is no button image, such as when you create buttons for macros that you've written yourself (see Chapter 19), or you might not like a particular button image.

Several of the commands on a button's Properties (right-click) menu deal with the button image. You can copy, paste, reset, edit, or change it as listed in the following:

◆ *Copy Button Image*: Copies the current image to the Clipboard, so you can paste it into an external drawing program and modify it.

◆ *Paste Button Image*: Places whatever is on the clipboard as the new image for the button. Use this after selecting an image in an external drawing program and using Edit➪Copy to copy it.

 Buttons must be exactly 16 by 16 pixels in size. If you are using an outside image editor, make sure you set your image size there to those values to make sure you are not creating an image that is too large to fit on a button.

◆ *Reset Button Image*: Returns the button image to its default.

◆ *Edit Button Image*: Opens a Button Editor window, which consists of a very simple image-editing program (see Figure 18-6).

◆ *Change Button Image*: Opens a palette of a few dozen sample pictures to choose from. Picking one of these can be useful as a starting point, but you will probably want to modify the image afterward.

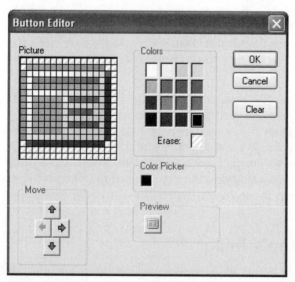

Figure 18-6: Right-click a button or menu command to display its Properties menu.

Perhaps a few words about the Button Editor are in order, as it's not the most intuitive graphic program in the world.

Click one of the colors in the Colors section, or click the Color Picker to open a dialog box with many more color choices. Or, to remove the color in a spot, click the Erase tool. After selecting the color of choice, click the little squares in the Picture area to change one or more of them to the chosen color.

The Move arrows move the entire image in the arrow direction; this is useful if you start creating a button image and then realize it isn't centered within the button area.

Using the Rearrange Commands Method

New in Office 2003 applications is the ability to arrange and modify commands and buttons via a dialog box. It's not as easy as drag-and-drop for most people, but it may be useful for people with less hand-eye coordination than average.

From the Customize dialog box, display the Commands tab and then click Rearrange Commands. The Rearrange Commands dialog box opens, offering a full-service environment for doing all the kinds of edits I've described so far in the chapter.

To use this dialog box, click either Menu Bar or Toolbar. A drop-down list of all the available items that fit that description appears. Select the one you want to work with (for example, choose Toolbar, then choose Formatting), and its commands/buttons appear in the Controls area.

From there, select an item in the Controls area and use the buttons at the right to modify it. You can add or delete buttons, move them around, and even modify the properties (through the Modify Selection button's menu). I won't belabor this dialog box here because it's pretty self-explanatory, especially after you've already mastered the methods I've described earlier. Figure 18-7 shows it.

Creating New Toolbars and Menus

Now that you know how to modify existing toolbars and menus, does it put you in the mood to create your own? You can build a toolbar or menu from scratch that contains exactly the commands you find useful. For example, you might create a toolbar that contained your "top ten" favorite commands, so they would always be close at hand.

The menu bar is considered a toolbar, and the menus on it are considered commands. If you want to create an alterative menu bar, simply create a new toolbar and then add menus to it. Toolbars can be a mixture of menus and buttons, although traditionally they are one or the other. (The Drawing toolbar is an exception; it contains the Draw menu as well as normal buttons.)

Creating a Toolbar

Here's how to create a new toolbar:

1. From the Customize dialog box, click the Toolbars tab.

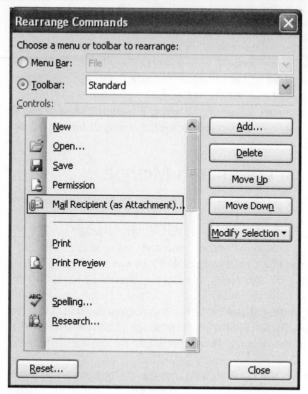

Figure 18-7: The Rearrange Commands dialog box offers an alternative to drag-and-drop.

2. Click New. Then type a name for it in the New Toolbar dialog box and click OK (see Figure 18-8).

3. A new, empty toolbar appears as a floating toolbar. If desired, drag it to the side, top, or bottom of the screen to dock it.

4. Add commands to it, as you learned earlier in the chapter.

Creating a Menu

New menus can be placed either on the Menu Bar or on a toolbar. They work the same either way. You could, for example, create a menu system similar to the Draw menu on the Drawing toolbar, where it exists alongside toolbar buttons but serves a different purpose.

To create a new menu, follow these steps:

1. From the Customize dialog box, click the Commands tab.

2. Scroll down through the left pane and find New Menu; then drag it to a toolbar or menu, the same as you would any new command or button.

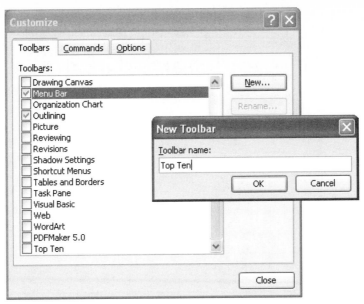

Figure 18-8: Create your own toolbars.

3. Name it by changing its properties (Name property), and add a hot key if desired, by placing an ampersand before the desired character.

4. Drag-and-drop other commands onto it. To do so, drag and pause over the menu name, and the menu will open; then drop the commands on the open menu. Figure 18-9 shows a custom menu bar I've created to hold some of the formatting commands I need quicker access to.

TIP

Want to assign keyboard shortcuts to things? Shortcut Manager for Power-Point is an add-in that lets you define your own keyboard shortcuts for menu items, macros, and VBA code and define shortcuts in specific templates. See http://officeone.mvps.org/ppsctmgr/ppsctmgr.html. There is an optional component called Shortcuts for PowerPoint that extends the program further by providing many predefined shortcuts that perform tasks such as erase the pen markings, change the pen color, change the volume, print the current slide, and more.

Setting Program Options

In addition to the customizable menus and toolbars, PowerPoint contains an amazing array of customizable settings. Some of them make purely cosmetic changes, whereas others enable or disable timesaving or safety features.

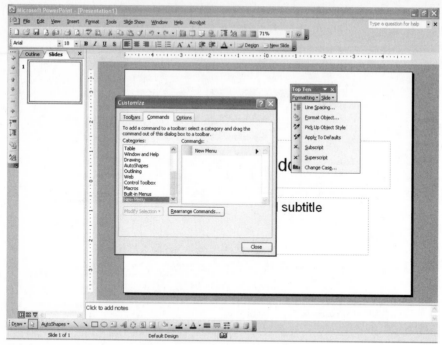

Figure 18-9: Create your own menu system.

Most options are accessed by selecting Tools⇨Options. In the Options dialog box, click a tab (there are seven to choose from) and then make your selections. Table 18-1 lists all the options, broken down by category.

TABLE 18-1 POWERPOINT OPTIONS

Tab	Section	Option	Description
View	Show	Startup Task Pane	Specifies whether the task pane appears when PowerPoint starts or when you start a new presentation.
		Slide Layout task pane when inserting new slides	Specifies whether the Slide Layout task pane appears when you insert a slide, so you can choose a layout for it.
		Status bar	Displays or hides the status bar at the bottom of the PowerPoint window.
		Vertical ruler	Displays or hides the vertical ruler when rulers are displayed.

Tab	Section	Option	Description
		Windows in Taskbar	Specifies whether each presentation will appear as a separate taskbar item, or whether a single item in the taskbar represents all open PowerPoint presentations.
	Slide show	Prompt to keep ink annotations when exiting	Clearing this checkbox keeps ink annotations automatically when exiting from Slide Show view.
		Show menu on right mouse click	Clearing this checkbox allows you to move backwards instead of accessing a shortcut menu when you right-click during a slide show.
		Show popup toolbar	Clear this checkbox to suppress the shortcut buttons and attached menus that normally appear on the lower-left corner of the slide when you move the mouse during a show.
		End with black slide	Deselect this option if you do not want a black slide after the last slide in the show.
	Default view	Open all documents using this view	Enables you to specify a starting view. The default is to reopen the file in whatever view it was last saved in.
General	General options	Provide feedback with sound to screen elements	When on, PowerPoint plays sounds associated with various system events (set up from the Windows Control Panel's Sound feature). Most people find these annoying, so they're off by default.
		Recently used file list	Remember that one way to open a file is to select it from the bottom of the File menu. To increase or decrease the number of files that appear there, change the number here.
		Link sounds with file size greater than	When you place a WAV sound file in a presentation, PowerPoint creates a link to it rather than embedding it if it is larger than the size you list here. (The maximum value you can enter here is 50MB.) All other sound file formats are linked regardless of size.

Continued

TABLE 18-1 POWERPOINT OPTIONS *(Continued)*

Tab	Section	Option	Description
	User information	Name and Initials	Fill in your name and initials if they don't already appear here. PowerPoint uses this information in several ways, including placing it on the Properties for the file (File ⇨ Properties) and marking any comments you make.
		Web Options	Click this button to open the Web Options dialog box, which I covered in Chapter 17.
		Service Options	Click this button to open the Service Options dialog box, where you can choose settings for shared workspaces, privacy, and online content.
Edit	Cut and Paste	Show Paste Options buttons	When this option is on and you paste text (see Chapter 4), the Paste Options icon appears, and you can click it for a menu of choices. Suppress that icon by turning this option off.
		Use smart cut and paste	When this option is enabled and you move things around with the Cut, Copy, and Paste commands, PowerPoint automatically removes excess spaces and adds spaces when needed.
	Text	When selecting, automatically select entire word	If this checkbox is marked and you select part of a word, the entire word becomes selected along with the white space after it.
		Drag-and-drop text editing	When enabled, this lets you move and copy by dragging with the mouse.
	Charts	New charts take on PowerPoint font	This option sets the font for inserted charts at 18-point for the default font used in the template. Clear this checkbox to use the chart's own fonts.

Tab	Section	Option	Description
	Undo	Maximum number of undos	This is the number of actions that PowerPoint remembers so you can undo them with Edit⇨Undo. The higher the number, the more memory used up by the feature.
	Disable new features	New animation effects, Multiple masters, Password protection	This section contains checkboxes for several of the features that are new to PowerPoint 2003. If you share files with someone who uses PowerPoint 97 or 2000, you might need to disable some or all of these.
Print	Printing options	Background printing	If you clear this checkbox, you won't be able to continue to use PowerPoint after issuing the Print command until the print job has been completely sent to the printer. Although inconvenient, it can speed up printing in some cases.
		Print TrueType fonts as graphics	This sends the fonts to the printer as pictures rather than outline font images. If you are having out-of-memory errors with the printer or inaccurately printed fonts, experiment with this setting.
		Print inserted objects at printer resolution	If a graphic has a higher resolution than the printer supports, this option dumbs down the object to match the printer, decreasing the size of the print file and making it print faster.
	Default print settings for this document	Use the most recently used print settings or Use the following print settings	This controls what happens when you click the Print button on the toolbar. It will either use whatever print settings were last specified in the Print dialog box, or it will use settings you specify yourself.

Continued

TABLE **18-1** POWERPOINT OPTIONS *(Continued)*

Tab	Section	Option	Description
Save	Save options	Allow fast saves	Fast saving speeds up the process by saving only the changes to the presentation each time. However, it tends to make the file size larger, and some experts suspect it of causing document corruption in some cases.
		Prompt for file properties	If this box is marked, the File Properties dialog box appears the first time you save a file. Some organizations manage their files based on this extra information; most people ignore it.
		Save AutoRecover info every___minutes	PowerPoint periodically saves your work in an AutoRecover file. You can specify the interval here.
		Convert charts when saving on previous version	When this is enabled and you save in an earlier format, charts are converted to be compatible with that format even if it means losing chart features.
		Save PowerPoint files as	You can save your PowerPoint files by default in any of several PowerPoint formats. Set the default here.
		Default file location	This specifies where new files are saved by default and where the Open dialog box opens to.
	Font options for current document only	Embed TrueType fonts	This setting specifies whether TrueType fonts will be embedded in the presentation file. It makes the file larger but can enable the presentation to be shown on another PC that doesn't have the same fonts installed. Not all fonts can be embedded.
Security	File encryption settings for this document	Password to open	Enter a password here that someone must enter in order to open the file. Optional: click Advanced to choose the encryption method to use.

Tab	Section	Option	Description
	File sharing settings for this document	Password to modify	Enter a password here that someone must enter in order to save changes to the file.
		Digital Signatures	Click to open a box for managing digital signatures set up for the document. You can then manage macro security according to the digital signatures. See Chapter 19.
	Privacy options	Remove personal information from file properties on save	Just what it says. Useful for people who do not want their name associated with the file in any way. It also strips out other identifying characteristics such as file path information.
	Macro security	Macro security	Click this button to adjust the security level for running macros in the presentation file. See Chapter 19.
Spelling and Style	Spelling	Check spelling as you type	Deselect if you do not want PowerPoint to run a spelling check in the background as you work.
		Hide all spelling errors	This option suppresses the wavy red lines that indicate spelling errors on a slide.
		Always suggest corrections	This option controls whether PowerPoint offers spelling suggestions or waits for you to click the Suggest button in the Spelling dialog box.
		Ignore words in UPPERCASE	When selected, all-uppercase words are not spell-checked.
		Ignore words with numbers	When selected, strings of letters that contain numbers are not spell-checked.
	Style	Check style	This enables/disables the Style Checker.
		Style Options	Click this button to open the Style Options dialog box, where you can configure how the Style Checker works.

Summary

In this chapter you learned how to make PowerPoint easier to use by customizing the menu and toolbar system and by setting program options. In the next chapter I'll show you how to work with the macros and add-ins functionality in PowerPoint.

Chapter 19

Working with Macros and Add-Ins

IN THIS CHAPTER

◆ Macro basics

◆ Macro playback

◆ Editing a macro with Visual Basic

◆ Dealing with macro security

◆ Reusing macros in multiple presentations

◆ Working with add-ins

AS YOU BECOME AN EXPERT POWERPOINT USER, you may want to extend PowerPoint to give it extra features or faster access to groups of activities. That's where macros and add-ins enter the picture. In this chapter I'll explain what macros and add-ins are, how to create and edit macros, and how to install, load, and use add-ins.

Macro Basics

Macros are recorded sets of steps that you can play back to perform tasks more easily. For example, suppose you frequently need to import your company logo, resize it, and move it to the top left corner of a slide. You can create a macro that does that, and save yourself several steps.

The most common way to create a macro is to record it. Macro recording works a lot like videotape recording. You click Record, and PowerPoint watches and records everything you do until you click Stop. The recording is saved under a unique name, and you can play back the recording any time to re-perform those actions.

You can also write your own macros using the Visual Basic Editor provided in PowerPoint, but this gets a little tricky. To write macros, rather than record them, you must know something about Visual Basic programming, and most business users don't have the time to spend learning a programming language. (It's fascinating stuff, though—take a class!)

There's no structural difference between a recorded macro and a written one; both are Visual Basic programs. Therefore, you can make changes to recorded macros in the Visual Basic Editor the same as you can a macro you created originally with the Visual Basic Editor. This comes in handy if you need to remove mistakes you made during the recording process as a shortcut for completely rerecording.

Macros don't work in Slide Show view. Why? See `www.mvps.org/skp/ppt00027.htm`.

Planning a Macro

Before you record a macro, think about exactly what you want to record and from what position you want it to start. Keep in mind that everything you do after clicking Record will be recorded. For example, suppose you want to create a macro that applies certain formatting to text. You would want to type the text before you recorded the macro so you would have something to format at recording time.

Macros work best when they store recorded keystrokes and menu commands. Mouse use sometimes does not record very well. So as you are planning your macro, try to come up with the keyboard equivalents of as many of the commands as possible.

You also need to think about where you are going to store the macro. If the macro should be used only in the active presentation, record it while that presentation is open. If you want it to be available in every presentation based on a certain template, open that template (the .POT file). If you create any dummy content in the process of recording the macro, don't forget to delete it before saving the template so that content does not become part of the template.

Recording a Macro

When you're sure you know what you need to do, and you're sure you want to start recording, follow these steps:

1. Choose Tools➪Macro➪Record New Macro. The Record Macro dialog box opens.

2. Enter a name for the macro in the Macro Name box. Be descriptive. For example, if you plan to record a macro that inserts a new slide and sets its layout to Title, you might call it *NewTitleSlide* (see Figure 19-1).

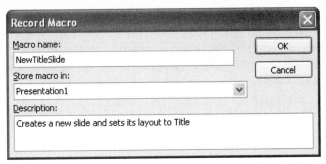

Figure 19-1: Name your macro and enter a description for it, if desired.

 Macro names must begin with a letter and can contain up to 80 characters. You cannot use spaces, and no symbols are allowed except the underscore character. You also can't use any Visual Basic reserved words for the name, such as Private, Public, Integer, or Sub.

3. If you have more than one presentation or template open, choose the one in which you want to store the macro from the Store Macro In drop-down list.

4. (Optional) Edit the description in the Description box, if desired. This is a good place to put an explanation of what the macro does if the name does not make it obvious.

5. Click OK. A tiny floating toolbar appears with a square in it, as shown in Figure 19-2. That is the Macro toolbar, and that square is the Stop button. You can click it at any time to stop the recording.

Figure 19-2: The Macro toolbar provides a Stop button for ending the recording.

6. Perform the steps that you want to record.

7. Click the Stop button to stop the recording.

When you finish the preceding steps, the Macro toolbar goes away, and it's as if nothing has happened. But don't be fooled; your macro is safely hidden away. I'll explain later in the chapter how to play it back and how to edit it.

When recording macros that involve selecting text, the macro records what text was selected even if you don't want it to, and that selection becomes part of the macro. See *Removing Text Selection from a Macro* later in the chapter to learn how to fix this.

Deleting a Macro

You can delete a macro only from the presentation in which it is stored, so switch to that presentation. Then, choose Tools➪Macro➪Macros to open the Macro dialog box. Select the macro you want to delete, click the Delete button, and click OK.

See this article if you are having trouble deleting a macro: www .rdpslides.com/pptfaq/FAQ00169.htm.

Macro Playback

There are two ways to play a macro. The basic way is to use the Macro dialog box, as I'll explain in the next section, but that's not very convenient. The alternative takes more time to set up but is easier in the long run—assigning the macro to a toolbar button or menu command.

Playing a Macro from the Macro Dialog Box

To play a macro from the Macro dialog box, choose Tools➪Macro➪Macros, or press Alt+F8 to open the macro dialog box.

If the macro is not in the active presentation, open the Macro In drop-down list and choose All Open presentations. Then select the macro name and click Run (see Figure 19-3).

If you're thinking "that's too much work," see the following section for a way of making a macro easier to run.

To play a macro from the Macro dialog box, the presentation or template in which you create it must be open. However, you can use a macro toolbar button regardless of which presentation is open. Therefore, it's a good idea to create a special Macros toolbar (see Chapter 18) and place buttons for all your macros on it. That way, all macros are available in all presentations.

Figure 19-3: Run macros from the Macro dialog box.

Assigning a Toolbar Button to a Macro

In Chapter 18 you learned how to modify toolbars by adding buttons for common commands. You can also add buttons for macros. Follow these steps:

1. Choose Tools ➪ Customize. The Customize dialog box opens.

2. On the Commands tab, scroll down and select Macros from the left side. A list of all the macros in the active presentation appears at the right (see Figure 19-4).

3. Drag the macro from the dialog box to a toolbar. (Create a new toolbar first if you want, as discussed in Chapter 18.)

4. (Optional) To change the button name, right-click it and type a new name in the Name box. You can also do any of the other things to the button that you learned about in Chapter 18.

5. When you have finished creating the button and setting its properties, click Close in the dialog box to return to normal operation.

You can also create ActiveX controls in PowerPoint 2003 and then write macros using Visual Basic for Applications for those controls. For example, you might add an ActiveX command button to a slide and then write a script defining what will happen when the user clicks that button. To place ActiveX controls on slides, view the Control Toolbox toolbar (choose View ➪ Toolbars ➪ Control

Toolbox) and use the tools there to place the controls. Then, right-click a control and choose View Code to edit the code behind it.

Figure 19-4: You can place macros on toolbars the same way as other commands.

Creating a Menu of Macros

You might decide to create a menu for your macros rather than a toolbar. This menu can be added either to an existing toolbar, or to a new toolbar you create, or to the existing menu bar. I won't get into the specifics here because Chapter 18 covered it pretty thoroughly. Go back to Chapter 18 and create a new toolbar if needed, and then add a New Menu item to it from the Commands tab of the Customize dialog box. Then, add your macros to that new menu. Figure 19-5 shows an example.

Figure 19-5: You can create a menu for easy access to macros, if desired.

Editing a Macro with Visual Basic

When you're recording a macro, errors inevitably occur. Perhaps you meant to click the Bold button and clicked Italic instead, so you had to turn italics back off again. Or, maybe you opened the wrong menu.

If the macro performs its function, even with the errors, you might just leave it alone. For example, it doesn't hurt anything if the macro turns Italics on and then off again because the end result is that it's off. However, if there are a lot of mistakes in a complex macro, it can take a little longer to run than normal. Some people, too, are sticklers for efficiency and can't stand the thought of their macro being longer and more convoluted than necessary, regardless of performance issues.

To edit a macro, you use the Visual Basic Editor. This is a complex application that might seem intimidating to the non-programmer, but as long as you stick to editing with it, you should be fine.

More intrepid types with Visual Basic experience might choose to try their hand at writing macros from scratch. Be aware, however, that Visual Basic for Applications (VBA), which is what PowerPoint uses, is slightly different from regular Visual Basic. To familiarize yourself with the version of Visual Basic within PowerPoint, I recommend that you create some fairly complex macros by recording, and then examine them in the Visual Basic Editor to see how it structures command lines.

To edit a macro, choose Tools➪Macro➪Macros or press Alt+F8 to open the Macro dialog box. Click the macro and click the Edit button. The Visual Basic Editor opens with your macro in it. If you have more than one macro recorded in the same presentation, all of them appear in the Module1 window, regardless of which one you chose initially (see Figure 19-6).

The `BoldItalicUnderline` macro in Figure 19-6 originally had a line at the beginning that selected text, but I removed it. I'll explain why—and how you can do the same in your own macro, if desired—later in the chapter.

To remove a line from the macro, highlight it and press Delete. You can figure out what a line does by reading it carefully. For example, the following line turns the Bold attribute on by settings its value to True:

```
ActiveWindow.Selection.TextRange.Font.Bold = msoTrue
```

When you are finished editing the macro, choose File➪Close and Return to Microsoft PowerPoint or press Alt+Q. Your changes are automatically saved.

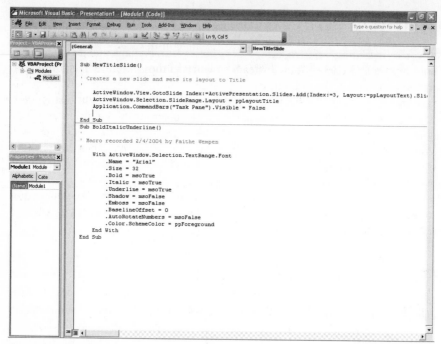

Figure 19-6: Editing a macro in the Visual Basic Editor.

Some VBA Fundamentals

Visual Basic is a rich programming language, and the version of it that works within Office applications enables you to write complex macros and even build mini-applications with dialog boxes that open with PowerPoint. This is way beyond what most business users would ever consider, but you may nevertheless be curious about the editor.

The Visual Basic Editor window has three panes: Project, Properties, and Code (see Figure 19-6). The Project window shows a hierarchy of the modules in the presentation. All the macros you record are stored in Module1, so you don't have to worry about this. The Properties panel shows the properties for the module. This pane is FYI-only too, as far as beginners are concerned.

The main panel that you work with is the Code window, the big one. It contains the lines of programming code that make up your macro.

Here are some things to note about the code:

♦ Each macro begins with the word Sub, followed by the macro name.

♦ Each macro ends with the words End Sub.

♦ Each command of the macro is on its own line.

♦ Each command in the macro narrows down what's being done through a series of words separated by periods. For example, in the

`BoldItalicUnderline` macro in Figure 19-6, `ActiveWindow` `.Selection.TextRange.Font` narrows down the activity to apply only to the font properties of the selected text range in the active window.

◆ Some lines begin with an apostrophe, such as the `Macro recorded...` line in Figure 19-6. These lines are comments and are ignored when the macro runs. If you want to temporarily disable a line of the macro for troubleshooting purposes, you can add an apostrophe in front of it.

 If you are interested in learning more about VBA, a good first place to start is the Help system. Don't think, however, that you can teach yourself programming just by reading the Help system. It's good, but the help there is slanted toward people who already know something about the topic. You won't find many easy explanations of how programming works. If you want to write your own VB macros from scratch, take a Visual Basic class at your local community college.

Here are a few additional Web resources for working with VBA in PowerPoint, all from the awesome `officeone.mvps.org` site that I've already referenced many times in this book:

◆ *VBA Controls Assistant.* If you are a VB wizard, you might have some VBA controls created. To use them in a presentation, check out the add-in, which supports VBA TextBox, VBAListBox, VBA ComboBox, and TreeView (http://officeone.mvps.org/ppvba/ppvba.html).

◆ *Event Generator.* Normally the event handler for events like `OnPresentationClose()`, `OnPresentationOpen()`, and so on can reside only in add-ins. The Event Generator add-in redirects many of the common program events to the presentations. Use for VBA programmers (http://officeone.mvps.org/eventgen/eventgen.html).

◆ *Quiz example.* Here's an article that shows how to create a quiz using VBA: www.mvps.org/skp/ppt00031.htm.

◆ *Tic Tac Toe.* Here's another PowerPoint demo using VBA: www.mvps .org/skp/downloads/tictactoe.zip.

Removing Text Selection from a Macro

Here's a quirk involving macros that apply text formatting, and how to fix it.

When recording a macro that formats text, you must either select some text before beginning the recording or select some text during the recording. If you don't, the macro will not record correctly.

However, selecting text has consequences you may not want. For example, suppose you select characters 10 through 14 of the text in a text box, and then record a macro that makes it bold. When you run that macro in the future, it will select characters 10 through 14 in the active text box and then make them bold. You probably don't want the selection to be part of the macro, though, right?

Here's how to fix that. Go into the Visual Basic Editor and either delete or comment out (by adding an apostrophe at the beginning) the code that specifies the selection.

For example, if the original was like this:

```
ActiveWindow.Selection.ShapeRange.TextFrame.TextRange.Characters
(Start:=10, Length:=5).Select
ActiveWindow.Selection.TextRange.Font.Bold = msoTrue
```

you would delete that first line, so all that remains is this:

```
ActiveWindow.Selection.TextRange.Font.Bold = msoTrue
```

Now when you run the macro, it will simply apply to whatever text you have already selected before running it, and the macro won't try to make any selection of its own.

Selecting the Right Steps to Record: An Example

In the course of examining your macros in the Visual Basic Editor, you will get an eye-opener as to the inner workings of PowerPoint. For example, you will see that commands that appear identical in everyday use are actually not identical at all. When you run into such cases, you may need to rethink the way you have a particular macro recorded, and possibly rerecord it.

Take, for example, the process of making some text bold, from the preceding section. One way of recording "bolding" is to record the clicking of the Bold button on the toolbar. That action creates this line in the macro:

```
ActiveWindow.Selection.TextRange.Font.Bold = msoTrue
```

(It also creates a line that selects the text, as described in the preceding section, but I have deleted it already here for simplicity.)

Another way of making text bold is to choose Format ➪ Font, click Bold, and click OK. Seems the same, right? But when you record that method, you are also recording all the other settings in the Font dialog box as well, so it would look something like this:

```
With ActiveWindow.Selection.TextRange.Font
    .Name = "Arial"
    .Size = 32
    .Bold = msoTrue
    .Italic = msoFalse
    .Underline = msoFalse
    .Shadow = msoFalse
```

```
    .Emboss = msoFalse
    .BaselineOffset = 0
    .AutoRotateNumbers = msoFalse
    .Color.SchemeColor = ppForeground
End With
```

This is called a "With" statement. Rather than repeating the text `ActiveWindow.Selection.TextRange.Font` on every line, it places it at the top of the statement and then just lists what has changed at the end of it on subsequent lines. Another way to have written this would have been:

```
ActiveWindow.Selection.TextRange.Font.Name = "Arial"
ActiveWindow.Selection.TextRange.Font.Size = 32
ActiveWindow.Selection.TextRange.Font.Bold = msoTrue
ActiveWindow.Selection.TextRange.Font.Italic = msoFalse
ActiveWindow.Selection.TextRange.Font.Underline = msoFalse
ActiveWindow.Selection.TextRange.Font.Shadow = msoFalse
ActiveWindow.Selection.TextRange.Font.Emboss = msoFalse
ActiveWindow.Selection.TextRange.Font.BaselineOffset = 0
ActiveWindow.Selection.TextRange.Font.AutoRotateNumbers = msoFalse
ActiveWindow.Selection.TextRange.Font.Color.SchemeColor =
ppForeground
```

The dialog box method recorded settings for font, size, italic, color, and many other settings that happened to be in effect on the text that I selected when I recorded the command. I didn't intend for those settings to be recorded, but there they were.

There are several possible solutions. I could delete the macro and rerecord it using the Bold button method, or I could edit the With statement to remove any of the lines that I didn't want to keep. For example, I could remove all the lines except the one that makes the text bold, so it would look like this:

```
With ActiveWindow.Selection.TextRange.Font
    .Bold = msoTrue
End With
```

Dealing with Macro Security

Macros are the primary way that data file viruses spread, so it's good to be cautious about them. For example, a Word macro virus was very common several years ago that forced documents to be saved as templates rather than as regular documents.

 Security is not an issue with macros that you created on the same PC on which you are running them. They run no matter what security settings are in effect because they have a private key associated with them that certifies that they are safe. Therefore, if you want to play around with the effects of various macro security settings, have a friend create a presentation file with some macros on his or her PC and send it to you for experimentation.

Setting the Macro Security Level in PowerPoint

Office 2003 offers greatly enhanced security features over earlier versions, especially in the area of macros. You can set four levels of macro security: Very High, High, Medium, or Low. Choose Tools⇨Macros⇨Security to set the level you want; the explanations next to each option button in that dialog box will explain the differences between the settings (see Figure 19-7).

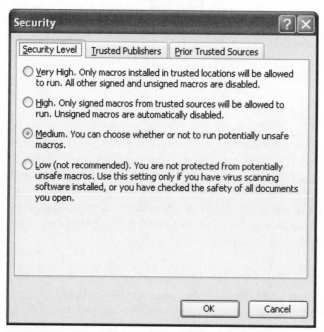

Figure 19-7: Set the macro security level in PowerPoint.

The Trusted Publishers tab lists the macro publishers whose macros will be allowed if you use the High setting. You cannot add to this list from within this window, but you can delete from it. There may also be a Prior Trusted Publishers tab, listing trusted sources that were migrated from a previous version of PowerPoint.

 Some PowerPoint add-ins that you can download from the Internet will require you to set your macro security to Low before they will install. Be sure you trust the author of the add-in before doing so, and don't forget to reset your macro security level to High or Medium afterwards.

Opening a Presentation Containing Macros

When you open a presentation that contains macros that are signed from trusted sources, the presentation simply opens, even if you have High security set.

For unsigned macros, or macros not from a trusted source, the behavior depends on the security settings you chose. With High or Very High, the presentation opens with the macros disabled. With Low, it opens with them enabled. With Medium, the dialog box shown in Figure 19-8 appears so you can decide what you want to do.

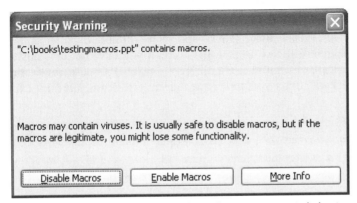

Figure 19-8: When Medium security is used, you are prompted about macros being enabled or disabled.

Understanding Digital Signatures

If you decide to create and distribute macros professionally, the best way to ensure that the macros you write and use have not been tampered with is to get a digital certificate from a certificate authority such as VeriSign and sign all your macro projects with it. A digital certificate is a code that matches up with a code stored on the certificate authority service, to verify that you are a legitimate certificate holder and that your work has not been changed since it was signed.

There are two ways that a digital signature helps in such situations. One is that it identifies the creator of the macro, giving the user a measure of ease in knowing that it has not come from some unknown source. The other is that the certificate authority verifies that it has not been changed.

CREATING YOUR OWN DIGITAL CERTIFICATE

You can create your own digital signature certificates, but you get only partial benefit from them. They do help in telling users who created the macro, but they do not certify that the content of the macro has not been changed. Because they are not connected to any central authority, they do not provide the ironclad verification of a certificate from a trusted source. Macros you create with a self-generated certificate are known as *self-signed*.

Self-signed macros are not considered secure and will not execute if macro security is set to Very High or High. If security is set to Medium, the Security Warning box appears, as shown in Figure 19-8. The exception is when the macro is being executed on the same PC as it was created or on a computer that has the private key for that certificate.

Create your certificates with the SelfCert.exe utility; from Windows, choose Start⇨All Programs⇨Microsoft Office Tools⇨Digital Certificate for VBA Projects. Then, just enter the name for the certificate and click OK. Simple enough!

SIGNING A MACRO DIGITALLY

After creating or acquiring a certificate, here's how to sign a macro with it.

Open the macro in the Visual Basic Editor, and in the Project Explorer pane, click the project. Then choose Tools⇨Digital Signature. If you have not previously selected a digital certificate or want to use a different one, click Choose, select the one you want, and click OK. Otherwise, to use the current certificate, just click OK.

 You should sign a macro only after it is completely finalized, because if you edit the signed macro later, the signature is removed. (However, it will automatically be resigned when saved if you have the proper certificate on your PC.)

VIEWING THE SECURITY CERTIFICATE

To view the certificate for the active presentation's macros, open the Visual Basic Editor, select the macro project (probably Module1), and then choose Tools⇨Digital Signature. In the Digital Signature dialog box, click Detail.

ADDING A MACRO PUBLISHER TO THE LIST OF TRUSTED SOURCES

Only macros with digital certificates from valid certificate authorities may be added to your list of trusted sources. Digital certificates created with SelfCert.exe may be added to the trusted source list only on the PC on which the macro was created.

In addition, the trusted sources list may be edited only when macro security is set to High or Medium.

To add a publisher to the list, when the security warning dialog box pops up to ask you about whether or not to enable the macros, choose Always Trust Macros from This Publisher. This will add that publisher to the list, and you won't be asked again.

To remove the publisher from the list, choose Tools⇨Macro⇨Security and on the Trusted Publishers tab, select a source and click Remove.

 If you had any trusted publishers set up in an earlier version of Office and you upgraded to Office 2003, there may be a Prior Trusted Publishers tab in the Security dialog box. You can remove any from there that you don't want. To move a publisher from the Prior tab to the regular Trusted Publishers tab, delete them from the Prior tab, then open a presentation that contains their macros, and choose Always Trust Macros from This Publisher, same as with a brand-new publisher source.

Reusing Macros in Multiple Presentations

A macro usually runs only in the presentation in which it is stored, or in all open presentations. If you create a macro in one presentation and then close that presentation, the macro is usually not available anymore.

To correct this, you can copy the macro to the other presentation. Macro security must be set to Medium or Low in order to do this.

Open both presentations, and then open the Visual Basic Editor. In the Project Explorer pane (top left corner), drag Module1 from the presentation containing the macros to the presentation that should receive them (see Figure 19-9).

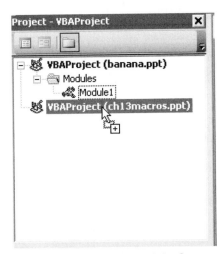

Figure 19-9: Copy macro modules from one presentation file to another.

If you want to copy macros into another presentation but the target presentation is not available on the same PC, you can export the macro module into a separate, free-standing file and import that file to the target presentation later. When you do this, you save the macros in a Visual Basic file (with a .BAS extension).

To export a macro module, open the presentation containing the macros in PowerPoint and then open the Visual Basic Editor. Right-click Module1 in the Project Explorer pane (top left) and choose Export File. Enter a name and location, and click Save.

To import the macro module somewhere else, open that presentation in PowerPoint and then open the Visual Basic Editor. Right-click the presentation file in the Project Explorer pane and choose Import File. Select the file and click Open.

Working with Add-Ins

An *add-in* is a helper file with a .PPA extension that you "add in" to PowerPoint to expand its capabilities. Most people reading this book won't be writing their own add-ins, but everyone should know how to find and install them.

Add-ins vary tremendously in terms of their complexity. The high-end add-ins (like many of the ones on the CD for this book) are almost like full-blown applications with their own Setup utilities. The low-end ones are so subtle you may not even realize they are installed. An add-in typically has a .PPA extension, but some may have .DLL, .EXE, or .PWZ extensions.

One of the coolest high-end add-ins for PowerPoint is Microsoft Producer, which you can get from the Microsoft Office Web site. It's a utility for creating flashy multimedia presentations that include video and sound based on PowerPoint. It's not just an add-in, but a full stand-alone application that you can run from outside of PowerPoint.

Finding Add-Ins

The Web is the best source of PowerPoint add-ins, and one of the best Web sites for listing and categorizing add-ins is Indezine (www.indezine.com/products/ powerpoint/addin/compatible.html). You can also find others by typing PowerPoint add-in in any search engine. There are also several good add-ins on the CD that comes with this book; see Appendix C for details. And of course, I've been mentioning various add-ins all throughout this book where one of them exists that will help with this or that specific task.

Installing and Removing Add-Ins

Most add-ins come with their own Setup programs, which may or may not automatically install the add-ins in PowerPoint. To check whether a particular add-in is installed, and install it if not, do the following:

1. Choose Tools⇨Add-Ins. The Add-Ins dialog box opens. If the add-in does not appear on the list, it is not installed yet. Figure 19-10 shows one add-in installed.

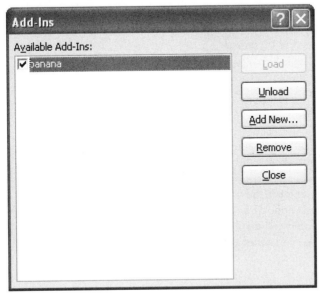

Figure 19-10: The Add-Ins box lists the installed add-ins and enables you to add more.

2. To install an add-in, click Add New. The Add New PowerPoint Add-In dialog box opens. It opens to the `C:\Documents and Settings\username \Application Data\Microsoft\Add-Ins` folder by default, but the add-in might be stored somewhere else.

3. Browse to the folder containing the add-in, select it, and click OK. Then back in the Add-Ins dialog box, click Load (if available) and then click Close.

If you don't know where the Setup program put the add-in, use the Search feature in Windows to locate files with a .PPA extension.

Loading or Unloading an Add-In

Notice the checkbox next to the add-in in Figure 19-10. You can use this to load or unload an add-in, which is useful because you can temporarily remove one without removing it from the handy list in the dialog box. Marking the checkbox is the same as clicking the Load button; clearing it is the same as clicking Unload.

If you have an add-in that does not load by default when PowerPoint starts up, but you would like it to do so, see this article at Microsoft's Web site: http://support.microsoft.com/?scid=kb;EN-US;q222685. The article refers to PowerPoint 2000, but the steps are also applicable for later versions. Also check out www.rdpslides.com/pptfaq/FAQ00031.htm and www.mvps.org/skp/ppafaq.htm for more information about add-ins. Also you can experiment on your own within the Visual Basic Editor by choosing AddIns ➪ Add-In Manager.

Summary

In this chapter you learned how to create your own macros, both by recording and by editing with the Visual Basic Editor. You also learned how to install and load/unload add-ins.

I hope you have enjoyed this book, and that you will continue to find it useful as a reference. I also hope you will take the time to explore the companion CD, which contains samples of many valuable PowerPoint-related add-ins, graphics, backgrounds, sounds, and other goodies.

Part VII

Appendixes

Appendix A

New Features in PowerPoint 2003

IN THIS CHAPTER

◆ New features in the latest version of PowerPoint

◆ Issues when opening files in previous versions

IF YOU HAVE USED AN EARLIER VERSION of PowerPoint before, or if you are sharing files with people who are still using an older version, this appendix is for you and will explain the differences you'll find between the versions.

The New Features

In terms of new features, PowerPoint 2003 is a rather minor update to PowerPoint 2002, the previous version. However, there are a few really great new features to enjoy!

The PowerPoint Viewer

One of the biggest benefits of PowerPoint 2003 over all earlier versions is its vastly improved version of the PowerPoint Viewer. The PowerPoint Viewer is an external program that you can distribute freely to anyone in your potential audience who might not have a full version of PowerPoint installed on his or her PC. It enables people to watch PowerPoint shows without having to shell out the money to buy PowerPoint.

The PowerPoint Viewer has not been updated in a long time. The last version of it came with PowerPoint 97, and that same old, tired version has been circulating ever since. Because that software was designed to display presentations created in PowerPoint 97, it does not support any of the new features that have been introduced in PowerPoint 2000, 2002, or 2003. That's why this new update is so important. At last you have a Viewer that can display almost all of the new features that PowerPoint itself can display.

Package for CD

Here's my favorite of the new features in PowerPoint 2003. Remember the old Pack and Go feature in earlier PowerPoint versions? You could use it to package a presentation and all its support files in one location so you could transfer it to some other location. That was all well and good, but the Package for CD feature lets you package the presentation—along with the PowerPoint Viewer—directly onto a writeable CD. Nothing has to be installed on the recipient's computer in order for it to run.

Windows Media Player Support

PowerPoint 2003 lets you play some media clips using the same internal controls as the Windows Media Player, rather than through separate media player controls. This makes clip playing faster, easier, and less buggy.

Research Pane

All Office 2003 applications now include a Research pane, which is connected to research sites on the Internet. The Thesaurus and Dictionary work as part of this pane now, and you can also look things up in online encyclopedias and news services with just a few clicks.

SharePoint Team Services

Here's another cool new Office-in-general feature for Office 2003 that also works with PowerPoint. With a server application called Windows SharePoint Services, users can set up Web-based SharePoint team sites that enable groups of people to share files and have discussions. This makes it much easier for groups of people to collaborate on draft presentations when they are not physically located in the same place.

Internet Faxing

PowerPoint 2003 comes with a Send to Fax Service capability that enables you to fax things without having to actually have a fax machine. This subscription-based service works through the Internet and it's not just for PowerPoint, but for all Office applications.

OneNote and Tablet PC integration

In all Office 2003 applications you can interact with a Tablet PC. For example, in PowerPoint you can use the writing capabilities of a Tablet PC to mark up a presentation and save your marked-up annotations. Handwriting integration is accomplished through a utility called OneNote, which can be used with any PC, not just the Tablet PC.

Saving Annotations

And speaking of annotations, with PowerPoint 2003 you can save all those marks, scribbles, notes, or whatever that you jotted down using the Pen feature in Slide Show view. They are called annotations, and you can now preserve them after leaving Slide Show view.

More Pen Options

In earlier versions of PowerPoint you had just one pen type to choose from in Slide Show view. In PowerPoint 2003 you have several pen types, each one with a different shape or thickness of tip. You can also choose from a rainbow of pen colors.

Issues When Opening Files in Previous Versions

As you learned in Chapter 1, the default file saving format results in a file that can be opened in PowerPoint 97, 2000, 2002, and 2003, and the PowerPoint 97-2003 & 95 format extends that to PowerPoint 95 as well.

However, just because the file will open in an older version does not necessarily mean that the older version will support all the features in the presentation. Table A-1 summarizes the feature losses when opening in various older versions.

TABLE A-1 PowerPoint 2003 Features Not Supported in Previous PowerPoint Versions

Feature	Issues
PowerPoint 2000 and Below:	
Password protection	Presentations with passwords do not open. The user receives an error message: "PowerPoint can't open the type of file represented by <filename>.ppt"
Multiple masters	Editing and resaving may result in loss of all but the first master of a certain type (for example, only one Slide Master, one Title Master, and so on)
Animation effects	Any unsupported effects are either converted to a supported effect or not used
Picture rotation	Windows metafiles do not appear rotated. Bitmaps change to the nearest 90-degree rotation
Transparency on a solid fill	May appear less smooth

Continued

TABLE A-2 PowerPoint 2003 Features Not Supported in Previous PowerPoint Versions (*Continued*)

Feature	Issues
Transparency on a fill effect or line	Cannot add transparency to a fill effect or line using the Transparency tool
Contrast and brightness adjustments on picture fills	Adjustments do not appear on some images
Fill rotates with shape	Fills do not appear rotated
Anti-aliasing	Not supported; text and graphics appear less smooth
Comments	Not visible or editable
Diagrams	Converted to groups of shapes
PowerPoint 97 and Below:	
Native tables	Converted to a group of shapes
Voice narration	Sound played with Windows Media Player as a WAV file. Not recognized as narration, and not synchronized to audio
Automatic numbered list	Appears as bulleted list
Picture bullets	Appear as regular bullets
Animated GIFs	First frame appears as a static image
PowerPoint 95:	
Animated chart elements	Appear as static chart objects that can be edited in Microsoft Graph
Custom shows	Slides appear in presentation, but Custom Show feature doesn't function
Native format movies and sounds	Converted to Windows Media Player objects
Diagrams	Converted to Windows Metafiles (WMF)
Play options for CD tracking and movie looping	Ignored
Document collaboration	Tracking and merging changes not supported
3-D effects	Converted to pictures
AutoShapes	Converted to freeform shape or picture
Connectors	Converted to freeform lines; automatic connecting behavior lost

Feature	Issues
Curves	Approximated with connected straight line segments
Transparency on a gradient fill	Appears as a transparent fill without a gradient
Joins and endcaps of lines	Appear as mitered joins on AutoShapes and round joins and endcaps on freeform shapes
Linked or embedded objects	Brightness, contrast, and color transformation settings are lost
WordArt drawing objects	Converted to picture objects
Picture fills	Converted to picture objects
Picture fills on shapes	Converted to picture objects with solid fill in which last foreground color is applied to object
Shadows, engraved	Appears as embossed shadow effect
Shadows, perspective	Converted to shapes or pictures and grouped with shape casting the shadow
Shapes or arcs with attached text	Converted to freeform shapes, arcs, or text boxes
Thick compound lines	Converted to picture objects
Hyperlinks that combine Play Sound with other Action settings	Play Sound settings are lost
Hyperlinks embedded within an object	Hyperlinks are lost
Action settings embedded in an object	Action settings are lost
Send a copy of a slide in e-mail as the body of the message	Message header information (recipient list, message options) is lost
Embedded fonts	Not supported
Embedded Excel charts	Not supported
Microsoft Graph charts	Editable only if the Convert Charts When Saving As Previous Version checkbox was selected when saving
Macros	Not supported
Unicode characters	Not supported

Appendix B

PowerPoint Resources Online

IN THIS CHAPTER

◆ PowerPoint-related Web sites

◆ PowerPoint-related newsgroups

LOOKING FOR MORE HELP, more templates, more add-ins—just *more*? Here are some of my favorite resources. I've broken down the list by category, but in many cases you'll find cross-category content on a site (for example, some sites have both support articles and downloads).

Help and Support

The following sites are general technical support sources.

Microsoft Office Online

`http://office.microsoft.com/home/office.aspx?assetid=FX01085797`
Here's the official home of PowerPoint and also one of the best and richest sources of information and extras. You can also get here from the Help menu within PowerPoint (select Help ➪ Microsoft Office Online).

Indezine

`www.indezine.com`
This is my favorite PowerPoint site overall. It's information-packed, with many articles by Geetesh Bajaj about PowerPoint usage. Don't miss the PowerPoint Links page here, with links to other PowerPoint resources—that page alone is worth the visit to this Web site.

Presentations.com

`www.presentations.com/presentations/index.jsp`
A very content-rich site, and a great resource for people who create and present presentations frequently. Though it's mostly PowerPoint-focused, there is some general content as well.

Sonia Coleman

www.soniacoleman.com/
A PowerPoint MVP with a lot of freebies to share, both in terms of tutorial information and in free downloads (including lots of templates). A definite must-see!

PowerPoint Answers

www.powerpointanswers.com/
There are many good articles here about using PowerPoint to its fullest, from Katherine Jacobs, another PowerPoint MVP.

Echo's Voice

www.echosvoice.com/
This is the Web site for Echo Swinford, who was the technical editor on this book. Several good articles here, including a tutorial on Bezier curves with lots of illustrations.

Add-Ins and Utilities

The following sites offer many extra add-ins and useful utilities.

WebAIM: PowerPoint Accessibility Techniques

www.webaim.org/techniques/powerpoint/
If you are interested in making Web-posted PowerPoint presentations more accessible to people with disabilities, this is a must-read. It contains a link to an Office Accessibility Wizard, which is an add-in that converts PowerPoint presentations to a format that is usable by screen-reading programs for the visually impaired and is easily navigable.

Steve Rindsberg/RDP

www.rdpslides.com/
Here's the Web site of a PowerPoint MVP who also has created some great add-ins and converters that you'll find included on the CD at the back of this book. He also runs www.pptfaq.com where you'll find PowerPoint FAQs.

Crystal Graphics

www.crystalgraphics.com/
Makers of the PowerPlugs for PowerPoint product, a set of add-ins that provide additional animation, 3-D, transition, charting, and graphics capabilities within PowerPoint.

Office Tips

www.mvps.org/skp

Source of dozens of wonderful add-ins for PowerPoint, many of which have been referenced throughout this book. This site is run by Shyam Pillai, another of the PowerPoint MVPs and an expert in extending PowerPoint with Visual Basic for Applications.

Backgrounds, Templates, and Graphics

The following sites are good sources for clip art, backgrounds, and a variety of templates that you may find useful.

A Bit Better Corporation

www.bitbetter.com

The home of the "Screen Beans" clip art. You may remember these little bean-headed stick figures from the Microsoft Office clip-art collection; well, you can get more of them (a lot more!) here. There is also a list of PowerPoint tips here.

PowerPoint Backgrounds

www.powerpointbackgrounds.com/

This is mostly a site with backgrounds for sale, but there are some free backgrounds here (you must subscribe to their newsletter to get them) and also some excellent PowerPoint usage tips and tutorials including a very good graphics tutorial that includes information on scanning.

PowerFinish

www.powerfinish.com/

A great source for PowerPoint templates. You'll find some samples of their templates on the CD that accompanies this book, as well as many more (over 14,000) for sale on their Web site.

Free Templates from Graphicsland

www.graphicsland.com/powerpoint-templates.htm

The above link takes you directly to a page where you can download a ZIP file containing dozens of free template files, with no fuss and no registration required. While you're here, though, check out the rest of Graphicsland, a service for printing various types of print materials such as bumper stickers.

PowerPoint Templates Pro

www.powerpointtemplatespro.com/
Very professional-looking template sets are for sale here. Buying a single template is very expensive here, but when buying multiple templates the price drops quickly.

aBetterPresentation.com

www.abetterpresentation.com/
A source of PowerPoint-related products and resources, including CD-based collections of graphics and templates and downloadable items. Most are for sale, but if you sign up for their newsletter you can receive two free backgrounds per month.

Slides Direct

www.slidesdirect.com/
A source of professional-quality PowerPoint templates, samples of which appear on the CD that comes with this book. This company also offers training services.

Zap It! Media

www.zapitmedia.com
Some very attractive and professional-looking templates are for sale here, and some for free download too.

Digital Juice

www.digitaljuice.com
Sellers of large collections of animations, clip art, and music. You'll find some of samples of their wares on the CD with this book.

Newsgroups and Mailing Lists

The following sites are general newsgroup and mailing list sources.

Microsoft Public PowerPoint Newsgroup

Microsoft.public.powerpoint
This is the official Microsoft PowerPoint newsgroup, and it's where many of the PowerPoint MVPs hang out on a daily basis to help answer tough questions. Therefore, it's a great starting point for troubleshooting and general information. Access this through a news reader program or through Google Groups (http://groups .google.com). You can also access the newsgroup through a Web interface at http://communities2.microsoft.com/communities/newsgroups/en-us/default.aspx.

Microsoft Office Freelist Group

www.freelists.org/cgi-bin/webpage?webpage-id=mso
A free public forum for people who want to talk "questions and answers" about Microsoft Office products.

Yahoo PowerPoint Group

http://groups.yahoo.com/group/powerpoint
A mailing list group for people interested in discussing PowerPoint. Many of the same people who participate in the previous two groups are also subscribers to this list. This is the same as eGroups, which merged with Yahoo Groups.

Appendix C

What's on the CD-ROM

THIS APPENDIX PROVIDES YOU with information on the contents of the CD that accompanies this book. For the latest and greatest information, please refer to the ReadMe file located at the root of the CD. Here is what you will find:

- System requirements
- Using the CD with Windows
- What's on the CD
- Troubleshooting

System Requirements

PowerPoint 2003 is part of Office 2003, which has a fairly rigorous set of system requirements for itself. If your system meets these, and you can run PowerPoint 2003 successfully, you should have no trouble with the CD that accompanies this book.

Office 2003 requires:

- PC with Pentium 233 MHz or higher processor, Pentium III recommended
- Microsoft Windows XP, or Microsoft Windows 2000 with Service Pack 3 or later
- 128MB of RAM or above
- 400MB of available hard disk space
- CD-ROM drive (if installing from CD)
- Super VGA (800 × 600) or higher resolution monitor

In addition you will need 300MB of space to install the materials on this CD.

Using the CD with Windows

To install the items from the CD to your hard drive, follow these steps:

1. Insert the CD into your computer's CD-ROM drive.

533

2. A window appears with the following options:

Install: Gives you the option to install the supplied software and the author-created samples on the CD-ROM.

Explore: Enables you to view the contents of the CD-ROM in its directory structure.

Links: Opens a hyperlinked page of Web sites.

Exit: Closes the autorun window.

If you do not have autorun enabled, or if the autorun window does not appear, follow these steps to access the CD:

1. Click Start⇨Run.

2. In the dialog box that appears, type *d:***setup.exe**, where *d* is the letter of your CD-ROM drive. This brings up the autorun window described in the preceding set of steps.

3. Choose the desired option from the menu. (See Step 2 in the preceding list for a description of these options.)

What's on the CD

The following sections provide a summary of the software and other materials you'll find on the CD.

Samples

The following sample PowerPoint materials are on the CD:

Digital Juice 2.0. Digital Juice, Inc. www.digitaljuice.com. Over 100 gorgeous full-color images with three remixes for each, representing a sampler of their complete collection. This is *quality stuff*!

PowerPointed. Geetesh Bajaj. www.powerpointed.com. A sampler pack including two templates, 10 background music scores, several seamless textures and backgrounds, and some special upgrade offers. Geetesh Bajaj is one of the PowerPoint MVPs.

Screen Beans Clipart. A Bit Better. www.bitbetter.com. You may remember seeing Screen Beans clip art in earlier versions of Microsoft Office; Microsoft licensed it from them. Well, there's a lot more where that came from! This sampler includes many samples in WMF format, which are free for your use; you can buy the entire pack at their Web site. Screen Bean clip art images are a registered trademark of A Bit Better Corporation.

Awesome PowerPoint Backgrounds. By Default. `www.powerpointbackgrounds`
`.com`. Just what the name says. Here are a half-dozen backgrounds you can use
freely. If you like them, look for more at their Web site. You will be amazed at the
number of collections and the breadth of subject.

PowerFinish Samples. Studio F Productions, Inc. `www.powerfinish.com`. These
beautiful free templates/backgrounds come from The Works for PowerPoint collection and are provided in both .pot and .jpg format. If you like them, check out
the full collection.

Applications

The following applications are on the CD:

Paint Shop Pro 8.0. JASC Software, Inc. `www.jasc.com`. This is my all-time favorite
image-editing program. I use it for almost everything—photo touch-up, graphics file
conversion, cropping, and so on. This is an evaluation version, but I'm thinking you
will probably fall in love with it and want to buy it, just like I did.

Impatica for PowerPoint. Impatica, Inc. `www.impatica.com`. This utility is the
fastest, easiest and most effective way to publish PowerPoint presentations to the
Web or deliver them through e-mail. Viewers do not require PowerPoint or any other
special software to receive online presentations. The CD-ROM contains more information about Impatica for PowerPoint and Impatica OnCue, with links to download
free, fully functional evaluation copies from `www.impatica.com/evaluation/`. Just
double-click the HTML page provided to find out more, then click the "Download"
button. Select the product in which you are interested and then fill in the form. As
soon as you have completed and submitted the form, you will be provided with your
evaluation Registration Code and a link to download the software.

RnR PPTools Starter Kit, Version 2. RDP. `www.rdpslides.com`. This is a suite of add-
ins accessible from toolbars that perform a host of useful functions in PowerPoint,
ranging from image positioning to VBA integration. These goodies are also courtesy
of one of the PowerPoint MVPs, Brian Reilly.

Scan Calculator. Freebyte! `http://freebyte.com/scancalculator`. This handy
utility helps you calculate the appropriate resolution at which to scan a photo in
order to get a certain result. Sure you could do it in your head, but this is much
easier.

NOTE: Scan Calculator doesn't provide an installer—it runs directly off the CD-
ROM. Simply open Scan Calculator's folder on the CD-ROM and double-click the
executable in order to run it. You can also copy the executable file to your hard
drive if you want to run it without the CD-ROM.

Camtasia Studio. TechSmith Corporation. `www.techsmith.com`. Here's a trial version of a very powerful program for capturing the action on a computer screen and

saving it as a video. There are many uses, including training and product demos, and the resulting files integrate nicely with PowerPoint.

SnagIT 7.x. TechSmith Corporation. www.techsmith.com. This is a trial version of a screen capture program that many of us professional authors use to get screen shots for our books. When you need still images of a computer screen, this is one of the best and most popular programs to capture them.

PANTONE® OfficeColor Assistant. Pantone, Inc. www.pantone.com. If you are preparing Microsoft Office files for professional printing using the PANTONE color system, you will appreciate this utility. It lets you select PANTONE colors from within Office applications, according to the PANTONE number.

PowerLink Pro Plus. Sonia Coleman. www.soniacoleman.com. This handy utility prepares your presentations for distribution by creating a "project" that contains your presentation file and all linked files. It also makes all the links in your presentation file relative so that the paths to them still work no matter where you run it from. While this ability is most useful in earlier versions of PowerPoint because they lacked the Package for CD feature, you may still find it helpful for PowerPoint 2003. This is a trial version that enables you to create two test projects. Sonia is one of the PowerPoint MVPs.

Autorun CD Project Creator Pro. Sonia Coleman. www.soniacoleman.com. This also creates an auto-running CD, like PowerLink Pro Plus, but it enables you to include other types of content as well, such as Adobe Acrobat, Word, and Excel. This is a trial version that enables you to create three test projects.

PowerWorship 3.0. Mysak Information Systems. www.mysak.com. This free utility is for churches that have sing-alongs where they show the song lyrics on PowerPoint slides to the congregation. You can maintain a library of songs and dynamically build slide shows and reusable song groups.

PowerSearch Plug-In. Accent Technologies. http://www.accent-technologies .com Powerpoint® PowerSearch Plug-In is easy to use and makes finding slides a snap. It saves hours in sorting through PowerPoint presentations looking for the slides you need.

Shareware programs are fully functional, trial versions of copyrighted programs. If you like particular programs, register with their authors for a nominal fee and receive licenses, enhanced versions, and technical support. *Freeware programs* are copyrighted games, applications, and utilities that are free for personal use. Unlike shareware, these programs do not require a fee or provide technical support. *GNU software* is governed by its own license, which is included inside the folder of the GNU product. See the GNU license for more details.

Trial, demo, or evaluation versions are usually limited either by time or functionality (such as being unable to save projects). Some trial versions are very sensitive to system date changes. If you alter your computer's date, the programs will "time out" and will no longer be functional.

Troubleshooting

If you have difficulty installing or using any of the materials on the companion CD, try the following solutions:

◆ **Turn off any anti-virus software that you may have running.** Installers sometimes mimic virus activity and can make your computer incorrectly believe that it is being infected by a virus. (Be sure to turn the anti-virus software back on later.)

◆ **Close all running programs.** The more programs you're running, the less memory is available to other programs. Installers also typically update files and programs; if you keep other programs running, installation may not work properly.

If you still have trouble with the CD-ROM, please call the Wiley Product Technical Support phone number: (800) 762-2974. Outside the United States, call 1(317) 572-3994. You can also contact Wiley Product Technical Support at www.wiley.com/techsupport. Wiley Publishing will provide technical support only for installation and other general quality control items; for technical support on the applications themselves, consult the program's vendor or author.

To place additional orders or to request information about other Wiley products, please call (800) 225-5945.

Index

A

continued

continued